DELIVERING JUSTICE

In this *Liber Amicorum*, leading experts and friends from around the world come together to pay tribute to Christopher Hodges and his multifaceted work by exploring what can be done to deliver justice and fairness, focusing on collective redress, consumer dispute resolution, court system reform, ethical business regulation and regulatory delivery.

After a decade-long career as a solicitor, Christopher Hodges became Professor of Justice Systems at the Centre for Socio-Legal Studies at the University of Oxford. Throughout his academic career he has worked on a variety of topics dealing with access to justice and dispute resolution: from product liability, procedural/funding systems and collective redress, to alternative dispute resolution and ethical business regulation. In 2021 Christopher Hodges was awarded an OBE for services to business and law. His ground-breaking research has not only inspired students and colleagues, but has also influenced policymakers worldwide.

Delivering justice, and 'making things better', runs like a thread through his work; the same thread connects the chapters in this book.

Delivering Justice

A Holistic and Multidisciplinary Approach

Liber Amicorum in Honour of Christopher Hodges

Edited by
Xandra Kramer
Stefaan Voet
Lorenz Ködderitzsch
Magdalena Tulibacka
Burkhard Hess

•HART•
OXFORD • LONDON • NEW YORK • NEW DELHI • SYDNEY

HART PUBLISHING

Bloomsbury Publishing Plc

Kemp House, Chawley Park, Cumnor Hill, Oxford, OX2 9PH, UK

1385 Broadway, New York, NY 10018, USA

29 Earlsfort Terrace, Dublin 2, Ireland

HART PUBLISHING, the Hart/Stag logo, BLOOMSBURY and the Diana logo are trademarks of Bloomsbury Publishing Plc

First published in Great Britain 2022

A catalogue record for this book is available from the British Library.

A catalogue record for this book is available from the Library of Congress.

Library of Congress Control Number: 2022943819

ISBN: HB: 978-1-50996-154-2
ePDF: 978-1-50996-156-6
ePub: 978-1-50996-155-9

Typeset by Compuscript Ltd, Shannon
Printed and bound in Great Britain by CPI Group (UK) Ltd, Croydon CR0 4YY

FSC www.fsc.org MIX Paper from responsible sources FSC® C013604

ACKNOWLEDGEMENTS

The editors warmly thank all the authors who have contributed to this book. Our thanks also go to Roberta Bassi (senior commissioning editor), Rosemarie Mearns (assistant editor) and Linda Goss (senior production editor) from Hart Publishing, Catherine Minahan (copy editor), Fiona Hodges (for a bit of inside information) and Edine Apeldoorn (student assistant of Xandra Kramer) for the administrative support.

CONTENTS

PART V
ETHICAL BUSINESS REGULATION, CORPORATE BEHAVIOUR AND REGULATORY DELIVERY

LIST OF CONTRIBUTORS

Mary E Bartkus is Special Counsel at Hughes Hubbard & Reed LLP, USA.

Alexandre Biard is Affiliated Senior Researcher at the University of Rotterdam and Senior Legal Officer at BEUC.

Harry Christophers CBE is the Founder and Conductor of The Sixteen and Conductor Laureate at the Handel and Haydn Society Boston.

Alex Chung is Honorary Lecturer at the Department of Science, Technology, Engineering and Public Policy (STEaPP), University College London.

Naomi Creutzfeldt is Professor of Socio-Legal Studies at the University of Westminster, UK.

Hilary Evans is Executive Director of the International Network for Delivery of Regulation (INDR), UK.

Jeremy Gray is the Artistic Director of Bampton Classical Opera.

Takuya Hatta is Professor of Law at Kobe University, Japan.

Burkhard Hess is Director of Max Planck Institute Luxembourg for Procedural Law.

Lorenz Ködderitzsch is Assistant General Counsel at the Law Department of Johnson & Johnson.

Xandra Kramer is Professor of Private Law and European Civil Procedure at the Erasmus University Rotterdam and Professor of Private International Law at Utrecht University.

Urs Leimbacher is Head of Public Affairs and Cultural Engagements at Swiss Re.

Sonia Macleod is a Researcher in Civil Justice Systems at the Centre for Socio-Legal Studies, University of Oxford.

Srikanth Mangalam is President of the PRISM Institute, Canada.

David Marks is former Partner and Solicitor with CMS Cameron McKenna.

Arundel McDougall is a former Executive Director of the European Justice Forum.

Hans-W Micklitz is Professor of Economic Law at the Robert Schuman Centre for Advanced Studies, European University Institute, Italy.

Graham Russell is Chief Executive of the Office for Product Safety and Standards at the Department for Business, Energy and Industrial Strategy, UK.

Lewis Shand Smith is Chair of the Business Banking Resolution Service, UK.

John Sorabji is a Lecturer at University College London.

Astrid Stadler is Professor of Law at the University of Konstanz, Germany.

Ruth N Steinholtz is Managing Partner at AretéWork, UK.

Magdalena Tulibacka is a Faculty Lecturer at Emory Law School, USA.

Eline Verhage is a Doctoral Candidate in Consumer ADR at Leiden University and an independent ADR consultant.

Matthew Vickers is Chief Executive and Chief Ombudsman at Ombudsman Services, UK.

Stefaan Voet is Professor of Law at KU Leuven, Belgium.

Sir Geoffrey Vos is Master of the Rolls and Head of Civil Justice in England and Wales.

Diana Wallis is a former Member and Vice-President of the European Parliament.

Stephen Weatherill is Emeritus Jacques Delors Professor of European Law at the University of Oxford and a Fellow of Somerville College.

Franziska Weber is Professor in Law and Economics at the Erasmus University Rotterdam.

Andrea Wechsler is Professor of Law at Pforzheim University, Germany.

Herbert Woopen is Director of Legal Policy at the European Justice Forum and a Board Member of the German Notaries' Mutual Fidelity Insurer (Notarversicherungsverein aG).

Ying Yu is a former Research Fellow at Wolfson College, University of Oxford.

PART I

Homage to a Polymath

1

The Multidimensional Career of a Polymath

XANDRA KRAMER, STEFAAN VOET, LORENZ KÖDDERITZSCH, MAGDALENA TULIBACKA AND BURKHARD HESS

I. A Unique Career of a Unique Man

In 2021, Professor Christopher Hodges – Chris – was given the status of emeritus professor and was awarded an OBE[1] for services to business and law. Throughout his academic career he has worked on a variety of topics dealing with access to justice and dispute resolution: from product liability, court systems, funding and collective redress, to alternative dispute resolution (ADR) and ethical business regulation. His ground-breaking research has not only inspired students and colleagues, but has also influenced policymakers worldwide. Delivering justice, and 'making things better', run like a thread through his work.

In this *Liber Amicorum*, longstanding friends and leading experts from around the world come together to pay tribute to Chris and his multifaceted work. The academic part explores what can be done to deliver justice and fairness, focusing on collective redress, consumer dispute resolution, reform of the court system, ethical business regulation and regulatory delivery.

The first 25 years of Chris's career were spent as a practising lawyer, based in leading international law firms in the City of London and for two years in Hong Kong (in 1984–85). At this time, he achieved the global distinction of Chair of the Committee on Product Liability, Advertising, Unfair Competition and Consumer Affairs of the International Bar Association. He is virtually unique in having then transferred to becoming a full-time academic. Within an astonishingly short time, he achieved global recognition, being appointed Erasmus Professor of the Fundamentals of Private Law, Erasmus University, Rotterdam (2011–14). Since 2004 he has been Head of a research programme at Oxford University, in 2014 being appointed Professor of Justice Systems at that same institution (the first person to hold that title).

He has been a Visiting Professor at the KU Leuven's Global Law School Programme (2013), Guest Professor of Wuhan University, Wuhan, China (2013–16), Honorary

[1] Officer of the Most Excellent Order of the British Empire.

Professor of the International Law School of the China University of Political Science and Law, Beijing, China (2013–16), and Visiting Fellow, Australian National University, Canberra (2014). He was elected a Supernumerary Fellow of Wolfson College, Oxford in 2015. A more detailed résumé of Chris's career can be found in chapter 2 of this book.

Chris combines rare gifts that are highly valued by a wide range of officials and businesses: the ability to undertake fundamental ground-breaking research, the intellectual ability to identify fresh and transformative visions of how things can be improved, and the ability to articulate them in a highly practical way and advocate enthusiastically for change. He has always been a man of vision and with a mission. His advice is widely sought and relied on by governments and businesses across the globe. He inspired many young scholars to embark on new, often interdisciplinary research projects. His manner of viewing civil justice systems, as a combination of problem-solving pathways rather than confined within the predetermined silos, challenged and inspired scholars and policymakers alike. If there is one phrase that he is remembered for by colleagues who had an opportunity to work with him, it is 'I have an idea!'

He has produced a steady stream of thoroughly researched books and articles across an exceptionally wide range of regulatory and dispute resolution topics – both his range and the quantity of output are far wider than almost any other contemporary academic. A list of his most important publications can be found in chapter 2 of this book.

Chris has had an enormous impact and influence in a number of different but related areas. His work has directly benefited consumers, businesses, regulators and economies. There is a consistent theme in these different areas of unbiased support for ethical and balanced improvements in how things are done, and the systems that are used. In the following paragraphs we try to give an overview of Chris's work. The fields of research correspond with the four academic parts of this *Liber Amicorum*: collective redress (part II), consumer dispute resolution (part III), court system reform and new technologies (part IV) and ethical business regulation, corporate behaviour and regulatory delivery (part V).

II. Collective Redress

For over a decade collective redress has been high on the European policy agenda. The European legislator has always struggled to take a clear position and establish a coherent legal framework. In June 2013, the European Commission published a Recommendation on common principles for injunctive and compensatory collective redress mechanisms,[2] which Chris famously labelled a *damp sqibb*.[3] The goal was not to harmonise the national systems but to list some common, non-binding principles relating both to judicial (compensatory and injunctive) and out-of-court collective redress that Member States should take into account when crafting such mechanisms.

[2] Recommendation of the European Commission of 11 June 2013 on common principles for injunctive and compensatory collective redress mechanisms in the Member States concerning violations of rights granted under Union Law [2013] OJ L201/60.

[3] C Hodges, 'Collective Redress: A Breakthrough or a Damp Sqibb?' (2014) 37 *Journal of Consumer Policy* 67.

In April 2018, the European Commission published its New Deal for Consumers package.[4] It included a proposal for a Directive on representative actions for the protection of collective interests of consumers. In December 2020, the new Directive of 25 November 2020 on representative actions for the protection of the collective interests of consumers was adopted, finally ending the struggle to establish a binding instrument on collective redress.[5]

The new Directive enables Qualified Entities (such as consumer organisations and independent public bodies) to request injunctive and compensatory redress measures. The Directive will be the leitmotiv for the debate and development of European class actions in the years to come.[6]

Since the launch of his academic career, collective redress has been an important part of Chris's research agenda. The fundamental question he has always asked is whether representative actions really offer (collective) redress?[7] Are there other (more efficient and effective) techniques to achieve the same outcome? How should these other techniques and representative actions be joined up to form an integrated dispute resolution framework?

In 2008, Chris laid down his framework for collective redress in Europe. In *The Reform of Class and Representative Actions in European Legal Systems. A New Framework for Collective Redress in Europe*,[8] he examines the principal trends and policy goals relating to collective redress mechanisms in Europe. He identifies three principal areas in which procedures and debates have emerged (within consumer protection and competition law, and from some national court systems) and looks at differing national models of public and private enforcement. The aim is to search for more efficient and inclusive procedures that would deliver increased access to justice and enhanced compliance with desired standards. A sequence of case studies in this work illustrates the pros and cons of differing models. Ultimately, he unravels and prioritises the various policy strands and recommends options for the future. The American 'private enforcement' model is contrasted with the more prevalent European public and mediated enforcement tradition. New developments involving ombudsmen and oversight of compensation by public enforcement bodies are identified, and underlying theories of restorative justice and responsive regulation are discussed. Public, private, formal, informal, ADR and voluntary methodologies are evaluated against criteria. The work concludes that the optimal options for collective redress in Europe involve a combination of approaches,

[4] See at https://ec.europa.eu/newsroom/just/items/620435/en.

[5] Directive 2020/1828 of the European Parliament and of the Council of 25 November 2020 on representative actions for the protection of the collective interests of consumers and repealing Directive 2009/22/EC (Representative Actions Directive) [2020] OJ L409/1.

[6] See in general A Uzelac and S Voet (eds), *Class Actions in Europe. Holy Grail or a Wrong Trail?* (Springer, 2021).

[7] D Hensler and C Hodges, 'What are People Trying to Do in Resolving Mass Issues, How Is It Going, and Where Are We Headed?' (2009) 66 *Annals of the American Academy of Political and Social Science* 330.

[8] C Hodges, *The Reform of Class and Representative Actions in European Legal Systems: A New Framework for Collective Redress in Europe* (Hart Publishing, 2008). In 2001, Chris wrote his well-respected classic on group and collective litigation in the UK (C Hodges, *Multi-Party Actions* (Oxford University Press, 2001); a second edition is forthcoming (C Hodges and G Webb (eds), *Multi-Party Actions*, 2nd edn (Oxford University Press, 2024)). See also C Hodges, 'Multi-Party Actions: A European Approach' (2001) 11 *Duke Journal of Comparative & International Law* 321; and C Hodges, 'Collective Actions' in P Cane and H Kritzer (eds), *The Oxford Handbook of Empirical Legal Research* (Oxford University Press, 2010) 705.

with priority given to public and voluntary solutions over private court-based mechanisms. Chris writes:

> Overall, therefore, reforms are called for in both civil justice systems and in policies on enforcement. The risk of producing ineffective, inappropriate and expensive systems is considerable if Europe gets the balance wrong. However, if Europe gets the balance right, it could produce a greater degree of virtuous behaviour in commerce and redress, more redress and overall lower cost, thereby enhancing both competitiveness and social and moral cohesion. Does this all sound too idealistic? Time may tell.[9]

That time came exactly a decade later. In 2018, and together with Stefaan Voet, *Delivering Collective Redress: New Technologies*,[10] was published. Building on Chris's previous work, this book charts the transformative shifts in techniques that seek to deliver collective redress, especially for mass consumer claims in Europe. It shows how traditional approaches of class litigation (old technology) have been eclipsed by the new technology of regulatory redress techniques and consumer ombudsmen.[11] The book describes a series of these techniques, each illustrated by leading examples taken from a 2016 pan-European Union (EU) research project. It then undertakes a comparative evaluation of each technique against key criteria, such as effective outcomes, speed and cost.[12] The book reveals major transformations in European legal systems, and shows the overriding need to view legal systems from fresh viewpoints and to devise a new integrated model.

The book puts forward a number of conclusions for future policy on collective redress in Europe.[13] The first, and most poignant, conclusion is that Member States and the EU should establish a robust policy on a coherent, modernised approach to market behaviour and enforcement, and that redress should not be considered on its own but as an integral part of contributing to strong and competitive markets. In his later work, Chris put this to the test and made this more concrete.

Part II of the present book is dedicated to collective redress: 'What is Collective in EU Collective Redress?' (Hans-W Micklitz and Andrea Wechsler) (chapter 8); '"*Je t'aime moi non plus*": Why Europe Needs Strong Collective Redress' (Alexandre Biard) (chapter 9); 'Collective Redress in EU Consumer Law: How It Is, How It Could Be' (Stephen Weatherill) (chapter 10); 'Let's Redress European Redress the Hodges Way! *Redressons redress en Europe à l'Hodgienne*! A Look at How Canada Resolves the Conflicting Collective Claims Cross-Border Conundrum and How May the Canadian Solution Help Us in the EU?' (Herbert Woopen) (chapter 11); 'Deadweight Loss and Collective Redress in Competition Law' (Franziska Weber) (chapter 12); 'Third-Party Funding in Collective Redress' (Astrid Stadler) (chapter 13) and 'Do Collective Redress Mechanisms Deliver Justice?' (Mary E Bartkus) (chapter 14).

[9] C Hodges, *The Reform of Class and Representative Actions in European Legal Systems: A New Framework for Collective Redress in Europe* (Hart Publishing, 2008) 249.

[10] C Hodges and S Voet, *Delivering Collective Redress: New Technologies* (Hart Publishing, 2018). See also C Hodges, 'Collective Redress: The Need for New Technologies' (2018) 42 *Journal of Consumer Policy* 59.

[11] See pt III of this book.

[12] See also C Hodges, 'Objectives, Mechanisms and Policy Choices in Collective Enforcement and Redress' in J Steele and W van Boom (eds), *Mass Justice* (Edward Elgar, 2011) 101.

[13] Hodges and Voet (n 10) 311–12.

III. Consumer Dispute Resolution

Another spearhead of Chris's research is consumer dispute resolution (CDR), which uses the traditional ADR techniques (arbitration, conciliation and mediation) but within the context of a dispute resolution structure that is entirely separate from the courts.[14] The CDR architecture encompasses a number of possible structures, including (regulated) private sector ombudsmen. It also encompasses online dispute resolution (ODR), which uses technology (the Internet) to facilitate CDR.

In 2013, the Consumer ADR Directive and Consumer ODR Regulation were adopted.[15] The latter establishes a free and interactive pan-European ODR platform through which consumers and traders can initiate ADR in relation to disputes concerning online transactions (offline transactions are excluded). National ADR entities receive the complaint electronically and seek to resolve the dispute. The Consumer ADR Directive promotes ADR by encouraging the use of approved ADR entities that ensure the following minimum quality standards: the entities should be impartial and provide transparent information, offer their services at no or nominal cost, and hear and determine complaints within 90 days of referral. The Directive applies to both domestic and cross-border disputes concerning complaints by a consumer resident in the EU against a trader established in the EU.

In 2012, Chris and his then Oxford team (Iris Benöhr and Naomi Creutzfeldt) published *Consumer ADR in Europe*,[16] the first systematic comparative study into how consumer ADR systems (usually ombudsmen[17]) work, the differing national architectures within which they operate and how they can be improved. The book describes ADR schemes in Belgium, France, Germany, Lithuania, the Netherlands, Poland, Slovenia, Spain, Sweden and the United Kingdom (UK), as well as emerging pan-EU dispute resolution schemes. It also covers EU measures on consumer ADR, and the then proposals for legislation on ADR and ODR (which later become the Consumer ADR Directive and Consumer ODR Regulation). Data on volumes, cost and the duration of ADR schemes are compared, both between different systems and with courts. As in his work on collective redress, relationships between ADR, courts and regulators are discussed, and the need for reforms is noted.

As Norbert Reich noted:

> The authors put forward a wealth of information about best practice in coverage, structure, visibility, and proceedings of CADR, certainly with a view to promoting CADR as an

[14] For a historical overview, see N Creutzfeldt, 'The Origins and Evolution of Consumer Dispute Resolution Systems in Europe' in C Hodges and A Stadler (eds), *Resolving Mass Disputes. ADR and Settlement of Mass Claims* (Edward Elgar, 2013) 223.

[15] Directive 2013/11/EU of the European Parliament and of the Council of 21 May 2013 on alternative dispute resolution for consumer disputes and amending Regulation (EC) No 2006/2004 and Directive 2009/22/EC (Directive on Consumer ADR) [2013] OJ L165/63 and Regulation (EU) No 524/2013 of the European Parliament and of the Council of 21 May 2013 on online dispute resolution for consumer disputes and amending Regulation (EC) No 2006/2004 and Directive 2009/22/EC (Regulation on Consumer ODR) [2013] OJ L165/1 (see at https://webgate.ec.europa.eu/odr). See in general P Cortés (ed), *The New Regulatory Framework for Consumer Dispute Resolution* (Oxford University Press, 2017).

[16] C Hodges, I Benöhr and N Creutzfeldt-Banda, *Consumer ADR in Europe* (Hart Publishing, 2012).

[17] See also C Hodges, 'The Private Sector Ombudsman' in M Hertogh and R Kirkham (eds), *The Research Handbook on Ombudsman* (Edward Elgar, 2018) 53.

> alternative to court-based access system and to improving existing ones. … The book is a very useful analysis to be recommended to all involved in shaping and using ADR schemes – governments, agencies, courts, lawyers' bodies, trade associations, consumer organizations, last but not least academics interested in consumer complaint handling and access to justice by learning from country experiences. The study is indispensable to understand and follow the legislative process provoked by the Commission proposals of 29 November 2011 – perhaps with an even greater emphasis and concern on coming ODR mechanisms.[18]

Consumer ADR in Europe was one of the first works underpinning that well-developed CDR systems can identify and process multiple claims, hence can offer collective redress,[19] and that they are able to trigger regulatory action – Chris ultimately sees the consumer as a regulator.[20] All these issues were developed more in detail in Chris's later work.

In this context of CDR, Chris again looked beyond the strict legislative and procedural framework. He regularly underlined the broader cultural context of CDR:

> Behind these considerations is an important cultural issue. One of the European Commission's motivations in developing CDR was that the EU is not, at heart, an adversarial culture, but seeks to build society based upon compromise and consensus. The principle of solidarity, for example, is seen in the final stage of EU lawmaking through conciliation between the major groups of the Council, Parliament and Commission. The core moral idea is that one who has morally wronged another person must do something about it and make amends.
>
> CDR seeks to support not just a society based on law and market exchange but also a fair and cohesive society.[21]

Chris's influence on the development CDR systems in various jurisdictions has been considerable. In the past years, he has had discussions on CDR and consumer ombudsmen with the UK Department of Business, Energy and Industrial Strategy (BEIS) and the Governments of Austria, Belgium, China, Denmark, Finland, France, Germany, Ireland, Lithuania, Netherlands, Norway, Portugal, Singapore, Spain and Sweden, as well as Ontario and UNCTAD.

Part III of this book focuses on consumer dispute resolution (CDR): 'Does CDR "Get It"?' (Lewis Shand Smith and Matthew Vickers) (chapter 15); 'Consumer Dispute Resolution in the Digital Era: Access for All, or Access for Some Consumers?' (Eline Verhage and Naomi Creutzfeldt) (chapter 16); 'Rise and Fall of Traffic Accident ADR

[18] N Reich, 'Book Review: Consumer ADR in Europe: Civil Justice Systems, by Christopher Hodges, Iris Benöhr and Naomi Creutzfeldt-Banda (Oxford: Hart Publishing, 2012)' (2013) 50 *Common Market Law Review* 913, 915.

[19] See C Hodges and A Stadler (eds), *Resolving Mass Disputes: ADR and Settlement of Mass Claims* (Edward Elgar, 2013) showing this integrative approach and combining collective redress and CDR

[20] C Hodges, 'The Consumer as Regulator' in D Leczykiewicz and S Weatherill (eds), *The Images of the Consumer in EU Law: Legislation, Free Movement and Competition Law* (Hart Publishing, 2016) 245. See also C Hodges, 'New Modes of Redress for Consumers: ADR and Regulation' in S Camarra Lapuente (ed), *La Revisión de las Normas Europeas y Nacionales de Proteccción de los Consumidores* (CIVITAS and Thomson Reuters, 2012) 227; and C Hodges, 'Fast, Effective and Low Cost Redress: How Do Public and Private Enforcement and ADR Compare?' in B Rodger (ed), *Competition Law: Comparative Private Enforcement and Collective Redress Across the EU* (Wolters Kluwer, 2014) 255.

[21] C Hodges, 'Implementing the Vision' in P Cortés (ed), *The New Regulatory Framework for Consumer Dispute Resolution* (Oxford University Press, 2017) 351, 367. See also, in the same sense, C Hodges, 'Unlocking Justice and Markets: The Promise of Consumer ADR' in J Zekoll, M Bälz and I Amelung (eds), *Dispute Resolution: Alternatives to Formalization – Formalization of Alternatives?* (Brill, 2014) 336.

in Japan: The Cause and the Possible Remedy' (Takuya Hatta) (chapter 17) and 'CDR: Catalyst for China's E-Commerce' (Ying Yu and Alex Chung) (chapter 18).

IV. Court System Reform and New Technologies

Chris never delved into strict procedural issues, except for litigation costs perhaps.[22] He is no hard-core proceduralist zooming in on technical details. Rather he has an overarching vision on (civil, criminal and administrative) procedure and on which role courts should play, and more particularly not play, in the dispute resolution arena.

The best example can be found in one of his more recent works, *Delivering Dispute Resolution. A Holistic Review of Models in England and Wales.*[23] This work, which focuses on England and Wales but undoubtedly also is relevant for other jurisdictions, reviews the techniques, mechanisms and architectures of the way disputes are processed in England and Wales. Adopting a comparative approach, it evaluates the current state of the main different types of dispute resolution systems, including business, consumer, personal injury, family, property, employment and claims against the state. It provides a holistic overview of the whole system and suggests both systemic and detailed reforms. Examining dispute resolution pathways from users' perspectives, the book highlights options such as ombudsmen, regulators, tribunals and courts, as well as mediation and other ADR and ODR approaches. It maps numerous sectoral developments to see if these also provide insights for other sectors. Several recurrent themes arise, including the diversification in the use of techniques; adoption of digital, online and artificial technology; cost and funding constraints; the emergence of new intermediaries; the need to focus accessibility arrangements for people and businesses that need help with their problems; and identifying effective ways for achieving behavioural change. This work analyses the shift from adversarial legalism to softer means of resolving social problems, and points to a major opportunity to devise an imaginative and holistic strategic vision for the jurisdiction.

The concluding chapter of the book, 'A New Design for Dispute Resolution Architecture',[24] where he aims to redesign the dispute resolution landscape, is a conclusion (or culmination) of Chris's previous work, in the sense that it brings together to a large extent all of his previous ideas and thoughts into a coherent mould. At the same time it can be seen as a blueprint or roadmap for his current and more recent work. At the outset are three over-arching design principles:

> First, complete pathways should be designed, that have steps that flow in a logical sequence and without interruption or barriers: in other words, an end-to-end design. Secondly, there should be a focus on solving the real problems that people have. Thirdly, the courts are no longer the sole or even possibly ultimate pathway.[25]

[22] C Hodges, S Vogenauer and M Tulibacka (eds), *The Costs and Funding of Civil Litigation. A Comparative Perspective* (Hart Publishing, 2010).

[23] C Hodges, *Delivering Dispute Resolution. A Holistic Review of Models in England and Wales* (Hart Publishing, 2019).

[24] ibid 550–70.

[25] ibid 550.

Regarding the last, perhaps the most provocative principle, Chris notes:

> Courts are not the only option. Courts – or anything else – might not be the best or appropriate option in a particular case. That realisation leads to the proposition that courts – or anything else – might not be the 'ultimate' or 'superior' solution. That proposition challenges some deeply held constitutional ideas, but it has to be faced in the contemporary world.[26]

Next, he lists the different stages in the relevant dispute resolution processes and pathways: information, assistance and triage, mediation, the ability to make a complaint or claim, case management, a decision and enforcement. In addition, the system should be able to identify, and apply, lessons, so as to avoid unnecessarily repeating the same problems and improve future behaviour and culture.

Again, as was the case for collective redress and CDR, the social dimension should not be forgotten:

> One aspect of the emerging mechanisms is that they promote a particular style of society, that identifies problems and solves them quickly and through cooperative engagement, rather than waiting for the litigation system to be invoked and to operate in a mode of conflict and adversarial legalism. The point is not just about the speed of problem identification and problem solving, it is about the values and style of society. What this means in relation to dispute resolution is a shift from adversarial legalism to softer means of resolving social problems. This trend has to be recognised in regulation, social behaviour, family, employment, or trading contexts, and expressed in the values, structures and systems that society uses for dispute resolution. There is a highly important underlying point here about the type of society that is being expressed and desired. It is that relationships (regulation-business, family, employment, citizen-state) should be based on mutual respect, identifying problems and resolving them quickly, fairly and without aggression. It is not an expression of desire for a society that values individual freedom and individual rights without much consideration for others. That society might be adversarial and fractured. It is an expression of desire for a society that values social cooperation and interaction in a supportive, discursive engagement. That society would be collaborative and healing.[27]

One notable example of Chris's new technologies is no-fault compensation schemes. In 2017, and together with Sonia Macleod, he published *Redress Schemes for Personal Injuries*.[28] This book offers the first systematic comparative study of over 40 personal injury compensation schemes. These include the comprehensive no-blame coverage offered by the New Zealand Accident Compensation Corporation; the widely used Patient, Pharmaceutical, Motor Accident and Workers Compensation Insurance systems of the Nordic states; the far smaller issue-focused schemes like the UK Thalidomide and vCJD Trusts; vaccine damage schemes that exist in many countries; as well as motor vehicle schemes from the USA. The study covers the drivers for their creation, the frameworks under which they operate, the criteria and thresholds used, the compensation offered, the claims process, statistics on throughput and costs, and analysis of financial costings. It also considers and compares the successes and failings of these schemes. Many different types of redress providers are studied. The authors draw

[26] ibid 551.
[27] ibid 569–70.
[28] S Macleod and C Hodges, *Redress Schemes for Personal Injuries* (Hart Publishing, 2017).

conclusions about the functions, essential requirements, architecture, scope, operation and performance of personal injury compensation systems. The relationships between such schemes, the courts and regulators – recurrent themes in Chris's research – are also discussed, and both calls and the need for reforms are noted. Making reference to the wide calls for reform of National Health Service (NHS) medical negligence litigation within the UK, and its replacement with a no-blame approach, the authors' findings outline options for future policy in this area.

In light of this, Chris's influence on the development of regulation and ethics in the medical devices sector needs to be underlined. Since the introduction of EU-wide regulation of medical devices around 1990, he has been the leading legal and later academic expert in this area. Around 2000, his leading position was recognised in his appointment by the Department of Health as co-chair (with the CEO of MHRA) of two regulatory strategy committees. He was Chair from 1992 for around 10 years of both the UK and EU trade associations' legal committees (Association of British HealthTech Industries (ABHI) and European Confederation of Medical Suppliers Associations (EUCOMED), now MEDTECH EUROPE), and of ABHI's regulatory committee, as well as latterly being a Board member of ABHI. As such, he inspired and led the successful introduction of industry codes of ethical practice. In 2012, he was asked by national regulators in the UK and Ireland to chair a committee on European strategic regulatory policy, which has continued and is expanding.

Moreover, Chris was the first non-pharmacist to be appointed Chairman of the Pharmaceutical Services Negotiating Committee (PSNC) (2007–11), representing the owners of all community pharmacies in England and Wales in discussions with the Department of Health on their strategic roles within the NHS and contractual conditions, not least on remuneration. Under his leadership, the PSNC maintained a stable and successful relationship between the Department of Health and community pharmacies, delivering effective healthcare in the NHS.

Part IV of this book looks at court system reform and new technologies: 'Digital Technology and the Development of Holistic Dispute Resolution' (Sir Geoffrey Vos and John Sorabji) (chapter 19); 'The Evolution of No-Fault Compensation Schemes for Personal Injuries' (Sonia Macleod) (chapter 20) and 'No-Fault Compensation Systems in the Pandemic Context' (Lorenz Ködderitzsch) (chapter 21).

V. Ethical Business Regulation, Corporate Behaviour and Regulatory Delivery

A common thread throughout Chris's work is the end of the traditional public versus private model. The binary and traditional classification of private versus public enforcement is outdated.[29] Traditional private law has become public private law and public law has been privatised.

[29] C Hodges and N Creutzfeldt, 'Transformations in Public and Private Enforcement' in H-W Micklitz and A Wechsler (eds), *The Transformation of Enforcement* (Hart Publishing, 2016) 115; and C Hodges, 'Public and Private Enforcement: The Practical Implications for Policy Architecture' in R Brownsword, H-W Micklitz, L Niglia and S Weatherill (eds), *The Foundations of European Private Law* (Hart Publishing, 2011) 437.

A first illustration of this is *Law and Corporate Behaviour. Integrating Theories of Regulation, Enforcement, Compliance and Ethics*,[30] which was published in 2015. This book examines the theories and practice of how to control corporate behaviour through legal techniques. The principal theories examined are deterrence, economic rational acting, responsive regulation and the findings of behavioural psychology. Leading examples of the various approaches are given in order to illustrate the models: private enforcement of law through litigation in the USA, public enforcement of competition law by the European Commission, and the recent reform of policies on public enforcement of regulatory law in the UK. Noting that behavioural psychology has as yet had only limited application in legal and regulatory theory, the book then analyses various European regulatory structures where behavioural techniques can be seen or could be applied. Sectors examined include financial services, civil aviation, pharmaceuticals, and workplace health and safety. Key findings are that enforcement has to focus on identifying the causes of non-compliance, so as to be able to support improved performance, rather than be based on fear motivating complete compliance. Systems in which reporting is essential for safety only function with a no-blame culture.

The book concludes by proposing a holistic model for maximising compliance within large organisations, combining public regulatory and criminal controls with internal corporate systems and external influences by stakeholders, held together by a unified core of ethical principles. In conclusion, the book proposes a new theory of ethical regulation. One Dutch reviewer concluded that 'If Hodges is right many authors – including legal economists – should revise their texts on the preventative effect of laws.'[31]

Two years later, in 2017, Chris and Ruth Steinholtz published *Ethical Business Practice and Regulation: A Behavioural and Values-Based Approach to Compliance and Enforcement*.[32] This book, which builds further on *Law and Corporate Behaviour*, explains the concepts of Ethical Business Practice (EBP) and Ethical Business Regulation (EBR), a new paradigm in compliance and enforcement based on behavioural science and ethics. The latter concept provides the basis for an effective relationship between a business and its regulators, resulting in better outcomes for both. It is attracting extensive attention from regulators and businesses around the world. The UK Government's 2017 Regulatory Futures Review draws on EBR as the foundation for its policy of 'regulatory self-assurance', while EBR draws on findings from behavioural science, responsive regulation, safety and business and integrity management to create a practical and holistic approach. Examples include the open culture that is essential for civil aviation safety, the Primary Authority agreements between regulators and national businesses, and feedback mechanisms provided by market vigilance systems and sectoral consumer ombudsmen. Both EBP and EBR are discussed more in detail in chapter 22 of this book: 'Ethical Business Practice and Regulation and Beyond: Challenging Traditional Approaches to Compliance and Enforcement' (Ruth N Steinholtz and Srikanth Mangalam).

[30] C Hodges, *Law and Corporate Behaviour. Integrating Theories of Regulation, Enforcement, Compliance and Ethics* (Hart Publishing, 2015).

[31] Ewoud Hondius in *Nederlands Tijdschrift voor Burgerlijk Recht* available at www.bloomsbury.com/uk/law-and-corporate-behaviour-9781782255833/.

[32] C Hodges and Ruth Steinholtz, *Ethical Business Practice and Regulation: A Behavioural and Values-Based Approach to Compliance and Enforcement* (Hart Publishing, 2017).

The impact that EBR has had within a short time is truly remarkable. Chris has assisted in the application of EBR with the following UK regulators: Civil Aviation Authority, the new Office for Students, MHRA, Food Standards Authority, Ofgem, Ofwat, Equality and Human Rights Commission, Health and Safety Executive. He has recently worked closely with the Cabinet Office on implementation of the Regulatory Futures Review, with the Regulatory Delivery Directorate of BEIS and with the Scottish Government (especially the Consumer and Competition Policy team, and Ministers of the Economy), and has explained his ideas to the Regulatory Policy Committee and the Financial Conduct Authority and Care Quality Commission.

In 2019, *Regulatory Delivery*, written by Chris and Graham Russell, was published.[33] It was the first product of members of the International Network for Delivery of Regulation (INDR).[34] The INDR is a membership organisation that aims to provide a Centre of Excellence to support improvement in the way regulation is delivered, namely how regulations are received and applied by businesses and others whose behaviour they seek to control, and the manner in which they are enforced. It is also a 'safe space' International Hub for the exchange of views and sharing of information on regulation and enforcement models, approaches and techniques, bringing together governmental policy and regulatory practitioners with academic support, to enable strong practical applications of best regulatory delivery practice.

At the outset of *Regulatory Delivery* is the Regulatory Delivery Model, developed by Graham Russell and his team at the UK BEIS. The model sets out a framework to steer improvements to regulatory delivery, comprising three prerequisites for regulatory agencies to be able to operate effectively (Governance Frameworks, Accountability and Culture) and three practices for regulatory agencies to be able to deliver societal outcomes (Outcome Measurement, Risk-based Prioritisation and Intervention Choices). Both INDR and regulatory delivery are discussed more in detail in chapter 23 of this book: 'The Evolution of INDR, 2017–2022' (Hilary Evans and Graham Russell).

VI. Tribute

This introduction and the following contributions are a tribute to the intellectual journey of Chris and the impact he has had on numerous fields of law. Starting with substantive law on product liability and regulation of medicines and medical devices, analysing the impact of aggregation of claims, its funding and safeguards, to exploring more effective dispute resolution in a consumer setting, leading on to ombudsmen, regulatory feedback loops to better regulation and ethical business practices, all while connecting dots where others are caught in their silos. We are indebted to Chris for his sharp analysis, lucid writing and creative ideas that have improved and will continue to improve legal policy and research.

[33] G Russell and C Hodges, *Regulatory Delivery* (Hart Publishing, 2019).
[34] See at www.indr.org.uk/.

2

Résumé and Main Publications

XANDRA KRAMER, STEFAAN VOET, LORENZ KÖDDERITZSCH, MAGDALENA TULIBACKA AND BURKHARD HESS

I. Résumé

18 March 1954	Born in Birmingham.
1972	A-levels (Physics, Chemistry, Mathematics) at King Edward's Birmingham; decided against studying metallurgy at university.
1972–73	Short Military Service Commission with Royal Signals, Germany.
1973–76	Choral Scholar at New College, Oxford, reading Law.
1976	BA, New College Oxford, Law/1980 MA.
1976–77	Part II Conversion Course at Guildford College of Law.
1977	Marriage Fiona; daughters: Elisabeth (b 1985), Helen (b 1987) and Lucy (b 1989).
1977–87	Articled clerk (= trainee) and then solicitor at Slaughter and May, City of London.
1984–85	Solicitor in Slaughter and May's Hong Kong office, admitted as solicitor in Hong Kong.
1987–89	Solicitor at Clifford Chance.
1990–2004	Partner at CMS Cameron McKenna.
1990–2006	Trustee and Director, The Sixteen.
1994	Beginning of PhD research on product liability law.
1995–2008	Chairman, Legal Committee, European Association of Medical Technology Manufacturers (EUCOMED).
2003–08	Vice-Chairman, Association of British Healthcare Industries, 2003–08 and Chair of its Legal Committee and Technical Policy Group.
2004	PhD King's College London: European Regulation of Consumer Product Safety.

2004	Joins Centre for Socio-legal Studies at Oxford and Fellow of Wolfson College.
2006–13	Chairman, Bampton Classical Opera.
2011–14	Professor of the Fundamentals of Private Law at Erasmus University, Rotterdam.
2013–16	Honorary Professor, the China University for Political Science and Law, Beijing, and Guest Professor, Wuhan University, Wuhan.
2014	Appointment as Professor of Justice Systems, University of Oxford.
2021	Appointed to the Order of the British Empire (OBE).
1 August 2021	Emeritus Professor of Justice Systems, University of Oxford.

II. Main Publications

1991

C Hodges, 'Harmonisation of European Controls over Research: Ethics Committees, Consent, Compensation and Indemnity' in A Goldberg and I Dodd-Smith (eds), *Pharmaceutical Medicine and the Law* (Royal College of Physicians of London and The Faculty of Pharmaceutical Medicine of the Royal Colleges of Physicians of the UK, 1991) 1067.

1993

C Hodges (ed), *Product Liability: European Laws and Practice* (Sweet & Maxwell, 1993).

C Hodges, 'Investigating, Reporting and Pursuing Fraud in Clinical Research: Legal Aspects and Options' in F Wells and S Lock (eds), *Fraud and Misconduct in Clinical Research* (BMJ Publishing, 1st edn 1993; 2nd edn 1995) 74.

1994

C Hodges, 'Product Safety Regulation' in M Mildred (ed), *Product Liability Law and Insurance* (Lloyd's of London Press, 1994 and subsequent editions).

C Hodges, 'The Consumer Protection Act 1987' in M Mildred (ed), *Product Liability Law and Insurance* (Lloyd's of London Press, 1994 and subsequent editions).

1995

C Hodges, ML Tyler and H Abbott, *Product Safety* (Sweet & Maxwell, 1995).

1998

C Hodges, 'Development Risks: Unanswered Questions' (1998) *MLR* 560.

1999

C Hodges, 'Factors Influencing the Incidence of Multiple Claims' (1999) *Journal of Personal Injury Litigation* 289.

C Hodges, 'European Regulation of Medical Devices' in J O'Grady, I Dodds-Smith, N Walsh and M Spencer (eds), *Medicines, Medical Devices and the Law* (Greenwich

Medical Media Limited, 1999); reprinted in J Griffin and J O'Grady (eds), *The Regulation of Medical Products* (BMJ Publishing, 2003); then a revised version in J Griffin and J O'Grady (eds), *The Textbook of Pharmaceutical Medicine*, 5th edn (BMJ Books and Blackwell Publishing, 2006).

2000

C Hodges, 'The Reuse of Medical Devices' (2000) 8 *Medical Law Review* 157.

2001

C Hodges, *Multi-Party Actions* (Oxford University Press, 2001).
C Hodges, 'Multi-Party Actions: A Approach' (2001) 11 *European Duke Journal of Comparative & International Law* 321.
C Hodges, 'Compensating Patients' (2001) 117 *LQR* 528 [Case Note].

2002

C Hodges, 'Product Liability of Suppliers: The Notification Trap' (2002) 6 *EL Rev* 758.
C Hodges, 'Directive 1999/44/EC on Sale of Consumer Goods and Consumer Guarantees' in M Kurer et al (eds), *Warranties and Disclaimers: Limitation of Liability in Consumer-Related Transactions* (Kluwer and International Bar Association, 2002) 601.

2004

C Hodges, 'Do We Need a European Medical Devices Agency?' (2004) 12 *Medical Law Review* 268.

2005

C Hodges, *European Regulation of Consumer Product Safety* (Oxford University Press, 2005).
C Hodges, 'Approaches to Product Liability in the EU and Member States' in D Fairgrieve (ed), *Product Liability in Comparative Perspective* (Cambridge University Press, 2005) 192.

2006

C Hodges, 'Competition enforcement, regulation, and civil justice: what is the case?' (2006) 43 *CMLR* 1.
C Hodges, 'Europeanisation of civil justice: trends and issues' (2006) 1 *Civil Justice Quarterly* 96.
C Hodges, 'Nordic Compensation Schemes for Drug Injuries' (2006) 29 *Journal of Consumer Policy* 14.
C Hodges, 'Product Liability: Suppliers, Limitation and Mistake' (2006) 122 *LQR* 393 [Case Note].

2007

C Hodges, 'Encouraging Enterprise and Rebalancing Risk: Implications of Economic Policy for Regulation, Enforcement and Compensation' (2007) 20 *European Business Law Review* 1231.

2008

C Hodges, *The Reform of Class and Representative Actions in European Legal Systems: A New Framework for Collective Redress in Europe* (Hart Publishing, 2008).

C Hodges, 'Regulating Risk or Advancing Therapies? Regulation and sustainability of medicines in a cash-limited economy' (2008) 19 *European Business Law Review* 365.

C Hodges, 'Group Actions' in P Cane and J Conaghan (eds), *The New Oxford Companion to Law* (Oxford University Press, 2008).

C Hodges, 'Product Safety' in P Cane and J Conaghan (eds), *The New Oxford Companion to Law* (Oxford University Press, 2008).

2009

C Hodges, 'Ensuring a High Level of Business Conduct in the EU' (2009) 17 *Regulatory Affairs Journal Devices* 13.

C Hodges, 'From Class Actions to Collective Redress' (2009) 28 *Civil Justice Quarterly* 41.

D Hensler and C Hodges, 'What are people trying to do in resolving mass issues, how is it going, and where are we headed?' (2009) 66 *Annals of the American Academy of Political and Social Science* 330.

C Hodges, 'United Kingdom' in F Cafaggi and H-W Micklitz (eds), *New Frontiers of Consumer Protection. The Interplay between Private and Public Enforcement* (Intersentia, 2009).

D Hensler and C Hodges, 'The Globalisation of Class Actions' (2009) 662(1) *Annals of the American Academy of Political and Social Science* 7.

2010

C Hodges, S Vogenauer and M Tulibacka (eds), *The Costs and Funding of Civil Litigation: A Comparative Approach* (Hart Publishing, 2010).

C Hodges, 'Collective Redress in Europe: The New Model' (2010) 7 *Civil Justice Quarterly* 370.

C Hodges, 'Collective Actions' in P Cane and H Kritzer (eds), *The Oxford Handbook of Empirical Legal Research* (Oxford University Press, 2010).

2011

C Hodges, 'The European Approach to Justice and Redress' (2011) 53(2) *Canadian Supreme Court Law Review* 301.

C Hodges, 'A Market-Based Competition Enforcement Policy' (2011) 22 *European Business Law Review* 261.

C Hodges, 'European Competition Enforcement Policy: Integrating Restitution and Behaviour Control' (2011) 34 *World Competition* 383.

C Hodges, 'Objectives, Mechanisms and Policy Choices in Collective Enforcement and Redress' in J Steele and W van Boom (eds), *Mass Justice* (Edward Elgar, 2011) 101.

C Hodges, 'Public and Private Enforcement: The Practical Implications for Policy Architecture' in R Brownsword et al (eds), *The Foundations of European Private Law* (Hart Publishing, 2011) 437.

2012

C Hodges, I Benöhr and N Creutzfeldt-Banda, *Consumer ADR in Europe* (Hart Publishing, 2012).

C Hodges, 'Consumer ADR in Europe' (2012) 6 *Zeitschrift für Konfliktmanagement* 195.

C Hodges, 'Current discussions on consumer redress: collective redress and ADR' (2012) 13 *ERA Forum* 11.

C Hodges, I Benöhr and N Creutzfeldt-Banda, 'Consumer-to-Business Dispute Resolution: The Power of CADR' (2012) 13 *ERA Forum* 199.

C Hodges, 'New Modes of Redress for Consumers and Competition Law' (2012) 11/12 *Revista de Concorrência e Regulação* 227.

C Hodges and R Money-Kyrle, 'Safeguards in Collective Action' (2012) 19 *Maastricht Journal of International and Comparative Law* 477.

C Hodges, 'New Modes of Redress for Consumers: ADR and Regulation' in S Camarra Lapuente (ed), *La Revisión de las Normas Europeas y Nacionales de Proteccción de los Consumidores* (CIVITAS and Thomson Reuters, 2012).

C Hodges, J Peysner and A Nurse, *Litigation Funding. Status and Issues* (Centre for Socio-Legal Studies, Oxford and Lincoln University, 2012).

C Hodges and R Money-Kyrle, 'Safeguards in Collective Actions' (2012) *FLJS Policy Brief.*

2013

C Hodges and A Stadler (eds), *Resolving Mass Disputes. ADR and Settlement of Mass Claims* (Edward Elgar, 2013).

C Hodges, 'Case C-168/05, Elisa María Mostraza Claro v Centro Móvil Milenium SL; Case C-4 0/08, Asturcom Telecomunicationes SL v Cristina Rodriguez Nogueira' (2013) *Intersentia Landmark Cases of EU Consumer Law in Honour of Jules Stuyck* [Case Note].

2014

C Hodges, 'Consumer ADR and Appeals' in A Uzelac and CH van Rhee (eds), *Nobody's Perfect. Essays on Appeals and Other Methods of Recourse against Judicial Decisions in Civil Matters* (Intersentia, 2014) 339.

C Hodges, 'Consumer Redress: Ideology and Empiricism' in K Purnhagen and P Rott (eds), *Varieties of European Economic Law and Regulation* (Springer, 2014) 793.

C Hodges, 'Delivering Redress through Alternative Dispute Resolution and Regulation in WH van Boom and G Wagner (eds), *Mass Torts in Europe: Cases and Reflections* (De Gruyter, 2014) 231.

C Hodges, 'Fast, Effective and Low-Cost Redress: How do Public and Private Enforcement and ADR Compare?' in B Rodger (ed), *Competition Law: Comparative Private Enforcement and Collective Redress Across the EU* (Wolters Kluwer, 2014) 255.

C Hodges, 'Unlocking Justice and Markets: The Promise of Consumer ADR' in J Zekoll, M Bälz and I Amelung (eds), *Dispute Resolution: Alternatives to Formalization – Formalization of Alternatives?* (Brill, 2014) 336.

N Creutzfeldt and C Hodges, 'Consumer Dispute Resolution (CDR) in Europe' (2014) 2 *Nederlands-Vlaams Tijdschrift voor Mediation en Conflictmanagement* 29.

2015

S Vogenauer and C Hodges (eds), *Civil Justice Systems in Europe: Implications for Choice of Forum and Choice of Contract Law* (Hart Publishing, 2015).

C Hodges, 'Verbraucher-Ombudsstellen: Besserere Regulierung und Beilegung von Streitigkeiten' (2015) 6 *Zeitschrift für das Privatrecht der Europäischen Union* 263.

2016

D Hensler, C Hodges and I Tzankova (eds), *Class Actions in Context: How Culture, Economics and Politics Shape Collective Litigation* (Edward Elgar 2016).

N Creutzfeldt and C Hodges, 'Parallel tracks in mass litigation: public and private responses to the Buncefield explosion in England' in D Hensler, C Hodges and I Tzankova (eds), *Class Actions in Context: How Economics, Politics and Culture Shape Collective Litigation* (Edward Elgar, 2016) 320.

C Hodges, 'The Consumer as Regulator' in D Leczykiewicz and S Weatherill (eds), *The Images of the Consumer in EU Law: Legislation, Free Movement and Competition Law* (Hart Publishing, 2016) 245.

C Hodges and N Creutzfeldt, 'Transformations in Public and Private Enforcement' in H-W Micklitz and A Wechsler (eds), *The Transformation of Enforcement* (Hart Publishing, 2016) 115.

C Hodges, 'US Class Actions: Promise and Reality' in H-W Micklitz and A Wechsler (eds), *The Transformation of Enforcement* (Hart Publishing, 2016) 199.

2017

C Hodges and R Steinholtz, *Ethical Business Practice and Regulation: A Behavioural and Values-Based Approach to Compliance and Enforcement* (Hart Publishing, 2017).

S Macleod and C Hodges, *Redress Schemes for Personal Injuries* (Hart Publishing, 2017).

C Hodges and S Voet, 'Consumer Dispute Resolution Mechanisms: Effective Enforcement and Common Principles' in B Hess and X Kramer (eds), *From Common Rules to Best Practices in European Civil Procedure* (Nomos and Hart Publishing, 2017) 353.

C Hodges, 'Consumer Redress: Implementing the Vision' in P Cortés (ed), *The New Regulatory Framework for Consumer Dispute Resolution* (Oxford University Press, 2017) 351.

C Hodges, 'The Regulation of Medicinal Products and Medical Devices' in J Laing and J McHale (eds), *Principles of Medical Law*, 4th edn (Oxford University Press, 2017).

2018

C Hodges and S Voet, *Delivering Collective Redress: New Technologies* (Hart Publishing, 2018).

C Hodges, 'Collective Redress: The Need for New Technologies' (2018) 42 *Journal of Consumer Policy* 59.

C Hodges, 'Delivering Data Protection: Trust and Ethical Culture' (2018) 4 *European Data Protection Law Review* 65.

C Hodges, 'The Private Sector Ombudsman' in M Hertogh and R Kirkham (eds), *The Research Handbook on Ombudsman* (Edward Elgar, 2018) 53.

2019

C Hodges, *Delivering Dispute Resolution: A Holistic Review of Models in England and Wales* (Hart Publishing, 2019).

G Russell and C Hodges, *Regulatory Delivery* (Hart Publishing, 2019).

C Hodges, 'Delivering Justice' (2019) 9 *International Journal of Procedural Law* 149.

A Biard and C Hodges, 'Médiation de la consommation: un bilan, des défis, des pistes de réflexion pour l'avenir' *Contrat Concurrence Consommation* n° 2, February 2019, study 2, 12.

C Hodges, 'Policy Brief: Developments and Issues in Consumer ADR and Consumer Ombudsmen in Europe' (2019) Foundation for Law, Justice and Society.

C Hodges, 'Consumer Alternative Dispute Resolution' in B Hess and S Law (eds), *Implementing EU Consumer Rights by National Procedural Law. Luxembourg Report on European Procedural Law*, vol II (Beck, 2019) 177.

2020

C Hodges, 'Achieving a Just Culture that Learns and Improves' in P Vines and A Akkermans (eds), *Unexpected Consequences of Compensation Law* (Hart Publishing, 2020) 123.

C Cole and C Hodges, *A Critical Analysis and Review of the Procedure and Substance of Appeal Rights to the First-tier Tribunal (General Regulatory Chamber)* (Centre for Socio-Legal Studies, 2020).

2022

C Hodges, *Outcome-Based Cooperation. In Communities, Business, Regulation, and Dispute Resolution* (Hart Publishing, 2022).

3

The Friend

DAVID MARKS

I. Rabbit Man

Christopher Hodges – I have always known him as Chris – entered my world at some point in 1990, bald as well as fully formed, or so I thought at the time. I was running my law firm's Brussels office when Chris joined the London practice as a partner. We visited his Brussels contacts together, he stayed with us and we got on famously.

I am sure that Chris has been called many things in his time, much as he has garnered titles and honours. I cannot vouch for his youthful nicknames, but to my daughters he is 'Rabbit Man', after a quantity of sleek brown fur which lived in a makeshift structure of wire and wood in his back garden. Although the rabbit succumbed to a local fox, 'Rabbit Man' endured. On a recent Zoom call I found myself telling one daughter, 'Rabbit Man's been made an OBE.'

At the outset Chris was another amiable colleague. Close acquaintance revealed more: the practising lawyer, the musician, the thinker and ultimately the academic. Improbable though I still find it, there was once Chris the soldier. Fully formed he may have seemed, but there remained a surprising amount of headroom for further growth.

II. The Colleague

Chris proved energetic and popular, and quickly established himself as a positive force within the firm. The highest possible compliment came from our pugnacious senior partner, 'I like that Chris Hodges – he's pushy.' Another senior colleague commented how much Chris had brought to the party.

His musical interests, on which more later, played their part. He was an enthusiastic choirmaster and set about organising a choir for the firm's Christmas carol service in the ancient St Bartholomew the Great in Smithfield near the office in London. As a skilled manager of quavering voices, Chris would deliberately under-rehearse, maximise nervous tension and snatch a peak performance on the night.

But above all it was his satirical order of service which caught the attention of his partners. We would all look forward to the email with spoof order of service, which skewered office politics and the firm's hierarchy.

His work rate was always prodigious. While Chris was building his practice he somehow found the time to write a book on product liability and establish an academic toehold at Oxford.

We had complementary practices, mine in EU law and his in product liability, medical device regulation and dispute resolution. We often paired up on client visits in Europe, North America and Japan. So we became regular hunting companions, fighting the jetlag and decompressing in the bar.

Japan in particular provided a rich outlet for his highly developed sense of fun. We would usually offer to give training talks to clients on a given range of subjects. After Chris had published his book on product liability that was all anyone wanted to hear about. Relegated to a supporting role in the Hodges roadshow, the rest of us would loyally catch his eye, distract him and try to make him corpse (for those unfamiliar, that means 'laugh involuntarily').

Chris buoyantly progressed through the hierarchy and was appointed one of the firm's six practice group managers and to the board. He led a disparate group of specialisations, including my own. His style was collegiate and supportive. Like the choirmaster, he would quietly get the best out of us.

In a fit of hubris he added his name to a wide field in the senior partner election. Of course everyone pledged to support whoever last canvassed them, leaving Chris quietly confident. Mercifully he lost, otherwise his later academic trajectory might have been very different and less fun.

The academic side was taking more of his energies as he began exploring alternative redress concepts and the proper role of regulation. I found myself heavily engaged in these themes over pints beer at The Hand and Shears, our local pub at the back of the office. Chris would hold forth and I would question, when awake. To a Chris in need of an audience, I passed for a good listener – and stifler of yawns.

As more books emerged it was clear that Chris planned to transition fully from legal practice into academia, preferably at his old university, Oxford. A move had always seemed to be a long way off, but when he finally said he was jumping ship I was shaken: it was like losing a leg, but I wished him joy.

When a colleague departs the personal relationship inevitably changes, because much of the common experience falls away. It was no different with Chris, but other things evolved to compensate. I helped develop a plan for our firm to support his academic research programme at Oxford and became involved in bringing his thinking to a wider business audience.

III. Early Days

Over time I have gained some insight into his earlier life. He was a pupil at King Edward's School, Birmingham where his father, a decorated war veteran, taught Romance languages. Chris does not always betray his origins but can still turn on the Midlands accent at will. He became a chorister in the school and developed a love for devotional music. When his voice broke, fortunately it did so in the right sort of way and became his passport to Oxford as a choral scholar.

In the year before taking up his place at Oxford, Chris enlisted with the army on a short service commission. This is something that I still find difficult to believe, and perhaps he does too. He emerged from this experience more worldly wise and apparently without killing anyone.

He studied law at Oxford, met his wife Fiona, who was studying classics, dutifully sang in the New College choir and became a founder member of the now internationally acclaimed choral group The Sixteen. He could readily have pursued a musical career, as a number of his contemporaries did.

There were other career opportunities. He was one of a group of students invited to a mountain hut on the Continent rumoured to be a recruiting ground for the British secret services. He declined.

He chose the law and trained as a solicitor with Slaughter and May, and after qualifying worked in both the London and Hong Kong offices. He was admitted to practice in Hong Kong, as well as in England and Wales. He worked at Clifford Chance before joining what is now CMS as a partner.

IV. Family

Chris is surrounded by strong and capable women. Fiona and he have three daughters, Elizabeth, Helen and Lucy. They keep him grounded and moderately sane. The importance of this strong family foundation to Chris's achievements should not be underestimated.

Fiona has a rapier wit and a rapid delivery. Chris needs to pay attention if he is to keep up. It is a joy to team up with Fiona in the often necessary task of deflating Chris (she usually refers to Chris as 'Sir' and in the third person). He takes it all in good part, most of the time.

V. Music

Music has also been a constant theme. Chris the choirmaster would occasionally disappear at a weekend to sing on tour with The Sixteen. I play The Sixteen's carol music every Christmas, and particularly relish a solo sung by Chris in medieval Spanish.

Chris's musical repertoire tends towards the sacred and ancient, with Haydn regarded as almost too modern. It follows that there are gaps in Chris's popular culture. On one of our early visits to Japan we were entertained to dinner and, because Chris was a singer, to karaoke. The songbook had just one page in English and Chris was initially horrified not to recognise anything. He had heard of The Beatles but was not overly familiar with their oeuvre. He finally settled on Sinatra's 'My Way', held the microphone at arm's length and set his voice at one-quarter power. People paid attention; someone was singing live.

Chris became involved with the management of The Sixteen and of country-house opera company Bampton Opera. Fiona would be in charge of costumes. He also joined with friends to form the occasional choral group Convivio, whose 'Teddybears' Picnic' will live long in my younger daughter's memory.

VI. Humour and Humanity

Chris tells a good joke and a good story. He has a well-developed sense of fun and a strong line in self-deprecation. Otherwise I would not have heard all of the following.

We were on a week's visit to Japan. On the Saturday I would return to Europe and Chris would fly on to Australia to testify on product liability before a government committee. As we were checking in at the airport the desk clerk examined Chris's passport and could not find his visa to enter Australia. 'But I'm British!' said Chris. 'You still need a visa sir.'

Sadly I had to take my leave before seeing how he would get himself out of this one. The solution was to phone the Australian consulate in Tokyo, where Chris had an involved discussion with the consul's infant son. Eventually he reached the consul, who was stuck in a Saturday morning Tokyo traffic jam. He would arrange for Chris to enter Australia, provided the person vouching for Chris was there on arrival.

At Sydney airport, immigration was, rightly, suspicious. 'So who is vouching for you?' Chris gave the name. 'What does he do?' 'He's Attorney General for New South Wales.' 'You're pulling my …' But he was there, a former London colleague at Clifford Chance, who had arranged for Chris to testify before the committee.

Chris tells this story end to end complete with excruciating accents, including that of the consul's infant son. He does not gloss over his superior assumption that as a Brit he be allowed into Australia without let or hindrance, or indeed a visa.

A common theme to all his interests is his pursuit of an audience. He loves to talk, hold forth, profess. He is in essence performative. But occasionally I have seen Chris misjudge his audience. This is likely a professorial trait: he might be telling the audience things which interest him but not them.

Then again, it could happen to anyone, but in this case it happened to Chris. The Brussels office of a US client was hosting its executive board on a visit to the EU. As part of the programme, I and the London client partner were invited to join a welcome dinner in their honour. The London colleague was unavailable and Chris deputised. This was during the first Gulf War, when there were concerns about terrorism and commercial airliners were flying mostly empty.

We showed up. The visitors were a tough looking bunch as we tried to make small talk over drinks. Chris's opening gambit was, 'So you weren't worried about flying over from the States with the war on?' The top man looked at him for a moment and replied without a smile, 'We took the jet'.

VII. What Makes Him Tick?

I still wonder. Chris excelled at what he put his mind to, put in extraordinary effort to achieve what he did, and took considerable risks to move between his various ambitions and interests. He has always had a book on the go from when I first knew him and his output has been truly prodigious. I am not sure this has made him universally popular with academic colleagues, who might suffer by comparison.

His drive must come from somewhere. Is it that Chris is an only child and only children frequently have a great capacity for sociability and friendship, as well as great self-motivation and self-belief? I doubt whether he has anything to prove to anyone other than to himself.

He has a strong sense of right and wrong, and it may be no accident that underlying his work on the proper role of regulation is the human instinct for doing the right thing. He is disappointed when he does not always find this quality in others: the only occasion I have seen him truly angry was when deliberately misled. Fundamentally he has a great belief in what he is doing and is convinced that he can make a difference. He can be evangelical – but is not saintliness the greatest of all temptations?

Chris is working across a range of legal, social and behavioural academic disciplines. His capacity for sociability and friendship are great assets in bringing people together and breaking down silos. The performer and choirmaster are other sides of the team builder and collaborator.

Whatever drives him, his achievements and collection of floppy hats speak for themselves. It never occurred to me that this new colleague would one day turn his back on a successful legal practice and become an Oxford professor.

VIII. So What Next?

Well, unsurprisingly, Chris has another book on the go. Who knows how many more there are in the can? Certainly, for as long as there is an audience for his ideas Chris will happily talk to it.

Fiona and Chris have just moved to Wells, a small cathedral city, which will have good sacred music. He will have a new home to knock about and make a study for himself, as well as a new garden to plant and enjoy. I personally hope there is a good cellar to do justice to his wine collection. Irrespective of whether the future brings more honours and opportunities to wear floppy hats, I wish him a belated happy retirement.

But as always with Chris there are other possibilities. And here I have a theory. What if the music, the law practice, the academic career were all an elaborate smokescreen? Did Chris in fact accept that invitation to the hut in the mountains when at Oxford, and was he tapped on the shoulder by the British secret services? Was he not in the military? It all makes sense now. His life's work has been nothing but an elaborate exercise in disinformation, and while we have been looking the other way he has subverted the traditional legal system and the vested interests of lawyers.

His next gig? We might be dealing here with the next agent 007. I hear there is a vacancy.

4

Policy Endeavour: Forging the Blueprint

ARUNDEL McDOUGALL AND URS LEIMBACHER

I. Introduction

The award of OBE to Chris Hodges in the Queen's New Year Honours 2021, as recognition for services to Business and Law, may seem the wrong end of the telescope for the start of this chapter, but the conjunction of those two components, Business and Law, is a useful shorthand for elucidating Chris's career.

These themes have played a large part in his work that we are celebrating here, and we explore how in what follows. It is true that in understanding the significance of Chris's subsequent career as a policy adviser in the realms of business and law, we must concede they are but two components of a complicated universe of moving parts. But they have been a driving force for what he has achieved over the years: what we might call the intelligent design of a new legal system, or philosophy, for determining legal disputes between consumers and business. Some call it by its relatively tried and tested formulaic ADR (Alternative Dispute Resolution), and that is a useful starting point, but it is a lot more.

In order to understand what the law does well and what it does not do so well, you need to understand how it works. This is why Chris's first career as a practising business lawyer is relevant to his success. His model has moved the consensus away from the axiom of the court system as the agent of resolution, what he terms an old technology, using private enforcement based on adversarialism and deterrence (litigation); to policies (Ethical Business Practice (EBP) and Ethical Business Regulation (EBR)) that support new technology to resolve consumer disputes. This new technology uses public enforcement based on human behaviour, particularly the behaviour of business. In doing so Chris has received the support of many businesses, regulators, judges and politicians.

That model relies heavily for its efficacy on two other components. One is the central role played by a non-judicial mechanism, either a sectoral regulator or ombudsman, or both, which is nonetheless determinative if the consumer agrees. Chris has planted his flag on that soil. And as an alternative to very costly, very messy, very one-dimensional litigation it is highly persuasive. Such ADR provides added dimensions of data capture from past disputes to manage future market turbulence, and consequent harms, and avoidance of capture by entrepreneurial litigation. In an increasingly digitalized and borderless transactional experience, his model for determining commercial disputes affecting not individual wrongs, but collective wrongs, is a winning formula.

The other component is that more troublesome ingredient referred to: human behaviour. The difficulty with a consumer redress system that relies on individuals, and corporate bodies, to behave and act ethically in a self-regulating environment, in return for absolution from penalties, civil and criminal, for observably good behaviour, is that it can look like an act of faith: people and organisations are good and bad in fluctuating proportions but ultimately equal measure. Decades of philosophy and psychology point to the Panglossian possibilities of theories of human behaviour, determining how people's instinctive adherence to rules brings about desirable outcomes. But rules can sometimes fossilise human endeavour. Chris's work has increasingly grappled with the dilemma of how to regulate individual and corporate behaviour in a way that encourages free enterprise and avoids having to invoke the black hole of civil litigation, or criminal penalties including imprisonment, for all but the most immoral or blatant criminal acts, and works for consumers.

His ADR model will no doubt have to be enshrined in legal frameworks of some sort appropriate to whatever business sector is concerned. So there will still be law involved. But his alternative model prioritises:

- functionality, not form;
- more reproducibility through data capture than is afforded by reliance on legal precedent;
- predictability of expectation and result, not as with litigation (the opposite); and
- competitive markets, not the market of lawyers' fees and third party funders.

The model, in its various forms, is developing deep and wide traction. The OBE is a national honour, but Chris's work is international in scope and application, to the benefit of business, regulators and consumers in many countries. That, if you like, is Chris's gift to posterity, though it remains a work in progress.

On the personal level, one can validly speculate about which of Chris's many characteristics have made him an international policy expert in consumer redress. The truth is that they have probably all contributed. But in terms of his lasting impact as a thinker, writer and proselytiser, the one feature that sets him apart and gives his ideas such traction is his background as a practising litigation lawyer before becoming an academic, having acted for many businesses, with a special insight into consumer redress across a wide range of business sectors. That experience is hard-welded onto his research.

Chris moved careers late in life. Before switching to the Centre for Socio-Legal Studies at Oxford University when he was 50, he had worked in the salt mines of a solicitors' practice for 27 years; in fact, in three very well-known and respected London law firms. By the time of his migration in 2004 he had become one of the UK's foremost product liability and regulatory law practitioners. As David Marks has explained, he had also, concurrently with his work as a lawyer in private practice, been intimately involved in running two business associations representing the medical device and healthcare industries. The experience he gained from this practical knowledge invested his career as an academic researcher and theorist with a rare empiricism, a sense of how legal mechanisms work, for and against businesses and consumers, which in turn has substantiated his ability to evaluate policy options in a balanced manner, advocating for functional change, and perhaps more importantly than all else, keep on the move in the sense of constantly expanding his horizon and being able to rationalise a self-standing holistic model of ADR.

As we shall see, an extra dimension to Chris's progress needs to be recognised as an integral part of his success. This is the involvement of European Justice Forum (EJF), a relatively small Brussels-based business association about which we say more section II, which has collaborated with Oxford University in supporting Chris's work at the Centre (and that of his research assistants), helping him gain the necessary 'bandwidth' to project his academic research into real-time policy-making based on Oxford's imprimatur.

The following pages combine personal reminiscences, from different standpoints, of two of Chris's many colleagues and friends. The two of us have worked alongside him internationally over the years in his endeavour to create a new consumer redress policy and want to express our appreciation of that journey.

II. Personal Reminiscences

Arundel

My long friendship with Chris began in 1999. He was writing his *Multi-Party Actions* book,[1] which he finished in July 2000. It was published the following year.

Chris was soliciting contributions to this analysis of multi-party actions (MPAs) in various jurisdictions, mainly from practitioners with personal experience of defending such cases. I was delighted to be asked to be one of his contributors.

It seems a long time ago now: MPAs were developing rapidly in the 1980s and 1990s as the main form of collective litigation in the UK, usually seeking consumer redress. Those of us defending such actions knew that this, the focus of Chris's work, was not only new and different, but exciting. Many of the claims involved a whole raft of new European law to which the UK subscribed, and therefore an entirely parallel but unknown legal territory superimposed upon existing UK regulatory and tort law.

A key component of this frontier was the inappropriately named 'no-fault' (but definitely not 'no-fault') European Product Liability Directive (Directive 85/374/EEC), which had been implemented in England and Wales through the medium of the Consumer Protection Act 1987. This conjunction of new European and English law with consumer rights presented not just fertile ground for plaintiffs – so they thought – but a whole new range of jurisprudential possibilities.

So it was interesting from a legal point of view, because we were dealing with new legal concepts and improvisational procedures. It was important for our business clients. And the intersection with the underlying matrices of numerous alleged mass harms made for fascinating work. Chris grasped the opportunity to define the zeitgeist by assembling a large number of UK case studies, and then analysing in enormous detail

[1] C Hodges, *Multi-Party Actions* (Oxford University Press, 2001).

the practical and procedural lessons from those examples. He superimposed on this a comparative analysis of class action models in the US, Canada and Australia. In so doing he was consolidating the learning on a rapidly evolving litigation model, which in turn gave him the knowledge base for everything that followed.

This encounter, though slightly arm's length, gives a good starting snap-shot of Chris's multi-disciplinary career. It showed prodigious work ethic, a collaborative method, and a slightly unnerving capacity for tying things down and formulating rules, which lawyers and academics have but which Chris has in spades. This may be partly because Chris was first a science student, and his technical mind has helped to define not only his approach to solutions but his trajectory across different disciplines.

On another level, those remote interactions with Chris over 20 years ago were the start of my travels with him and, looking back, predictive. What it showed was the empiricism that has distinguished his academic enquiry: the ability to convert collective redress ideas derived from wide research, into practical policy proposals with functionality at their core. This functionality comes from lessons learned in his many years as product liability and regulatory lawyer. I recognised this from my own experience defending businesses in MPAs and knowing the shoreline.

It was the starter's gun for a career shift: from practitioner to a thinker, a compendious and prolific writer, and a person wanting to formulate frameworks, using all the lessons learnt from his lived experience of litigation and alternative redress systems. In short, a policy expert based on a strategy in the front line. But it was only ever going one way: towards alternatives to litigation.

So much for the start of the story. If predictive it was not prophetic at the time, and the trail went cold until I actually met Chris for the first time in 2007, three years after he had left the law to become an academic at Oxford. He was working at the Centre for Socio-Legal Studies, part of the Oxford Law Faculty and a focus for the broader sociological implications of law and the development of policy. That period of eight years (1999–2007) was transformative.

In 2007, I recommended that Ashurst, a City law firm where I was a litigation partner, become a member of EJF, a small but prestigious business association in Brussels that had been formed in 2005 to promote alternatives to collective litigation in Europe, as a foil to initiatives by the European Commission intended to push class actions as part of its revamped consumer agenda.

I started to get involved in EJF because, very quickly, it struck me as being professionally run, with major global businesses as members, having a network of external law firm advisers in most EU member countries and a secretariat in Brussels. It articulated serious, knowledgeable, well-thought-through ideas addressing specifically the European issues emerging on the consumer redress agenda, and used these to effect with useful institutional contacts in Brussels. I also swiftly came to appreciate that the individuals who represented the corporate members, whom I met regularly and who all became friends, were also equally dedicated to the goals of EJF and were prepared to spend the effort, beyond their normal schedules, in thinking the messages through.

At the same time Chris was widening out his previous research into common law MPAs. As Head of the CMS Research Programme on Civil Justice Systems at the Centre, he was now analysing a whole new world of parallel, but very different and divergent consumer protection systems across Europe, examining the principal trends and policy goals relating to such mechanisms in Europe. Two results emerged from this research.

The first was another holistic rationalisation of redress systems, this time in a much broader context, in the form of an influential monograph, published in 2008 as a further book: *The Reform of Class and Representative Actions in European Legal Systems: A New Framework for Collective Redress in Europe*.[2] This identified the technique of 'regulatory redress', which no one else had noticed. This was but the beginning of Chris's taking a leading role in academic debates about class actions.

The second, and for me much more immediate, result was that he became involved in helping to formulate EU-wide policy considerations for EJF's members to evaluate. So it was that our two paths intersected. It was in this context that I came to know Chris, by seeing him repeatedly at EJF meetings, hearing him present his ideas for alternative forms of consumer redress and talking to him.

Those meetings were usually held at CMS Cameron McKenna's offices in Aldersgate (he had been a partner of CMS Cameron McKenna for many years but by then had retired from the partnership), lasting maybe three hours with a short break for lunch. It was a short walk from Ashurst's offices in Appold Street, so I could attend the meetings, catch up with the law and policy, and confer with a number of interesting individuals, all very efficiently in the space of a few hours, and then return to my desk mid-afternoon. I was encouraged to think that as product liability defence specialists, Ashurst received added value from our membership in the form of contemporary intelligence, and were better able to translate the European dimension of our defence work and implications for the future to our clients, because we were more on the button.

Chris is a superb speaker, the very antithesis of a dry academic. Because of his by now wide European credentials, his was an authentic, credible and lucid voice for the European lawyers attending; there were several UK lawyers, but most came from civil code countries in the EU. His presentations were a magnet. I sensed a disparate audience of in-house and external lawyers coalescing around his themes. Most of them travelled significant distances (not infrequently from the US) and if they minded about the journey, rarely showed it because the technology transfer was worth it.

Because the organisation came to benefit so materially from Chris's ideas, it is worth explaining who was behind EJF. The key player in those early days was Malcolm Carlisle OBE, who founded the organisation with a few far-sighted general counsel from other international businesses with experience of defending US class actions and awareness of the abuses such actions could generate. Malcolm was an able in-house lawyer in the medical device industry, with long experience of medical device regulations and advocacy with the EU institutions. He had known Chris from the mid-1990s, when they had both been involved in EU regulation of medical devices.

Malcolm ran the show until, very sadly, he died in November 2011. He was hugely supported by Dr Lorenz Ködderitzsch, a senior in-house lawyer at Johnson & Johnson, who helped to give (indeed still does) the organisation enormous credibility both externally in Brussels and also amongst the membership. The members admire and respect

[2] C Hodges, *The Reform of Class and Representative Actions in European Legal Systems: A New Framework for Collective Redress in Europe* (Hart Publishing, 2008).

his drive, vibrancy and intellectual ballast. After Malcolm's death, Lorenz assumed the mantle of Chairman until 2015, which as a busy senior in-house lawyer was a significant additional responsibility.

But it was Chris who, whilst scrupulously preserving his academic independence (and being required to do so by CMS and Swiss Re, who have supported his Oxford research programme), provided the ideas, the intellectual capital, for EJF's outreach. It gave EJF the confidence of knowing that the messages EJF crafted were supported by original, independent and voluminous research, and expressed ideas for rational and balanced policy objectives for consumer dispute resolution that were functional and clearly effective.

Two strands of Chris's work thus came together in 2007–08. On the one hand there was his body of empirical research on European redress systems, his evaluation of the options to collective litigation and his conclusions on what worked best, all enunciated in his 2008 book, and his further outreach across academic networks. And on the other hand there was his advocacy of practical alternatives, through presentations not just to EJF but to policymakers at EU level and in the Member States, collaborations across the EU with academics, regulators and lawyers, and written papers, journal articles and other publications. From 2007–08, Chris's approach to these two initiatives started to transform the landscape of public debate at EU level.

The idiom was changing from a purely litigation focus to an approach based on 'consumer redress', and the debate was changing to the relative merits and demerits of litigation as compared with those of alternative forms of redress. Although many experienced US defence counsel were familiar with class action deficiencies, no one else had attempted to challenge the primacy of the class actions shibboleths with such focus and precision. The tide had been mainly one way, and Chris was swimming against it. Yet his Oxford imprimatur provided the intellectual platform for becoming the thought-leader in consumer redress policy.

And thus, whilst keeping his MPA/class actions irons in the fire (and continuing to deliver undergraduate lectures on product liability at Oxford from 2004 to 2019), his research projects focused increasingly on how to construct an entirely fresh model for resolving consumer disputes that was versatile (which answered the idiosyncrasies of numerous different legal systems), functional (which was proved to work and simple) and used familiar mechanisms (no need to re-invent the wheel), and which was not, or did not have to be, adversarial (it was not axiomatically litigious).

It happens that this evolution in his thinking coincided with the 2008–09 financial crisis. Funding of MPAs had always been a troubling component in the mix. It was an effect of the crisis in the UK that there was a consequent reduction in the budget available for civil legal aid over the following years, which threatened the existence of publicly funded MPAs. Hitherto these had been the proliferating type of collective litigation discussed in Chris's 2001 *Multi-Party Actions* book.

These budget reductions had a disastrous effect on state funding, not just for MPAs but for family disputes and almost all or any form of litigation involving private claimants on low incomes, as well as on criminal legal aid. But the virtual wiping out of civil legal aid led to privatisation of litigation. It turbo-charged conditional fees and fuelled the emergence of a third-party-funding industry to fill the vacuum of class action funding, which in turn prompted fears of entrepreneurial litigation, which would not be geared to achieving the plaintiffs' personal objectives but to realising investors' returns.

In Brussels, the debate about the introduction of an EU-wide class action, and how much of the policy behind it was to mimic the US class action and how much was to be indigenous to the EU, was fomenting. But at the same time, the Commission under the second presidency of Barroso was agitating for legislation on ADR to enhance the operation of the single market, working from the perception that the existing EU legislative measures for ADR were inadequate in a digital age, in particular to encourage the resolution of disputes arising from the increasing volume of cross-border transactions.

Urs

The EU legislative dynamics outlined above had also triggered Swiss Re's interest and led to the company's active engagement as an EJF member in 2008. Swiss Re had learned its lessons from the US. In its Annual Report 2020, then Chairman Walter B Kielholz wrote:

> During the early years of my career, so in the 1970s and early 1980s, but especially after 1986, a massive wave of asbestos and environmental liability claims in the US crashed over the insurance industry. This resulted in huge claims payments around the world, especially for reinsurers. This also posed a threat to the future of your company, Swiss Re. We had to adapt to a completely new environment characterised by very aggressive plaintiffs' lawyers in the US. It took years for the US to bring the excesses of a legal industry specialised in liability lawsuits under greater control.

According to its 2020 Annual Report, Swiss Re still reserves over $1.4 billion for asbestos and environmental liability claims, mainly in the US.

Based on this US experience, it was clear that US collective action, with its inherent conflicts of interest, was not a model that Swiss Re wanted to see introduced in Europe. Consequently, when the EU initiated plans for collective redress in Europe, Swiss Re found the cross-sectoral coalition formed by EJF provided a good platform to encourage and support an informed debate about alternative approaches to redress. Our initial contacts with Chris Hodges soon established that here was indeed an eminent expert, whose ideas were compelling in a double sense: they had the advantage of being based on research of actual civil justice systems and, thus, they had the potential to make a real difference.

Against the background of these long-term goals, Swiss Re decided that a long-term partnership with Oxford University in support of Chris's academic research was a good way to underpin a constructive legislative and regulatory dialogue. Swiss Re's analysis of the perspectives for Swiss Re was clearly positive: collective redress was – and continues to be – of high business interest to Swiss Re and the re/insurance industry globally, because it shapes the legal and regulatory environment for important areas of liability insurance and the resulting claims.

Arundel

Chris's academic career continued to make headway against the prevailing tide that asserted that deterrence through the medium of class action litigation was a panacea for all corporate ills. During the years 2008 to 2012, he directed a research project with colleagues in Oxford, Iris Benoehr and Naomi Creutzfeldt, into national and cross-border consumer ADR systems in the EU, examining the different national architectures within which they operated and how they could be improved. The scope was wide: it covered France, Germany, Lithuania, Poland, the Netherlands, Slovenia, Spain, Sweden and the UK, as well as a number of pan-EU systems. This was the first systematic comparative study on this subject and resulted, in 2012, in the publication of the three co-authors' seminal analysis *Consumer ADR in Europe*,[3] thus providing the template for the discussions then coming to fruition within the EU institutions about the appropriate ADR legislation.

At this time, Chris also formed a highly productive and influential collaboration with Professor Stefaan Voet of Leuven University, compiling information and case studies that enabled empirical comparison between the different models of litigation, class actions, ADR, ombudsmen and regulatory redress. They became embedded with the national Ombudsmen in their respective countries, acting as strategy policy think tanks for the leading Ombudsmen and influencing governments. That collaboration has produced a number of highly significant publications evaluating different mechanisms and showing that the techniques of regulatory redress and Ombudsmen are far preferable to litigation-based class action mechanisms in effectively and efficiently delivering good outcomes to consumers and others; and the collaboration continues to the present day.

In February 2012, I became Executive Director of EJF. This meant I was much more personally and closely involved in getting to grips with Chris's work at Oxford. This necessitated a paradigm shift for me in studying, in detail, sections of his large corpus of work and the direction of his ideas, not this time as a lawyer but as someone in charge of a think tank and a lobbyist; making sense of his ideas as a precursor to explaining their alignment (or not) with EJF's objectives to EJF members, fashioning the appropriate messages and advocating them to policymakers in London and Brussels.

Chris had so many calls on his time that our contact was limited and intermittent, but on the occasions when we could discuss his work in person he was a willing indoctrinator, which was invaluable to understanding the background to his ideas when I was learning the ropes and ladders of Brussels advocacy.

What made this task easier was Chris's very unusual combination of talent, to which I have referred previously, the cross from practising lawyer, with substantial European regulatory experience, to Oxford academic, then triangulating these influences into being an internationally recognised legal policy guru. His background as a practitioner resonated with the EJF membership, business lawyers who saw that his practical experiences as a litigator allowed him to convert his work product from the Oxford research

[3] C Hodges, I Benoehr and N Creutzfeldt-Banda, *Consumer ADR in Europe* (Bloomsbury Publishing, 2012).

engine into practical ideas for policy change that could work in their world, as they did for consumers.

Urs

At the outset we at Swiss Re were intrigued by the good mix of independent research and result-oriented outreach and advocacy that the cooperation with Chris and the EJF could deliver. It was clear that, in order to shape European legislation in such a way as to prevent the negative effects of the US class action system, a forward-oriented and concrete alternative was needed. Chris's ADR research provided an innovative framework that, in Swiss Re's view, had the potential to create a real win-win situation both from an EU political viewpoint and from an industry perspective: it could facilitate access to justice in the broad sense of the term; deliver redress. And it could do so in a timely way and with low access thresholds. It thus matched an important political ambition of the EU, namely, to complete the single market goal by providing equitable access to justice for all throughout the EU, including for smaller amounts over which no one would usually go to court, and including cross-border cases.

Swiss Re's 10-year endowment in support of the Oxford research programme in Civil Justice Systems covered the period 2012–21. This arm's-length arrangement with the university allowed for long-term legal empirical research and legal analysis that has yielded many ideas and new perspectives.

Starting with our first meetings at Swiss Re, we have been inspired by Chris's ability to develop a compelling regulatory narrative based on his enormous expertise from comparative research. He knows what works and what does not! This knowledge is invaluable from both a political and an industry perspective. And from that body of practical knowledge and research insights he has been able to develop a highly innovative and convincing framework for an ADR approach that effectively delivers redress. Given the cost of litigation in general, the risks associated with court processes, and the specific experience with US asbestos and environmental litigation, such an alternative framework for collective redress had high attractiveness for our industry: it provided a balanced approach to justice while also deterring abuse.

The endowment's long-term orientation thus helped to provide continuity for Chris's prolific research efforts over a decade at a time when the policy and legislative debate in the EU was at a crucial juncture. And the partnership with Oxford University, a renowned institution with an excellent reputation and a global network, proved most productive also for outreach and access to stakeholders. Chris was thus able to present and discuss his ideas in countries around the world, from Poland to Canada and from Italy to China.

Arundel

None of this would have been possible without Chris's enormous reserves of energy, his indefatigable international travel to promote his ideas for a new ADR model in priority to collective litigation and his gift for collaboration. The breadth of this influence was soon seen in his academic appointments outside Oxford from 2011 onwards. He was appointed the Professor of the Fundamentals of Private Law at Erasmus University, Rotterdam in 2011, for four years. That facilitated the work with Professor Voet, and also brought opportunities to engage with Dutch, Belgian, German and Italian academics and officials; various further publications were also produced. And then in 2013 he was made an Honorary Professor at the China University for Political Science and Law, Beijing and a Guest Professor at Wuhan University. To this should be added his lecturing in Singapore and Australia.

When Chris was appointed Professor of Justice Systems at Oxford in 2014, I was initially puzzled by the breadth of this title, because those of us who worked closely with him knew him as a passionate advocate of ADR systems and of the societal benefits of redress outside litigation, whilst 'justice' certainly implied judicial systems, in particular court-regulated systems, which ADR is clearly not. But it was an inspired title, because it recognised that ADR in all its infinite variety could be a function of providing systematic justice. Again, that Oxford imprimatur, the adoption of ADR as a part of justice, helped to establish the legitimacy of the theory.

Since then his contributions from Oxford have continued to frame the debate on the consumer redress agenda across a range of projects. Using his widening research into behavioural psychology and economics, deterrence theory and business ethics, linking these to policy, expanding the profile of regulatory redress systems, his extensive writing converting these insights into policy initiatives, his numerous exchanges with policymakers at all levels, not just in the UK and EU but in all other common law jurisdictions, have been inspirational. They were instrumental in keeping EJF in the limelight in Brussels throughout my time as Executive Director, and they still are under Ekkart Kaske's stewardship. In 2014–21, assisted by changes to the UK judicial infrastructure caused mainly by massive budget reductions, they permanently moved the dial towards a recognition of the utility of alternative forms of redress, (new technology) and away from mass litigation (old technology).

Urs Continues

As a global company, Swiss Re very much appreciated Chris's truly global network. The company benefited greatly from the insights from his relentless travels and intense dialogue with practitioners, legislators, regulators and governments in countries around the world. Swiss Re's experts and clients have gained fresh insights from the inspiring interactions with Chris Hodges. No doubt his deep knowledge and his prolific work as an academic writer, a gifted advisor and lively conference speaker have planted the seed for ADR-based regulatory and legislative frameworks in numerous countries. This is his enduring legacy.

An EJF meeting hosted by Swiss Re in Zurich in June 2016 is illustrative of the synergies that Swiss Re was able to use as a company member being in close touch with one of the foremost experts on comparative research on civil justice systems. The dialogue could build on Chris's recently published book, *Law and Corporate Behaviour.*[4]

[4] C Hodges, *Law and Corporate Behaviour: Integrating Theories of Regulation, Enforcement, Compliance and Ethics* (Bloomsbury Publishing, 2015).

In sharing copies of this seminal work with key stakeholders, Swiss Re took the opportunity to remind them of the challenge at hand:

> You will, like us, be concerned at the potential spread across Europe of US-style class actions and huge fines … that do little but inflict unnecessary damage on business and innocent employees, shareholders, suppliers and others.

Also in 2016, in its report *Striking the Balance: Upholding the Seven Principles of Public Life in Regulation*,[5] the UK Government acknowledged Chris's highly relevant contributions:

> Professor Hodges' research confirms that:
>
> - Regulatory bodies need to be both effective and ethical. As well as their specific responsibilities, they have a broader leadership role to bring about a more ethical environment within and beyond public life.
> - Promoting an ethical approach to compliance can be seen simultaneously as a sound commercial and regulatory strategy. There are positive gains in terms of commercial reward, better compliance and reduced enforcement costs.
> - Reinforcing such an approach, the active development of collaborative relationships brings benefits for both sides and can be seen as a further dimension of the ethical leadership that the Committee expects of regulatory bodies.
>
> Best Practice: Regulators should actively engage with those they regulate and take a leadership role by encouraging positive attitudes towards compliance.
>
> Recommendation: Such promotion of an ethical approach to compliance would be supported by a suitable amendment to the Regulators' Code.

Indeed: what more could an academic expert wish for than for his research insights to translate into a straightforward regulatory recommendation?

The UN Commission on Trade and Development (UNCTAD) also picked up Chris's research insights in its 2016 UNCTAD *Manual on Consumer Protection*:

> Professor Christopher Hodges mounts an eloquent plea for a collaborative approach to consumer protection and regulation: 'The basic idea is one of a collaborative approach between businesses, their stakeholders and public officials, based on a shared ethical approach.'
>
> He argues that the findings of behavioural psychology suggest that the regulatory system will be most effective in affecting the behaviour of individuals where it supports ethical and fair behaviour. He finds that individuals will not volunteer information if they fear attracting criticism or blame, and that a 'blame culture' will inhibit learning and the development of an ethical culture, so businesses and regulators should support an essentially open collaborative culture in which complaints are treated as gifts. This may sound fanciful, but some private sector companies have indeed adopted this model and sought out complaints. Nevertheless he acknowledges that 'where people break rules or behave immorally, people expect to see a proportionate response.' Bearing this in mind, one could apply many criteria to both CSR [Corporate Social Responsibility] and SR [Self Regulation].[6]

[5] Committee on Standards in Public Life, *Striking the Balance: Upholding the Seven Principles of Public Life in Regulation* (Cm 9327, 2016) para 8.43.

[6] UNCTAD, *Manual on Consumer Protection* (2016) available at https://unctad.org/system/files/official-document/webditcclp2016d1.pdf, 48.

In its 2018 survey *Collective Redress in the Member States of the European Union* (for the JURI Committee), the European Parliament made clear that Chris Hodges' research provided valuable perspectives for future legislation:

> The main issues in respect of collective actions are: funding, the ability to secure it for collective actions is the most significant issue in respect of the efficacy of such a mechanism; efficient management of such claims; ensuring that claims do not result in over-compensation for weak claims, under-compensation for strong claims; conflicts of interest between class members; an absence of effective control of litigation by the class representative. In terms of the regulatory or deterrent effect of collective actions it can be questioned whether they are effective in this respect. Hodges has written widely on this and has done so compellingly in questioning the utility of such mechanisms to achieve regulatory compliance and to deter, for instance, tortfeasing.[7]

Chris's ideas and proposed solutions were heard as far as China: in 2014, the Foundation for Law, Justice and Society, Oxford, and the Swiss Re Centre for Global Dialogue jointly published a Chinese report co-authored by Chris Hodges and Ying Yu: *The Status of Public and Private Enforcement of Law in the EU: Innovation and Transformation.*[8]

As Lord Thomas of Cwmgiedd, Kt PC, Lord Chief Justice of England and Wales 2013–17, states in his Foreword to Chris Hodges' 2019 book *Delivering Dispute Resolution*, 'An accessible, fair and cost-effective system of dispute resolution is essential to the Rule of Law.'[9] This sums up in a perfectly concise manner the supreme goal that Chris has pursued in his research, which spans across all five continents. His endeavour was always to enable equitable access to justice for all by providing the conceptual framework for an ADR approach that really works.

For over a decade of close engagement with Swiss Re, Chris Hodges has driven forward innovative research based on an enormously broad body of comparative studies. He has combined insatiable academic curiosity as a researcher with a strong entrepreneurial spirit and an enormous capacity for productive work, plus a true gift to engage with people in the political and regulatory world.

In fact, to have an eminent academic expert who also knows what works in practice – and what does not – is a unique asset that links conceptual research to everyday life. Chris Hodges has provided the essential guidance to enable policymakers to install redress systems that deliver justice. From a citizens' and business perspective, his innovative thinking has created new building blocks for what we call 'good government'. This will be his lasting contribution to creating better, more equitable justice systems around the world.

Upon his retirement from Oxford, in June 2021, Swiss Re gratefully acknowledged Chris's enormous contribution:

> We could not have found a better cooperation partner to manage the 'Swiss Re Research Programme on Civil Justice Systems' at Oxford University! Throughout the many years of our cooperation we have been impressed again and again by the way you have created links

[7] JURI Committee, *Collective Redress in the Member States of the European Union* available at www.europarl.europa.eu/thinktank/en/document/IPOL_STU(2018)608829, 263.

[8] C Hodges, Y Yu, *The Status of Public and Private Enforcement of Law in the EU: Innovation and Transformation*, (Foundation for Law and Justice in Society & Swiss Re, 2014).

[9] Lord Thomas, 'Foreword' in C Hodges, *Delivering Dispute Resolution: A Holistic Review of Models in England and Wales* (Hart/Beck, 2019).

> between theory and practice. You have developed highly original thinking in all areas of your research. And you have also been highly prolific in putting your thoughts and insights to paper. Numerous renowned books and publications in this field testify to the depth of your mastery of the subject matter.

Arundel and Urs Conclude

We hope that our respective recollections amply demonstrate how the award to Chris of the OBE in the 2021 New Year's Honours List was well deserved. It was recognition from the UK Government of his unique contribution to changing not just consumer redress policy but wider justice policy in establishing a modern, working alternative to an adversarial (and somewhat discredited) litigation system.

On a personal note, we wish to record our appreciation of the deep friendship we have enjoyed with Chris over the many years we have had the pleasure of working with him on his endeavours.

5

A Love of Music: From Oxford to The Sixteen

HARRY CHRISTOPHERS CBE

Oxford – that city of dreaming spires, academia and great music. It was in 1973 when I went up to Magdalen College, Oxford as an Academical Clerk and a certain Christopher Hodges went to New College as a Choral Scholar. In typical Oxford fashion the two posts meant the same – we sang in the chapel choirs of our respective colleges, and thus were thrown into a readymade student group, each person possessing a love of singing whether or not we were actually studying music. In our cases, we weren't, I read Classics and Chris, Jurisprudence. There was a real camaraderie between the colleges, not surprising as they are just around the corner from each other.

Looking back and unbeknown to us at the time, there was quite a pool of talent which would emerge in later years. Two highly decorated people of the cloth, Bernard Longley (New College, tenor), now Archbishop of Birmingham, and Paul Ferguson (New College, Organ Scholar), now Bishop of Whitby, Michael Briggs (Magdalen, bass) now Lord Briggs and a Supreme Court judge, and so the list goes on. But back in the 1970s, we sang every day in chapel, different music on each occasion, covering music of six centuries, from John Sheppard or William Byrd to Kenneth Leighton or Edmund Rubbra. In addition to our academic studies, we would be expected to come fully prepared and fulfil our singing duties to the best of our ability; evensong every day, including the weekends, sundry concerts, tours and a recording each year. But it didn't stop there, we as students put together our own concerts, and naturally Chris and I sang in numerous groups together. And so an eternal friendship began.

I formed The Sixteen after I left Oxford, and Chris was very much an active part of its formation. He helped me realise what I actually really wanted to do, and that, in its embryonic form, was to continue our simple love of performing sixteenth-century sacred music, a tradition with which we had been imbued by our respective Directors of Music, Bernard Rose at Magdalen, David Lumsden at New, and groups like The Clerkes of Oxenford and the very early days of The Tallis Scholars. Through singing we had been taught discipline, working as one and a sort of telepathy. Singing in a choir is not just about getting the notes right, good ensemble and singing in tune, it's about thinking and breathing together and above all supporting your colleagues.

Of this group of singers I assembled in 1977 only very few pursued a career in music – most took up other careers and many, like Chris himself, have been highly successful. In those very early years we were a choir *sine nomine* performing occasional concerts, mostly seasonal, Christmas or Easter; so how did we come up with The Sixteen? Early in 1979, we really felt we couldn't just be a disembodied choir, a name had to be conjured up. It didn't take long to decide really; once Richard Price had deigned to suggest it should be called the Richard Price Singers, I believe it was Chris who said 'Look, there are sixteen of us, we perform sixteenth-century music so why not just … simply … The 16." Chris, ever practical, ever succinct. So we toyed with it numerically; that didn't last long, and in May 1979, The Sixteen was christened; and so it has remained ever since, causing critics much jollity and audiences more often than not a numerical challenge. Suffice it to say, I use the smallest number of singers I consider to be musically viable for the type of music we are performing. Chris sang regularly for us in those early days while he was working for Slaughter and May. It was all very cavalier; we enjoyed each other's company and we all just loved singing together. There were, fortuitously, certain turning points that altered our perception of what the future might offer.

Hugh Keyte, then one of the main producers for BBC Radio 3, came to our concert in Oxford just prior to our London debut at St John's Smith Square. He enjoyed it so much that he asked us to do a BBC lunchtime concert – we were the first choir (apart from the BBC's very own BBC Singers) to have been invited to do so. Our Smith Square debut also proved to be fortuitous – Stephen Pettitt, then a critic for *The Times*, reviewed the concert with the immortal words 'If the sound of the choir was a revelation, so too was the music itself.'

The name had been chosen in May 1979 – however, it was almost exactly a year later when I realised that 16 was not the perfect number. I had purchased those magnificently presented *Musica Britannica* volumes of the *Eton Choirbook*, and it was soon apparent that I needed to add to the soprano line. I had been schooled at Magdalen in the David Wulstan theory of transposing this music up a minor third, thus needing more females (trebles and means) and fewer of the lower voices. Chris had been a mainstay of the bass line in Wulstan's group, The Clerkes of Oxenford, and so was well versed in the style of this complex early music. The following year we did a concert in Marylebone Parish Church of some of this amazing music – amazing in its variety and complexity and amazing in its difficulty. On the advice of my old friend, David James (the sound of the Hilliard Ensemble) I had written to Meridian Records to invite them to this concert with a view to making an LP. They enjoyed the concert immensely and said let's do something. And so on 4 October 1980 we made a record of *Eton Choirbook* music. We rehearsed on the Friday evening and recorded for six hours on the Saturday in St Anne and St Agnes, Gresham Street, in the heart of the City of London. That was it – long takes, very little patching – hard work but a fabulous achievement; well, the recording was, the LP cover was shockingly poor, black with a smudgy blob of gold, which was supposed to have been a statue of the Virgin Mary. The second volume followed in January 1982 – this was not so successful. The sessions (again the same schedule – incredible really, considering how things were to change) were rather fraught. The engineer (also the owner of Meridian Records) had his very fixed ideas about recording technique; he wouldn't contemplate anything more than 25 minutes a side (we are still talking LPs). We had too much music, or rather these *Eton Choirbook* antiphons last about 15 minutes each, so I had to find a piece a little shorter in length to put on the LP. I hadn't brought my *Musica Britannica* volumes with me, so in the lunch break (we had exactly one hour) we bombed down in Robin Barda's car (barrister) to Westminster Music Library, dug out the volumes, found a men's voice piece that would work, made a copy; and on the drive back Sally Dunkley (soprano and musicologist), Francis Steele (bass and musicologist) and I made a few editorial decisions and amendments, Chris popped to his office at Slaughter and May, by chance just round the corner from the church, to photocopy the piece, and in the afternoon session we sight-read it onto tape.

I realised things needed to change, I was still singing professionally at Westminster Abbey and in the BBC Singers, but in 1985 I gave up my singing career for that of conducting. Although I had decided that my career was solely in music, for many members of the choir, Chris included, other professions were being pursued. Looking at our massive CD catalogue (160 titles and rising), the choir did not consist of solely professional singers until about 1992, with Chris, Robin Barda and Peter Burrows (who became our Development Director for many years) being the last to depart the ranks. Chris is immortalised on one particular CD, and that is a recording of Christmas Music from Medieval and Renaissance Europe. It's on the Hyperion label, released in 1987 and still available (CDA66263). *The Guardian* called it 'a most unusual and attractive record', principally, I suspect, for Chris's amazing rendition of a Spanish '*villancico*' carol '*Riu, riu chiu*', a genuine shepherd song. Chris had special language coaching on this to get as close to medieval Spanish as he could. It's brilliant, although in a subsequent concert performance one critic, who clearly wasn't acquainted with the authentic feel, referred to his 'execrable Spanish' – Chris has dined out on that review for many years! The percussion player also deserves special mention – Robin Barda – and being The Sixteen, we couldn't simply list him as playing a tambourine, we preferred to use the more exotic Spanish title, *panderete*.

Let us now go back to the point at which I decided to devote myself to conducting and the future of The Sixteen. We were getting pretty busy as an ensemble, with concerts, tours and regular recordings for Hyperion, and we decided that we needed to become a Registered Company with charitable status. How fortunate we were to have top legal brains amongst our ranks. The Sixteen Ltd was formed on 15 July 1985, with me as Chairman and Chris as a Trustee and Company Secretary. Among the other trustees were other founder members of The Sixteen: Robin Barda, who is a highly respected barrister, who also happens to be the present Chairman of the Board, and Richard Price, who at the time had his own company, European Marketing Consultants. Chris remained a Trustee for many years until stepping down in 2007.

I am still astounded to this day how Chris found time to spend supporting our existence and ensuring that we ran the company in exemplary fashion, amidst being a partner at McKenna & Co, consulting, lecturing at Oxford and writing enormous tomes on pharmaceutical law, but time he found. And there were some pretty hour-consuming issues to sort out, not least recording contracts, first with Virgin Classics then with Collins Classics; there were constantly complex situations to untangle. We had the best part of 10 years recording for Collins Classics, but in 1998 they closed. The company had been swallowed up by Zomba in 1996, and from that point their interest in classical music dwindled rapidly. Ever since 1990, I had had the freedom to record whatever I wanted (Collins being an artist-led label) and we had 34 titles, ranging from the *Eton Choirbook*, Victoria, Purcell, Handel and Bach to Poulenc, Britten, Stravinsky and Messiaen. I reckon they had probably invested well over a million pounds in us, and it had been a vintage recording period, but when we realised that our art was being siphoned off to some budget label, very poorly packaged with chocolate-box type covers, scanty notes, no text or translations and dirt cheap, we knew we had to do something.

So we decided that we had to make a move to retrieve our Collins Classics catalogue. Not only had Collins pumped thousands and thousands of pounds into our recordings, I had personally invested a lot of time and energy researching new recording ideas and poring over scores; and needless to say, all our artists and production team had worked tirelessly. We asked Anne Rushton, who had been the linchpin of Collins' management in its heyday, to look at the pros and cons of (i) licensing the titles back from Collins (Zomba by then) to release under our name, or (ii) buying the catalogue. She came to a board meeting and presented findings that showed the second option was strongest, although it carried considerable risk. We opted for the latter, and Chris was instrumental in guiding us through the process. After detailed negotiations with Zomba and their lawyer and months of stalemate, we suggested to Zomba that we all spent a day in a room together with the aim of coming out with a deal, which we did. The Sixteen didn't have the cash to buy up front, so we agreed to the release of up to 10 titles a year for a scheduled annual payment.

And so one of our proudest moments as an organisation was realised – I can still see that wide smile of success shining from Chris's face – our trading company, The Sixteen Productions, was formed in October 2001.

Practically everyone said we were stark raving mad to start a record company, especially when the classical record industry was in decline, but our aim was to tour and sell loads of CDs and, shock horror, even do a tour CD. Well, after all, how had the pop industry survived? That's simple – the group records an album, tours said album and sells thousands as a result of that tour. We started the Choral Pilgrimage in 2000, and each year we record an album to go with that tour; as a consequence we sell a fair number at our concerts, not quite on the scale of UB40 et al but still pretty good, and a whole lot better than almost all of our colleagues. Simple logic.

So how did it all work? In a nutshell, The Sixteen (the charity) retains ownership of all the catalogue; a subsidiary company, The Sixteen Productions Ltd, was formed, which worked with one of the top UK distributors to re-release and market the 30+ titles that made up that Collins back catalogue. We re-packaged them and they were released over the next four to five years, thus giving us a bed on which to build CORO, the record label of The Sixteen, into what it is today. We secured a good media profile and developed a marketing relationship, initially with *Gramophone Magazine* as media sponsor of the Choral Pilgrimage. By the end of 2004, we had made the final payment for the back catalogue, and by the end of 2005 all of the Collins discs had been re-released on CORO.

We owe Chris a lot, but most importantly it has been his moral support of our 'thinking outside the box' and ensuring that we had a good business structure, which was not only legally sound but also allowed us to keep faith with our ideals. Chris takes pride in what we do, and even though he is not directly involved any more, either as a singer or as trustee, his enthusiasm for our continuing success is there for all to see.

6

'In Modern Comic Opera One Sometimes Has to Wing It. If It's Too Absurd to Say It, Then Sing It!'*

JEREMY GRAY

This chapter offers a personal appreciation of our dedicatee and his interest in music. It mostly charts some of the achievements of the small specialist British company Bampton Classical Opera, during an exciting period of development under the chairmanship of Christopher Hodges between 2005 and 2013.[1]

However, my appreciation of Chris Hodges the musician must begin in King Edward's School, situated in spacious grounds opposite the University of Birmingham. Chris's father John taught modern languages there for 31 years, and this historic and well-respected academic school served his son well. Young Hodges joined the school in 1967 in the third year, known as the Upper Middle, but it was probably not until we were both in the sixth form years that musical activity brought us together. It all seems a very long time ago now and my memories are unhelpfully vague, but perusing the *Chronicle*, the termly school newsletter (conveniently posted online by a helpful archivist), has jogged my recollections and paints a rewarding picture of Chris's high-profile and multi-faceted school career.[2] In our final two years, the sixth form, Chris and I frequented the 'music school', built in the 1960s with an impressive raked concert hall and a music library that, for us and a close-knit group of friends, became our social centre of choice. The library room was dominated by a monster of a two-manual harpsichord, which the BBC had reputedly ditched as unplayable after a visiting lunchtime broadcast, and was further blessed with a comprehensive collection of music scores. For my own education, and I'm sure for Chris's as well, easy access to orchestral and vocal music books was important in shaping and broadening tastes, which could be supplemented by after-school visits to the outstanding collection of Birmingham Central Library. The City of Birmingham Symphony Orchestra, then performing under

* Figaro, in Paisiello's *The Barber of Seville*: libretto translation for Bampton Classical Opera by Gilly French.

[1] www.bamptonopera.org.uk. Details of all productions mentioned in the text, including extensive programme booklet articles and press reviews, can be accessed via the Events/Past Productions tab. An overview of the early years of the company is given by F Maddocks, 'Not country-house …' *Opera* (2012) 804.

[2] Available at www.oldeds.kes.org.uk/chronicles.

Louis Frémaux's direction in the impressive classical temple of the Town Hall, was also seminal in the musical education of our group, whilst the nearby Backyard Bar provided illicit refreshment for naughty schoolboys.

But what does the King Edward's *Chronicle* reveal about our dedicatee? We encounter 'CJSH' as a keen member of the Combined Cadet Force, recounting with typically dry wit a school army camp in Dorset in July 1970 – he enjoyed the 'platoon attacks with lots and lots of blank ammo', and left the experience 'exhausted but triumphant'. We read of him as secretary of the film society, which showed scratchy black-and-white projections in one of the lecture rooms, and we read him critically but sensitively assessing a curricular innovation, a sixth-form lecture series on *The Background of Western Culture*, which was obviously inspiring, if not to most teenage schoolboys. We also discover that Chris acted in *The Winter's Tale*, giving 'an accomplished and precise performance'. But most frequently the *Chronicle* relates 'Hodges' as a remarkable musician, a fine baritone and trumpeter – he even ran a handbell team, which rang in the 1972 New Year live on local television. The reviewer of the school's Individual Music Competition in May 1970 called it 'the Christopher Hodges show' and heaped generous praise: 'he combines technical skill both in trumpet playing and voice production with dedication and, being a first-rate musician, is not content merely to make a noise on the right note at the right time – he works hard to achieve a high standard of performance'. We read appreciations of his performances of trumpet concertos by Haydn and Hummel, and of his singing of arias from the *St Matthew Passion* ('even the longest and most intricate phrases were admirably controlled'). Chris even gave 'a very good account of the difficult solo baritone part' in the première (fortunately also the dernière) of a pretentious piece of sub-Messiaen (*Creamini omni*) composed by one Jeremy Gray. With less embarrassment, I am delighted to be reminded of Chris's excursions into operatic repertory – Papageno's aria, accompanied by piano and panpipes, showed Chris's 'humour and light, confiding tones which realised Mozart's intentions exactly'. In an account of an annual House Music Competition, it is noted that Chris made an arrangement from *Le nozze di Figaro* – although I am sorry to report that on this occasion that particular House was judged at the bottom of the eight Houses.

School music was a formative breeding ground for our own musical enterprises. Encouraged by the school's Director of Music, Roy Massey, then organist at Birmingham Cathedral, an enthusiastic group of us schoolboy musicians organised quite frequent concerts in various venues, mostly churches, across the Birmingham area. Mr (now Dr) Massey never seemed distressed by the free use we made of his private office in the Music School, including his typewriter. We discovered and encountered pitfalls and successes in music programming, marketing, event management – and, of course, performance.

After we completed our school careers in 1972–73, Chris and I went our separate ways – he to Oxford, I to Cambridge – and thus new friendship circles and musical opportunities changed our perspectives. We fell out of contact for many years, until Bampton Classical Opera happily restored our friendship.

I consider that the birth of Bampton Classical Opera in 1993 in part evolved from that spirit of musical enterprise that had been honed at King Edward's. Bampton is an attractive and historic village about 15 miles west of Oxford, where my wife Gilly French and I had moved two years previously. Gilly, a soprano, was enamoured with the role of Galatea in Handel's *Acis and Galatea* and, with the assistance of the local arts organisation, we embarked on an al fresco staged performance in the lovely garden of the historic Deanery, adjacent to the magnificent medieval St Mary's Church. It was only intended as a one-off event, but we attracted a modest but appreciative audience, and our intentionally relaxed ethos – the audience even had to bring their own garden chairs – seemed to appeal. One gentleman who had never been to an opera before praised it as 'the best evening of his life', and in the following months we were asked what we intended to perform next. And so the show went on – and continues today.

The second year included Mozart's unfinished 1784 comedy *L'oca del Cairo* (*The Cairo Goose*), for which we were given access to a manuscript performing edition by the musicologist Erik Smith, who became a good colleague in our efforts. From then on, our artistic policy was set: no *Traviatas* or *Carmens* at Bampton – we would concentrate instead on little-known operas of the eighteenth century, works for small forces suitable for our garden venue and modest finances, and to be sung in English.

By the time Christopher joined our Board of Directors in 2005, we had progressed a long way and had established a secure reputation in the national press, especially for our enterprising repertory and the strength of our generally young professional singers. I forget now the circumstances in which he came back onto our lives – I think he and his wife Fiona attended one of our performances at St John's Smith Square, our regular London venue, and his combination of musicianship and legal expertise made him a firm candidate to be a director of the company. When we needed a candidate for a new Chairman, as we were about to lose the incumbent who was emigrating, Chris readily accepted that position. We were delighted.

But Chris's involvement had already been preceded by that of Fiona. Skilled in needlework and creative costume, she agreed to design and make costumes for a small-scale Haydn production that we were invited to take to the delightful niche English Haydn Festival at Bridgnorth in Shropshire in June 2004. With only five characters and a modest length, *L'infedeltà delusa* was to prove an enjoyable and useful addition to our repertory, and we revived it with different casts several times through until 2007.[3] Haydn's operas are not widely performed, although the much grander Garsington Opera, also then based in Oxfordshire, had explored many of them in the 1990s. We have since gone on to perform several others.[4] The initial Bridgnorth performance was of necessity hastily rehearsed, but was much enhanced by the tasteful splendour of Fiona's eighteenth-century period costumes. She displayed an appealing expertise in petticoats and corsetry, and her copious notes, sketches and swatches of fabrics, which we still hold in our archive, remind me of her sensitivity to colour and texture.

Chris's period of tenure as Chair lasted from 2005 until 2013. It was a period of both consolidation and exciting expansion, and Chris's guidance and legal expertise were critical to our success during these years. Although Bampton has always been restrained by minimal infrastructure and very limited funding, this period saw several new and worthwhile projects and venues, with growing audiences and reputation. The year 2005 was an exciting year for us: we were invited to perform at the lively and prestigious Buxton Festival in July in the Buxton Opera House, a gloriously sumptuous creation

[3] These included a performance in 2007 in the private theatre at Buscot House, Oxfordshire, as a surprise for the Diamond Wedding party of our Patron, Sir Charles Mackerras, and Lady Mackerras.

[4] In 2022 we will continue this series with *Il mondo della luna* (to be sung in English as *Fool Moon*).

of 1901–03 by one of the greatest theatre architects, Frank Matcham. An invitation to Buxton was an important step forward for us, and our pursuit of rare repertory closely fitted Buxton's own interests and profile. The invitation came from the general manager Glyn Foley, and necessitated a shift in our ambition and working methods. Following an intriguing line of Bampton rehabilitations of well-known opera plots set by less familiar composers, we selected to perform *The Barber of Seville* – but not the famous Rossini version. Ours was the earlier setting from 1782 by Giovanni Paisiello (1740–1816), which had been enormously successful in its day across Europe until Rossini knocked it off its perch. Whereas our previous staged activities had been presented with light-weight, locally-produced scenery, Buxton required a professional design and build for its grand theatre stage. Glyn suggested Nigel Hook as designer, and we entered into a happy partnership. Nigel's sense of humour and inventiveness matched the Bampton ethos well, and the *Barber* proved to be one of the funniest and best-performed of all our productions. Nigel suggested setting the production in a 1960s caravan at a grotesque English seaside holiday camp 'of timeless ghastliness'.[5] We engaged a marvellous and energetic young cast, including Rebecca Bottone, Paul Carey Jones, Adrian Dwyer and Nicholas Merryweather, and with two performances at Bampton before swiftly moving to Buxton, we reached an impressive total audience of 2,500. The only drawback of performing at the Opera House was that we discovered that the plastic 'Seville oranges', which were thrown copiously and cheerfully onto the stage during a crazy and climactic storm scene in Act 2, gently rolled down the rake and into the unsuspecting orchestra pit – fortunately the discovery was made before any orchestral players suffered head-aches, and we replaced the oranges with a purchase of softer and less mobile teddy bears.

The Hodges' seventeenth-century 'Grammar House' at Aynho, about an hour's drive from Bampton, became a regular destination for meetings and opera social events over these years. Fiona continued to design costumes for some of our productions, including the compilation opera *The Jewel Box*, performed in 2006 in Mozart's 250th birthday year, various revivals of *L'infedeltà delusa*, and a double-bill of Gluck's *Le cinesi* and Mozart's juvenile but charming *Apollo and Hyacinth* in 2008 and revived for the 2009 Cheltenham Festival.[6] The 'Grammar House' had extensive attics where, amidst the hefty roof beams, Fiona curated a growing collection of costumes. The Hodges' splendid dining room hosted both creative suppers and meetings of our Board, as well as of a Development Board that Chris set up around this time to nurture our work. A visit to Aynho was always accompanied by a satisfying meal and a tour around the extensive and impressive garden into which Chris put amazing energy and effort. Chris's chairmanship of the board of Bampton Classical Opera was always enthusiastic and constructive, and we valued his legal expertise. He was always supportive of our plans and generous with his time and money. He helped us acquire new figurehead patrons, including Bampton's Member of Parliament, David Cameron, later to become leader of his party and Prime Minister, as well as singer and broadcaster Brian Kay and opera director David Pountney. Our financial turnover gradually increased, and

[5] R Thicknesse, 'Comic romp takes a holiday by the sea' *The Times* (21 July 2005) 32.

[6] *The Jewel Box* is a compilation of isolated and little-known Mozart arias and ensembles, edited by and with a libretto by Paul Griffiths. Its première had been given by Opera North in 1991. *Le cinesi* launched an interest for us into the little-known short operas by Gluck; we have gone on to perform *Il parnaso confuso* and *Bauci e Filemone*, as well as one of his major reform works, *Paride ed Elena*.

for a few years it became easier to acquire sizeable grants from charitable trusts and foundations, although the global financial crash of 2008 inevitably led to a reversal. It is hardly surprising that our busiest year was 2007, when, amongst several other events, we took *L'infedeltà delusa* to four new venues. One of these was to prove especially useful and enjoyable to us: the magnificent Wotton House in Buckinghamshire, where owner David Gladstone promoted a recital series of quality and charm and where we continued to perform small-scale operas until 2015.

During the Hodges years we continued to tackle intriguing rarities with confidence and panache, often selecting operas to throw light on the contexts of more familiar composers and masterworks. In 2006 we gave the first UK performances since probably 1798 of *La capricciosa corretta* by the Spaniard Vicente Martín y Soler (1754–1806), whose gift for charming and memorable melody shaped a glittering career that took him to Italy, Austria, Russia and England. Arriving in Vienna in 1785, he collaborated with the equally peripatetic poet Lorenzo da Ponte (1749–1838) on three works that were to enjoy a prodigious success: *Il burbero di buon cuore*, *Una cosa rara* and *L'arbore di Diana*. In Vienna he was encouraged by the young Anglo-Italian soprano superstar Nancy Storace (1765–1817), whom he had met in Venice, and Nancy was to star in his Viennese works as well as developing a close collaboration with Mozart, most notably as Susanna in *Le nozze di Figaro*. At Bampton, beginning with performances in 2000 of *Gli equivoci* (*The Comedy of Errors*), libretto by Da Ponte), composed in Vienna by Nancy's brother Stephen (1762–96), we have developed something of an obsession with this talented singer-actress who was such an instrumental link in the creation of classical opera.[7] When Da Ponte came to London in 1792, after Mozart's death and prompted by Casanova, he renewed his friendship with the Storaces, as well as with Irish tenor Michael Kelly (who had created Don Basilio and Don Curzio in the Vienna première of *Figaro*). At the King's Theatre, Haymarket, London, Da Ponte attempted to nurture the best standards of Italian opera and, of course, to further his own interests. Martín y Soler joined him there, travelling from St Petersburg where he was court composer, and they collaborated on two new works, *La capricciosa corretta* and *L'isola del piacere*.

La capricciosa corretta was widely popular throughout Europe for a couple of decades but, like so many eighteenth-century operas, then fell into semi-oblivion. Our modern-day UK première at Bampton in July 2006 was during an especially hot spell of weather, and our audiences were the largest yet. As Da Ponte's story about the 'taming' of a vain and shrewish wife, Ciprigna, was originally located in a villa at the foot of Mount Vesuvius, we set our production in a Roman-era villa and designed scenery based on Pompeian paintings and artefacts. As in so many comic operas of the period, the denouement is preceded by a cataclysmic storm – which provided our local set builder, Mike Wareham, with great scope for ingenuity, building in his back garden in Bampton an eruptible Mount Vesuvius. One of Bampton's most supportive press critics, Roderick Dunnett, wrote in *Opera Now*:

> The setting is Pompeii, AD79, with Vesuvius in sight; and during the opera the balloon actually goes up. It is typical of Bampton's ingenuity to attempt something as bizarre as staging

[7] Amongst these have been Salieri's *The School of Jealousy* (*La scuola de' gelosi*) in 2017 and a celebratory concert *Songs for Nancy* in St John's Smith Square in March 2018.

> an eruption amid the herbage and shrubberies of an English country garden, and even more typical of them to pull it off. The lighting and set effects were both hilarious and chokingly realistic. I still have the smoke in my nostrils.[8]

The following year we received a second Buxton invitation and took a very different opera from these Italianate comedies – Georg Benda's 1776 singspiel *Romeo and Juliet.* The choice was encouraged by our previous successes with Shakespearian subjects – Storace's *The Comedy of Errors* and Salieri's *Falstaff* – and we had long been mesmerised by a recording of this work, written by a historically significant Bohemian-born composer, whose influence on Mozart was crucial. Once again we collaborated at Buxton with Nigel Hook as designer, and settled on an austere Victorian look, lit atmospherically by John Bishop (a lighting designer with a rare depth of operatic knowledge) and with costumes created by our talented Bampton volunteer Pauline Smith. On this occasion the show opened at Buxton before moving to Bampton, and I recall the trepidation of seeing the set for the first time as it was unloaded from the delivery lorry behind the Buxton Opera House – we only had a single rehearsal on stage with the set. Although the piece was well worth performing for the quality of its music, it is an uneasy work dramatically, and perhaps not all our singers managed to shape and propel it convincingly on stage. The libretto, by Friedrich Wilhelm Gotter, is an awkward reduction from the Shakespeare, with only four main characters and no crowd scenes, although it was successful in the late eighteenth century and beyond, helping to encourage a general revival of Shakespeare's plays in Germany. The following week at Bampton proved memorable, when rain of monsoon ferocity marooned the village as an island, complete with problematic power cuts. We had to resort to performances by candlelight in the church. Our orchestral players travelling from outside were unable to reach the village, and instead the conductor played an out-of-tune piano lit by a lamp powered from a car parked outside the church porch. They were in fact wonderful and memorable performances for the tiny audiences who could reach us.

One of our most ambitious choices was *Leonora* by the Parma-born Ferdinando Paer (1771–1839), performed as the UK première at Bampton in July 2008 and later at St John's Smith Square; we were disappointed that we were not able to tempt Buxton to take this magnificent and fascinating work. *Leonora, ossia L'amore coniugale* continued our interest in alternative settings of popular libretti or subjects, following Gazzaniga's *Don Giovanni*, Salieri's *Falstaff* and Paisiello's *The Barber of Seville*. The stirring account of the plucky cross-dressing Leonora, who infiltrates the revolutionary prison in which her husband Florestano is incarcerated, was first performed in Dresden in 1804 to great acclaim, with Paer's wife Francesca Riccardi in the title role. The musical legacy of the narrative, based on a play by Jean-Nicola Bouilly, is particularly strong, with operatic versions by Pierre Gaveaux (*Léonore, ou l'amour conjugal*, 1798) and by Simon Mayr (*L'amor coniugale*, 1805). As Peter Conrad has explained, these early *Leonoras* treat the subject as a sentimental comedy, an approach that was to disturb and tax Beethoven as he wrestled with versions of libretto and music between 1804 and 1814, ultimately to create *Fidelio*.[9] Although it seems there was no love lost between Paer and Beethoven,

[8] R Dunnett, 'Live reviews' *Opera Now* (November/December 2006) 109.

[9] D Johnson, 'Fidelio', *The New Grove Dictionary of Opera* (London, Macmillan, 1992) ii, 182, provides a useful summary of Beethoven's versions of *Leonore/Fidelio*. For the Paer version, see SL Balthazar, 'Leonora', *The New Grove Dictionary of Opera* (Macmillan Publishers Limited, 1992) vol 2, 1150.

the latter certainly came to know Paer's opera, attending a performance in 1808 and keeping a score of it in his study. Sir Charles Mackerras, one of our figurehead Patrons, who had conducted and recorded *Fidelio* to great acclaim, joined us at a Bampton performance: I fondly remember him wrapped up in a blanket on a cool evening, barely able to contain his enthusiasm as he spotted musical references that he felt convinced must have influenced Beethoven. The critics were impressed as well, not least the redoubtable Andrew Porter, who wrote 'It was a fascinating evening, honestly, decently and ambitiously performed: a page of musical history brought to life, a first encounter that for opera-goers with long memories recalled the rewarding St Pancras adventures long ago.'[10]

Success with *Leonora* led to our further enthusiasm for this 'familiar story, unfamiliar composer' approach. We were disappointed to learn that Salieri had only sketched initial and unperformable thoughts for *Così fan tutte* before Lorenzo da Ponte passed on the libretto to Mozart; but, once again, *The New Grove Dictionary of Opera* revealed an exciting possibility, a post-Mozart *Marriage of Figaro* by a Portuguese composer then unknown to us, Marcos Portugal (1762–1830). *La pazza giornata, ossia Il matrimonio di Figaro* was first performed in Venice in late December 1799. The libretto by Gaetano Rossi, who went on to write for Rossini, Meyebeer and Donizetti, can be seen as a critique of Da Ponte's edition and reinstated certain sections from Beaumarchais' original play. As with *Leonora* and some others of our operas, we were faced with the need to commission a performing music edition for an unpublished work. The task proved surprisingly easy to organise when we discovered that Dr David Cranmer, an English musicologist based in Lisbon at the Centro de Estudos da Sociologia e Estética Musical at the Universidade Nova, was engaged in a long-term, funded project of editing manuscripts of Marcos Portugal. *Il matrimonio di Figaro* was already on his list and, once our determination to perform was established, he was able to bring forward the proposal to meet our needs. Consequently, on 23 July 2010 at Bampton we were able to give the first performances anywhere since 1800. We performed the work four times that summer and revived it for three performances at the Buxton Festival in 2012. We located the production as was appropriate 'outside Seville' in a colourful Spanish Moorish setting, built locally by Anthony Hall around large fretwork screens donated to us from the Tate gallery, and the costumes were by Fiona Hodges. Our English translation was subsequently used for the New York American première in 2016 by On Site Opera.

These years saw us develop several worthwhile new enterprises. My own art history teaching post at Queen's College, a girls' independent school in central London, led to several operatic projects with the teenage students, including *Apollo and Hyacinth* in 2007 and Schubert's captivating *Die Verschworenen* (*The Conspirators*) in 2009. Such productions pitted the young female students against professional male singers from the company, which really encouraged their vocal skills and confidence. The Schubert, which was conducted by Gilly French, was attended by a critic from *Opera* magazine, who beautifully judged it with these memorable comments:

> Few of the period opera companies, who spend so much time and effort trying to recover the original feel of a work through elaborate digging, come close to conjuring up the atmosphere of authenticity of these performances. Schubert and his friends would surely have felt at

[10] A Porter, 'Leonora', *Opera* (2008) 1207. His reference to St Pancras recalls the Camden Festival in London between 1954 and 1987, which also specialised in rare opera.

> home with Bampton's small production … so full of warmth, personality and camaraderie, all charmingly frayed at the edges. The young raw voices were the highlight.[11]

A significant London development during this period was an extended series of occasional concerts of rare operatic music given at the renowned Wigmore Hall, beginning with Gluck's *La danza* and *Le cinesi* in 2009. For these we convened a small orchestra of some of the leading period instrument players on the London and national circuit, performing under the name Bampton Classical Players. Christian Curnyn conducted the Gluck; Benjamin Bayl conducted works by Thomas Arne in 2011; and Christopher Bucknall conducted Handel, Eccles and Bononcini in 2012. In 2011 we also added the Purcell Room at the Southbank to our venues, with a concert of Gluck's *Il parnaso confuso* and arias by Mozart. However, these proved expensive enterprises for us, and we found it difficult to attract the scale of audiences that would make them worthwhile. Both Arne's *The Judgment of Paris* and Handel's *The Choice of Hercules* then toured a number of public and private venues, including the historic Holywell Music Room in Oxford where we began to establish an occasional presence, a venue still being used for the Final of our biennial Young Singers' Competition.

Our major works at this time included our first visit into the French repertory with a delightful double bill in 2012 of Philidor, *Blaise le Savetier* and Grétry, *L'amant jaloux* (both operas centre around a large wardrobe, and aspects of the Grétry appear to have influenced Mozart in *Figaro*) and Cimarosa's *The Italian Girl in London*. Costumes for all these were by Fiona. I remember being slightly uncertain about our repertory choice of the Cimarosa, wondering if the music could be considered a little pedestrian. But – as with Paisiello's *Barber* – it proved that these hardworking and very successful Italian composers from the generation before Rossini, who could produce operas with extraordinary frequency and facility, well understood how to fashion engaging comedies that are well-paced and can still entertain in the twenty-first century. For *The Italian Girl* we employed a wonderfully adept cast (Kim Sheehan, Caryl Hughes, Adam Tunnicliffe, Nicholas Merryweather and Robert Winslade Anderson) and worked for the first time with a new conductor, Thomas Blunt.[12] We took the *Italian Girl* to Buxton in 2011 and Nigel Hook again excelled with the set, creating a gloriously dilapidated lounge from c1982 in the fictitious Hamilton Hotel, complete with the (also fictitious) Trafalgar Square underground station entrance outside. As Claire Seymour judged, Cimarosa provided 'a perfect scenario for a barmy yet sentimental comic romp of the kind in which Bampton Classical Opera excels'.[13]

I realise that this volume's dedicatee, Christopher Hodges, has rather disappeared from sight in the above paragraphs, but minutes from board meetings hardly make compelling reading. The complexity involved in any live music enterprise, if it is to be successful, is built on a hidden foundation of administration, business insight and funding. Strategy, legal compliance and regulation, fundraising enterprises and myriad details of event planning are vital to quality, and during these years our Chair steered a confident course through often uncertain, even difficult, waters. But at some time

[11] I Toronyi-Lalic, 'Die Verschworenen' *Opera* (2009) 719.
[12] In 2022 Blunt will be working with us for the fourth time, on Haydn's *Il mondo della luna*.
[13] C Seymour, 'The Italian Girl in London' *Opera* (2011) 1135.

the curtain had to fall on this exciting Act, and so the minutes of our board meeting on 11 May 2013 record that

> Chris has resigned from the Board, with regret, because of the increasing pressures of his work. He has seen us through a period of considerable development and expansion and his contribution was warmly noted and appreciated.

These seem dry words but our appreciation was, and remains, sincere. Bampton Classical Opera's 20th birthday was in 2013, which, in the summer, we celebrated with Mozart's early opera *La finta semplice* and with the launch of a new biennial Young Singers' Competition. The latter has since proved a vital innovation and, although initiated with Chris's encouragement, it was especially nurtured by his protégée, Hilary Reid Evans, who had recently joined our Board and then took over as our Chair. Her close links with Christopher are expressed by a further contribution to this volume (chapter 23, with Graham Russell), and we are grateful to her for continuing in her own distinctive way his firm and balanced management of our Board. Happily, Chris and Fiona continue their loyal interest and remain most generous in their support.

A fittingly vocal conclusion to this essay is suggested by the unforgettable, if seemingly absurd, King Edward's School Song, 'Where the iron heart of England throbs beneath its sombre robe', which Chris and I bellowed out on many occasions in our youth:

> Forward, where the knocks are hardest, some to failure, some to fame;
>
> Never mind the cheers or hooting, keep your head and play the game.[14]

But what more especially comes to mind is the appropriateness of the congratulatory line 'a school whose sons have made her great and famous round the globe': Christopher Hodges, with his global legal work and esteem, has certainly proved those words, as the present volume with its internationalist flavour surely demonstrates.

[14] Words by Alfred Hayes (1857–1936), set to music by Arthur Somervell.

7

Solicitor, Academic, Policymaker!

DIANA WALLIS

'Tinker, Tailor, Soldier, Sailor' ... so runs the old English counting nursery rhyme. Here, as I hope the title will suggest, I rather wanted to muse on the very varied legal career that Chris Hodges has had, and how I have observed that intersecting with my own as we both traversed similar but different aspects of lawyering. In doing so I hope to pay tribute to his substantial impact on the evolution of thinking around civil justice systems and indeed their development. Also, along the way, to give some small thanks for the kind personal and professional friendship that I have been fortunate to enjoy.

In early April 2007, then a Member of the European Parliament for Yorkshire & The Humber and much involved in EU civil justice policy, I wrote a 'Letter to the Editor' of the *Financial Times*:

> Sir, While your editorial ('A bogeyman abroad?', March 15) made many cogent points about class actions, surely the real bogeyman abroad is the continuing failure to provide a coherent European system of cross-border access to civil and commercial justice. The European Commission rightly champions many proposals to facilitate the ease of cross-border business to free up the internal market, but what about redress when things go wrong? This remains a tangled and costly nightmare for most consumers.
>
> The growing ethos behind much current European Union regulation is increasingly a so-called 'light touch' approach which European companies and employers' representatives tell us they want. If this is indeed wanted, then the companion of this must be informed and active consumers who are able to take action together to obtain redress when things go wrong. This is currently a gaping hole in the EU's civil justice architecture.
>
> Of course, any such system must be European and respect many of the points raised in your editorial, but this is the other side of a liberal and just internal market that some of us have been waiting to see the Commission get to grips with. You could say there should be no mobility in the internal market without liability!
>
> Diana Wallis MEP

Of course, to those who know him, they will realise that this was like an open invitation to Chris; here was a real live policymaker and politician writing about civil justice and class actions. I must have appeared a dream target! Whilst having a recent clear-out of papers I came across what is now a very rare thing, which I received in response – indeed it was pretty remarkable even at the date received – a carefully handwritten letter from an Oxford academic to me on these subjects, after he had seen my letter to the Editor. The letter of course was from Chris, then 'Head, Research Project on Civil Justice Systems' at the Centre for Socio-Legal Studies. It has been filed with other personal letters, like a 'thank you' note from an Icelandic PM and other such intriguing memorabilia from my parliamentary career. Chris alluded in his letter to our having met earlier when he was still at CMS Cameron McKenna. It may have been when we both were still solicitors, before I had embarked on the policy-making part of my career. Sadly, I cannot recall, but these letters serve just as well as a starting point and we are probably more evidentially secure. In addition, what I am sure of is that following this exchange we did meet and continued to meet, as our shared interest in issues around access to justice meant that our paths continued to cross regularly, and indeed ultimately as both colleagues and friends.

It is perhaps useful to give some more context to the timing of our original contact. Like Chris, I was a former practising solicitor. As I became a politician and lawmaker, I headed for the area of policy I knew best, and where I hoped I might be most effective and helpful: 'Legal Affairs' was the name of my main committee in the European Parliament, which dealt mainly with instruments pertaining to civil and commercial law and their relationship with the EU's Internal Market. In a sense for me this was a continuation of legal practice, trying to secure access to justice but in a wider way. In some ways I guess the transition Chris made from practice to academia was similar, allowing him time and space for that wider viewpoint. In the letter mentioned above he admitted to me 'academia is much more interesting and offers opportunities to think' – and one should add in Chris's case, 'to write'; I never came away from a meeting without an armful of publications or books! I note that even his original letter referred to at least two publications he was working on; this was of course typical. I guess I was a bit jealous, politicking only ever allows time for rather brief interventions.

I also think it is worth digressing to think about solicitors transitioning to academia. In other jurisdictions, as I had become aware during periods spent both in Belgium and Switzerland whilst a young lawyer, it is almost a normal occurrence for practising lawyers to combine practice with academia. It is far rarer in our jurisdiction: perhaps some barristers manage the combination, but for solicitors hardly ever. I speak from experience: I tried for a while to work part-time as a solicitor and to lecture; let us just say most of your professional partners find it a distracting and strange choice. So I think Chris was absolutely correct to make the complete transition, and I am sure we are all the richer for it in terms of his output and contribution.

To return to the time of our first interaction: Chris's earlier publications were very much around the subject of class actions and mass claims. I was then in my second parliamentary term of five years; I had just become a Vice President of the European Parliament and I knew the things I wanted to achieve. One of them was a European class action. The moment seemed propitious: as a 'Liberal' I had the luxury of two female Commissioners from the liberal family in charge of respectively consumer policy (Meglena Kuneva, Bulgarian) and competition policy (Neelie Kroes, Netherlands); we all shared a similar vision. It looked like full steam ahead, although we knew there would be opposition. At the same time the other policy area that increasingly took my attention was that relating to alternative dispute resolution (ADR) in general and mediation in particular. Some try to put these two in opposition to each other; in fact I believe, and I think Chris too saw and sees, that they are both valid paths to access to justice, although if we can avoid antagonism and blame so much the better. I recall an event in the European Parliament that an organisation Chris was involved in, although not him, had approached my office for me to host, an event my staff were told was about ADR. On the day, it turned out the event was rather more about undermining the arguments in favour of a European class action. I remember my staff were furious, however both issues were surely valid in any discussion about the future of European civil justice. It is there that I think Chris and I recognised our mutual interest. Parliamentary staff are always loyal guard dogs in respect of their members, and I think my office initially felt that Chris was possibly on the wrong side of the argument for my taste, and there may therefore have been an early attempt to keep us apart!

However, I think that, given our interest in similar issues, we were bound to keep meeting, even if that was sometimes as it were by proxy, meeting his then assistant Naomi Creutzfeldt at an ADR conference at the Academy of European Law (*Europaische Rechtsakademie* (ERA)) and learning how they were criss-crossing Europe looking at different ADR and Ombuds systems. Again, I thought this was an incredible project – one that could give us real input as policymakers into what was actually happening on the ground. We had our fears about the diversity of ADR systems and whether European regulation was either a help or hindrance. Here was someone, along with his team, going out and looking at and speaking to those running a multiplicity of ADR schemes.

It seemed to me that our thinking began to align increasingly around ideas of 'coherence' and the need for a 'holistic' justice system in European level, using both the court and other dispute resolution methods. This rather than what seemed to be being constructed, which was a patchwork of instruments contorted to fit in with appropriate legal bases normally giving pre-eminence to the good functioning of the Internal Market whilst not really delivering a comprehensible justice system. One of the memorable times we spent together was at a conference hosted in the small Portuguese city of Leiria by the polytechnic there. The overall conference theme related to electronic or e-justice. Over *pastel de nata* at coffee time and in the evenings copious amount of tapas and red wine, there was the chance to discuss further and to appreciate our shared views. I remembered we exchanged the papers we produced after that conference, again finding ourselves much in agreement about the need for a holistic approach. By this time, I had left the Parliament and had become involve with the fairly newly formed European Law Institute (ELI), of which I was to be President for a period of four years between 2013 and 2017. At the same time I returned to a part-time post at the Law School within the University of Hull. Thus we were both involved in thinking about the future of legal policy of civil justice, whilst beginning to focus much more on the need for wider use of ADR.

Perhaps the most memorable day we shared was the day of the referendum on the UK's continued membership of the European Union. We had arranged to meet in Oxford for lunch, and I was then going on to Hart Publishing to discuss my ideas for a monograph on European civil justice. I was apprehensive about the referendum result, especially being a resident of Yorkshire and being familiar with the political terrain there, which had the possibility to produce such large votes in favour of UKIP. However, lunch in Oxford was quite a different experience: it was sunny and Chris was definitely upbeat, with all sorts of ideas. My mood was improved by the number of 'Yes' posters; even a woman pushing a pram past our restaurant with the pram covered in 'Yes' banners. I thought maybe, just maybe, it will all be OK. Chris promised to provide support to my proposal to Hart and again I had a positive meeting there. A perfect day, topped off by seeing a production of *A Midsummer Night's Dream* at Stratford. As we all know, by next morning the nightmare had arrived and my publication fell by the wayside: I did not have the heart for it anymore. Chris, kindly as ever, found a way to involve me with the Centre at Oxford where I became an honorary fellow. So would begin a series of visits to Oxford either for the annual ADR conferences or just to meet.

Around the same time, as President of the ELI, I was approached by Sir Geoffrey Vos, then a Justice of the High Court and President of the European Network of the Councils for the Judiciary (ENCJ). He suggested a joint project between our two institutions on the relationship between the courts and ADR bodies, or, put another way, the relationship between formal and informal justice, as the final project was to become known. Apart from a group of scholars and practitioners from around Europe, who joined us in this endeavour to be part of the project team, all such projects had a team of advisors, and who better in this case than Chris? The ELI was in the habit of hosting an annual conference, which every other year would take place away from its home base of Vienna; in 2016 the choice fell on the University of Ferrara and its beautiful and historic city.

It was also the custom to host several panel discussions surrounding on-going project work, so of course our project related to ADR formed one such panel; Sir Geoffrey was a key part of the panel, which I had to chair, and I had also invited Chris to participate. I think he arrived only on the day and did not really have the chance to discuss with Geoffrey in advance, although to be fair I think he warned me he would be provocative. We had a full hall, which became fuller. Chris had mistaken his man, or rather his judge, in Sir Geoffrey: here was a judge who understood, and indeed has gone on to champion, the use of ADR. Chris made some comments about judicial attitudes to ADR that would have left a less controlled panellist apoplectic; it was too much, but certainly provided some fireworks for the participants. Chris had totally misread his judge; but in fairness to both, they have gone on to be great collaborators, which shows the benefit of such events, although as Chair it gave me a few sticky moments. Indeed, later in the finalisation of the project, we held a small conference at the European Law Academy in Trier, where Chris was again involved as was Geoffrey, who sadly could not attend in person but did so remotely due to a health issue. By this time, I seem to recall they were already good colleagues, and Chris was doubtless in touch with him as he is with most of us, full of ideas.

This was borne out by the fact that Geoffrey was both present and an active participant at the last Oxford ADR conference before the pandemic hit us. Indeed, I could not write this without mentioning those conferences. I am not sure how many I have attended now; certainly I think three, it may be more. They have always been such a positive occasion, bringing together many practitioners of different aspects of ADR and academics in a way that is not so common. They are always good for meeting old friends, but importantly for hearing and understanding what is going on at street level in the delivery of justice, be it in relation to parking fines, furniture, or any consumer issue, then putting it all together to consider what we have and, more importantly, what we might be able to create going forward. This is the type of lawyering I respect, and that Chris has achieved.

Lawyers can be just lawyers who spend a lifetime advising and helping individuals, and that is a valid and needful choice, especially at a time when, certainly in the UK, lawyers are somewhat beleaguered and criticised. However, lawyers can also choose to use that practical experience to think and advise more widely as to how society can do things better, deliver justice more fairly. It is of course both fun and a privilege to be able to travel those diverse paths as a lawyer, and I think that we would have to acknowledge that Chris has, by virtue of his various roles as a lawyer, been more impactful than most on that wider stage. I recall an instance at a conference at Trier that ostensibly had nothing to do with Chris, when Professor Hugh Beal made a comment about something to the effect that it sounded like a Chris Hodges' idea, which in turn led to a series of texts from various of us in the audience to Chris in the UK and back. It is some achievement to get your ideas implanted and discussed in that way!

So solicitor, academic, policymaker … I wonder what next we can add to the rhyme? But we can certainly wish *bon voyage* along with our thanks for the journey so far!

PART II

Collective Redress

8

What is Collective in EU Collective Redress?

HANS-W MICKLITZ AND ANDREA WECHSLER

We need to think about how to organise best enforcement of consumer law in the EU.

(C Hodges, a summary of many conversations over many years)

A Personal Note

Dear Chris, the intellectual community of EU lawyers benefitted over decades from your relentless commitment and insistence on the overwhelming importance of law enforcement in the EU. Your power and your energy drove us all in new areas and forced us to break down boundaries between substantive and procedural law, and to combine the law in the books with the law in action. Three areas stand out: ADR/ODR, administrative enforcement and representative/collective actions.[1] In each of the three, you left us with comprehensive monographs that serve as a kind of fundament on which we your colleagues are building our own research. One of the key issues is the question of what is collective in collective action, whatever its name might be – collective, representative or class action – and whoever the regulator or the claimant might be – an administrative body, a lawyer, a business or a consumer organisation. The following contribution is meant to improve clarity in the notion of 'collective', which dominates the European discourse. It will be conceptual and theoretical; we will restrict the references to the minimum so as to gain space, literally and metaphorically, to lay the ground for future research.

[1] C Hodges, *The Reform of Class and Representative Actions in European Legal Systems: A New Framework for Collective Redress in Europe* (Hart Publishing, 2008); C Hodges, I Benöhr and N Creutzfeldt, *Consumer ADR in Europe* (Oxford, Hart Publishing, 2012); C Hodges, *Law and Corporate Behaviour: Integrating Theories of Regulation, Enforcement, Compliance and Ethics* (Hart Publishing, 2015); C Hodges and S Voet, *Delivering Collective Redress New Technologies* (Hart Publishing, 2018).

I. Collective Redress as Regulatory Litigation

Recent years have seen ever more global disputes as a result of globalisation, the rise of multinational companies and the transformation of transnational trade into Global Value Chains.[2] The extended geographical reach goes hand in hand with the rise of transnational legal disputes and an ever greater concern of policymakers and citizens of how to effectively and efficiently enforce established private rights against transnational players.[3] In recent years, this concern has also come to the forefront of attention in the European Union (EU) and its Member States. The given legal constraints of harmonising enforcement[4] did not prevent the EU from considerably Europeanising collective enforcement through public and private entities, as well as through alternative and online dispute resolution (ADR, ODR).[5]

The phenomena of 'massification',[6] mass production, consumption and large-scale economic development have endowed economic dispute resolution with yet another dimension. In the area of business-to-consumer (B2C) transactions, in particular factual and legal issues have become replicable over a wide variety of transactions. Whilst resolution of commonality of disputes has a long-standing tradition in the United States (US) in the form of class actions,[7] it is only in the last three decades that policymakers worldwide – and in particular in Europe – have begun to engage in legislative activities for the resolution of mass disputes in the form of class actions, public interest litigation, group litigation, aggregated litigation, representative action and collective redress mechanisms.[8]

This chapter asks the question 'What is collective in collective redress?' It exposes the lack of definitional clarity of 'collective', enquires into the terminology and meaning of 'collective' in collective redress, and conceptualises the respective policy levers for designing collective redress mechanisms. Here are the arguments:

1. 'Collective' has never been sufficiently defined. Its significance has been substantially underrated and its complexity underestimated.
2. Collective redress is being used as a proxy for 'regulatory' redress, ex-ante through deterrence and ex-post through compensation.
3. Collective redress is complementary to and supportive of administrative and alternative enforcement mechanisms and their rationales.

[2] R Baldwin, *The Great Convergence: Information Technology and the New Globalization* (The Belnap Press, 2016).

[3] A Stadler, 'Cross-border mass litigation: A Particular Challenge for European Law' in J Steele and W van Boom (eds), *Mass Justice, Challenges of Representation and Distribution* (Edward Elgar, 2011).

[4] W van Gerven, 'Of Rights, Remedies and Procedures' (2002) 37 *CML Rev* 501.

[5] F Steffek and H Unberath (eds), *Regulating Dispute Resolution, ADR and Access to Justice at the Crossroads* (Hart Publishing, 2013); B Hess and P Ortolani, *Impediments of National Procedural Law to the Free Movement of Judgments: Luxembourg Report on European Procedural Law*, vol I (Beck/Hart/Nomos, 2019); B Hess and S Law, *Implementing EU Consumer Rights by National Procedural Law: Luxembourg Report on European Procedural Law*, vol II (Beck/Hart/Nomos, 2019).

[6] M Cappelletti, 'Vindicating the Public Interest through the Courts: A Comparative Contribution' (1975–1976) 25 *Buffalo Law Review* 645.

[7] R Nagareda, *The Law of Class Actions and other Aggregate Litigation* (Foundation Press, 2009).

[8] A Uzelac and S Voet (eds), *Class Actions in Europe Holy Grail or a Wrong Trail?* (Springer, 2021).

4. The regulatory dimension of collective redress restructures civil justice systems in three ways:

   (a) The promotion of collective redress increases the significance of conciliatory and alternative dispute resolution mechanisms. Thereby, the power balance between judicial and non-judicial, national and European initiatives is substantially tilted towards non-judicial and European dispute resolution mechanisms.
   (b) The integration of collective redress mechanisms redraws the boundaries between procedural and substantive law, thereby reducing regulatory compensation and transaction costs and eroding the principle of procedural autonomy.
   (c) The drive towards plaintiff-run collective redress goes along with a move from producerism to consumerism.[9]

II. Collectivity, Commonality and Economies of Scale

The following section not only discusses the rise of collectivity and collective redress in policy and law, but also introduces six case scenarios that exemplify the conceptual and theoretical approach.

A. Collectivity and Collective Redress

As corporations have learnt to capture economies of scale and scope, so now do policymakers devote their policy initiatives to capturing economies of scale and scope in consumer redress mechanisms. However, it is the diversity of collective redress issues and instruments that makes a common definitional foundation of collectiveness difficult in collective redress.

Historically, class actions were the rule in medieval England.[10] Deficiencies in transportation, communications and administrative structures revealed the impossibility and inefficiency of individual litigation. The commonalities in close-knit communities provided the legitimacy for group litigation. With ongoing industrialisation, however, group litigation eventually disappeared from the European procedural portfolio in 1850. On the other hand, class action proceedings in the US increased following *West v Randall* in 1820.[11] It would take more than a century for Europe – as well as other leading jurisdictions in the world, such as Canada, China, India and Japan – to (re-)open procedural instruments for mass disputes. The 'massification' of society – to use Cappelletti's terminology[12] – triggered the rise of commonality and collectivity of issues. As in medieval times, though, the inefficiency, ineffectiveness and impossibility

[9] JQ Whitman, 'Consumerism versus Producerism: A Study in Comparative Law' (2007–2008) 117 *Yale Law Journal* 340.

[10] S C Yeazell, *From Medieval Group Litigation to the Modern Class Action* (Yale University Press, 1987) 38.

[11] *West v Randall*, 29 F Cas 718 (No 17, 424) (1820).

[12] Cappelletti (n 6).

of just compensation and redress led to acknowledgement of the need for collective redress within and across boundaries. Ever since 1990, nation states have included collective consumer protection either in national consumer protection laws or in civil procedure laws.[13] In the EU, subsequent to the judgments of the European Court of Justice (ECJ) in *Courage* and *Manfredi*,[14] the European Commission devoted extensive attention to antitrust injuries as well as collective redress for consumers.[15]

Figure 8.1 European collective redress initiatives

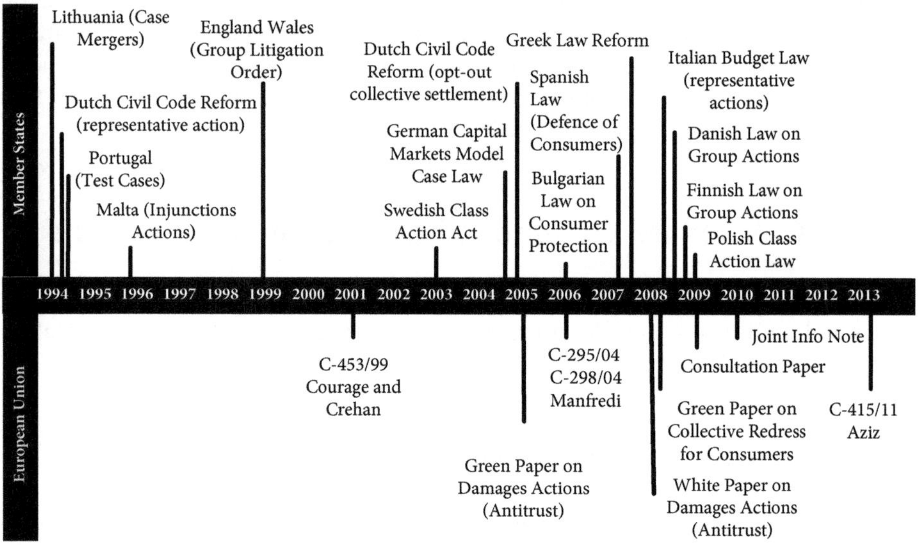

Reconstructing the history of collective redress in the EU demonstrates a bewildering use of the word 'collective'. There are two different strands of regulation – that aimed at the protection of national consumers and that dealing with transborder litigation. The first has its origins in Directive 84/450/EEC on misleading advertising (later Directive 2005/29/EC) and Directive 93/13/EC on unfair contract terms, which introduced the action of injunction as a stop order mechanism on behalf of national administrative authorities and national consumer organisations in order to create a common platform for national action. There is no explicit reference to 'collective action' or any other form of 'collectivity'. The second strand starts with Directive 98/27/EC, in which the notion of 'collective interests' is introduced, connected to entities that legitimately represent consumers. Collectivity is equated with the respective interest of the

[13] Hodges, *The Reform of Class and Representative Actions in European Legal Systems* (n 1).

[14] Case C-453/99 *Courage Ltd v Bernard Crehan and Bernard Crehan v Courage Ltd and others* ECLI:EU:C:2001:465, [2001] ECR I-6297; Case C-295/04 *Vincenzo Manfredi v Lloyd Adriatico Assicurazioni SpA ea* ECLI:EU:C:2006:461, [2006] ECR I-6619.

[15] Inter alia, the 'Green Paper on Consumer Collective Redress' (2008) available at https://ec.europa.eu/commission/presscorner/detail/en/MEMO_08_741; 'Proposal for a Directive of the European Parliament and of the Council on certain rules governing actions for damages under national law for infringements of the competition law provisions of the Member States and of the European Union' COM/2013/0404 final – 2013/0185 (COD).

Member States' consumers who need to be defended in transnational litigation via the action of injunction. This line of thought is reiterated in Regulation 2006/2004 – later Regulation 2017/2394 – on cooperation in transborder enforcement. The nation state-bound understanding of collective interests is confirmed and specified in Article 3(4) of the 2017 Regulation, depending on the degree to which more than one Member States' collective consumer interests are affected through 'widespread infringement' (meaning at least three Member States) or 'widespread infringement with a Union dimension' (meaning 'a widespread infringement that has done, does or is likely to do harm to the collective interests of consumers in at least two-thirds of the Member States, accounting, together, for at least two-thirds of the population of the Union').

The old and longstanding political debate about collective compensation schemes gained momentum in the debate about remedies against antitrust injuries, which affected consumer protection policy. As Hodges pointed out,[16] the 2008 Green Paper on *Damages Actions for Breach of EC Antitrust Rules*[17] referred to 'collective action'. The 2008 White Paper on *Damages Actions for Breach of the EC Antitrust Rules*,[18] by contrast, immediately abandoned 'collective action', whilst 'collective redress' is taken to denote representative actions, on the one hand, and opt-in collective actions, on the other. The finally adopted Directive 2014/104 is limited to individual enforcement. Recital 13 states 'this Directive should require Member States to introduce "collective redress" mechanisms for the enforcement of Articles 101 and 102 TFEU'.

The 2008 Green Paper on *Consumer Collective Redress*[19] avoided any rhetoric about collective actions. The Commission Work Programme 2012 mentions 'collective redress' rather than using any other terminology.[20] The 2010 Joint Information Note *Towards a Coherent European Approach to Collective Redress: Next Steps*[21] finally ventures into a definition of 'collective redress':

> 'Collective redress' is a broad concept encompassing any mechanism that may accomplish the cessation or prevention of unlawful business practices which affect a multitude of claimants or the compensation for the harm caused by such practices. There are two main forms of collective redress: by way of injunctive relief, claimants seek to stop the continuation of illegal behaviour; by way of compensatory relief, they seek damages for the harm caused. Collective redress procedures can take a variety of forms, including out-of-court mechanisms for dispute resolution or the entrustment of public or representative entities with the enforcement of claims.

Directive 1828/2020 finally realised what consumer advocates had been longing for over the decades. It goes beyond 'collective interests of consumers' to cover injunctions and integrates 'collective redress' (recital 5). The Directive merges the purely national and the transborder dimension in drawing a distinction between injunctions, where the collective interests of the respective Member State – or states in transborder litigation – have

[16] Hodges *The Reform of Class and Representative Actions* (n 1).

[17] SEC (2005) 1732.

[18] SEC (2008) 404.

[19] COM (2008) 794 final.

[20] Communication from the Commission to the European Parliament, the Council, the European Economic and Social Committee, and the Committee of the Regions, Commission Work Programme 2012, Delivering European renewal, COM (2011) 777 final.

[21] SEC (2010) 1192.

to be affected, and collective redress to the benefit of the affected group of consumers, which can be national or even transnational. Article 3 reads as follows:

> (3) 'collective interests of consumers' means the general interest of consumers and, in particular for the purposes of redress measures, the interests of a group of consumers …

The degree of collectivity follows the type of action. Consumer redress remains primarily bound to a group of national consumers, but Article 4(2) opens the path for representative action – injunctions and collective redress – through consumer organisations that 'represent consumers from more than one Member State'. In theory, it would be possible to identify European consumers as the targeted group.

What looks like a huge step forward in the advancement of the consumer acquis still does not bring clarity on the proper meaning of the term 'collective'. The European minimum standard on collective redress is 'opt-in', so as to evade conceptual comparability with US class action mechanisms.[22] This conclusion can be corroborated by reference to the ever-prominent rhetoric of the avoidance of abusive litigation. The reservations in the diverse preparatory documents[23] ended up in a set of rules that oblige the Member States to supervise and monitor collective litigation of consumer organisations (see Article 5(3) and (4) of the Directive).

In consequence, the term 'collective' in collective redress has – still – not sufficiently been defined and analysed, with the implication that its significance has been substantially underrated and its complexity underestimated. The usage of the terminology of 'collective' and 'collective redress' denotes a rather narrow understanding of 'collective' in collective redress, which is restricted to a description of the group of victims or plaintiffs. The term reflects a decision to explicitly avoid 'class' terminology and substitute it through 'group action', with the clear message that the standard case is the equation of consumer group with the collective consumer interests in one nation state.

B. A Heuristic Approach to Collective Redress: Scenarios

A doctrinally coherent and theoretically conclusive approach to collective redress requires comprehensiveness in application to a large variety of scenarios. Out of the five scenarios identified in this subsection, three are taken from the realm of economic law, two from the realm of non-economic law. Even though non-economic redress mechanisms are rarely discussed in a collective redress context, they have become an integral part of the enforcement system and have increasingly reached the ECJ.

The *first* case scenario relates to the realm of capital markets and securities law:

> A big telecommunications company is going public. In its prospectus issued at the initial public offers, the companies valued its real property holdings en bloc rather than on an individual basis. In 2001, these valuations proved to be grossly overstated and the telecommunications company wrote down the land values by 2 billion euros.

[22] SEC (2010) 1192, 6.

[23] Information Note SEC (2010) 1192, 6 firmly opposing US class actions, Commission Staff Working Document, Public Consultation: *Towards a Coherent European Approach to Collective Redress* (SEC (2011) 173 final, 4 February 2010) 9.

> As a result, the stock's value plummeted by 92%. Consequently, the question arises whether the affected shareholders were entitled to individual or collective relief on the grounds of misrepresentation in the prospectus. The sheer quantity of the claims brought in German courts against Telecom threatened to clog the courts' docket for years so that the legislator passed the Capital Investors Model Proceeding Law (KapMuG) in 2005.[24]

The *second* case scenario is placed in the realm of credit agreements and consumer protection:

> A large number of citizens were called uninvited at their homes and induced to purchase flats, ie to invest in the construction industry by entering into loan agreements. However, as these loan agreements, these secured credit agreements, fell under the Door-Step Selling Directive, citizens thus induced to enter into such secured credit agreements could exercise a right of cancellation. The legal result of such a cancellation of a credit agreement was that such consumers were obliged to pay back the credit valuta to the bank, while the bank had to return all received payments on interest. The problem for investors, however, was the fact that the flats were sold to them at a price that doubled the market value. And even 10 years after the loan agreement, investors were not able to pay back the credit by selling the flats. Likewise, the income of the investors from renting out the flat was not sufficient to cover the monthly credit rates. Consequently, the question arose whether the affected investors were entitled to relief for the losses sustained between having entered into the contracts and their cancellation.[25]

The *third* scenario is situated in the realm of competition law, and more specifically hardcore cartels:

> For decades, wholesale grocers bought potatoes at a price prescribed by potato wholesalers. As an investigation by the competition authorities shows, however, potato producers conspired to fix prices. Consequently, the question arose whether the wholesale grocers affected (1,900) were entitled to compensatory relief on the grounds of overcharging. It is noticeable in this context that it was not only the wholesale grocers that had suffered losses due to overcharging but consumers as well, who suffered from artificially high potato prices – meaning essentially the general public. Comparable cartel allegations were investigated by German competition authorities.[26]

The *fourth* fact scenario stems from the realm of environmental law and environmental pollution:

> An individual lives close to a busy central road in a European inner-city centre. Measurements of air quality taken near his home have shown that in several

[24] Kapitalanleger-Musterverfahrens-Gesetz (6 August 2005) BGBl 2437. The case has still not come to an end. The competent court has made a proposal to settle the case. Whether the proposal will be accepted by the claimants is still open.

[25] Facts essentially taken from Case C-481/99 *Georg Heininger and Helga Heininger v Bayerische Hypo- und Vereinsbank AG* ECLI:EU:C:2001:684, [2001] ECR I-9945.

[26] See in context at www.bundeskartellamt.de/wDeutsch/aktuelles/presse/2013_05_10.php.

> consecutive years, the limit value fixed for emissions of particulate matters was exceeded far more than 35 times, even though that is the maximum number of instances permitted under the Federal Law on combating pollution. Not being the only citizen living on that street, the question arises whether or not individuals affected have the means for collective redress available against this instance of collective air pollution. And the decisive question is whether relief – as, for instance, in the form of an action plan – can be sought from the responsible municipal, state or federal authorities rather than directly from the polluting individuals? *Janecek*[27] dealt with the question of whether or not Article 7(3) of Directive 96/62 confers an individual right to require the competent national authorities to draw up an action plan where there is a risk that the limit values or alert thresholds for emissions may be exceeded.

The *fifth* case scenario is taken from the realm of social regulation, specifically anti-discrimination law:

> Feryn[28] sells and installs doors. It placed a 'vacancies' sign on its premises, hoping to recruit fitters to install doors at customers' houses. At the same time, one of the directors of the company was quoted in the national newspaper as saying that the company would not hire Moroccan immigrants because the customers were reluctant to give such persons access to their homes. The national Centre for Equal Opportunities and Opposition to Racism (CGKR), which was set up to promote equal treatment, applied to the labour court for a finding that that particular company applied a discriminatory labour policy. The relevant question was whether or not public statements that an employer did not recruit persons of certain ethnic origin constituted direct discrimination, even though there was no identifiable claimant but rather a large group of potentially affected Moroccan job applicants. The ECJ answered the question in the affirmative.

III. Conceptualising Collective Redress

This section aims at analysing various legislative and judicial approaches to collectivity in the EU, the institutional environment of collective redress, its cause of action and its procedural requirements: legal standing. It dives deeply into the law and also uses the five cases set out in section II.B for illustrative and paradigmatic purposes. The emerging logic is claimed to characterise the European approach to collectivity.

A. The Institutional Environment

Conceptualising redress requires a look at the institutional environment – both in terms of enforcement avenues and in terms of distribution mechanisms. The analysis is

[27] Case C-237/07 *Dieter Janecek v Freistaat Bayern* ECLI:EU:C:2008:447, [2008] ECR I-6221, for a full reconstruction of the case; B Kas, '"Hybrid" collective remedies in the EU social legal order' PhD thesis, European University Institute (2017).

[28] Case C-54/07 *Cemrum voor gelijkheid van kansen en voor racismebestrijding v Firma Feryn NV* ECLI:EU:C:2008:397, [2008] ECR I-5187, reconstructed by Kas (n 27).

based on the premises that the newly established enforcement mechanisms, especially Directive 2020/1828, have the potential to lead to fundamental changes in national civil justice systems by challenging the traditional role of courts.

Historically, we have witnessed a diversity of national systems and, thus, inconsistent approaches to collective redress at EU level. The result is an uneven enforcement of rights and even an undermining of the enjoyment of rights by European citizens. Prior to EU harmonisation, there were four different types of instruments used in the then 16 Member States that applied collective redress schemes: group actions, representative actions, test case procedures and procedures for skimming off profits.[29] Every national system had introduced collective redress by a different mix of instruments, thus demonstrating a broad variety of understandings of collectivity and collective institutional environments. In the light of this diversity, the question for the policymaker was how universally European such an institutional environment for collective redress should and could be construed to be.

Directive (EU) 2020/1828 demonstrates how legal reform in the EU redraws the balance of power in collective consumer redress. Qualified entities may now bring not only a cross-border action for injunction, which has been possible since Directive 98/27/EC, but also a representative action. The aim of the revised Directive is to 'ensure that at Union and national level at least one effective and efficient procedural mechanism for representative actions for injunctive measures and for redress measures is available to consumers in all Member States'.[30] In the light of this overall aim, it is, on the one hand, left to the Members States to specify the local rules of procedure, thereby leaving ample space for national legislatures. On the other hand, it is explicitly stated that the Directive 'should not replace existing national procedural mechanisms for the protection of collective or individual consumer interests'.[31] Therefore, Member States may adopt further and additional provisions with the objective of protecting collective consumer interests. Enforcement avenues remain largely defined at a national level, though subject to EU law scrutiny, to be exercised by the European Commission in the infringement procedure and by the ECJ in the preliminary reference procedure.

A look at national regimes and one of our case examples shows that the institutional environment for collective redress is far from comprehensive harmonisation. The telecommunications case is a telling example of how slowly procedural approximation moves within Europe and even within individual Member States. In 2001, some 17,000 shareholders of Deutsche Telekom had filed about 2,500 individual lawsuits against the company. The starting point was, thus, individual claims. Responding to this flood of lawsuits, the German legislature enacted the Capital Markets Model Case Act (*Kapitalanleger-Musterverfahrensgesetz* (*KapMuG*)) in 2005. The Act tries to provide mechanisms for courts to handle cases of mass investor damages, whilst avoiding the introduction of US-style class actions into German law. The second step is thus national evolution of procedural law by way of model laws leaving space for European approximation.

[29] G Jones, 'The Role of the Legislators in developing collective remedies: institutional perspectives' in *Legislating for Collective Redress under European Law: Perspectives from National Judiciaries*, Conference Paper, 1 (copy on file with author).

[30] Recital 7.

[31] ibid.

Directive (EU) 2020/1828 shows tentative steps being taken towards exactly that missing link of European approximation. According to Caponi, new procedural rules can stimulate and alter the culture of parties, judges and lawyers in remarkable ways.[32] However, collective redress mechanisms by themselves will not be potent enough to promote harmonisation of civil procedure: EU initiatives are just one driver – operating on a normative level. The procedural handling of cross-border conflicts requires further procedural approximation, which could only be realised on the basis of common understandings of the value of effective redress and of substantive rights. Whilst such a consequence seems to lie in the logic of the European integration process, it highlights the instrumental use of giving full and effective value to substantive rights. Collective interests or collectivity in whatever shade is no more than a proxy for 'regulatory' redress. Collective redress instruments function as deterrent-based regulatory – almost quasi-criminal – litigation mechanisms, which are complementary to and supportive of administrative and alternative enforcement mechanisms. The term 'collective' disguises regulatory initiatives leading to a fundamental reconstruction of civil justice, enforcement is privatised and courts turn into 'regulators'.[33] Procedural rules are reclassified as substantive ones, ADR/ODR/arbitration is promoted as an alternative to access to courts, settlement mechanisms in collective redress are transforming the role of courts, not to mention the increasing importance legally binding compliance mechanisms to be enforced through administrative fines. The General Data Protection Regulation (GDPR) and the current EU proposals on the Digital Market Act, Digital Services Act, Digital Governance Act, the Artificial Intelligence Act and the Data Act demonstrate elements of a new institutional enforcement environment, one that is based on the strong interaction between compliance and 'fines and a reduced role for private actors, and the representation of collective interests and of collective redress.

The institutional environment across borders determines distribution mechanisms for mass justice. The aggregation of claims across borders requires appropriate mechanisms for the distribution of relief. Essentially, collectivity needs to be justly dissolved and redress redistributed back into individual claims. Inappropriate mechanisms to protect and enforce rights have the potential to undermine the effectiveness of judicial protection and thereby the trust in judicial protection.[34] Without individual rights to get compensated, any form of collective redress is doomed to fail. Reality at EU level looks different. Ineffective judicial protection is visible in the realm of competition and consumer law. In competition law, the Court of Justice has consistently emphasised the importance of allowing citizens to claim compensation for antitrust injuries, and triggered the elaboration of Directive 2014/104/EC on antitrust damages.[35] However, the Directive by and large neglects the role of consumers as possible victims of antitrust

[32] R Caponi, 'Harmonizing Civil Procedure: Initial Remarks' in B Hess and XE Kramer (eds), *From Common Rules to Best Practices in European Civil Procedure* (Hart Publishing/Nomos, 2017) 43.

[33] H-W Micklitz, 'The Transformation of Enforcement in EU Private Law: Preliminary Considerations' (ERPL, 2015) 491.

[34] C Backes, 'Effective environmental protection: towards a better understanding of environmental quality standards in environmental legislation' in L Gipperth and C Zetterberg (eds), *Miljörättsliga perspektiv och tankevändor, Vänbok till Jan Darpö & Gabriel Michanek, Iustus Förlag AB* (Ad Libris Uppsala, 2013).

[35] Case C-453/99 *Courage Ltd v Bernard Crehan and Bernard Crehan v Courage Ltd and others* ECLI:EU:C:2001:465, [2001] ECR I-6297; and Case C-295/04 *Vincenzo Manfredi v Lloyd Adriatico Assicurazioni SpA ea* ECLI:EU:C:2006:461, [2006] ECR I-6619.

injuries, and sets aside any form of collective redress. The missing European rules to compensate consumers highlights the role of domestic legal systems. But domestic legal systems rarely provide opportunities to obtain reparation for low-profile harm.

An example of this is clearly the German potato cartel case. Two German potato-packing firms were fined by the German competition authorities (Federal Cartel Office, *Bundeskartellamt*) for price-fixing for potatoes and onions in their contracts with retail group Metro. A fine of €13.2 million had to be paid as an administrative penalty. However, the question remained how the individual losses could be compensated in that case. In fact, loss had occurred at the level not only of wholesale grocers, but also of consumers through overcharging.[36] Consumers as victims failed to obtain reparation for the harm, even though we can witness an increasing tendency towards civil litigation to seek damages by buyers of overpriced products. The White Paper on damages actions for breach of EC antitrust rules[37] had explicitly concluded that domestic rules of Member States to compensate victims of infringements of antitrust rules were insufficient and that EU action was needed, albeit with limited results. The potato case not only points to a regulatory gap in the design of antitrust injuries; it also demonstrates the difficulties in compensating individual consumers if the level of damage is low and does not provide an incentive to take action. However, even if the overall damage to individual consumers in antitrust injuries is high, there are still no European-wide mechanisms to dissolve consumer collectivity in antitrust injuries.

Despite these obvious shortcomings, it seems unlikely that national legal systems will be forced by European institutions to introduce collective redress mechanisms in order to overcome these deficiencies. Individual redress will remain undercompensated. A web of alternative policy levers, like simplifying individual redress or resorting to ADR instruments, could in part – and in theory – address these deficiencies. Likewise, insurance could play a crucial role as a loss distribution mechanism. However, as has been argued by Backes,[38] it would be crucial to rethink distribution mechanisms in light of the principle of effective judicial protection.

A recent judgment of the German Supreme Court provides for such an occasion.[39] The Court had declared void a standard term that allowed banks to increase their fees without seeking the explicit consent of consumers. The unwillingness of the banks to take action so as to reimburse the affected consumers was brought to light in German newspapers, and might lead to a collective action organised by law firms, who are currently seeking consumers who are ready to use the German opt-in mechanism. The immoral behaviour of the banks seems to increase the readiness of consumers to fight for their rights, even if the potential compensation remains below €100 in each case. Chris Hodges[40] would have pointed to the superiority of agencies, which should take action not only to prohibit such practices but also to compensate consumers. He might be right, in that the German BaFin (Federal Financial Supervisory Authority) took regulatory action to push the banks into action. However, the banks immediately went

[36] See Press Release of the German Cartel Office (Bundeskartellamt) (3 May 2018).
[37] COM (2008) 165 def.
[38] Backes (n 34).
[39] Bundesgerichtshof, Urt v [27.04.2021] – XI ZR 26/20.
[40] Hodges, *The Reform of Class and Representative Actions in European Legal Systems* (n 1).

to court and challenged the competence of the BaFin.[41] The European Commission strove for such competencies in the revised Regulation on the cooperation of transborder enforcement. The remainder of this initiative is far from administrative collective redress, though.[42]

B. The Cause of Action: Substantive Collective Redress

Conceptualising redress requires an analysis of the types of harm, loss and damage, as well as remedies. The argument is that the increase in mass dispute resolution mechanisms equally increases consumer expectations for compensation, and substantially strengthens deterrence against violating consumer rights. In consequence, collective redress mechanisms might be apt to reduce the amount of social harm.

The move towards the 'more economic approach' in EU law, driven by efficiency considerations, has gone on to accurately capture and compensate both for individual private losses and for social collective losses. Individual loss describes damage that individual citizens or entities have incurred, while social loss describes the social cost imposed on the society. Collective redress mechanisms are meant to compensate for both individual loss and social loss.[43] However, two difficulties have to be overcome: first of all, we need to find mechanisms to calculate *collective* damage that allow us to adequately compensate *individual* private losses. And, second, we need to find mechanisms that maximise the related insecurity for market participants, so that they are prevented from violating the law. It is this latter point that is claimed to contribute to the avoidance of collective social losses that can rarely be compensated.

The diversity of law enforcement mechanisms has boosted expectations of receiving compensation for economic losses, or at least encouraged the seeking of redress for non-economic deficiencies. A telling example is the *Janecek* case.[44] Mr Janecek lived on a central ring road in Munich, rather close to an air-quality measuring station. Measurements taken at that station had shown that, in 2005 and 2006, the limit value fixed for some emissions been exceeded much more than 35 times, even though that is the maximum number of instances permitted under the Federal Law on combating pollution. Therefore Mr Janecek brought an action before the Administrative Court of Munich for an order requiring the Freistaat Bayern (the land of Bavaria) to draw up an air-quality action plan for the precise district in which he lived, so as to determine the measures to be taken in the short term to avoid exceeding the emission limit. His action was dismissed. He appealed to the Higher Administrative Court and eventually to the

[41] VG Frankfurt a.M., Urt v [24.06.2021], Az 7 K 2237/20.F. *Verbraucher und Recht* 2021, 430 with annotation P Rott.

[42] Art 9(4)(c) Regulation 2017/2394: 'Competent authorities shall have at least the following enforcement powers … the power to receive from the trader, on the trader's initiative, additional remedial commitments for the benefit of consumers that have been affected by the alleged infringement covered by this Regulation, or, where appropriate, to seek to obtain commitments from the trader to offer adequate remedies to the consumers that have been affected by that infringement.'

[43] P Cortés, 'Conclusion. Ensuring the Provision of Consumer Dispute Resolution' in P Cortés (ed), *The New Regulatory Framework for Consumer Dispute Resolution* (Oxford University Press, 2016) 465.

[44] Case C-237/07, *Dieter Janecek v Freistaat Bayern* ECLI:EU:C:2008:447, [2008] ECR I-6221; for a full reconstruction of the case, see Kas (n 27).

Federal Administrative Court. The latter referred questions to the ECJ for a preliminary ruling asking, inter alia, whether

> a third party whose health is impaired is entitled to the preparation of an action plan even if, irrespective of any action plan, he is in a position to enforce his right to avoid any detriment to his health as a result of the emission limit value being exceeded, by bringing an action for intervention by the public authority.[45]

Eventually, Mr Janecek was granted the right to require the competent national authorities to take measures to combat atmospheric pollution. Citizens were granted a right to minimise the social costs of air pollution by forcing public authorities to draw up action plans to reduce air pollution. Thereby the judgment is apt to protect collective interests such as life, health and the property of the citizens of Munich against infringements, even in cases where causes of actions were not initially recognised.

Likewise, the Capital Markets Model Case Act (*Kapitalanleger-Musterverfahrensgesetz* (*KapMuG*)) enhanced the expectation of thousands of investors to have their losses compensated. In *Heiniger*,[46] the ECJ extended the right of cancellation to cases where consumers had not received the information specified in Article 4 of Directive 87/102 when the contract was negotiated away from business premises. Mr and Mrs Heininger wanted to withdraw from a loan agreement, as they had been induced – by an uninvited call at their home – to purchase a flat and to enter into the loan agreement. The couple maintained that they had not been informed about their right of cancellation. In its judgment, the ECJ stated that the period for withdrawal would not start until the information had been provided. This judgment essentially established a possibly eternal right of withdrawal, to the benefit of thousands of German consumers who were in a similar situation. Thus the judgment is likely to protect individual consumers, and prevents social loss from happening by extending the right of withdrawal.

Both cases differ in their impact on individual compensation and the future prevention of social loss. The thousands of investors, as well as the thousands of 'Heinigers', might not have received what they expected in the end, but the two judgments have unfolded a deterrent effect that leads to a reduction of social losses and the future protection of interests such as life, health and property. The difficulty of calculating retrospective collective remedies triggered vindicatory damages in both public and private settings. Vindicatory damages are defined as remedies that are not meant to provide compensation but determine that a legally protected right has been infringed and how the loss can be addressed. In both cases, it could be shown that novel rights were created, thereby instituting novel rights as a regulatory instrument for the avoidance of social loss.

An analysis of collective redress and an analysis of which types of remedies are best suited to address collective harm and damage are crucial for the effectiveness of judicial protection. Rarely has the attempt been made to analyse the nature of remedies and the implications of different remedies with regard to collective redress.[47] The most common of all remedies, and maybe the one on which all victims set their hopes, is

[45] *Janacek* (n 44) 21.

[46] Facts essentially taken from Case C-481/99 *Georg Heininger and Helga Heininger v Bayerische Hypo- und Vereinsbank AG* ECLI:EU:C:2001:684, [2001] ECR I-9945.

[47] T Kaye, 'A Sound Taxonomy of Remedies' (2017–2018) 36 *Quinnipiac Law Review* 79, 82.

the remedy to recover debt. As we have seen in the context of competition law cases, however, economic loss compensation can rarely be an appropriate remedy for individual consumers. The following section attempts to classify remedies and to analyse their aptness as instruments of collective redress.

One taxonomy of remedies model was suggested by van Boom (see Figure 8.2). He distinguished between retrospective remedies to address past violation or infringement and prospective remedies to deter future violation or infringement. In addition, there are vindicatory damages that are designed to vindicate the claimants violated rights, in public law as a mechanism not to recover material loss but to provide for extra-compensatory redress, for instance cy-près, coupon settlement, apology, declaratory judgment. Again, collective redress is tilting the balance towards deterrence thereby relying on the prevention of future infringements and avoidance of prospective damages and possibly vindicatory damages.

Figure 8.2 Taxonomy of remedies

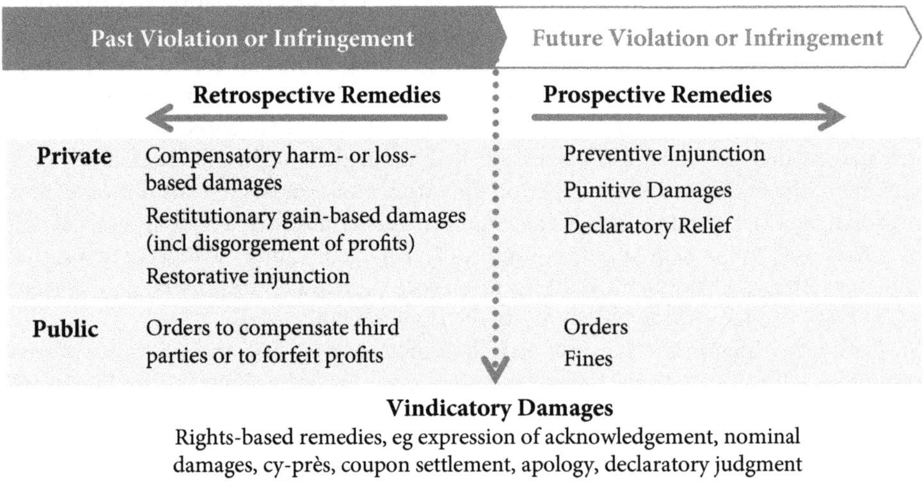

Source: cf Willem H. van Boom (2010).

In another taxonomy model of remedies, Kaye argued that the only sound basis for a taxonomy of remedies is a taxonomy of rights.[48] Remedies need to be distinguished as replicative, substitutionary and transformative. *Replicative* remedies, such as liquidated damages, ejectment or a statutory declaration, are said to vindicate primary rights. *Substitutionary* remedies are claimed to vindicate secondary rights: they do not substitute for a loss of value the plaintiff might have suffered; rather, substitutionary remedies sanction the defendant for its wrong. The *Feryn* case[49] demonstrates what is at stake. A Belgian equality body claimed that Feryn, a Belgian sales and installation company, had applied a discriminatory recruitment policy, following public statements made by

[48] ibid 86.

[49] Case C-54/07 *Cemrum voor gelijkheid van kansen en voor racismebestrijding v Firma Feryn NV* ECLI:EU:C:2008:397, [2008] ECR I-5187, reconstructed by Kas (n 27).

its director regarding the recruitment of immigrants. The Court held that the protection against discrimination under Directive 2000/43/EC does not require a concrete victim in order to deduce the discriminatory effects of a public (commercial) statement. Thus, by classifying a public statement made by an employer in a recruitment drive as direct discrimination, the Court granted substitutionary damages for a great number of potentially affected citizens. *Transformative* remedies, the third type, are claimed to create a special kind of tertiary right that puts the plaintiff in an entirely new position.[50] *Janecek*[51] provides for such a transformative remedy, as the Munich authorities are obliged by law to take action to reduce the emissions.

The two models reveal an increasing tendency in collective redress to combine prospective and transformative remedies. Thus, litigation and the design of remedies demonstrate regulatory characteristics. The collectivity of redress, in whatever 'collectivity' encompasses, transforms the doctrinal underpinnings of EU law from compensation to deterrence, thereby reconstructing the European civil justice system.

C. Standing: Procedural Prerequisites for Collective Redress

Last but not least, an analysis of collective redress requires a look at standing, and thus the procedural prerequisites for collective redress. Both an analysis of plaintiff and defendant constellations and an analysis of how collective interests are aggregated show how power balances have been shifted. Overall, there is a strong move towards granting private collective entities, but also public collective entities, standing in going to court in the collective interests of a particular sub-group of society, be they workers, consumers or those discriminated against. Such a move goes hand in hand with the introduction of new means of supervision and monitoring of the use of collective redress through private or public collective entities. A prominent example is the new Directive 1828/2020 on representative action. Time will tell in which direction things are developing, whether the newly introduced rules on standing will lead to a considerable increase in collective redress, or whether nation states will use the newly introduced powers to exercise control over private, but also public, collective redress.[52]

An important classification relates to the parties in litigation. Most of the current debates about collective redress primarily concern plaintiff group litigation, where the plaintiff constitutes a collective aggregation while the defendant is an individual entity. However, this is merely one of three group litigation constellations. As Figure 8.3 demonstrates, defendant group litigation is also conceptually conceivable, with the defendants being aggregated individuals, as is bilateral group litigation, with both plaintiff and defendant being collectives. The academic discourse focuses on collectivity on the part of the plaintiff, thereby defining the mechanisms on how collectivity can properly be sustained. Various mechanisms are in place and discussed prospectively to design plaintiff group actions.

[50] Kaye (n 46) 82.

[51] *Janecek* (n 44); for a full reconstruction of the case, see Kas (n 27).

[52] S Voet, 'Where the wild things are: reflections on the state and future of European collective redress' in A Keirse and M Loos (eds), *Waves in Contract and Liability in Three Decades of Ius Commune* (Intersentia, 2017) 150.

Figure 8.3 Classification of group litigation

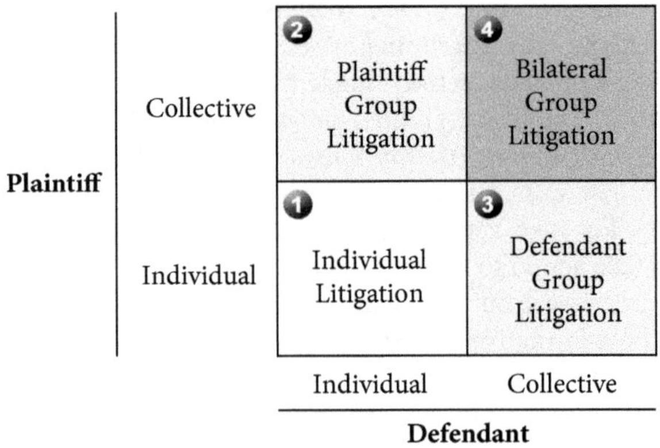

The five exemplary cases provide the background for a deeper insight. The first case involves a great number of plaintiffs while having only an individual defendant – a big telecommunications company. The second case scenario on the Door-Step Selling Directive equally involved collectivity on the part of the plaintiff, whereas on the opposite side there is only one defendant. The competition law case on the potato cartel, the third case, involves both several plaintiffs and several defendants, which is characteristic of cartel cases. In *Janecek*, the fourth example, we had one citizen representing every inhabitant living close to his home, and an individual defendant. And in *Feryn*, there are a great number of possible affected plaintiffs and one individual defendant. Essentially, these cases show that most collective redress case constellations – apart from competition law – involve several plaintiffs but merely one individual defendant.

Like the academic discourse, the law focuses primarily on collective plaintiff constellations. Thus, the collective redress Directive 1828/2020 requires all EU Member States to put in place at least one effective procedural mechanism to enforce collective interests. This is done by allowing so-called qualified entities to bring representative actions to court for the purpose of injunction and redress. Such qualified entities will primarily be consumer organisations and public bodies, national consumer agencies. The qualified entities will have to comply with the same criteria in cross-border actions, whilst merely domestic actions will be subject to criteria established under national law. It remains for the Member States to decide whether to harmonise the criteria for cross-border and domestic actions.

The EU focuses primarily on representative actions rather than mechanisms of class action or aggregated individual claims.[53] A representative action describes a situation where an organisation, an authority or an individual, which is not the real party to the litigation, brings an action on behalf of a group of individuals. Within the representative action mechanisms, the Member States will be given the discretion to choose to opt in or opt out. Many European countries rely on representative mechanisms such

[53] A Uzelac, 'Why no class actions in Europe? A view from the side of dysfunctional justice systems' in V Harsági and CH van Rhee (eds), *Multi-Party Redress Mechanisms in Europe: Squeaking Mice?* (Intersentia, 2014) 53.

as complaint boards or consumer councils in terms of ADR.[54] In the Nordic countries, the Consumer Ombudsman plays a crucial role as public enforcer of the collective, if not the public, interest. Private group actions are often linked with actions taken by the Consumer Ombudsman, so that there is a cost-effective and generally efficient approach to securing consumer rights.

Collectiveness on the part of plaintiffs in EU law defines redress mechanisms as core procedural law in specialised areas, such as consumer and competition law. It thereby redraws the boundaries between procedural and substantive law. The principle of procedural autonomy is subtly eroded, with the positive effect of a reduction in transaction costs, on the one hand, but also, on the other hand, with the negative effect of eliminating regulatory competition and, thus, eliminating learning effects for a bottom-up, more coherent procedural harmonisation.

A second crucial point in discussing collectivity is the question of aggregating collective interests through compensation, property interests or even essential public interests, such as clean air in the *Janecek* case. The terminology 'aggregated action' derives from the US context.[55] The common starting point for relief in both public and private enforcement actions is a valid cause of action, that is the plaintiff's right to sue a defendant for relief in the light of an alleged violation of a prohibition, or an alleged infringement of a right or a civil wrong, that causes physical or economic harm or loss to a plaintiff or his property. One of the overarching questions is the question of what role collectivity plays and should play in triggering liability in various causes of action – whether in economic law or other areas of law. The law in the US differs, in that the term 'aggregated claims' is meant to cover all types of collective actions, as long as there is 'aggregation and collectivity'. One difficulty remains: the EU darling of qualified entities looks rather alien in the US legal system, where collective action turns around class action, the delineation of the class and the legitimacy of the lead plaintiff to speak on behalf of the class. However, litigation brought forward by qualified entities typically contains an element of collectivity; equally typically, this element remains rather diffuse – the collective interests of consumers, of workers or of those discriminated against. Thus far it would make sense to use the notion of aggregated claims in the EU context too.

The current European legal environment, however, is ridden by jurisdiction issues in cross-border collective redress. In consumer contract claims, Section 4 of Chapter II of the Brussels I Regulation provides that if a contract falls within the protective scope, a consumer is always entitled to sue a business defendant in the consumer's domicile. Such a focus is incompatible with the nature of cross-border collective redress, where consumers may come from different Member States. Whether such deep reflection was behind the ECJ's decision[56] when it rejected the applicability of Section 4 of Chapter II to consumer organisations as plaintiffs is far from clear. The result, though, is more leeway for the building of 'groups of injured consumers' in a cross-border context for

[54] H Oe, 'Consumer Ombudsman Denkar, Collective Redress and the Role of Ombudsman', Jean Monnet Conference at the European University Institute, Florence (2013), paper on file with the authors.

[55] B Smith, 'Class Action and Aggregate Litigation: A comparative international analysis' (2020) 124:2 *Penn State Law Review* 303, 345.

[56] Case C-167/00 *Verein für Konsumenteninformation v Karl Heinz Henkel* ECLI:EU:C:2002:555, [2002] ECR I-8111 and Case C-191/15 *Verein für Konsumenteninformation v Amazon EU Sàrl* ECLI:EU:C:2016:612; see P Rott, 'Das IPR der Verbraucherverbandsklage' (2016) *Europäische Zeitschrift für Wirtschaftsrecht* 733.

the aggregation of claims. The problem remains that the Brussels Regulation does not provide rules for aggregated claims in whatever form. The clear focus on protecting the individual consumer sets incentives for using test cases, with one individual standing as a disguised form of aggregated claim, disguised because the collectivity standing behind the individual plaintiff will have to be identified in each and every case. However, in *Facebook*[57] the ECJ set narrow limits to using the consumer's domicile as a tool for aggregated claims. Schrems, a legal activist, had collected 25,000 complaints against Facebook. Seven of them, coming from Austria, Germany and India, had transferred their rights to Schrems. The ECJ rejected the applicability of the consumer's domicile for such aggregated claims, but confirmed the individual standing of Schrems. This leads to the rather strange consequence that only one individual can have his or her voice heard before the ECJ on behalf of the European or even world-wide community of Facebook users, but that Luxembourg cannot be used as a platform for aggregated complaints. The ideology of an individual-based determination of the place of jurisdiction to the benefit of one single person is maintained but at the same time distorted, as the 'individual' is representing not only the European community but also the global community. It lies within the logic of such argumentation that Mathias Schrems will probably manage to bring further disguised aggregated claims before the ECJ, as long as the Austrian courts are willing to refer cases to the ECJ.

In the light of the foregoing, one can only assume the types of legal problem that may result from the opportunity introduced in Directive 1828/2020 for qualified entities to take action on behalf of consumer groups in more than one country. The Directive does not contain rules on jurisdiction, nor rules on the applicable law. What has been presented so far – the types of conflict around the issue of jurisdiction – is only a small foretaste of the problems that arise when it comes to the question of applicable law. Neither Brussels nor the Rome Regulations are prepared for collective legal disputes. Not surprisingly, disputes regarding dogma are flourishing. The reality, the current practice of the qualified entities – the consumer organisations and the consumer agencies – looks very different, though. They shy away from legally complicated cross-border actions and prefer to coordinate collective actions under the auspices of BEUC, the European umbrella organisation for consumer protection.[58] From such a perspective, a common European problem – such as, for instance, *Dieselgate* – once identified, leads to collective litigation in the respective Member States, each consumer organisation relying on its own legal means and its own substantive and procedural laws.[59]

[57] Case C-498/16 *Maximilian Schrems v Facebook Ireland Limited* ECLI:EU:C:2018:37.

[58] G Howells and H-W Micklitz, *Consumer Law Enforcement Forum Project, Guidelines for Consumer Organisations on Enforcement and Collective Redress* (September 2009) available at www.mpo.cz/assets/dokumenty/40585/45442/550298/priloha001.pdf; Consumer Justice Enforcement Forum, Guidelines for enforcement on consumer rights (prepared with the support of Geraint Howells and Hans-Wolfgang Micklitz) (2013); Consumer Justice Enforcement Forum II, Enforcement of Consumer Rights: Strategies and Recommendations (prepared with the support of Evelyn Terryn, Geraint Howells, Hans-Wolfgang Micklitz) (May 2016) available at www.beuc.eu/publications/beuc-x-2016-051_cojef_ii-enforcement_of_consumer_rights.pdf.

[59] 'Volkswagen Dieselgate four years down the road: An overview of enforcement actions and policy work by BEUC and its members since the Dieselgate scandal' (2019) available at www.beuc.eu/publications/beuc-x-2019-050_report_-_four_years_after_the_dieselgate_scandal.pdf; 'The Long and Winding Road, Two Years of GDPR: A cross-border data protection enforcement case from a consumer perspective' (2020) available at www.beuc.eu/publications/beuc-x-2020-074_two_years_of_the_gdpr_a_cross-border_data_protection_enforcement_case_from_a_consumer_perspective.pdf.

IV. Revisiting Collective Redress

Addressing the ambiguities, collective redress in Europe is still at an experimental stage. One of the core questions of mass litigation remains whether the party bringing a collective action has the standing and ability to represent the interests of the class of claimants and what alternative mechanisms to aggregate claims are available. A number of mechanisms can be cited: test-case procedures (such as the Telecom case), group actions, opt-in collective actions and opt-out collective actions. The last of these are rarely available in the EU but prevalent in the US. They grant the advantage of wider representation of the victims and are thus more efficient and of greater deterrent effect, but they are also more prone to generating excesses in compensation. Essentially, the aggregation of collective interests will remain one of the major tasks of procedural approximation in the EU. Figure 8.4 suggests that there is a move from negative to positive integration, via the enhancement of fundamental rights to judicial protection, towards procedural approximation.

Figure 8.4 Procedural approximation as the fourth wave of European integration

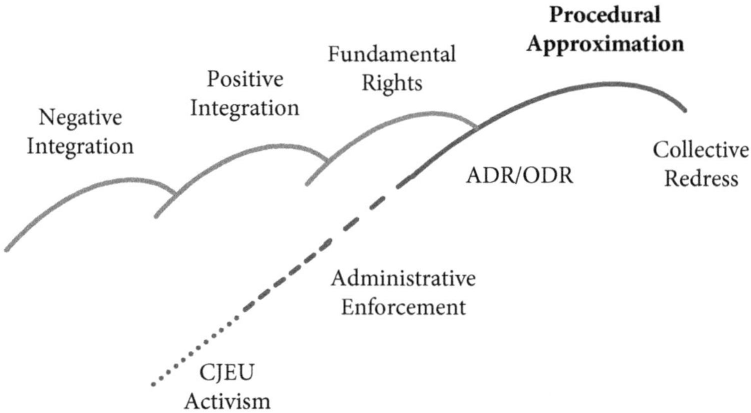

The visualisation is not meant to suggest that the development is sequential. The different steps – negative/positive integration, fundamental rights, procedural approximation – exist side by side, although negative integration through judicial activism is no longer of major importance.[60] The decisive step still consists in the adoption of the Single European Act and the move to positive integration through the Europeanisation of all sorts of social policies, environmental protection, health and safety, non-discrimination and consumer protection. The EU legislature, not least with the strong support of the ECJ, did not confine itself to laying down social standards for the EU as a whole. Gradually but steadily, the EU interfered in the procedural dimension, embedding individual and collective rights in the Charter of Fundamental Rights and enabling citizens to implement social policies in their daily lives through individual and collective

[60] J Zglinski, *Europe's Passive Virtues, Deference to National Authorities in EU Free Movement Law* (Oxford University Press, 2020).

enforcement. Inherent in these social policies is an element of collectivity, as the EU intends to strengthen the environment, to improve health and safety, to put an end to discrimination, and to guarantee a high level of protection in the name of and to the benefit of all those who are concerned by the respective policies. These may be the citizens of the EU as a whole, or particular sub-groups within the society to which the EU grants status-related rights. So far, the EU rules on collective redress are fragmented, inconsistent and more often than not related to particular policy fields. Sometimes it is even hard to identify a clear line of reasoning in the development of EU law. The broader window seems helpful to place the later developments into a wider conceptual and theoretical context.

Over the past 50 years, analytic philosophers have been exploring the nature of collective action in the sense of acting together, from very different angles from economic theory but also from political science.[61] Legal scholarship in the US seems to be ahead of that in the EU, not least due to the introduction of the US class action in 1966 and long-standing experience. The term 'collective action problem' describes the situation in which multiple individuals would all benefit from a certain action, but the associated costs make it implausible that any one individual can or will undertake and solve it alone. The rational choice is then to undertake collective action, the cost of which is shared. The economic theory of collective action is concerned with the provision of public goods (and other collective consumption) through the collaboration of two or more individuals, and the impact of externalities on group behaviour. It is more commonly referred to as Public Choice.[62] The collective action problem is still a dominant feature in US legal scholarship, and so is the potential abuse of the class action.

The EU discourse, however, is less prone to economic theory and more connected to looking at the organisation of collective interests through the lens of social change, shifting the language from 'collective action problem' to 'public interest litigation'.[63] Kelemen, by pulling together the different strands of collective action in the wider EU context, argues that the EU, just like the US, is moving towards what he terms 'adversarial legalism'. The term goes back to Kagan,[64] who defines 'adversarial legalism' as 'policymaking, policy implementation, and dispute resolution by means of party-and-lawyer-dominated legal contestation'. The five selected cases – where each stands for a particular policy field – demonstrate indeed that there is a strong move in EU law to fight out different policy positions before the ECJ and before domestic courts. Contrary to the US, in the EU, collective redress remains first and foremost in the hands of national courts. It would certainly be of scholarly interest to compare the federal structure of collective redress in the US and the EU. The ever stronger

[61] N Bardsley, 'On collective intentions: collective action in economics and philosophy' (2007) 157 *Synthese* 141, 142.

[62] See M Olson, *The Logic of Collective Action: Public Goods and the Theory of Groups* (Harvard University Press, 1965).

[63] J Handler, *Social Movements and the Legal System, A Theory of Law Reform and Social Change* (Academic Press, 1978).

[64] RA Kagan, *The American Way of Law* (Harvard University Press, 2003; 2nd edn, 2020); looking more into similarities between developed countries, LM Friedman, 'The Same Only Different: Reflections on Robert Kagan's Adversarial Legalism' (2020) 45 *Law and Social Inquiry* 1170.

restrictions on class actions through federal laws and the growing tensions between the federal and the State level in the US have certainly strengthened the importance of class actions at the State level. In this respect, the US might be coming closer to Europe, where a strong procedural design of collective redress at the EU level is missing and where the enforceability of the collective redress depends to a large extent on the law of the Member States. Whether such an interaction can still be called adversarial should be left to a different occasion.

9

'*Je t'aime moi non plus*': Why Europe Needs Strong Collective Redress

ALEXANDRE BIARD*

In the 21st century, the civil justice system may change dramatically.
(C Hodges, 'Current discussions on consumer redress: collective redress and ADR' (2012))

I. Introduction

The name of Professor Hodges is for many closely associated with the world of collective redress. It is in particular for me. As I have the privilege to contribute to the *Liber Amicorum* in honour of Christopher, I would like to start with some personal memories. As a PhD researcher working in the area of collective redress, I became quickly acquainted with Professor Hodges's research, which is a must-read for anyone interested in such a complex topic. I met Christopher for the first time in December 2011 during a lecture he gave at Erasmus University Rotterdam. At that time, Christopher was a Professor of the Fundamentals of Private Law there. This first meeting marked the start of a long journey, and our paths crossed again several times afterwards, whether in Leuven, Brussels, Oxford, Paris or again in Rotterdam.[1]

Exchanging ideas and thoughts with Professor Hodges has importantly contributed to shaping the way I am conducting research. I am particularly grateful to Christopher for two important pieces of advice he gave me in my early academic career. His first recommendation was 'go and talk to people'. Professor Hodges is the opposite of the academic shut away in his ivory tower, disconnected from the real world and playing with ideas without considering their applications and implications on the ground. In fact, I do not know many scholars like Professor Hodges (except maybe Stefaan Voet,

* The point of view and ideas expressed in this contribution are exclusively those of the author. They do not represent the opinion of BEUC, nor those of its member organisations.

[1] Professor Hodges was a member of the advisory committee for a research project on access to justice set up by Xandra Kramer at Erasmus University Rotterdam, which I joined as a post-doctoral researcher in 2017–19.

one of the co-editors of this book), who has travelled the world to exchange ideas with policymakers and stakeholders, with the intention of better understanding what works in other countries. I had the chance to accompany Christopher to Paris in 2019, where we held several meetings with representatives of the French consumer authority (DGCCRF) and several ombudsmen. The objective was to collect first-hand evidence on the way they were doing their work.[2] Since then, I have tried to follow Christopher's advice and have engaged with public and private stakeholders, with the intention of connecting evidence-based research and policy discussions.

Christopher's second recommendation was 'contemplate the toolbox as a whole and weigh all the available alternatives'. If collective redress has been one of Professor Hodges' areas of expertise, it is far from being the only one (as the various contributions in this book clearly demonstrate). In the area of consumer protection in particular, Christopher has considered the enforcement toolbox as whole, and has contemplated the different enforcement techniques, especially alternative dispute resolution (ADR) and other regulatory measures.

More than a decade ago, Christopher drew the attention of (European) academics and policymakers to several pivotal issues that one should consider carefully in the area of collective redress.[3] For example, in 2009 he pointed out that the financing of mass claims would be among the most important questions upon which the success or the failure of collective redress mechanisms would ultimately depend.[4] On the one hand, without proper funding, collective redress actions, which are usually very costly for claimant organisations, would be doomed to fail. On the other hand, too much funding might provide parties with the wrong incentives. In 2022, the discussions on the financing of collective redress continue to score high on the policy agenda, at both the European and national levels.[5] In parallel, Christopher also made several early predictions, which turned out to be verified on the ground. For example, while commenting on the 2013 European Commission's Recommendation on collective redress,[6] which was intended to be a roadmap for Member States when implementing collective redress mechanisms into their national systems, Professor Hodges took the view that the Recommendation looked more like a 'damp sqibb' rather than a real breakthrough, in particular because the text tended to give too much leeway to Member States and hence did not allow

[2] Our field visit to Paris resulted in the following article, describing the state-of-play of consumer ADR in France: A Biard and C Hodges, 'Médiation de la consommation: un bilan, des défis, des pistes de réflexion pour l'avenir' in *Contrats Concurrence Consommation* (February 2019).

[3] C Hodges, 'From Class Actions to Collective Redress' (2009) 28 *Consumer Justice Quarterly* 41.

[4] D Hensler and C Hodges, 'What are people trying to do in resolving mass issues, how is it going, and where are we headed?' (2009) 66 *Annals of the American Academy of Political and Social Science* 330; C Hodges, *The Reform of Class and Representative Actions in European Legal Systems – A New Framework for Collective Redress in Europe* (Hart Publishing, 2008) 319.

[5] In November 2021, the European Commission organised a workshop on the EU Representation Action Directive, with one session dedicated to the topic of funding and financing (see at https://rad-workshop-2021.eu).

[6] Commission, 'Recommendation of 11 June 2013 on common principles for injunctive and compensatory collective redress mechanisms in the Member States concerning violations of rights granted under Union Law' [2013] OJ L201/60.

for a consistent approach across Europe.[7] Five years later, the report of the European Commission on the impact of the 2013 Recommendation ultimately concluded that there had been indeed 'a rather limited follow-up to the Recommendation'.[8]

While Professor Hodges' relationship with collective redress has been passionate (Christopher is the author and co-author of dozens of papers published in highly regarded academic journals, as well as the writer and co-writer of several books on the topic), it has also been complicated, hence the title of this contribution, which is a reference to the famous song, *Je t'aime moi non plus*, written by the French songwriter Serge Gainsbourg in the late 1960s. Professor Hodges has taken the view that collective redress mechanisms may not be a suitable solution for ensuring compensation for consumers in mass-harm situations. He has described collective redress as belonging to the 'old technologies' for delivering redress.[9] According to Christopher, other routes – in particular consumer ADR (especially in the form of ombudsmen) and redress through regulatory bodies – may be more appropriate and more effective.[10] Professor Hodges has thus described these two techniques as belonging to what he has called the 'new technologies' for delivering redress. As a consequence, according to Christopher, the European Union (EU) would be pursuing the wrong route when pushing for generalisation of collective redress in all Member States.

While keeping one foot in academia, I joined the consumer movement several years ago, working in particular in the area of consumer law enforcement. Although the EU probably has one of the highest levels of consumer protection in the world, the enforcement of the rules on the ground continues to be one of its main Achilles' heels. Several initiatives are currently ongoing to strengthen the enforcement of consumer rights in the EU.[11] In this capacity, I came to the belief that collective redress mechanisms may not belong to the so-called 'old technologies'. At least, collective redress does not belong to old technologies *yet*. Along with ADR and other public enforcement techniques, collective redress continues to be a necessary complementary tool for strengthening the enforcement of consumer rules in Europe and for ensuring compensation to consumers when they are involved in mass-harm situations. In this contribution, I try to explain why Europe crucially needs strong collective redress mechanisms (section II). In fact, the real issue is not whether we need collective redress, but rather what these

[7] C Hodges, 'Collective Redress: A Breakthrough or a Damp Sqibb' (2014) 37 *Journal of Consumer Policy* 67.

[8] Commission, 'Report on the implementation of the Commission Recommendation of 11 June 2013' COM (2018) 40 final 21.

[9] C Hodges and S Voet, *Delivering Collective Redress: New Technologies* (Hart Publishing, 2018); C Hodges, 'Collective Redress: The Need for New Technologies' (2018) 42 *Journal of Consumer Policy* 59.

[10] C Hodges, 'Delivering Redress through Alternative Dispute Resolution and regulation' in W van Boom and G Wagner (eds), *Mass Torts in Europe: Cases and Reflections* (De Gruyter, 2014) 231; C Hodges, I Benöhr and N Creutzfeldt, 'Consumer-to-Business Dispute Resolution: The Power of CADR' (2012) 13 ERA Forum 199; and C Hodges, 'Current discussions on consumer redress: collective redress and ADR' (2012) 13 *ERA Forum* 11.

[11] (Among many examples) Commission, 'New Consumer Agenda Strengthening consumer resilience for sustainable recovery' COM/2020/696 (final); BEUC, 'Stepping up the enforcement of consumer protection rules' (*BEUC* September 2020) available at www.beuc.eu/publications/stepping-enforcement-consumer-protection-rules/html.

mechanisms should look like if one wants to ensure that they fully deliver for consumers. Directive 2020/1828 on representative actions for the protection of the collective interests of consumers (hereinafter the 'Representative Action Directive'), which was adopted in November 2020 and will enter into effect in June 2023, may not offer answers to all the challenges brought by collective redress; this was never the intention of the EU policymakers. Rather, this legislation constitutes an important starting point upon which we should now build (section III).

To conclude this introduction, let me draw a parallel with the world of opera, another of Christopher's passions. In 1853, the first performance of Giuseppe Verdi's *La Traviata* took place in Venice, at La Fenice. The event turned out to be … a disaster. As Verdi wrote to one of his friends, '*La traviata ieri sera, fiasco. La colpa è mia o dei cantanti? Il tempo giudicherà*' ('La Traviata last night, a failure. Was the fault mine or the singers'? Time will tell').[12] Another observer also noted of this disastrous start, '*l'un des fours les plus noirs de l'histoire de l'opéra*' ('one of the biggest failures in opera's history').[13] Notwithstanding its early difficulties, there is no doubt that Verdi's *La Traviata* is today one of the most acclaimed and famous operas worldwide. Of course, the comparison between Violetta and Alfredo's tragic romance and collective redress stops here. This shows, however, that things one may initially view as total flops can actually, with time, also become success stories …

II. Why Collective Redress is a Must-Have for Europe

Several reasons justify the recent efforts of the EU to make collective redress mechanisms available in all Member States. First, the EU enforcement toolbox in the area of consumer protection builds on an equilibrium between public and private enforcement, where actions launched by public authorities, ADR/ODR and court actions coexist. Today, the other mechanisms (ADR and regulatory techniques) cannot in many cases by themselves secure compensation in mass-harm situations, whereas large-scale damage claims have been multiplying. Second, in the context of budgetary constraints, collective redress can be an important procedural tool for all stakeholders, including claimants and judiciaries, but also defendants. Third, the purported excesses of collective redress often used by business representatives have not materialised in practice, and nothing today demonstrates that collective redress leads to abuses or is detrimental to economies. Fourth, the limited effects of collective redress in some countries should not lead to our pre-judging its effect in the future. It will take time before collective redress can 'get into a groove'. Fifth and finally, with or without collective redress, collective litigation is already happening, and is here to stay. It is surely better if it takes place in the structured context of collective redress rather than in the unstructured 'wild west'.

[12] H Krehbiel, *A Book of Operas: Their Histories, Their Plots and Their Music* (Macmillan, 1983).
[13] P Saint-André, *La Traviata – Guide des opéras de Verdi* (Fayard, 1990) 570.

A. Because the Other Options for Delivering Redress Are Not Ripe (Yet)

Professor Hodges has convincingly showed that ADR, when adequately set up (in particular in the form of ombudsmen) and sufficiently resourced, may deal with mass litigation in an effective manner.[14] However, this situation is limited to a few countries and/or sectors today (essentially some sectors in the United Kingdom (UK) and in a few Nordic countries). In the other European countries, most ADR entities continue to be ill-equipped and may not have sufficient available resources to deal with individual claims, and hence would not be able to cope with mass claims. In addition, the existing national architecture for consumer ADR in many European countries continues to be problematic and may have precluded its development. Among other reasons, this may be because Member States have not structured their national ADR landscapes around a few key sectorial ombudsmen, or because, where they exist, these ombudsmen continue to compete with other private schemes.[15] In addition, the confidentiality of ADR procedures, which is often perceived as a golden principle upon which the success of ADR would depend, is controversial when applied in the area of mass claims. One may indeed wonder whether the resolution of mass claims, which generally have important societal consequences and high media impact,[16] should be placed under public scrutiny rather than be dealt with behind closed doors. In 2022, the European Commission announced its intention to evaluate the existing regulatory framework for consumer ADR.[17] This evaluation process might lead to changes in the existing regulatory framework. In parallel, by June 2028, the European Commission is also expected to evaluate the relevance of establishing a 'European ombudsman' for cross-border representative actions.[18] Things may thus get moving in the future, albeit slowly. In a few years, consumer ADR could become an effective tool for dealing with mass claims in Europe. However, to date, in many cases, we are still far from reaching this result.

Regulatory redress may be another tool to secure compensation in the context of mass-harm situations. This refers to situations where public enforcement authorities directly secure compensation for the consumers harmed. The idea is appealing, and some countries have indeed started to discuss this possibility. Discussions are ongoing

[14] C Hodges, 'Policy Brief: Developments and Issues in Consumer ADR and Consumer Ombudsmen in Europe', The Foundation for Law Justice and Society, Oxford (2019) available at www.fljs.org/developments-and-issues-consumer-adr-and-consumer-ombudsmen-europe; and C Hodges, 'Consumer ombudsmen: better regulation and dispute resolution' (2015) 15 *ERA Forum* 593.

[15] European Commission's Report of 25 September 2019 on the Application of Directive 2013/11/EU on consumer ADR, COM (2019) 425 final. See also, eg, in France, A Biard, 'Impact of Directive 2013/11/EU on Consumer ADR: Evidence from France and the UK' (2018) *Journal of Consumer Policy* 1; and A Biard, 'Towards High-Quality Consumer ADR: The Belgian Experience' in L Cadiet, B Hess and M Requejo Isidro (eds), *Privatising Dispute Resolution – Trends and Limits* (Nomos, 2019) 79.

[16] B Stier and I Tzankova, 'The Culture of Collective Litigation: A Comparative Analysis' in D Hensler, C Hodges and I Tzankova (eds), *Class Action in Context – How Culture, Economics and Politics Shape Collective Litigation* (Edward Elgar, 2016) 27.

[17] As announced by the European Commission during the 2nd 'ADR Assembly', which took place in October 2021.

[18] Art 23(3) of the Representative Action Directive.

in the UK, for example, as to whether the Competition and Markets Authority (CMA) should have the power to secure redress for consumers. To date, however, only a handful of national authorities have the ability to secure redress for consumers. In its 2016 initial legislative proposal for a revision of the Consumer Protection Coordination Regulation (CPC Regulation), the European Commission proposed to confer on national enforcement authorities the power to 'order the trader responsible … to compensate consumers that have suffered harm as a consequence of the infringement'.[19] But this proposal did not make it into the final text of the CPC Regulation. Many authorities today do not have the power to secure compensation. In parallel, those authorities that do have this power may not be willing to use it actively. This was evidenced, for example, when the CPC-Network and the European Commission issued a statement in the context of the Dieselgate scandal, which urged Volkswagen to compensate all European consumers affected.[20] Ultimately, only a few national authorities imposed fines on Volkswagen, and none of them ordered Volkswagen to compensate consumers (although at the same time, several national court decisions had already established the liability of the car manufacturer and had ordered Volkswagen to compensate consumers). Some authorities take the view that securing compensation for consumers is not part of their job, and that it is up to consumers (or their representatives) to follow up on their decisions to seek compensation when this is needed. For example, the practice of the Polish consumer Authority (UoKiK) illustrates this two-stage approach. In January 2020, the UoKiK imposed a record fine on Volkswagen. When issuing its decision, the authority also highlighted that 'once UOKiK's decisions become legally binding, they become a precedent, which makes it easier for consumers to pursue possible claims in court … Consumers may also refer to UOKiK's decisions when making a complaint'.[21]

Arguably, another method for national authorities to secure compensation for consumers may be through voluntary commitments, where traders proactively commit to compensating consumers. According to the CPC Regulation, all consumer enforcement authorities today have the power to receive commitments from traders. That being said, traders may have an incentive to actively propose compensation to consumers only when they fear being targeted by a collective redress action. Put simply, traders' willingness to compensate consumers occurs in the shadow of collective redress.

Finally, another important limitation to the role of public authorities in this area is related to their status and the fact that several of them are not fully independent from ministries and from the political sphere. For example, the French consumer authority (DGCCRF) is embedded in the Ministry of Economic Affairs. Conversely, in Italy, the Autorità Garante della Concorrenza e del Mercato (AGCM) is an independent public entity. Because of their lack of independence, some authorities may be influenced by political considerations, and this may stop some of them from ordering infringing traders to facilitate compensation for consumers in situations of mass harm.

[19] COM (2016) 0283, 25 May 2016, Art 8.

[20] A Biard, 'Retour sur 6 ans de Dieselgate en Europe du point de vue des consommateurs' (2021/2) *DCCR – Consumentenrecht* 131.

[21] See at https://icpen.org/news/1025.

In 2022, the European Commission announced its intention to evaluate the CPC Regulation, with a report expected in the first quarter of 2023. This evaluation might lead to a possible revision of the existing framework. This may be a good opportunity to once again put this topic on the discussion table. However, given the existing differences between the national enforcement approaches and philosophies, and the fact that, because of their status, several enforcement authorities are still insufficiently independent, it will take several years before we finally reach a point where authorities can indeed actively secure compensation for consumers in mass-harm situations.

The current situation may thus be summarised as follows. On the one hand, ADR has still not fully taken off in many Member States and is often still not adapted to deal with mass claims.[22] On the other hand, in many Member States, regulatory bodies do not have the powers to order compensation. When they have this power, authorities may not be willing to use it proactively. Meanwhile, mass-harm situations caused by defective products or large-scale unlawful practices continue to multiply. In this context, collective redress has an important role to play in the enforcement toolbox and can contribute to strengthening the other enforcement techniques.

B. Because Collective Redress Can Be an Important Tool for All Stakeholders

Studies[23] have long shown that consumers usually decide not to take any legal action when they believe this will take too long (42 per cent), that the sums involved are too small (39.7 per cent), that a complaint will not lead to a satisfactory solution (36.6 per cent), when they are unsure about their rights (21 per cent) or when they do not know to whom and how to address their complaint (20.1 per cent). Many consumers are also deterred from bringing claims against multinational companies that many see as lost battles. Collective redress is a tool to mitigate the rational apathy problem precluding many valid claims from being brought in the first place. Collective redress tools serve as mechanism to re-balance the relationship between traders and consumers, and empowers consumers and their representatives against unfair and illegal practices. Relying on traders' collaborative approach to correct harmful situations is not sufficient. Collective redress is needed to trigger changes in traders' behaviour.

In parallel, collective redress can also be useful and relevant for courts, as it can contribute to the better administration of justice in a period of constrained budgets. Collective redress allows judges to find a solution to a problem once and for all, which otherwise would have triggered a rash of individual complaints. This was illustrated recently in Germany, where the judiciary had to deal with thousands of individual Dieselgate-related claims. The added value of mass litigation was also well illustrated by Judge Rubin while deciding on the Bendectin class action in the United States. He

[22] BEUC, 'Stepping the enforcement of consumer rights in Europe' *BEUC* (September 2020) available at www.beuc.eu/publications/stepping-enforcement-consumer-protection-rules/html.

[23] See, eg, Commission, 'Consumers' attitudes towards cross-border trade and consumer protection' (2018) doi:10.2818/209599.

calculated that adjudicating all pending cases separately and individually would require approximately 182 years of his time. He further added 'it takes little mathematical calculation to determine that if each of over 1100 cases were tried separately for 38 trial days a substantial number of the District Judges in this country could do nothing for a year but try Bendectin cases'.[24]

Finally, collective redress can also be beneficial to defendants. Traders may be willing to clarify and end a litigious situation in order to find a 'global bill of peace'.[25] In some countries, like for example in the Netherlands, traders have played key roles in the adoption of tools to resolve mass claims.

C. Because the Purported Excesses of Collective Redress Have Not Materialised

For years, businesses lobbies have been 'crying wolf' and arguing that collective redress will endanger economies and lead to a wide variety of abuses. They have often used the example of the US class actions sometimes described as a 'Frankenstein monster'.[26] Yet the excesses of the US class action have in reality been rather limited. In 2017, the so-called Institute for Legal Reform (actually set up by the US Chamber of Commerce) published a report that argued that 'there are a number of very powerful indicators that all of the same incentives and forces that have led to mass abuse in other jurisdictions are also gathering force in the EU'.[27] Several of the conclusions made in this report had to be approached with scepticism, however.[28] Thus far, collective redress mechanisms – in countries where they are available – have not led to any abuses, nor contributed to jeopardising economies.[29] In many ways, the current heated discussions on collective redress resemble the one that took place in Europe 40 years ago about the Product Liability Directive (another of Christopher's areas of expertise), which was finally adopted in 1985 (and which the European Commission may consider revising in the near future).[30] At that time, industry already strongly opposed this legislation and

[24] Judge Rubin in *In Re Richardson-Merrell, Inc*, 624 F, Supp 1212 (1985).

[25] R Nagareda, 'Mass Resolution of Mass Torts: Emerging issues in the United States and the Global Future' in J Steel and W Boom (eds), *Mass Justice: Challenges of Representation and Distribution* (Edward Elgar, 2011) 27; and R Nagareda, 'Autonomy, Peace, and Put Options in Mass Tort Class Actions' (2002) 115 *Harvard Law Review* 747.

[26] A Miller, 'Of Frankenstein Monsters and Shining Knights: Myths, Reality and the Class Action Problem' (1979) 92 *Harvard Law Review* 664; I Veillard and B Volders., 'La consécration des actions de groupe en Europe – La traversée de l'Atlantique aurait-elle adouci le Monstre à la Frankenstein?' (2008) 2 *Revue de jurisprudence commerciale* 67; and D Hensler, 'Revisiting the Monster: New Myths and Realities of Class Action and Other Large Scale Litigation' (2001) 11 *Duke Journal of Comparative and International Law* 179.

[27] Institute for Legal Reform, 'The Growth of Collective Redress in the EU: A Survey of Developments in 10 Member States' (Institute for Legal Reform, March 2017) available at https://instituteforlegalreform.com/research/the-growth-of-collective-redress-in-the-eu-a-survey-of-developments-in-10-member-states/

[28] See, inter alia, at https://conflictoflaws.net/2017/dutch-collective-redress-dangerous-a-call-for-a-more-nuanced-approach/.

[29] This was also one of the conclusions of the Institute for Legal Reform's report when highlighting that 'the EU is not currently gripped by waves of abusive litigation'.

[30] See at www.altroconsumo.it/auto-e-moto/automobili/news/altroconsumo-contro-volkswagen.

argued that it would adversely affect the European economy and led to frivolous litigation. More than 36 years after the adoption of the Product Liability Directive, we are still waiting for these purported excesses to materialise. The same observation holds for collective redress in Europe.

D. Because the Limited Effects of Collective Redress Today Should Not Lead Us to Pre-Judge Its Effect in the Future

A claim often made against the generalisation of collective redress in Europe is that such mechanisms – where they are available – have generally yielded limited results for consumers. In several countries, this observation may indeed be true. I have myself written about the limited impact of the French group action, which was adopted in 2014 and whose effects have been so far still inconclusive.[31] Things are, however, changing progressively. In early January 2022, for the first time, a group action against the pharmaceutical company Sanofi paved the way for the compensation of thousands of individuals who took the drug *depakine* (valproate Sodium), causing malformation in babies.[32] In February 2021, the collective redress action launched by the Spanish consumer organisation OCU was successful and triggered compensation for thousands of Spanish consumers.[33] A few months later, an Italian court similarly ordered Volkswagen to compensate more than 63,000 consumers in the context of a class action brought by the Italian consumer organisation Altroconsumo against the German manufacturer.

At the time of writing, most of the defendants in the above-mentioned cases have appealed the decisions. It may thus still take a while before individuals actually receive compensation. This shows, however, that consumers can successfully collectively fight for their rights before courts and that collective redress actions are not doomed to fail. Ultimately, it might be erroneous to consider that because of their limited impact in the past, collective redress actions will continue to fail in the future. Contexts, dynamics and mindsets are progressively changing. It will take time, though, before all stakeholders, in particular judges and claimant organisations, become fully acquainted with the new tool.

E. Because Collective Litigation is Already Here Anyway

In many ways, collective litigation is already present in Europe, and is here to stay. It takes many different forms. In some countries, some lawyers and other 'mass litigation entrepreneurs' have decided to position themselves on the emerging mass litigation

[31] A Biard, 'A ação de grupo na França: um OVNI no direito processual francês com efeitos ainda inconclusivos apos sete anos' (2021) 344 *Revista do Processo* 405; and A Biard, 'Sale temps pour l'action de groupe … la nécessaire recherche d'outils alternatifs pour résoudre les litiges de masse' (2018) 157 *Revue Lamy Droit Civil* 21.

[32] See at www.challenges.fr/entreprise/sante-et-pharmacie/la-premiere-action-de-groupe-dans-la-sante-contre-sanofi-est-validee.

[33] Madrid Tribunal Mercantil no 01, judgment no 36/202, *OCU v VW Group Espana Distribucion SA*, 25 January 2021.

markets.[34] They are using the possibilities offered by digital tools (eg, web platforms) to aggregate individual claims and to structure mass claims. This happens outside the formal scope of collective redress mechanisms, however, and mass litigation entrepreneurs often resort to traditional procedural tools (such as joinders) and not to collective redress mechanisms, for which they usually do not have legal standing.[35] These practices are problematic since they contribute to a certain degree of confusion and put consumers at risk, as many are not aware of the possible legal consequences for them if the action fails. To avoid such a proliferation of mass litigation entrepreneurs, structured collective redress mechanisms are necessary. It is better if mass litigation takes place within clear boundaries, with identified actors and on a fair playing field, rather than in the 'wild west'.

III. European Collective Redress: A Promising Future?

In November 2020, the EU adopted the long-awaited Representative Action Directive (see section I). Member States have until the end of 2022 to transpose the rules into their national systems, and the Directive will then enter into effect in June 2023. The Directive raises several doubts and concerns. This should not, however, eclipse its important added value and the fact that this legislation remains a key building block, paving the way for European collective redress. The success of collective redress in Europe will ultimately depend on the procedural choices made at national level and on changes in the mindsets of all stakeholders.

A. The Representative Action Directive: Concerns and Pending Issues …

The Directive has been the result of long and difficult preparatory discussions between the EU institutions.[36] The final result raises several doubts and concerns. For example, one may question the distinction introduced by the Directive between domestic representative actions and cross-border representative actions. The Directive foresees requirements for qualified entities designated for the purposes of bringing cross-border representative actions, leaving Member States free to decide on the requirements applying to qualified entities designated for the purpose of bringing domestic representative actions. Member States may therefore decide on more or less stringent requirements for

[34] A Biard and X Kramer, 'The EU directive on representative actions for consumers: a milestone or another missed opportunity?' (2019) 2 *Zeitschrift für Europäisches Privatrecht* 249.

[35] This is, for example, the case in France (see A Biard and MJ Azar-Baud, 'The Dawn of Collective Redress 3.0 in France' in A Uzelac and S Voet (eds), *Class Actions in Europe: Holy Grail or a Wrong Trail?* (Springer, 2021) 73; A Biard, 'Do all roads really lead to Rome? Group actions and alternative pathways for claiming compensation in mass harm situations in France' (Leuven Blog for Public Law, February 2022) available at www.leuvenpubliclaw.com/do-all-roads-really-lead-to-rome-group-actions-and-alternative-pathways-for-claiming-compensation-in-mass-harm-situations-in-france/.

[36] A Biard and S Voet, 'Collective Redress in the EU: Will it Finally Come True?' in Uzelac and Voet (eds) (n 35) 287.

qualified entities bringing domestic actions, the only rule being that these requirements should be consistent with the objective of the Directive. Undoubtedly, it would have been easier and less confusing for all stakeholders to have one set of requirements applying to all representative actions, regardless of their domestic or cross-border nature. Furthermore, the Directive does not say much on the issue of financing and assistance to qualified entities. Its Article 20, for example, merely provides that

> Member States shall take measures aiming to ensure that the costs of the proceedings related to representative actions do not prevent qualified entities from effectively exercising their right to seek the [injunctive or redress] measures.

Moreover, one may question the relevance of Article 15, which provides that

> Member states shall ensure that the final decision [in the context of a representative action] of any member state concerning the existence of an infringement ... can be used by all parties as evidence in the context of any other action.

To ensure legal clarity and to avoid divergent decisions, it would probably have been better to make the final court decision binding on the other courts as well. Finally, and more worryingly, the Directive is silent on the private international law aspects of mass claims. This is a missed opportunity given that (i) the 'New Deal for Consumers' package[37] (of which the Representative Action Directive was part) was (at least partly) triggered by the Dieselgate scandal, which has been in itself a clear example of a cross-border mass claim, (ii) the many Dieselgate-related court cases across Europe have raised many private international law problems,[38] which have importantly contributed to delaying compensation to consumers, have facilitated opportunistic behaviour by Volkswagen and enabled the car manufacturer to discriminate between European consumers,[39] and (iii) the issue of private international law rules in this context has been identified by many scholars and practitioners for several years as being of the utmost importance for the resolution of cross-border mass claims.[40]

B. ... Should Not Eclipse Its Achievements

Notwithstanding the concerns highlighted, the Representative Action Directive remains an important achievement for Europe. It concludes several decades of tense discussions at European and national levels. Consumers across Europe now have the possibility to act jointly to seek injunctive and/or redress measures in mass-harm situations. One

[37] Commission, 'A New Deal for Consumers', 11 April 2018, COM (2018) 0183 final.

[38] It is noteworthy that one case reached the CJEU (Case C-343/19, *VKI v Volkswagen*, 9 July 2020). Private international law issues were also discussed in early 2022 in the context of collective action brought by the organisation Verbraucherzentrale Südtirol against Volkswagen; see at www.bundesjustizamt.de/DE/Themen/Buergerdienste/Klageregister/Klagen/202008/KlagRE_8_2020_node.html.

[39] Biard (n 20).

[40] See, inter alia, A Stadler, 'The Commission's Recommendation on common principles of collective redress and private international law' (2013) 4 *Nederlands Internationaal Privaatrecht* 483; T Bosters, *Collective Redress and Private International Law in the EU* (Asser Press, 2017) 268; A Pato, *Jurisdiction and Cross-Border Collective Redress: A European Private International Law Perspective* (Hart Publishing, 2019) 368; and D Fairgrieve and E Lein (eds), *Extraterritoriality and Collective Redress* (Oxford University Press, 2012).

should not expect the Representative Action Directive to establish a fully-fledged collective redress mechanism in Europe. This was not the intention of the EU policymakers. As Recital 12 clearly states, 'in line with the principle of procedural autonomy, this Directive should not contain provisions on every aspect of proceedings in representative actions'. As a consequence, the Representative Action Directive should rather be seen as a pivotal building block for European collective redress, and one should also not forget that in some European countries at least, it will represent the very first building block in this area.

Furthermore, if the problems highlighted above may not be justified, at least they can be explained. They are the direct consequence of the many political compromises that were necessary to bring this legislation to life. For example, the split between cross-border and domestic representative actions and the differences in the requirements for qualified entities result from the preparatory legislative discussions. Such distinctions did not exist in the European Commission's initial proposal. They were imposed by the Council and the Member States, several of which wanted to protect their pre-existing national collective redress mechanisms.

Finally, although the absence of clear private international law rules for collective redress is regrettable, it is also obvious that addressing such a controversial issue in the context of the Directive would have considerably delayed (and probably undermined) the adoption of the Directive as a whole. Given that collective redress itself has already been a very controversial topic among Member States, such a step-by-step approach disentangling the Representative Action Directive and the revision of private international law rules turned out to be necessary, and ultimately probably the right thing to do. One might also wonder whether the revision of the existing European private international rules will not require broader discussions, including but not limited to the area of collective redress. This seems to be the approach followed by the European Commission, and the latter will assess in late 2022–early 2023 the relevance of the Brussels I Regulation to deal (in particular but not only) with collective redress.

C. The Future of European Collective Redress Still Needs To Be Written

The EU has paved the way, but the success of collective redress in Europe is now highly dependent on the choices made by Member States.[41] At the time of finalising this contribution,[42] many Member States appear to be late in the transposition process, which officially should be concluded by December 2022. The Covid-19 pandemic has certainly and importantly contributed to disrupting the national legislative agenda. An exception seems to be Luxembourg, as this country has been among the very first Member States to present draft legislation transposing the Directive.

There is still some uncertainty today as to whether Member States will manage to convert the try scored by the EU in November 2020.[43] Will the French legislature use

[41] Biard and Voet (n 36).
[42] That is, early March 2022.
[43] To re-use a rugby-based comparison (see Biard and Voet, n 36).

this possibility to revise the rules applying to French group actions? (For example, until now, consumer group actions in France could only be brought to claim compensation for material harm. This limitation has been pivotal in the context of Dieselgate and has precluded some consumer organisations from starting collective redress actions.) Will Portugal change the rules of its 'popular action'? (To date, the Portuguese collective redress action based on the opt-out system has turned out to be a rather effective way for delivering redress to Portuguese consumers.) Will Denmark broaden the possibility to use the opt-out mechanism? (So far, the possibility to use the opt-out mechanism has been limited to collective redress actions brought by the Danish Consumer Ombudsman. However, the Danish Consumer Ombudsman has never used this possibility and all actions to date have been following the opt-in model.) Will Member States decide to introduce rules to avoid lengthy collective redress proceedings (eg, by deciding that preliminary court decisions should be handed down in a given timeframe)? Will Member States decide to provide strong assistance to qualified entities for bringing collective redress actions or, on the contrary, will they limit their sources of funding and financing? Will Member States decide to set up specialised courts for the purposes of dealing with mass claims? Most of these questions are today still being discussed by several Member States.

Finally, the Member States will not be the only ones deciding on the success of collective redress in Europe. All stakeholders will also need to become acquainted with the new tool. For example, qualified entities will have to be equipped to be able to bring representative actions and to process individual claims in a cost-effective way. They will also have to learn how to manage consumers' expectations and interests during the different steps of the procedure. Qualified entities will have to set up new online tools, such as web registries and other platforms, to ensure swift communication with individual consumers. In parallel, they will also have to ensure that consumers with limited digital literacy can remain well informed about representative actions and the fact that they also have the possibility to exercise their rights. From their part, judges and members of judiciaries (who will have key roles to play for the management and resolution of mass claims)[44] might need to show some creativity to be able to deal with mass claims in the most effective way. Collective redress has the potential to be a game changer in Europe. As a consequence, changes in mindsets will progressively be necessary to fight possible initial reluctance vis-à-vis these new tools (in some countries, judiciaries have expressed some mistrust with regard to collective redress mechanisms).[45] Training and guidelines for judges, as well as a European network where judges will have the possibility to share best practices, will be needed in the coming years. Put simply, the introduction of collective redress in Europe will now importantly require some pedagogy at different levels and with all stakeholders.

* * *

At the end of *La Traviata's* first Act, Violetta sings 'Follie! Follie! Delirio vano è questo!' ('It's madness! It's empty delirium!'). One may take the view that the current efforts of

[44] A Biard, *Judges and Mass Litigation – A (Behavioural) Law & Economics Perspective* (2014) available at http://hdl.handle.net/1765/77279.

[45] Biard and Azar-Baud (n 35).

the EU to enhance collective redress across Europe are vain or doomed to fail. However, there may be many reasons to believe that another (and brighter) future is also possible for collective redress. As all European consumers need strong collective redress, let us hope that, like for *La Traviata*, European collective redress will be a successful story in the years to come.

10

Collective Redress in EU Consumer Law: How It Is, How It Could Be

STEPHEN WEATHERILL

> Collective redress is an issue that has been around – and not solved – for many years … It is time to abandon old technology that does not work well and adopt new technology that works better.
>
> (C Hodges, 'Collective Redress: The Need for New Technologies' (2019))

I. Introduction

The Court of Justice has interpreted Directive 93/13 on unfair terms in consumer contracts to require that national judges shall consider of their own motion whether a violation of European Union (EU) law has occurred in cases that arise before them. It has justified this incursion into national procedural law, which goes beyond the terms of the Directive, as a means to protect the consumer as the weaker party. The Court has, however, refused to extend this logic to cases involving consumer representative organisations. They, it seems, must operate on the assumptions laid down by national law, without the extra procedural help provided by EU law to individual consumers. This is a missed opportunity. The Court has improved the position of the individual consumer litigant, but that litigant would be much better off if those improvements were also extended to collective action routed through consumer representative associations. Collective action is likely to be far more valuable than individual action in vindicating the interests protected by consumer law. This chapter reflects on the Court's unwarranted caution, and explains this case study as an illumination of the point that EU consumer law owes much to the Court but that legislative solutions are apt to deliver more systematic progress. That in turn encourages inspection of the legislative acquis, but here too one finds further evidence of ad hoc solutions and abundant caution. This is clear in particular from examination of Directive 2020/1828 on representative actions for the protection of the collective interests of consumers. It makes a real and useful contribution to the effective enforcement of EU consumer law, but its coverage is far from comprehensive. So, reflecting on collective redress in EU consumer law, the overall picture is one that is familiar to EU consumer lawyers: a patchwork – a bit here, a bit there. For a vision of a more ambitious and sophisticated regime governing collective redress in the EU there is one place to look – the work of Chris Hodges.

II. Directive 93/13 on Unfair Terms in Consumer Contracts

A. The Nature and Purpose of Directive 93/13

Directive 93/13 on unfair terms in consumer contracts is by no means the only EU Directive that promotes the protection of the consumer, but it is probably the most prominent.[1] This is in part because it was the first Directive adopted by the EU that reached beyond the regulation of the bargaining environment within which consumer contracts are formed and instead addressed directly the *content* of the contract. Article 3(1) of the Directive provides that a contractual term that has not been individually negotiated shall be regarded as unfair 'if, contrary to the requirement of good faith, it causes a significant imbalance in the parties' rights and obligations arising under the contract, to the detriment of the consumer'. Article 6(1) of Directive 93/13 requires the Member States to provide that unfair terms shall not bind the consumer.

The Directive was accordingly a watershed. National contract lawyers now had to take EU law seriously as something more than a source of the type of mandatory disclosure rules and 'cooling-off' periods that had characterised earlier EU legislative initiatives in the field.

The Directive's prominence is also attributable to the torrent of case law it has generated. The Court of Justice, fed a rich and varied diet of preliminary rulings by national courts seeking interpretative guidance on the meaning and effect of the Directive, has shaped for itself statements of principle that frame its understanding of the purpose of the Directive as a means to regulate the EU's internal market according to common rules that promote consumer protection.

The assertion that the system of protection introduced by Directive 93/13 is based on the idea that the consumer is in a weak position vis-à-vis the seller or supplier as regards both bargaining power and level of knowledge is a very regular visitor to the Court's judgments. The Court describes Article 6(1) as a mandatory provision that, taking into account the weaker position of one of the parties to the contract, aims to replace the formal balance the contract establishes between the rights and obligations of the parties with an effective balance that re-establishes equality between them.[2]

In this way the Court treats the direct check on the enforceability of contractual terms that lies at the heart of Directive 93/13 as motivated by concern to tackle the

[1] [1993] OJ L95/29.

[2] Eg Case C-168/05 *Mostaza Claro v Centro Móvil Milenium* ECLI:EU:C:2006:10421, para 36; Case C-137/08 *VB Pénzügyi Lízing* ECLI:EU:C:2010:10847, para 47; Case C-618/10 *Banco Español de Crédito v Joaquín Calderón Camino* ECLI:EU:C:2012:349, paras 40, 63; Case C-415/11 *Mohamed Aziz* ECLI:EU:C:2013:164, para 45; Case C-470/12 *Pohotovosť s.r.o. v Vašuta* ECLI:EU:C:2014:101, paras 39–41; Case C-169/14 *Sánchez Morcillo* ECLI:EU:C:2014:2099, para 23; Case C-8/14 *BBVA SA* ECLI:EU:C:2015:731, para 17.

imbalance that flows from permitting contractual freedom free rein in the economically asymmetric relationship that typically prevails between the supplier and the consumer. In this sense Directive 93/13 is about promoting the autonomy of weaker parties. It is not about undermining freedom of contract. It is about granting it real meaning and effect.

B. Giving Shape to the Directive: The Active Role of the Court

This understanding of the Directive as a means to make real the autonomy of the consumer as the weaker party to the transaction is not mere rhetoric. At a concrete practical level this perspective has guided the Court in its treatment of some rather specific questions about the proper interpretation of the Directive.

So, for example, the Court has stated that since the system of protection introduced by the Directive is based on the idea that consumers are in a weak position vis-à-vis sellers or suppliers, in particular as regards their level of knowledge, the requirement of transparency of contractual terms, stipulated by Article 4(2) and Article 5 of Directive 93/13, cannot be reduced merely to an obligation that they be formally and grammatically intelligible. Instead, in order to comply with the Directive, contractual terms must be drafted in plain and intelligible language. This is to understand transparency in a broad sense – one that takes a realistic view of consumer fallibility.[3]

Consider too the Court's treatment of Article 6(1) of the Directive. This provision requires deletion of the offending unfair clause, which dictates that it is not open to a national court to revise the clause in order to remove its worst effects. According to the Court, this interpretation is necessary to protect the aim of the Directive, for if a national court were to be granted such a power of revision the consequence would be to weaken the dissuasive effect on sellers or suppliers minded to use unfair terms.[4] However, the Court's case law, provoked by national litigation interrogating blind spots in the legislative regime that have generated preliminary references, has been lured into addressing related questions of sophisticated nuance and detail. Revision is not excluded in *all* circumstances. The Court has held that a national court may delete an unfair term and replace it with a supplementary provision of national law to avoid the annulment of the contract where that annulment would prejudice the consumer.[5]

The Court's plentiful case law not only deals with particular consequences of invalidity, but also has attracted attention in specific sectors where, at national level, unfairness is attacked by reliance on the protection envisaged by the Directive. In this vein the Directive has been used with striking frequency in cases involving the terms applicable to mortgage repayment, especially but not only in Spain. The background to many of these

[3] See eg Joined Cases C-776/19 to C-782/19 *VB et al* ECLI:EU:C:2021:470; Case C-212/20 *MP, BP* ECLI:EU:C:2021:934; Case C-125/18 *Gómez del Moral Guasch* ECLI:EU:C:2020:138; Case C-186/16 *Andriciuc and others* ECLI:EU:C:2017:703.

[4] Case C-488/11 *Asbeek Brusse* ECLI:EU:C:2013:341.

[5] See, eg, Case C-26/13 *Árpád Kásler* ECLI:EU:C:2014:282; Joined Cases C-482/13 et al *Unicaja Banco SA* ECLI:EU:C:2015:21; Case C-90/14 *Banco Grupo Cajatres v Pinilla* ECLI:EU:C:2015:465; Case C-212/20 (n 3); Case C-655/20 *Marc Gómez del Moral Guasch v Bankia SA* ECLI:EU:C:2021:943.

cases lies in the wave of debt and house repossessions in consequence of the economic crisis, and in some circumstances the Directive has proved a valuable source of protection. So, for example, in *Sánchez Morcillo*,[6] Spanish rules governing the enforcement of mortgages were successfully attacked before the Court on the basis they failed to provide effective protection of the consumer as required by Directive 93/13. The ruling draws on the long-standing thematic and principled concern to adopt an interpretation that achieves protection of the consumer as the weaker party.[7] Consumers have not always found the Court willing to interpret the Directive in so helpful a manner,[8] but the overall narrative tells of how the Directive, applied through national legal practice and nurtured by the Court in receipt of preliminary references, is invoked as a response to and as compensation for inadequate *ex ante* regulatory control.[9] Contracts concerning the exchange of foreign currency offer another example of regular recourse to the protection for the consumer envisaged by the Directive, generating a stream of preliminary references made by national courts to Luxembourg in circumstances where effective *ex ante* control of unfair terms is lacking.[10]

C. The Court's Expectations of the Role of the National Judge

The most high-profile group of cases decided under Directive 93/13 are those in which the Court has chosen to rely on the need to ensure the achievement of the Directive's aims as a basis for interpreting it to affect matters of civil procedure that lie beyond the explicit text of the Directive. In this vein the Court has gone so far as to insist that a national court has a duty to evaluate the fairness of terms of its own motion.

The line of case law began in 2000 in *Oceano Grupo Editorial SA v Rocio Murciano Quintero*, in which the Court insisted that achieving the effective protection of the consumer envisaged by the Directive entails that a national court shall acknowledge that it has power to evaluate the unfairness of terms of its own motion.[11] Subsequently the Court altered the obligation of a national court from *power* to *duty*. It first made this change in 2006 in *Elisa María Mostaza Claro v Centro Móvil Milenium SL*,[12] though subsequently, in 2016, in its ruling in *Milena Tomášová*,[13] the Court admitted the past inconsistency in its case law but chose to fix on its 2009 ruling in *Pannon GSM Zrt* as

[6] Case C-169/14 *Sánchez Morcillo* ECLI:EU:C:2014:2099.

[7] Esp paras 22–23. See also eg Case C-8/14 (n 2).

[8] Contrast, eg, Case C-34/13 *Monika Kušionová* ECLI:EU:C:2014:2189 (Slovakia); Case C-32/14 *ERSTE Bank* ECLI:EU:C:2015:637 (Hungary). See for the full context J Mayoral and A Torres Pérez, 'On judicial mobilization: entrepreneuring for policy change at times of crisis' (2018) 40 *Journal of European Integration* 719.

[9] See esp M Józon, 'Unfair contract terms law in Europe in times of crisis: Substantive justice lost in the paradise of proceduralisation of contract fairness' (2017) 6 *Journal of European and Consumer Market Law* 157.

[10] Eg Case C-186/16 (n 3); Case C-212/20 (n 3); Case C-932/19 *OTP Jelzálogbank Zrt.* ECLI:EU:C:2021:673.

[11] Joined Cases C-240/98 to C-244/98 *Oceano Grupo Editorial SA v Rocio Murciano Quintero* ECLI:EU:C:2000:346.

[12] Case C-168/05 *Elisa Maria Mostaza Claro v Centro Móvil Milenium* ECLI:EU:C:2006:10421, para 38.

[13] Case C-168/15 *Milena Tomášová* ECLI:EU:C:2016:602.

the key case in which it had placed the matter beyond doubt.[14] Provided the national court has available to it the necessary legal and factual elements, it is in fact a matter of *duty* – not simply *power* – to rule on the possible unfairness of a contractual term falling within the scope of the Directive, irrespective of whether the consumer has raised the matter in the proceedings.[15]

Cases involving consumer arbitration provide a good illustration of what is at stake. Imagine that the terms of a contractual commitment to pursue dispute resolution through arbitration are tainted by inclusion of an unfair clause. A consumer may raise the point. Even if he or she does not, the national judge should raise it. But what if there exist national rules that forbid any disturbance of the process of arbitration by the judicial process? Arbitration, after all, is designed to achieve quicker and cheaper results than conventional judicial process, and so is typically the subject of insulation from intervention. The Court of Justice has, however, taken the view that the importance of protecting the consumer from unfair terms in accordance with Directive 93/13 may prevail over such concerns about the economical administration of justice. So in *Elisa María Mostaza Claro v Centro Móvil Milenium SL*, a Spanish court had no doubt that an arbitration agreement was tainted by inclusion of an unfair contractual term; but equally it had no doubt that under Spanish procedural law Ms Mostaza Claro, a consumer, had failed to plead that the arbitration agreement was invalid during the arbitration proceedings and therefore it was now too late for her to raise the matter in a subsequent action of annulment. Thus, under Spanish law, the arbitration award against her must stand, notwithstanding an underlying violation of the Directive. A preliminary reference was made to the Court in Luxembourg.[16] Directive 93/13 itself has nothing explicit to say about such procedural questions, but the Court, basing its reasoning on its understanding of the system of protection for the consumer as the weaker party to the transaction, concluded that the effective protection of the consumer envisaged by the Directive can be achieved only by requiring the reinforcement that is supplied by casting an obligation on the national judge to intervene, if necessary of his or her own motion, to check for the contaminating presence of unfair terms. The Court noted that 'it is in the interest of efficient arbitration proceedings that review of arbitration awards should be limited in scope and that annulment of or refusal to recognise an award should be possible only in exceptional circumstances'.[17] It found, however, that the circumstances prevailing in the case *were* exceptional. The Directive is a means to protect the consumer who is in a relatively weak position.[18] So a court dealing with an action for annulment of an arbitration award must be able to determine whether that award is void because the agreement contains an unfair term, even where the consumer has failed to plead the invalidity of the arbitration agreement in the course of the arbitration proceedings.

[14] Case C-243/08 *Pannon GSM Zrt* ECLI:EU:C:2009:350, para 32.

[15] See also, eg, Case C-397/11 *Erika Jőrös* ECLI:EU:C:2013:340, para 28; Case C-618/10 *Banco Español de Crédito* ECLI:EU:C:2012:349, paras 42 and 43; Case C-472/11 *Banif Plus Bank* ECLI:EU:C:2013:88, para 22; Case C-32/14 (n 8) para 41. For book-length examination, see A Beka, *The Active Role of Courts in Consumer Litigation* (Intersentia, 2018).

[16] Case C-168/05 (n 12).

[17] ibid para 34.

[18] ibid paras 25, 36.

The consequence is that an area one might have assumed belonged within a sphere of national procedural autonomy, given the absence of any direct engagement with such matters of civil procedure in the Directive, has instead been converted into a matter of mandatory EU law. In this way the Court has accentuated the contours of consumer law as a distinct category within national legal orders. Appreciation of the significance of this shift is sharpened when one realises that the Court has taken a quite different attitude when asked to disturb national rules aimed at securing the finality of arbitration in cases involving commercial parties. In the context of commercial litigation the Court has refused to set aside rules of national law even where the result of their application is that misapplication of EU law is allowed to stand.[19] Cases decided in the light of Directive 93/13 where the Court imposes a duty on national courts to raise relevant points of EU law of their own motion are 'justified by the need to ensure that consumers are given the effective protection' the Directive seeks to achieve, but this logic does not spill over beyond the particular context of consumer protection.[20] The aim to strengthen the position of the individual litigant prevails where he or she is a consumer; the concern with the finality of arbitration and the efficient administration of justice prevails in the absence of a consumer. This is not collective redress, but it is to understand the consumer as needing a helping hand in the courtroom.

D. The Actual and Potential Influence of the Court's Case Law

All this means that no one can sensibly undertake inquiry into Directive 93/13 in particular and EU consumer law generally without having a shrewd awareness of the contribution, both actual and potential, of the Court of Justice. This is visible in academic treatments.[21] It also leaps out from the Notice providing guidance on the interpretation and application of Directive 93/13, which the Commission published in 2019.[22] Stretching over 89 pages of the *Official Journal*, it contains an immense amount of intricate detail on the nature, purpose and content of the Directive, and, in order to provide a complete picture, it is larded with references to the case law of the Court of Justice, a list of which is provided in an Annex to the Notice. Its very first page deserves credit for recognising the necessary breadth of that inquiry:

> The Court's interpretation is not limited to the criteria for the substantive assessment of contract terms and to the consequences to be drawn from the unfairness of contract terms, but also has implications for the national rules of procedure insofar as those rules are relevant to the effective protection against unfair contract terms.

[19] Eg Joined Cases C-222/05 et al *J van der Weerd* ECLI:EU:C:2007:318; Joined Cases C-392/04 and C-422/04 *i-21 Germany and Arcor v Germany* ECLI:EU:C:2006:586; Case C-455/06 *Heemskerk BV* ECLI:EU:C:2008:650.

[20] Joined Cases C-222/05 et al (n 19) para 40.

[21] See, eg, H-W Micklitz and N Reich, 'The Court and Sleeping Beauty: The Revival of the Unfair Contract Terms Directive' (2014) 51 *CML Rev* 771; O Gerstenberg, 'Constitutional Reasoning in Private Law: The Role of the CJEU in Adjudicating Unfair Terms in Consumer Contracts' (2015) 21 *ELJ* 599. See also N Reich, *General Principles of EU Civil Law* (Intersentia, 2013); S Weatherill, *Contract Law of the Internal Market* (Intersentia, 2016).

[22] [2019] OJ C323/4.

The vigour of the Court's contribution further means that those involved in the practical world of consumer protection should always be asking themselves not simply whether EU law may help on its face, but also whether the Court could be induced to offer help in circumstances reaching beyond the legislative text. This is clearly a current trend. The number of references made to the Court that raise questions about Directive 93/13 is remarkably high, and they frequently involve matters of intricate detail arising not only out of the Directive itself but also out of the Court's abundant case law interpreting the Directive. So for example, in a case lodged with the Court in September 2021, a Romanian court asked the Court once again to revisit its treatment of terms concerning currency conversion, as well as its approach to the power of a national court to adjust a term that offends against the Directive's fairness test, asking detailed questions and citing a whole series of the Court's own existing decisions as a means to frame the inquiry.[23] There is a dynamic here: the more the Court chooses to embroider the text of the Directive with ambitious rulings about its consequences, the more likely it is to be invited to go further and deeper.[24] Preliminary reference breeds preliminary reference.

The Court has a principled preference for consumer protection as an interpretative paradigm, and it can draw on Article 12 of the Treaty on the Functioning of the European Union (TFEU) and Articles 38 and 47 of the EU Charter of Fundamental Rights as sources of constitutional support for its approach. But the Court's sense of adventure should not be allowed to pass without criticism. It deserves to be noted that in some of these decisions the Court has embarked on a path that is not mapped by any concrete EU rules. A clear risk is that national procedural rules – on matters such as the proper role of the judge, on the finality of arbitration – will be overthrown as a result of resort to the claim that EU law requires effective protection of the rights it has created. The Court may make choices that deserve criticism for disregard of values other than the effectiveness of EU law. Specialists in arbitration might, for example, question whether the efficient administration of justice, promoted by holding arbitral proceedings to be final, is tarnished by the Court's eagerness to open up such proceedings where consumers are involved.[25] More generally, the Court's approach may generate uncertainty. Where consumer protection is at stake, one has at least a plausible expectation of success in using EU law to lever open a blockage under national law to effective application of EU law, even where the matter in hand escapes the formal reach of the relevant EU measure. Hence the flow and flood of preliminary references.

This anxiety about the uncertainty injected by the Court's flexible reading of the demands of EU law is accentuated when one appreciates that it is not always the case that consumer protection exerts transformative effect. The Court is not unfailingly ready to leap to the rescue of the consumer litigant faced by obstructive rules of national law. So, for example, whereas in *Mostaza Claro* the consumer had raised the matter of unfairness

[23] Case C-566/21 *S*, pending before the Court.

[24] See also, combining detailed questions with citation of existing case law, eg, Case C-598/21 *Všeobecná úverová banka*, Case C-567/20 *Zagrebačka banka*, both pending before the Court.

[25] See eg G Bermann, 'Navigating EU law and the Law of International Arbitration' (2012) 28 *Arbitration International* 397; MJ Sørensen, 'In the name of effective consumer protection and public policy' (2016) 24 *European Review of Private Law* 791; J Brett, 'EU Law and Procedural Autonomy in International Commercial Arbitration' (2021) 29 *European Review of Private Law* 583.

in proceedings contesting an earlier adverse arbitral finding, by contrast in *Asturcom Telecomuncaciones* the consumer had been much less active.[26] She had failed even to challenge the arbitral award within the time limit stipulated by national (Spanish) law. In this case, the Court of Justice refused to offer a helping hand. It accepted that the importance of *res judicata* and ensuring the sound administration of justice should prevail over the consumer interest in re-opening the matter. So, provided it applied also to similar domestic actions, the national rule would survive scrutiny despite the impediment to effective consumer protection. It seems that EU law treats the aim of consumer protection, which is given concrete shape by Directive 93/13, as a motivating force that is strong enough to require adaptation of national rules of civil procedure in some but not all circumstances.

E. Brushes with Collective Redress

To turn – finally! – to matters associated with collective redress, a similar tale is visible of useful yet ad hoc and limited protection achieved by the Court's case law on the interpretation of Directive 93/13.

The Court has proved unwilling to invest consumer *associations* with any special protective status. *Asociación de Consumidores Independientes de Castilla y León v Anuntis Segundamano España SL* concerned Spanish rules on territorial jurisdiction in litigation that worked to the advantage of the trader rather than the consumer representative organisation seeking to act against unfair terms.[27] The Court was not here dealing with something novel. Several years earlier, in *Océano Grupo Editorial*, it had addressed the compatibility of this type of rule with Directive 93/13.[28] It had taken the view that a clause that confers jurisdiction in respect of all disputes arising under the contract on the court in the seller's territorial jurisdiction has an effect that is exclusively to the benefit of the seller. Since it confers no conceivable compensating advantage on the individual consumer, it was to be treated as unfair within the meaning of Directive 93/13. But in *Asociación de Consumidores Independientes de Castilla y León v Anuntis Segundamano España SL* the Court did not embrace this approach. Instead it explained that its case law was based on the perception that an *individual* consumer is in an inferior position to a trader, but that this does not apply to a consumer association. Consumer associations acting collectively are, it seems, treated as powerful enough to counteract the economic power of suppliers, even where suppliers are privileged by domestic procedural rules. Directive 93/13 does not help. The Court took a comparably cautious approach in *Pohotvost' s.r.o. v Vašuta*.[29] This concerned a Slovak law that prevented a consumer protection association from intervening in support of a consumer in procedures for enforcement of an arbitration award against the consumer. The Court did not find any violation of the requirements of effective protection pursued by the Directive.[30]

[26] Case C-40/08 ECLI:EU:C:2009:615.
[27] Case C-413/12 ECLI:EU:C:2013:800.
[28] Joined Cases C-240/98 to C-244/98 (n 11).
[29] Case C-470/12 (n 2).
[30] See also Joined Cases C-381/14 and C-385/14 *Jorge Sales Sinués* ECLI:EU:C:2016:909; Case C-448/17 *EOS KSI Slovensko* ECLI:EU:C:2018:745.

Such a ruling preserves national autonomy but at the expense of the pursuit of consumer protection, which in many other cases the Court has actively embraced.

The Court's determination to draw a bright line between consumer associations and individual consumers is regrettable and its reasoning is unpersuasive. Its observation that the real problem in these circumstances is not the procedural rule on jurisdiction but rather the association's financial position is peculiar.[31] Most obstructive rules are ultimately unproblematic if a litigant is rich enough! In reality some consumer associations are doubtless sufficiently well resourced to able to enter into combat with traders on an equal footing, while others – probably most – are not. It would have been more in the spirit of the Court's earlier case law had the Court left national courts to make a context-specific inquiry into whether such rules obstruct the effective protection of consumers in the particular circumstances that have arisen.

In this area – as in so many areas of EU law – there are big questions to address about whether the Court has gone beyond the judicial function in its assertive approach to interpretation of EU law, and, if so, how this impacts on its proper relationship with the political process of lawmaking, both at EU level and at national level. The concern of this chapter is more modest: it is to explore the protective effect of Directive 93/13. That effect is vigorous, and part of that is attributable to the Court's own interpretative ambition. But the case law on consumer representative organisations shows the limits and eccentricities of consumer protection delivered by judicial creativity. It is bitty. Case law always is. Legislative solutions are more likely to generate systematic reform.

And in the EU we have some legislative solutions! But we need more. The EU's legislative acquis on collective redress in the consumer sphere is illuminatingly ad hoc and patchwork in its character. It adds to the sense of incrementalism already created by inspection of the Court's case law, rather than moving confidently beyond it. This is the subject of the next section.

III. Directive 2020/1828 on Representative Actions for the Protection of the Collective Interests of Consumers

A. Directive 2020/1828 as Renovation

The centrepiece of the EU's legislative acquis is Directive 2020/1828 on representative actions for the protection of the collective interests of consumers.[32] It is a measure of legislative harmonisation adopted pursuant to Article 114 TFEU as a means to improve the functioning of the EU's internal market. As its first recital asserts, technological and economic trends (summarised as 'globalisation and digitalisation') have 'increased the risk of a large number of consumers being harmed by the same unlawful practice'. What is therefore required, the recital continues, is 'effective means to bring unlawful practices to an end and to obtain redress for consumers', thereby to enhance 'consumer confidence

[31] Case C-413/12 (n 27) para 37.
[32] [2020] OJ C409/1.

in the internal market'. The issue, then, is to promote a high level of consumer protection within the internal market, which is the thematic core of much of EU consumer law as it has developed over the last few decades. The Treaty foundations that underpin this dual purpose are Articles 114 and 169 TFEU combined with Article 38 of the EU Charter of Fundamental Rights, and these are dutifully cited in recital 4 to Directive 2020/1828. The aim: to improve consumers' access to justice within the internal market.[33]

Make no mistake, the Directive is valuable. It replaces Directive 2009/22 with effect from 25 June 2023.[34] That Directive provided that qualified entities – that is, entities designated by Member States as qualified to bring representative actions on behalf of consumers – shall be entitled to bring representative actions aimed at suppressing violations of EU law that are harmful to the collective interests of consumers. Moreover, Directive 2020/1828 moves beyond Recommendation 2013/396 on common principles for injunctive and compensatory collective redress mechanisms in EU Member States.[35] That Recommendation is not limited to consumer protection; it also addresses, inter alia, environmental protection and competition law. It seeks to elucidate basic principles that should apply in common across the Union, although in line with its status as a soft-law instrument the Recommendation is expressed in a rather general style.

Directive 2020/1828 follows the model of its two predecessors, the binding 2009 Directive and the non-binding 2013 Recommendation, but it seeks to improve, update and strengthen the system of protection.[36] The 2020 Directive is part of the 'New Deal' package dedicated to the modernisation of EU consumer law.[37] It therefore forms part of the Commission's determined campaign of recent times to lend fresh impetus to the shaping of a consumer policy for the EU.

B. The Reforms Promised by Directive 2020/1828

In order to achieve this regulatory renovation, the Directive contains rules that are designed to make sure that a representative action[38] is available in all 27 Member States. It shall lie in the hands of qualified entities, that is any organisation or public body representing consumers' interests that has been designated by a Member State as qualified to bring representative actions in accordance with this Directive.[39] Article 4 explains the process to be followed in making this designation. The Directive's scope covers such representative actions brought against violations by traders of the provisions of EU law listed in its Annex I that harm or may harm the collective interests of consumers.[40] The structure, then, is the structure found in Directive 2009/22: the intent is not to create

[33] Art 1(1).
[34] [2009] OJ L110/30.
[35] [2013] OJ L201/60.
[36] See COM (2018) 184 for the Commission's thinking.
[37] See at https://ec.europa.eu/info/law/law-topic/consumer-protection-law/review-eu-consumer-law-new-deal-consumers_en.
[38] Defined in Art 3(5).
[39] Art 3(4).
[40] Art 2(1).

new types of protection but rather to enhance the enforcement of existing protection. The Directive's Annex I contains 66 EU measures – familiar fare to the EU consumer lawyer. Only 13 featured in the Annex to Directive 2009/22. Consumer law moves on and it gets wider: data protection, for example, is on the 2020 list but was entirely absent in 2009. The scheme applies to domestic and to cross-border infringements.[41] Article 7 of Directive 2020/1828 provides more detail on the nature of the representative action. As a minimum, qualified entities shall be entitled to injunctive measures and redress measures, the nature of which is elaborated in Articles 8 and 9 respectively. This is an improvement on the narrower reach of measures envisaged by Directive 2009/22.

Article 3(3) of the Directive provides that 'collective interests of consumers' means the general interest of consumers and, in particular for the purposes of redress measures, the interests of a group of consumers. This is the key. The Directive wants to look beyond vindication of rights by an individual consumer. Under an assumption that individuals are highly unlikely to go to law to pursue relatively small-scale claims, with the result that multiple such small-scale harms may go unpenalised and therefore undeterred, the Directive envisages the establishment of a system of redress that harnesses the collective power of individual affected consumers. Thematically this is very familiar to consumer lawyers and policymakers in any jurisdiction on the planet. It is one of the great challenges of consumer law to find ways to make its enforcement effective and its impact on the market therefore tangible. Reliance on individuals acting solo is highly unlikely to do the job. Recital 9 of Directive 2020/1828 taps into exactly this perspective. Allowing qualified entities to pursue representative actions has

> the aim of ensuring that traders comply with relevant provisions of Union law and to overcome the obstacles faced by consumers in individual actions, such as those relating to uncertainty about their rights and about which procedural mechanisms are available, psychological reluctance to take action and the negative balance of the expected costs relative to the benefits of the individual action.

C. The Limits and the Inadequacies of Directive 2020/1828

So far, so good: Directive 2020/1828 deserves a welcome for its contribution to effective consumer protection. But only up to a point.

The Directive does not aspire to comprehensive coverage. Its broad aspiration is to create a single mechanism operative throughout the territory of the EU that will improve the enforcement of consumer protection law, but its limits need to be borne in mind. It has been compellingly noted that the most conspicuous feature of the Directive is the 'reluctance of the EU legislature to prescribe binding uniform and precise standards'.[42] Several matters covered by the Directive permit choices to be made

[41] Art 2(1).

[42] B Gsell, 'The New European Directive on Representative Actions for the Protection of the Collective Interests of Consumers – a huge but blurry step forward' (2021) 58 *CML Rev* 1365, 1370. See also P Poretti, 'Collective Redress in the European Union – Current Issues and Future Outlook' (2019) 3 *EU and Comparative Law Issues and Challenges Series* 339.

at national level, which is not conducive to the establishment of a common regime. Moreover other important matters are beyond the scope of the area harmonised by the Directive and are therefore left to be handled according to national preferences, which will doubtless vary across the 27 Member States and which in some cases will doubtless fall short of what is required to secure effective enforcement of the EU rules.

The most immediately obvious example of this is that the EU does not lay down with precision which bodies shall be treated as qualified entities and which shall not. The Directive puts shape on the concept, in particular in its Article 4. But the Directive is written to make clear that it is in principle for the Member States, not the EU, to designate which entities qualify for these purposes.

In similarly reticent vein, the Directive does not spell out whether a representative action may be brought in judicial proceedings, administrative proceedings or both. It leaves this choice in the hands of the Member States in implementing the Directive. Recital 19 explains that 'both judicial proceedings and administrative proceedings could effectively and efficiently serve to protect the collective interests of consumers', and so the matter is left to the discretion of the Member States.

The nature of a representative action is also not spelled out exhaustively in the Directive. It is common in EU legislation to find that the text of a measure provides detail on what the measure covers, while the Preamble, typically written in looser and less formal style, explains (inter alia) what is *not* covered. Directive 2020/1828 follows this model. In this vein, let its recital 12 speak for itself:

> In line with the principle of procedural autonomy, this Directive should not contain provisions on every aspect of proceedings in representative actions. Accordingly, it is for the Member States to lay down rules, for instance, on admissibility, evidence or the means of appeal, applicable to representative actions. For example, it should be for Member States to decide on the required degree of similarity of individual claims or the minimum number of consumers concerned by a representative action for redress measures in order for the case to be admitted to be heard as a representative action. Such national rules should not hamper the effective functioning of the procedural mechanism for representative actions required by this Directive …

At one level this is simply how EU Directives function. Unlike EU Regulations, they are expected to be fitted into existing national arrangements. They do not create a new free-standing regime. But at another level this offers an insight into how difficult the creation of common rules may be in the EU. A harmonisation directive operates only within its material scope, and frequently leaves a lot of matters close to, but formally outwith, that material scope unharmonised, and so subject to persistently diverse national treatment.

It is helpful here to re-connect with the discussion in section II.E of consumer representative organisations in the case law of the Court. Under the Directive, it follows from the point that it is for Member States to designate 'qualified entities' that consumer representative organisations are not automatically entitled to such designation as a matter of EU law. However, that statement requires qualification in the light of careful inspection of the relevant provisions of the Directive. A 'qualified entity' means any organisation or public body representing consumers' interests that has been designated by a Member State as qualified to bring representative actions in accordance with the

Directive.[43] The Directive stipulates that Member States shall ensure that entities, 'in particular consumer organisations, including consumer organisations that represent members from more than one Member State', are eligible to be designated as qualified entities for the purpose of bringing representative actions.[44] Member States *shall* designate such an entity that has made a request to be so designated for the purposes of cross-border representative actions if that entity complies with all of a series of stipulated criteria.[45] These require that it is a legal person constituted in accordance with the national law of the Member State of its designation and can demonstrate:

- 12 months of actual public activity in the protection of consumer interests prior to its request for designation;
- that its statutory purpose demonstrates that it has a legitimate interest in protecting consumer interests as provided for in the provisions of EU law referred to in the Directive's Annex I;
- it has a non-profit-making character;
- it is not the subject of insolvency proceedings and is not declared insolvent;
- it is independent and not influenced by persons other than consumers, in particular by traders, who have an economic interest in the bringing of any representative action, including in the event of funding by third parties, and, to that end, has established procedures to prevent such influence as well as to prevent conflicts of interest between itself, its funding providers and the interests of consumers;
- it makes publicly available in plain and intelligible language by any appropriate means, in particular on its website, information that demonstrates that the entity complies with these criteria and information about the sources of its funding in general, its organisational, management and membership structure, its statutory purpose and its activities.

These, to repeat, are the criteria applicable to designation for the purpose of bringing a cross-border representative action. The Directive is less prescriptive on the criteria applicable to designation for the purposes of bringing a domestic representative action, although a Member State may choose to apply the same criteria.[46]

These criteria, taken together, set a rather high bar. The background that explains that legislative outcome is lobbying by industry to confine what has been claimed as the risk of over-aggressive litigation consequent on the creation of procedural rights at EU level. However, legally, the point is that although it follows that a consumer representative organisation is not entitled as a matter of EU law to be treated as a qualified entity for the purposes of the Directive, a consumer representative organisation that meets these stipulated criteria is, it seems, so entitled. So although the structure of the Directive is to grant to Member States the choice of which entities to designate

[43] Art 3(4).
[44] Art 4(2).
[45] Art 4(3) (emphasis added).
[46] Art 4(4) and (5).

for the purposes of bringing representative actions, it explicitly embraces the eligibility of consumer representative organisations,[47] and it requires their designation for the purposes of bringing a cross-border representative action if they meet the stipulated criteria.[48] Practice confirms the prominence of consumer representative organisations. Directive 2009/22, which will be replaced by Directive 2020/1828 with effect from 2023, is considerably less prescriptive than its successor in setting out the criteria applicable to designation, but several consumer representative organisations have been notified as entitled to be treated as qualified entities under it.[49]

So the EU legislative process has recognised the importance and value of consumer representative organisations in bringing proceedings to enforce the body of EU measures listed in Annex I to the Directive in supplement to individual actions; and in the particular matter of cross-border representative actions it seems that a consumer representative organisation is entitled to be designated as a qualified entity pursuant to the Directive, provided it meets all the criteria stipulated by the Directive.

This is a positive step. But nevertheless it falls far short of a comprehensive regime.

Critical to effective consumer protection is funding. A consumer representative organisation is only as effective as its resources permit it to be. Directive 2020/1828 addresses the matter of funding, but in a rather feeble way. Article 20 leaves the matter in the hands of the Member States. The provisions are written with great caution and absence of detailed obligation, and even though EU law imposes a general obligation on Member States to ensure the effective enforcement of obligations contained in Directives, this is not readily translated into a concrete requirement to provide a budget of a specific size to an enforcement agency. In fact – still worse – the Directive goes so far as to exclude methods Member States might usefully have employed to ensure a funding stream apt to encourage effective enforcement. So it is sceptical about the use of punitive damages[50] and it limits the scope for funding by competing traders.[51] The Directive's failure to tackle the matter of funding with any vigour – plausibly another manifestation of industry lobbying during its drafting – has been convincingly criticised as a real weakness.[52]

Nor does the Directive address matters of civil procedure of the type the Court has plunged into in the case law discussed in section II. The Directive does not address the *ex officio* role of national judiciaries at all, nor does it dive into matters of civil procedure more generally. In this sense the Directive is an ad hoc and limited response to the blockages to effective enforcement of consumer law. In the matter of civil procedure the Court is more boldly interventionist – in some matters, though, as discussed in section II.E, not in support of consumer associations – than the legislative institutions,

[47] Art 4(2). See also recital 24 'Consumer organisations … should all be considered well placed to apply for the status of qualified entity in accordance with national law.'

[48] Art 4(3).

[49] See, eg, [2019] OJ C237/3.

[50] Recitals 10, 42. Punitive damages are not addressed in the text of the Directive proper so there is scope for doubting the legal force of this scepticism.

[51] Art 10.

[52] See L Visscher and M Faure, 'A Law and Economics Perspective on the EU Directive on Representative Actions' (2021) 44 *Journal of Consumer Policy* 455, 472–75; also Gsell (n 42) 1397–99.

but neither is doing more than adding an adjustment here, an adjustment there, when permitted by the accidents of litigation in the case of the Court and when the window of political opportunity opens in the case of the legislative process. This is not a comprehensive regime governing collective redress.

IV. Overview and Prospective

A survey of EU rules on collective redress reveals a pattern that is readily familiar to EU consumer lawyers. There is a bit here, a bit there. The Court has amplified Directive 93/13 not only to make more elaborate and concrete the nature of the control it exercises over unfair terms, but also to draw out implications for procedural protection at national level that is apt to secure the effective protection of the rights envisaged by the Directive. But when invited to use this logic in order to strengthen the position of consumer representative organisations before national courts, it was unwilling to do so. Directive 2020/1828 does strengthen the position of consumer representative organisations before national courts, but in a way that leaves open, and under-developed, a number of matters untouched by the Directive, such as determination of the degree of similarity of individual claims required for the case to be admitted to be heard as a representative action, and that is also feeble in its treatment of some matters which are touched, such as funding[53] and disclosure rules.[54] So, surveying the EU landscape of collective redress, there is a mix of legislation and judicial ambition that should certainly be greeted with warmth on its own terms as a means to provide a protective content within the internal market that stretches across the territory of the 27 Member States, and yet which should also be viewed with appreciation of its limits. It is not a comprehensive scheme of collective redress. It is not remotely close to a comprehensive system of collective redress.

So what can be done? And what should be done?

A system that is based on an expectation that individual consumers will take action when they are confronted by a violation of their legal rights is based on unrealistic assumptions. Consumers are frequently only dimly aware of their legal rights. They are easily fobbed off by unscrupulous traders, even if the consumer is assertive enough to make a fuss in the first place. But, and still worse, a consumer who is fully aware of his or her legal rights may rationally conclude that it is not worth pursuing the matter. If it will take time, money and energy, scarce resources all, to secure redress for a trifling loss, then the rational consumer will likely sigh, accept the pain and move on. The result is that a large aggregate loss, made up of multiple small losses, may be absorbed by a bloc of affected consumers, while the trader is protected from any consequences. In this gap lies failed consumer protection and an absence of any incentive for the trader to improve in future. Here lies the appeal of collective redress (and of related phenomena such as class actions and representative actions). Access to justice is the slogan: the

[53] Arts 10, 20.
[54] Art 18.

promise is to provide effective means for compensating consumers and deterring trader malpractice. By looking beyond the inadequacies of individual enforcement, collective redress offers a means to secure vindication of consumer rights that is realistic rather than theoretical, effective rather than formal.

The elements of a successful system of collective redress are plausibly several. They conventionally include court-focused procedures that in some form permit an action to be pursued by or on behalf of a group of consumers who have suffered similar harms. There arise important questions about detailed design, such as who shall have standing to bring the claim, how it shall be funded (including whether third-party funding is allowed), how similar the harm must be for consumers to be entitled to act collectively rather than individually, whether an opt-in or an opt-out model should be preferred, what forms of redress should be available and what degree of protection from unmeritorious claims should be included. Every jurisdiction has its own particularities.[55] Choosing focus and priorities is a major issue. It is well known that the United States has tended to prefer an emphasis on private enforcement and litigation, whereas in Europe a more mixed approach, drawing on strategies of public regulation as well as private action, is visible. There is much to be said in favour of an integrated approach that ranges over several distinct policy instruments in order to construct a coherent and systematic scheme of effective enforcement. In this vein, the full picture should include market supervision and enforcement by public bodies, while other forms of alternative dispute resolution and mediation, including the role of ombudsmen, should also be endorsed.[56]

The pattern of EU law in the field of collective redress is especially peculiar and especially unsatisfactory. Most of all, it is not integrated and it is not coherent. It is a commonplace criticism that the EU has been far more successful in creating an integrated space for transfrontier economic activity within its internal market than it has in creating administrative and civil justice systems that offer effective and readily enforceable protection from market failures and inequities within that space. That is a criticism not limited to consumer law in the EU – consider from this perspective both generally and as candidates for improvement through resort to collective redress also environmental law,[57] competition law,[58] equality law[59] and labour law[60] – but consumer law serves as a well-chosen illustration of this imbalance. And here, in tracking the concrete and frankly eccentric shape of the EU's contribution to collective redress, is confirmation based on a vivid and detailed case study.

[55] See eg A Uzelac and S Voet (eds), *Class Actions in Europe: Holy Grail or a Wrong Trail?* (Springer, 2021); C Hodges and S Voet, *Delivering Collective Redress: New Technologies* (Hart Publishing, 2018); E Lein et al, *Collective Redress in Europe: Why and How?* (BIICL, 2015); also R Amaro et al, *Collective Redress in the Member States of the European Union* (European Parliament, 2018).

[56] See esp Hodges and Voet (n 55).

[57] See, eg, M Eliantonio, 'Collective Redress in Environmental Matters in the EU: a Role Model or a Problem Child' (2014) 41 *Legal Issues of Economic Integration* 257.

[58] See, eg, E Şahin, *Collective Redress and EU Competition Law* (Routledge, 2019).

[59] See, eg, S Benedi Lahuerta, 'Enforcing EU Equality Law through Collective Redress: Lagging behind?' (2018) 55 *CML Rev* 783.

[60] Z Rasnača, 'Collective redress in labour and social law disputes: an (attractive) option for the EU?' (2021) 12 *European Labour Law Journal* 415.

In trying to explain these inadequacies, one must reckon with constitutional questions associated with the EU's limited competence to legislate; but most of all it seems that the EU is politically incapable of doing more than a bit here, a bit there. Incremental development is the story of EU consumer law. It has always been the story of EU consumer law.[61]

Chris Hodges has shown how it can be done better. Let me move towards a conclusion by referring to his paper published in 2019 in the *Journal of Consumer Policy*, 'Collective Redress: The Need for New Technologies'.[62] He treats the (then proposed rather than adopted) Directive as 'old technology', in the sense that it focuses only on a litigation-based representative action model. Think more broadly and ambitiously, he urges! And not for the first time: already in 2014 he had criticised the Commission Recommendation 2013/396[63] for its narrow litigation-based focus, and had pressed for a more holistic approach.[64] Now in his 2019 article Chris points out (with an understandable tone of disappointment) that the Commission remains guilty of failing to consider all available options; albeit that, as he acknowledges, there is no apparent appetite among the Member States for a more thorough intervention pursued at EU level. But the unimaginative focus on private enforcement according to a litigation-based model, which characterised Recommendation 2013/396 and which, for all its improvements at the level of detail, also characterises Directive 2020/1828, is not simply a missed opportunity – it is a whole series of missed opportunities. As Chris demonstrates, a range of new ideas – 'new technologies', as he felicitously puts it – exists and can profitably be drawn on, most notably empowering regulatory authorities to pursue and require redress and securing an enhancement of the role of Consumer Ombudsmen. In this matter Chris has shown intellectual leadership, so much so that an analysis of the Directive in one of the most prestigious of all EU law academic journals is – quite properly – attentive to his 'fundamental criticism' of the Directive's relatively narrow focus and its failure to engage with the full breadth of available regulatory strategies.[65]

Collective redress in the EU can be improved. The agenda exists, and Chris Hodges has done much to shape it. But, as consumer lawyers, we must ruefully accept that history cautions us that the EU is likely to complete it, if at all, only by slow steps and incremental development.

[61] S Weatherill, 'Consumer Policy' in P Craig and G de Búrca, *The Evolution of EU Law*, 3rd edn (Oxford University Press, 2021).

[62] C Hodges, 'Collective Redress: The Need for New Technologies' (2019) 42 *Journal of Consumer Policy* 59.

[63] See n 35.

[64] C Hodges, 'Collective Redress: A Breakthrough or a Damp Sqibb?' (2014) 37 *Journal of Consumer Policy* 67.

[65] Gsell (n 42) 1399. See also for due homage, Poretti (n 42) 353; Visscher and Faure (n 52) 456; Rasnača (n 60) 418.

11

Let's Redress European Redress the Hodges Way! *Redressons redress en Europe à l'Hodgienne!*

A Look at How Canada Resolves the Conflicting Collective Claims Cross-Border Conundrum and How May the Canadian Solution Help Us in the EU?

HERBERT WOOPEN

> Further, if the ability of the collective action to deliver mass compensation is not particularly impressive, and the mechanism is outperformed by other newer intermediaries and mechanisms, a serious question arises about the ongoing justification for the mechanism.
>
> (C Hodges and S Voet, *Delivering Collective Redress. New Technologies* (2018))

I. Introduction

A major challenge for collective redress to be effective in the EU will be how to ensure cross-border coordination of more than one national collective proceeding in related cases. This problem has likewise been experienced in Canada over the last few decades, and in order to resolve it all provinces adopted the 'Canadian Judicial Protocol for the Management of Multi-Jurisdictional Claims'[1] in 2011. The Canadian

[1] 'Canadian Judicial Protocol for the Management of Multijurisdictional Class Actions' (*CBA*, 13 August 2011) available at www.cba.org/Our-Work/Resolutions/Resolutions/2011/Canadian-Judicial-Protocol-for-the-Management-of-M?lang=en-CA; www.cba.org/getattachment/Our-Work/Resolutions/Resolutions/2011/Canadian-Judicial-Protocol-for-the-Management-of-M/11-03-A-Annex01.pdf.

Bar Association supports such coordination by a voluntary platform for Pan-Canadian coordination (National Class Action Database),[2] which had been recommended by a Uniform Law Conference of Canada's Working Group on Multi-jurisdictional Class Actions.

The rules in Québec, the first[3] province to introduce collective actions in Canada in 1978, are of particular interest because each application for authorisation also needs to be served on the Fonds d'aide aux actions collectives.[4] This institution, which is apparently unique in the world, is of particular interest, because enforcing the Law in general is an integral task for a public body (*res publica*) that is associated with its monopoly on the use of force. Law enforcement and the public body's monopoly of power are two sides of the same coin. This monopoly should prohibit the placing of the infrastructure and funding that are needed for law enforcement in the hands of private entities. Conversely, when the creation of such private entities is observed, in a best-case scenario this may be indicative of systemic weaknesses in core areas of public infrastructure; and in a worst-case scenario it could lead to a culture where 'private mercenaries' provide services only for those cases where such gaps in the public infrastructure can be turned into maximum profits.

The Canadian model of cross-border coordination may assist in finding a shortcut to resolving the cross-border challenge in the European Union (EU); and taking a closer look at the model in Québec in particular may also serve to reduce the potential in the EU for financial exploitation of such frictions in the EU framework for collective redress. Taking inspiration from Christopher Hodges, a broad view that also covers the modus operandi of the Québec Fund may suggest using such a model, at both EU Member State and even EU level, for *non-court dispute resolution procedures* too, that is, to fund ombuds entities and infrastructure to ensure early access to ('capturing in a versatile infrastructure'), as well as swift and cheap resolution of, such disputes. Digitalisation is a megatrend in judicial systems worldwide; efforts to this effect in Germany are strongly increasing, and the new governing coalition has in particular agreed in their coalition agreement[5] to create citizen-friendly digital procedures for small claims in specialised courts to ensure simple enforcement of such claims. A German author[6] points to well-functioning systems in other countries, particularly to the leading role of Canada, specifically to the British Columbia Civil Resolution Tribunal (CRT), which is Canada's first online court.[7]

[2] 'Class Action Database' (*CBA*) available at www.cba.org/Publications-Resources/Class-Action-Database.

[3] C Pichet, 'Public Financiers as Overseers of Class Proceedings' (2016) 12(3) *New York University Journal of Law & Business* 777, 787.

[4] Art 58 sentence 2 of the Regulation of the Superior Court of Québec in civil matters available at http://legisquebec.gouv.qc.ca/en/pdf/cr/C-25.01,%20R.%200.2.1.pdf.

[5] 'Koalitionsvertrag' (Coalition Treaty 2021–2025) paras 3537–3540 available at www.bundesregierung.de/breg-de/service/gesetzesvorhaben/koalitionsvertrag-2021-1990800; www.bundesregierung.de/resource/blob/974430/1990812/04221173eef9a6720059cc353d759a2b/2021-12-10-koav2021-data.pdf?download=1.

[6] Lawyer Prof Dr Wilfried Bernhardt, Staatssekretaer aD, 'Quo vadis Ampel? – Digitalisierung der Justiz' in juris (Beilage zum Anwaltsblatt) March 2022, 90, 91, fn 13.

[7] 'Civil Resolution Tribunal' available at https://civilresolutionbc.ca/.

II. Unresolved Issues in the EU Directive on Representative Actions

As the author has shown elsewhere,[8] neither the new EU Directive on Representative Actions[9] nor the existing Brussels I (Recast) Regulation[10] provides solutions to the challenges resulting from parallel domestic and cross-border collective actions in multiple Member States. The Directive instead requires Member States to resolve these issues individually.[11] This looks like a 'mission impossible' and has prompted the author to severely criticise the Directive for the irresponsible approach that it adopted of not legislating on issues that were perfectly predictable.[12]

In an attempt to assist in finding solutions as negotiations were underway in the EU's Council, the author proposed to create two distinct information technology (IT) solutions: one for the purposes of cross-border coordination among courts and other public entities, and the other for collection and storage of the data of contentious cases ('capturing') that merit further consideration, initially by alternative dispute resolution (ADR)/ombuds bodies even before any court is involved.[13] The first of these ideas has been retained, at least to a certain extent, in that the IT coordination tool under construction for National Contact Points (NCPs) is now planned to connect not only the NCPs but also courts and administrative authorities.[14] Moreover, it will go beyond the limited provisions of the Directive on identifying and checking national designation of qualified entities by allowing for communication among the various courts and administrative authorities that could be seised by collective actions. This progress had

[8] H Woopen, 'Kollektiver Rechtsschutz – Chancen der Umsetzung, Die Europäische Verbandsklage auf dem Weg ins deutsche Recht'['Collective Redress – Opportunities of the Directive's Transposition, The European Representative Action on its Way into German Law'] [2021] *Juristenzeitung* 601, 603–05.

[9] Directive (EU) 2020/1828 of the European Parliament and of the Council of 25 November 2020 on representative actions for the protection of the collective interests of consumers and repealing Directive 2009/22/EC [2020] OJ L409/1.

[10] Regulation (EU) No 1215/2012 of the European Parliament and of the Council of 12 December 2012 on jurisdiction and the recognition and enforcement of judgments in civil and commercial matters (Recast) [2012] OJ L351/1.

[11] Art 9(4) reads 'Member States shall lay down rules to ensure that consumers who have explicitly or tacitly expressed their wish to be represented in a representative action can neither be represented in other representative actions with the same cause of action and against the same trader, nor be able to bring an action individually with the same cause of action and against the same trader. Member States shall also lay down rules to ensure that consumers do not receive compensation more than once for the same cause of action against the same trader.'

[12] Woopen (n 8): it seems to be the unanimous view that the rules of Brussels I (Recast) do not fit, one voice even deploring this in respect of the resulting impossibility of having competition in favour of a 'race to the bottom' of standards: B Rentsch, 'Kollektiver Rechtsschutz unter der EU-Verbandsklagerichtlinie' [2021] *Europäische Zeitschrift für Wirtschaftsrecht* 524 (524 introduction, 525, 533 section V, thesis 6). And yet no other proposals to resolve the issues could so far be found, except for those made by the author, supported by the European Justice Forum – www.europeanjusticeforum.org – Representative actions, Message no 5 – no domestic effects of procedures in other Member States (without separate exequatur procedure).

[13] Contribution by European Justice Forum to the EU Consultation on 'Consumer policy – the EU's new "consumer agenda"' (available at https://ec.europa.eu/info/law/better-regulation/have-your-say/initiatives/12464-A-New-Consumer-Agenda), 'Legal Tech for Justice, Not for Profit – A new Governance for Consumer Law Enforcement in the Union Should Rely on Electronic Registries and Communication as State-of-the-Art Response, namely to insufficient provisions in the recent Representative Actions Directive' at 4–9 for coordination (and beneficiary participation in representative actions) and at 9–12 for ADR/ODR.

[14] Art 14 para 4(b) adds 'if necessary under national law'.

been disclosed by the Commission at the end of the Workshop on the Implementation of the Representative Actions Directive (EU) 2020/1828 on 26 November 2021, and the tool's name will be 'REACT' – the Representative Actions Communication Tool.

The 'conflicting collective claims cross-border conundrum' has thus, albeit timidly, been addressed by the Commission for the first time. It had surfaced many years earlier in Canada, which does not have a comprehensive federal collective procedure. The federal procedure can only be used against the federal government or in matters over which the federal government has exclusive jurisdiction.[15] The regular class action procedures consist of different comprehensive opt-out models in Canada's provinces. These collective instruments can, based on a ruling by the Supreme Court of Canada, even be used for those parts of the country that do not have their own formal collective claims legislation (these being the province of Prince Edward Island and the three territories: Northwest Territories, Yukon and Nunavut).[16] In some provinces, such as British Columbia,[17] residents of other provinces may participate in a collective procedure across the provincial border only via opt-in, as had been recommended by the Uniform Law Conference of Canada in 1995, although Manitoba did not heed this advice and allowed extra-provincial opt-out classes. With the exception of Québec, all the provinces follow the model according to which the procedure starts as an individual claim and can later be 'certified' as a class action, thus opening it up to an opt-out collective action. In contrast, in Québec – based on Articles 53 to 62 (Chapter X) of the Québec Superior Court's Rules of Civil Procedure[18] – the courts must be asked to 'authorise' a class action that is introduced as such from the start, and this action is terminated if such authorisation is denied.[19]

The structural set-up in Canada thus looks largely comparable to that in the EU, which forms an umbrella for its 27 Member States with different judicial traditions and various collective action models, some already existing, some still to be created. It should therefore be legitimate and instructive to have a look at how Canada may have resolved the issues mentioned above, study of several practical and up-to-date cases from Canada being the best way to achieve these aims.

III. The Current Approach to the Conflicting Collective Claims Cross-Border Conundrum in Recent Canadian Judgments

The Canadian legal database 'CanLII' (Canadian Legal Information Institute) currently shows 150 hits for 'multijurisdictional class action' of which 83 are court decisions,

[15] GM Zakaib and J Saint-Onge, *A Summary of Canadian Class Action Procedure and Developments* (booklet edited by law firm Borden Ladner Gervais, 2018) 1.

[16] See, eg, US Chamber Institute for Legal Reform, *Perspective d'un horizon incertain – Recours collectifs au Canada 2011–2014* (2015) 5.

[17] ibid, 54, note 5.

[18] Chapter C-25.01, r 0.2.1 – Regulation of the Superior Court of Québec in civil matters, Code of Civil Procedure (chapter C-25.01, a 63) available at www.legisquebec.gouv.qc.ca/en/document/cr/C-25.01,%20 r.%200.2.1%20/.

[19] Zakaib and Saint-Onge (n 15) 5–6.

22 legislation and 45 commentaries.[20] Among the court decisions, two judgments stand out as offering good advice on how to handle the same problem in an EU context: the first for an overview from a systemic perspective; and the second from an individual court's perspective regarding guidance on how to best anchor such a solution for multi-jurisdictional coordination into the respective national civil procedural laws while transposing the EU Directive on Representative Actions.

A. The Result: Systemic Disentanglement

In *Micron Technologies Inc c Hazan* of 2 September 2020 (date of hearing: 1 November 2019),[21] the Court of Appeal in the Canadian Province of Québec rejected the Appeal against a judgment rendered on 11 February 2019 that had dismissed an application for a stay of the class action. This case is extremely instructive because of its underlying appraisal of relevant facts and rules.

On 30 April 2018, the Respondent filed an Application for Authorisation to Institute a Class Action against the Appellants in Québec Superior Court for damages based on a price-fixing conspiracy among the Appellants that led to artificially inflated prices for dynamic random-access memories (DRAMs). The group, which claimed to be entitled to damages and, under provincial consumer protection law, to punitive damages as well, was described as:

> All persons or entities in Canada (subsidiarily in Quebec) who, between at least June 1, 2016 and February 1, 2018, acquired dynamic random-access memory ('DRAM') directly from one of the Defendants (the 'Direct Purchasers') or who acquired DRAM and/or products containing DRAM either from a Direct Purchaser or from another indirect purchaser at a different level in the distribution chain (the 'Indirect Purchasers'), or any other Group(s) to be determined by the Court.

Two days later, on 2 May 2018, a person by the name of Chelsea Jensen filed a Statement of Claim in the Federal Court for damages for price fixing against the same seven defendants, including a motion that the action be certified as a class action on behalf of largely the same group, defined as:

> All persons or entities in Canada who, from June 1, 2016 to February 1, 2018 (the 'Class Period'), purchased DRAM or products containing DRAM. Excluded from the Class are the defendants and their parent companies, subsidiaries, and affiliates.

A further proposed class action filed in the Federal Court was discontinued after the Jensen statement of claim was amended to include the second plaintiff and his lawyers.

Similar proceedings were also filed in the British Columbia and Ontario courts but not moved forward. The Ontario plaintiff, now a co-plaintiff in the Federal proceedings, declared to hold the Ontario proceedings while advancing the Federal proceedings.

[20] Available at www.canlii.org/en/#search/type=decision&text=Multijurisdictional%20class%20action.

[21] *Micron Technology Inc c Hazan*, 2020 QCCA 1104 (CanLII) available at https://canlii.ca/t/j9hhj.

i. Intra-Québec Cases

A second application for authorisation was also filed on 3 May 2018 at the Québec Superior Court and suspended on 14 June 2018 under the 'first to file' rule, which applies to 'intra-Québec cases' following the leading case of *Hotte c Servier Canada Inc.*[22] In this case, the general rule on *lis pendens* between two or more pending actions was made applicable to class actions under the following reasoning: *lis pendens* is fulfilled if the two claims meet the conditions for *res judicata*, that is, the demand is based on the same cause and is between the same parties acting in the same qualities and the thing applied for is the same (Article 2848 of the Civil Code of Québec (CCQ)). When there is *lis pendens*, the court will proceed with the first action filed and dismiss the second and any subsequent actions, under Article 168 of the Code of Civil Procedure of Québec (CCP) (former Article 165 CCP). Given that the general rules on *lis pendens* do not apply neatly to motions for authorisation to institute class actions due to different claimants taking the initiative, the Court found instead '*une apparence de litispendance*'. It concluded that, contrary to initial appearances, the ultimate identity of the parties in these different actions was the same even though there were three different petitioners, because the petitioners proposed representing the same group and 'the group was the real party'.[23] The Court held that the first motion filed should proceed by applying the 'first to file' rule. It did not, however, dismiss the other motions – which would have been the consequence if Article 168(1) CCP had been directly applied – but rather suspended them until the first motion for authorisation was decided, at which time it left open the possibility to seek the dismissal of the suspended motions under the principle of *res judicata*. This rule was confirmed, in principle, in *Schmidt c Johnson & Johnson Inc*,[24] on the grounds of its ease of application in contrast to the alternative of an expensive debate to determine which petitioner was better qualified, but was also modified with regard to the best interests of the members of the class:

> [52] Thus, it is admissible to show that the first motion filed with the Registry suffers from serious deficiencies, that the lawyers who are responsible for it are not hurrying to advance it, that they have filed similar proceedings elsewhere in Canada for the same putative members, etc, ie, indications that the lawyers behind the first proceeding are only trying to occupy the field and are not motivated by the best interests of the putative Quebec members.[25]

ii. Interprovincial and International Cases

The solution for a conflict between a Québec action and a *foreign* procedure or judgment is treated in Article 3137 CCQ,[26] which authorises the Québec court to stay its

[22] *Hotte c Servier Canada Inc*, 1999 CanLII 13363 (QC CA) available at https://canlii.ca/t/1mvw6.

[23] *Micron Technologies Inc c Hazan* (n 21) para 26.

[24] *Schmidt c Johnson & Johnson Inc* 2012 QCCA 2132.

[25] Original text in French: 'Ainsi, est admissible la démonstration que la première requête déposée au greffe souffre de graves lacunes, que les avocats qui en sont les responsables ne s'empressent pas de la faire progresser, qu'ils ont déposé des procédures similaires ailleurs au Canada, et ce, pour les mêmes membres putatifs, etc, c'est-à-dire des indices que les avocats derrières la première procédure tentent uniquement d'occuper le terrain et ne sont pas mus par le meilleur intérêt des membres putatifs québécois.'

[26] Art 3137 CCQ provides 'On the application of a party, a Québec authority may stay its ruling on an action brought before it if another action between the same parties based on the same facts and having the same

proceedings, but only if the foreign action was filed first. If the Québec court is 'first seised of the dispute', Article 3155(4) CCQ[27] provides that a foreign judgment will not be recognised if there is *lis pendens* with the Québec action.

Before staying an application to authorise a class action or an already authorised class action when a motion to certify a class action or a class action is already under way outside of Québec, the court must, however, pursuant to Article 577 CCP, have regard to the protection of the rights and interests of the Québec members in the non-Québec court:

> **577.** The court cannot refuse to authorize a class action on the sole ground that the class members are part of a multi-jurisdictional class action already under way outside Québec.
>
> If asked to decline jurisdiction, to stay an application for authorization to institute a class action or to stay a class action, the court is required to have regard for the protection of the rights and interests of Québec residents.
>
> If a multi-jurisdictional class action has been instituted outside Québec, the court, in order to protect the rights and interests of class members resident in Québec, may disallow the discontinuance of an application for authorization, or authorize another plaintiff or representative plaintiff to institute a class action involving the same subject matter and the same class if it is convinced that the class members' interests would thus be better served.

The relationship between the rule in Article 3137 CCQ and the 'first to file' rule was first defined in such a way that the Superior Court had no jurisdiction to stay the Québec proceedings if they were instituted first, and a discretion to do so if they were not instituted first.[28] But based on the general clause on judicial powers in Article 49 CCP,[29]

subject is pending before a foreign authority, provided that the latter action can result in a decision which may be recognized in Québec, or if such a decision has already been rendered by a foreign authority.'

[27] Art 3155 provides:

> A decision rendered outside Québec is recognized and, where applicable, declared enforceable by the Québec authority, except in the following cases:
>
> (1) the authority of the State where the decision was rendered had no jurisdiction under the provisions of this Title;
> (2) the decision, at the place where it was rendered, is subject to an ordinary remedy or is not final or enforceable;
> (3) the decision was rendered in contravention of the fundamental principles of procedure;
> (4) a dispute between the same parties, based on the same facts and having the same subject has given rise to a decision rendered in Québec, whether or not it has become final, is pending before a Québec authority, first seized of the dispute, or has been decided in a third State and the decision meets the conditions necessary for it to be recognized in Québec;
> (5) the outcome of a foreign decision is manifestly inconsistent with public order as understood in international relations;
> (6) the decision enforces obligations arising from the taxation laws of a foreign State.

[28] *Micron Technology Inc c Hazan* (n 21) para 33; in the *FCA* case, three concurrent applications were filed in Québec, Ontario and British Columbia, and the Superior Court still held that the Québec application could not be stayed under international *lis pendens* and Art 3137 CCQ because it had been filed before the others: *Garage Poirier & Poirier Inc c FCA Canada inc*, 2018 QCCS 107, paras 37–39.

[29] Art 49 CCP provides:

> The courts and judges, both in first instance and in appeal, have all the powers necessary to exercise their jurisdiction.
>
> They may, at any time and in all matters, even on their own initiative, grant injunctions or issue protection orders or orders to safeguard the parties' rights for the period and subject to the conditions they determine. As well, they may make such orders as are appropriate to deal with situations for which no solution is provided by law.

the Superior Court is also allowed to suspend Québec class action proceedings if they were filed first, provided that the interests of the Québec members and the proper administration of justice militate in favour of such suspension.[30] As a result, the Superior Court can suspend Québec class action proceedings in favour of proceedings filed outside Québec, even if the Québec proceedings were filed first.

iii. Federal Court versus Superior Court

Considering the conflict between claims filed at the Québec Superior Court and the Federal Court, no precedent had existed as to whether the 'first to file' rule applies in these particular circumstances. The judicial rules so far quoted do not apply, as Article 3137 CCQ does not apply to proceedings in Federal Court, and the 'first to file' rule only applies in the Québec Superior Court on claims introduced at the same court. *Micron Technology Inc c Hazan* acknowledges this and develops 'other considerations' that will be relevant, without turning the conflict into a 'beauty contest'. Each court can suspend only its own proceedings and not the other's in another province or at the federal level. The fact that Canada is a federation where there is comity amongst the courts should therefore lead to their all applying similar tests and reaching similar outcomes on such issues.

The appropriate test for a suspension can be based on Article 49 CCP and on the mandatory language of the second paragraph of Article 577 CCP (emphasis added): 'If asked to decline jurisdiction, to stay an application for authorization to institute a class action or to stay a class action, *the court is required to have regard for the protection of the rights and interests of Québec residents*.' While this provision did not appear to apply neatly, given that the first paragraph requires that there is a 'multi-jurisdictional class action already under way outside Québec', the Court suggested in *FCA* that the limitation in the first paragraph does not apply to the second paragraph, and that anyway the Superior Court would have the duty to ensure that the rights and interests of the members are adequately protected.[31]

Generally, it will not be in the interests of justice or of the parties to have two class actions proceed on the merits in parallel in front of different courts, due to the risk of conflicting judgments, costs to the parties and the waste of judicial resources. Each court should therefore assess whether either proposed class action includes issues, remedies or class members not included in the other, whether such differences be the result of a strategic decision by a party or of limits on the territorial or subject-matter jurisdiction of one of the courts. A difference in the scope of the proposed class actions may be relevant, because it suggests that additional proceedings may be necessary in the other forum to address all of the issues, remedies and class members.

The court must also ensure that the rights and interests of Québec residents are adequately protected and that the proposed representative is in a position to represent them properly. This would include, for example, that the Québec residents be treated

[30] *FCA Canada Inc c Garage Poirier & Poirier Inc*, 2019 QCCA 2213, paras 73, 78.
[31] *Micron Technology Inc c Hazan* (n 21) paras 46–50.

in the same way as residents of other jurisdictions, that they receive the benefits of any applicable Québec legislation, and that any notices and other communications be disseminated in Québec and in French.[32] Given that at the time of the court's required decision nobody knows how the other courts will decide, all of the parties can consent and present a litigation plan to the Superior Court showing how they will conduct the litigation and protect the rights and interests of the Québec members, that again may be sufficient for the judge to grant the suspension before either proceeding is authorised or certified. However, the lack of authorisation or certification may be problematic in cases where the application for a suspension is contested and the parties make representations as to what the Superior Court and the other court may or may not do with respect to authorisation or certification. While the Superior Court may suspend the Québec proceedings pending before it at any stage, the judge might, depending on the circumstances, dismiss such a request as premature if it was made before the other concurrent class action has been authorised or certified.[33]

The appellate court in *Micron Technology Inc c Hazan* thus confirmed that the court of first instance was right in not staying the Québec procedure but that it should continue for further clarification. The appellate ruling confirmed (obiter) as examples several points of interest that were unknown to the court of first instance at the time of its decision, and which provided justification for postponing its decision on the application to stay its own action as it awaited clarification of these unknowns:[34]

- Will the class actions be authorised in the Superior Court and certified in the Federal Court?
- What will be the classes? The two proposed definitions are essentially identical (national, same period, same activities and same defendants), but the Appellants urged the limitation of the class definition to residents of Québec in the Superior Court. This can only be decided at the authorisation stage.
- What issues will be litigated? Both courts have concurrent jurisdiction, but in the Québec Proceedings the Respondent also invoked provincial consumer protection legislation and advanced on that basis a claim for punitive damages – a claim that could not be included in the Federal Court Proceedings while counsel for the Respondent was unable to substantiate such claims.
- What timetables are to be expected? The Québec judge concluded without conclusive reasons that the case at the Superior Court would be less complex and dealt with more quickly.

The issues described above were still unresolved at the time of its decision; therefore, the court of first instance (Québec Superior Court) was right in not staying its own procedure at this point in time.

[32] ibid paras 51–53.
[33] ibid paras 55–57.
[34] ibid paras 68–69.

iv. Summarising the Result under an Inadequate Regulatory Framework – What Micron Technology Inc c Hazan *Teaches Us about Designing Coordination*

Ultimately, the main outcome of this judgment boils down to granting the courts involved the flexibility to adapt to the requirements of each individual case, to engage in a consensual procedure, to apply test criteria in a comparable way in order to achieve the best possible use of judicial resources, whilst minimising costs for the parties involved, in a spirit of mutual trust and cooperation ('comity').

This somewhat disappointing result becomes better understandable when looking back in time in the next subsection, which shows the size of the challenge ahead for the EU legislator to resolve the predictable problems with conflicting claims in the EU.

B. The Painful Journey to Reach Comity – How Did They Get There?

It must be in the EU's interest to take a shortcut towards resolving the predictable problems that have been mentioned so far. Therefore, it should be instructive for us to take a closer look at how the same challenges have been addressed in Canada.

i. First Phase of the Canadian Approach: The 'Subclass Deference Model'

Looking back at the years before 2009, courts in Canada had used an approach that looks like a kind of 'self defence' against illegitimate over-demand, an approach that could also be employed by European countries as an initial solution if they continue to be left out in the cold by the European Commission. Scott Maidment summarised this as follows:

> With the enactment of class action legislation throughout the Canadian provinces, the commencement of multiple duplicative or overlapping national class actions had become commonplace. In many cases, duplicative class actions had been commenced by a consortium of class counsel acting in concert across provincial borders. In other cases, duplicative class actions were commenced by class action law firms acting in competition with one another. In either circumstance, each firm of class counsel may seek to maximize its own participation in the same action and thereby maximise its share of associated fees.[35]

As a lawyer, he specifies that when the profit motive for individual law firms is combined with an absence of effective forum selection rules, this encourages the commencement of duplicative national class actions that offer no marginal benefit to class members and encourage practices that create unnecessary chaos, confusion and cost.[36]

The courts struck back by adopting a 'subclass deference model' in response to disputes regarding the choice of forum. Thus, any court in which a national class action

[35] S Maidment, 'Exclusive Forum Selection in National Class Actions: A Common Issues Approach' [2009] *The Canadian Class Action Review* 133, 133–34.

[36] ibid 134, fn 3.

was brought would generally refuse to engage in comprehensive forum selection for the whole procedure. Instead, the court would generally 'defer' that part of the action to the superior court of another province that consists of the sub-class of persons residing in that other province. This 'deferential approach' produced disorder and unfairness, inefficiency, confusion and uncertainty for defendants and class members alike.[37] Legislative reform was not to be expected, as Canada's Constitution confers exclusive jurisdiction over the administration of justice within the provinces upon the provincial legislatures, in a formula that is comparable in spirit to the EU's split of legislative competencies between the EU and Member States. Article 81 of the Treaty on the Functioning of the European Union (TFEU), the only article in Chapter 3 'Judicial Cooperation in Civil Matters', which in its German version is at the same time the unofficial title of Article 81 in German text editions, reads:

1. The Union shall develop judicial cooperation in civil matters having cross-border implications, based on the principle of mutual recognition of judgments and of decisions in extrajudicial cases. Such cooperation may include the adoption of measures for the approximation of the laws and regulations of the Member States.
2. For the purposes of paragraph 1, the European Parliament and the Council, acting in accordance with the ordinary legislative procedure, shall adopt measures, particularly when necessary for the proper functioning of the internal market, aimed at ensuring:
   (a) the mutual recognition and enforcement between Member States of judgments and of decisions in extrajudicial cases;
   (b) the cross-border service of judicial and extrajudicial documents;
   (c) the compatibility of the rules applicable in the Member States concerning conflict of laws and of jurisdiction;
   (d) cooperation in the taking of evidence;
   (e) effective access to justice;
   (f) the elimination of obstacles to the proper functioning of civil proceedings, if necessary by promoting the compatibility of the rules on civil procedure applicable in the Member States;
   (g) *the development of alternative methods of dispute settlement*;[38]
   (h) support for the training of the judiciary and judicial staff.

And yet the Representative Actions Directive does not even mention this explicit and limited legislative competence in *procedural* matters. The Directive is meant to be based on an 'annex competence' to the competence of the Union for the harmonisation of *substantive* consumer protection law. Nevertheless, the Directive includes provisions on cross-border issues;[39] therefore, it may have exceeded the legislative powers that were

[37] ibid 134, 135–43; also reported in Woopen (n 8) 611.
[38] Emphasis added with respect to the last bullet of the conclusion of this piece in section V.
[39] Cross-border impacts come with: suspension or interruption of limitation periods (Directive, Art 16 and recital 65); a prohibition on admitting a settlement for court approval or approval by an administrative authority if there is any other ongoing representative action in front of the court or administrative authority of the same Member State regarding the same trader and regarding the same practice (Directive, Art 11 and Art 9(4)); a rule on conflicting actions in Art 5b(3a) ('cannot be represented in other representative actions nor bring an individual action'); a possibility for individual consumers concerned to accept or to refuse to be bound by a settlement approved by a court or administrative authority (Directive, Art 11(4), sentence 2); effects of final national court or administrative authority decisions establishing an infringement harming collective interests of consumers (Directive, Art 15 'effect of final decisions'); rules regarding orders by courts

bestowed upon the EU legislative bodies by the Member States, because the EU cannot have legislative powers exceeding what has been delegated to it by the Member States (ultra vires).[40] Such concerns will have to be taken into consideration not only by the European Court of Justice but also by the legislators, including at the EU level, as they attempt to head off the predictable collisions.

The lesson from Canada in this respect is that administrative arrangements among provincial superior courts ultimately cannot deprive a determined litigant of the right to pursue litigation in the forum of his choice. Thus, without either coordinated legislative action taken by all provinces or a constitutional amendment to transfer necessary powers to the federal Parliament, it was not possible to address this problem meaningfully in Canada through legislative or administrative reform.

Maidment suggested resolving this problem through application of a proper *contextual* application of the common law principles of *forum non conveniens* in identifying the issues truly common to various actions, and having them decided in the one forum closest to the location of parties and witnesses, evidence, factual matters and experience in applying the relevant substantive law. Common issues would be evidence related to the conduct and knowledge or duties of care of the defendants. Any issue that turns on the conduct or evidence of any particular individual plaintiff would be an individual issue and not a common issue – up to the place of residence of class members – with individual issues having to be determined without trial through some form of reference, private arbitration, summary procedure or settlement grid.[41] The tool to stop conflicting claims in jurisdictions less suitable for the common issues would be anti-suit injunctions.[42] But this proposed approach has apparently not caught on.

ii. Second Phase of the Canadian Approach: The Canadian Judicial Protocol for the Management of Multijurisdictional Class Actions – Cooperation and Comity

A more successful development was started by the Uniform Law Conference of Canada (ULCC) in 2004 with a 'National Class Actions Project', which published its first report at the ULCC's 2005 conference in Vancouver,[43] followed by a Supplementary Report by the Special Working Group on Multi-Jurisdictional Class Proceedings at the conference

and administrative authorities to defendants to submit evidence to support a representative action (Directive, Art 18); rules concerning the standing and authorisation of qualified entities to bring collective actions for redress in other Member States (Directive, Arts 6(1), 7(1), 4(6)) and the unresolved issue of which cross-border effects, ie res iudicata, lis pendens and international competence implications, 'domestic' actions, eg by a domestic ad hoc entity, may have against non-domestic defendants), and for several qualified entities to do so jointly in a single representative action, including if they are from different Member States (Directive, Art 6(2)–(3) and recital 31).

[40] 'Legal Tech for Justice, not for Profit' (n 13) 14–15.

[41] Maidment (n 35) 135, 143–53.

[42] ibid 150, 152.

[43] The Report of the Uniform Law Conference of Canada's Committee on the National Class and Related Interjurisdictional Issues: Background, Analysis, and Recommendations (Vancouver, BC, 9 March 2005) warned that the potential for chaos and confusion remains high unless the problem of duplicative class actions is resolved; available at https://ulcc-chlc.ca/ULCC/media/EN-Annual-Meeting-2005/Interjurisdictional-Class-Actions.pdf.

in Edmonton, Alberta, in 2006.[44] Following terrible confusion with conflicting collective cross-provincial-border claims,[45] it suggested creation of an on-line Canadian Class Proceedings Registry of all class action filings in each Canadian jurisdiction, for use by the public, counsel and courts, and various options and duties for the courts and plaintiffs to make choices, liaise and coordinate. Specific Guidelines Applicable to Court-to-Court Communications in Cross-Border Cases promulgated in the insolvency area by the American Law Institute were to be adopted by the courts hearing cases certified in relation to the same issues in multiple jurisdictions.

The coordination efforts between the provinces and the federal level proposed in those papers developed further slowly, resulting in the current respective rules to be followed and that meanwhile have been adopted by all Canadian provinces with slight variations, which can be found in Schedule A to the Judicial Protocol. From the Québec Superior Court Rules of Civil Procedure they can be partly paraphrased and summarised as follows:

> **Article 55 Documents accompanying the application**. The application [on the form published on the website of the Superior Court] is accompanied by a copy of all other applications for authorization to bring a class action dealing in whole or in part with the same subject matter and an attestation from the applicant or the applicant's lawyer indicating that the application will be entered in the national class action register. …
>
> [Failure to follow this rule or not to serve it on the adverse party at the same time gives the judge leeway to postpone the date of presentation of the application and order the application to remedy the failure.
>
> Within five days of filing, a copy of the application for authorisation to institute a class action must be registered in the registry of class actions (Article 56 and Article 573 of the Québec Code of Civil Procedure – chapter C-25-01). A settlement proposal ('Transaction' – Article 58) submitted for approval of the court needs to indicate the amounts that will be reimbursed to the *Fonds d'aide aux action collectives* if it contributed financial assistance to the representative, and every application of approval must be served on the *Fonds d'aide aux action collectives.*]
>
> **Article 59 Report on administration**. If a judgment orders the collective recovery of the claims made with individual payment of the members' claims, the special clerk or third person designated by the court must file with the court, after the time limit for members to file their claim has expired, a detailed report on its administration and give notice to the parties and the Fonds d'aide aux action collectives.
>
> **Article 60 Remaining balance**. If the report filed under section 59 mentions a remaining balance the representative, within 30 [days] after the report is filed, must present an application to the court to dispose of the amounts, giving notice of presentation to the special clerk or the third person designated by the court and to the Fonds d'aide aux action collectives, if applicable.[46]

[44] Available at https://classactionlitigation.com/Class_Actions_Supplementary_Report.pdf.

[45] See the impressive practical example of the Baycol litigation across the provinces of British Columbia, Saskatechwan, Manitoba, Ontario, Québec as well as Newfoundland and Labrador, laid out in the 2005 Report (n 41) in paras 10–12, and of the Vioxx litigation, ibid para 13.

[46] For an example of the reverse case where the lawyers of the claimant group had to pay back to the Fonds d'aide aux actions collectives the support they had received from it, see *Monique Charland c Hydro-Québec*, case no 27, Report 2020–2021 of the Fonds d'aide aux actions collectives, 17.

> **Article 61 Legal costs and fees.** When the Fonds d'aide aux action collectives has granted financial assistance, an application to determine the legal costs and the fees of the representative's lawyer, or to obtain the approval of a transaction [ie settlement] on fees, legal costs, or professional fees is served on the Fonds d'aide aux action collectives with notice of presentation.
>
> **Article 62 Multi-jurisdictional class action.** In the case of a prospective, authorized or certified class action having the same object as a prospective, authorized or certified class action instituted in 2 or more provinces, the court may, on application, direct the parties to apply the Canadian Judicial Protocol for the Management of Multijurisdictional Class Actions.

This framework offered to the courts involved for voluntary adoption in 'comity' is supported by the Canadian Bar Association (CBA), which has set up the National Class Action Database[47] for information about the existence and status of class actions across Canada, so that the public, counsel and courts need consult only one source for this information, and without cost to them. It comprises all class actions filed in Canada after 1 January 2007 and sent to the CBA. Once posted, a class action proceeding remains on the database unless and until it is dismissed as a class action by the court. Counsel who wish to have proceedings posted on the database must complete the Database Registration Form[48] and send it, along with the original pleadings and certification motion, to the CBA website Strictly speaking, however, this remains a primarily voluntary commitment on the part of class action counsel, thus the CBA cannot guarantee the exhaustiveness of the class actions listed or the accuracy of the information posted.

The Protocol also includes the possibility to terminate proceedings by means of a Multijurisdictional Class Settlement Approval to be granted by all the courts that are involved. The list of the formalities to be fulfilled for such a procedure extends over three pages (in two languages) of the Protocol (no 7, 8a–j, 9a–f, and 10–14), but an adequate means for holding a Settlement Hearing jointly is provided for by allowing for a video link or other means to permit all parties and all judges to participate in the hearings (no 10).

iii. Evaluation of the Procedure Under the Canadian Judicial Protocol for the Management of Multijurisdictional Class Actions

The Protocol with its coordination procedures and formalised steps, as well as the supporting infrastructure consisting of the CBA Registry and the tools for audiovisual conferencing between courts, appears to be working properly: counsel and courts agree which court will take the lead in establishing the evidence and the legal analysis, while being monitored in these efforts by the other courts that have been seised with the same matter and that have not terminated but only stayed their own proceedings while receiving regular updates on the progress in the leading court.[49]

[47] Available at www.cba.org/Publications-Resources/Class-Action-Database.

[48] Available at www.cba.org/CBAMediaLibrary/cba_na/PDFs/LLR/ClassActionForm2019.docx.

[49] Recent example of a staying order: *Ibarra c Corporation Cadillac Fairview limitée*, 2021 QCCS 5092 (CanLII) available at https://canlii.ca/t/jl7dv.

What the Protocol does not describe further is the infrastructure for the distribution of the compensation either agreed on by settlement or decided by court judgment. The Protocol just mentions in its section 'Settlement Approval' (paragraph no 8 lit j) that the address and phone number of the appointed 'Claims Administrator' for settlements need to be communicated, and Articles 55–62 of the Québec Superior Court Rules of Civil Procedure (see section III.B.ii) outline in their Article 59 the reporting duties of a 'special clerk or third person designated by the court' regarding his filing of group members' individual claims after their 'opting-in' period has expired.

C. Taking the Courts' Perspective: How to Cooperate and Decide Best

In the recent judgment in *Benamor c Air Canada*,[50] the Québec Court of Appeal had reason to discuss the size of the class to be admitted – two judges voting for a limitation of the class to all residents of Canada, and the dissenting rapporteur of the case favouring admission of a worldwide group of class members. Joseph Benamor had objected to additional payments to be made for using flight credits – bought as several coupons called 'Air Canada Consumer Flight Pass' – either later than these coupons had been declared valid or for their use by different persons. His case has received funding from the *Fonds d'aide aux action collectives*.[51]

i. Possibility of Worldwide Actions

All three judges concur that it would in principle be possible to include non-residents of Canada in a class in a Québec class actions procedure,[52] even though this has never been done before in a consumer law case, and only parsimoniously in securities cases, and even this was primarily for the simple purpose of obtaining court approval for a settlement that had already been reached among the parties, and that with the exclusion of securities bought on US markets.[53]

Starting from the obiter considerations of Judge LeBel in a case decided in 2009,[54] the majority in *Benamor c Air Canada* deem it justified to use similar considerations with respect to the adequacy of setting up a worldwide class. Judge LeBel wrote in 2009:

> [56] In addition to its conclusions of law, the Quebec Court of Appeal seems to have had reservations or concerns about the creation of classes of claimants from two or more provinces. We need not consider this question in detail. However, the need to form such national classes does seem to arise occasionally. The formation of a national class can lead to the delicate problem of creating subclasses within it and determining what legal system will apply to them. In the context of such proceedings, the court hearing an application also has a duty to

[50] *Benamor c Air Canada*, 2020 QCCA 1597 (CanLII), available at https://canlii.ca/t/jbvm9.

[51] Case no 12 p 11 of the most recent report of the *Fonds d'aide aux actions collectives*, available at www.faac.justice.gouv.qc.ca/doc/RapportAnnuel2020–2021.pdf.

[52] *Benamor c Air Canada* (n 50) paras 75, 116.

[53] ibid para 105.

[54] *Canada Post Corp v Lépine*, 2009 SCC 16 (CanLII), [2009] 1 SCR 549, available at https://canlii.ca/t/22zdq, paras 56–57.

ensure that the conduct of the proceeding, the choice of remedies and the enforcement of the judgment effectively take account of each group's specific interests, and it must order them to ensure that clear information is provided.

[57] As can be seen in this appeal, the creation of national classes also raises the issue of relations between equal but different superior courts in a federal system in which civil procedure and the administration of justice are under provincial jurisdiction. This case shows that the decisions made may sometimes cause friction between courts in different provinces. This of course often involves problems with communications or contacts between the courts and between the lawyers involved in such proceedings. However, the provincial legislatures should pay more attention to the framework for national class actions and the problems they present. More effective methods for managing jurisdictional disputes should be established in the spirit of mutual comity that is required between the courts of different provinces in the Canadian legal space. It is not this Court's role to define the necessary solutions. However, it is important to note the problems that sometimes seem to arise in conducting such actions.

ii. Proportionality as a Requirement

Based on these thoughts for coordination at the national level, the majority in the *Benamor c Air Canada* judgment sum up the decisive points for consideration as

> the difficulties of relationships between the different courts involved, of the choice of suitable remedies and of enforcement, of the ability of the class representative to properly move the action forward and to communicate clearly with all involved, along with the 'complexification' of the file.[55]

In order to deal with this, they deem, as in any civil procedure, 'proportionality' to remain a key consideration for the authorising judge to make decisions, particularly on the group to be described as being bound by a future judgment:

> There is no doubt that an application for authorization is not immune from the principles that underlie the procedural system, so that such an application and the proceeding it gives rise to are subject to Article 18 CCP,[56] whether it concerns the description of the proposed group, the conditions for authorization, the notification of members, the replacement of the representative, the review of a common issue, the conduct of the trial on the merits, the approval of a settlement or any other step provided for in the Code of Civil Procedure. Consequently, proportionality, by the very nature of things, will be measured within the procedural edifice erected by the legislator.[57]

[55] *Benamor c Air Canada* (n 50) para 102; author's translation as this judgment is not available in English.

[56] Art 18 CCP provides:

> The parties to a proceeding must observe the principle of proportionality and ensure that their actions, their pleadings, including their choice of an oral or a written defense, and the means of proof they use are proportionate, in terms of the cost and time involved, to the nature and complexity of the matter and the purpose of the application.
>
> Judges must likewise observe the principle of proportionality in managing the proceedings they are assigned, regardless of the stage at which they intervene. They must ensure that the measures and acts they order or authorize are in keeping with the same principle, while having regard to the proper administration of justice.

[57] *Benamor c Air Canada* (n 50) para 103; author's translation as this judgment is not available in English.

Catherine Piché, in her report for the Ministry of Justice of the Province of Québec on potential reforms of the régime for class actions in Québec, explicitly recommended the introduction of the principle of proportionality either as a general principle, into title III of book IV that deals with the Québec Code of Civil Procedure on class actions, or even as a fifth criterion for the authorisation of class actions.[58]

iii. Towards a Dynamic Interpretation of the Brussels I (Recast) Regulation

As long as the coordination mechanism proposed is not in place, the Canadian Phase I solution is the only viable alternative option that could be replicated in the EU. This means that recognition of foreign judgments will depend on the degree of judicial cooperation that is truly achieved within the EU. Canadian courts and legislators have recommended making the degree of consolidation of collective actions to be realised dependent on the effective support that exists for implementing such consolidation ('reality check'). This looks like a recipe for a way forward for the EU:

- As long as no cross-border coordination mechanism is in place nor properly defined, the Canadian Phase I solution must be maintained. This means that national courts are bound to limit the ambition of their decisions to beneficiaries domiciled in their own territory, excluding any effects on residents of other Member States.
- As soon as a well-defined coordination mechanism for collective actions similar to Canada's Phase II is in place, cross-border recognition could be decided upon, taking into account the proportionality criterion developed in the *Benamor c Air Canada* judgment. This should start no earlier, though, than when this procedure can be exercised via an IT infrastructure that relieves the courts of paper-based work and is capable of recording the essential key data of the individual beneficiaries at such an early stage that conflict resolution in ways other than resolution by the court – namely before ombuds offices or public authorities – is still possible, thus preventing lengthy and expensive court proceedings from being the only way forward.

iv. Following the Ontario Class Proceedings Act

An extremely helpful approach can be seen in the Ontario provincial law, which sets up a *superiority* requirement. It demands that the class action procedural vehicle be *preferable to all reasonably available means of resolving the class members' claims*, including, as applicable, a quasi-judicial or administrative proceeding, the case management of claims in a civil proceeding, or any remedial scheme or programme outside of legal proceedings.[59] This coincides with the reading we have already given to the criterion of proportionality, and is at the same time a smooth transition to the next subsection.

[58] C Piché, *Perspectives de réforme de l'action collective au Québec – Rapport préparé à l'attention du ministère de la Justice du Québec* (2019) 5, 'les coûts de l'instance (notamment les honoraires d'avocats souvent pharamineux) sont préoccupants toutefois'; and ibid 60, 71–76 (available at www.justice.gouv.qc.ca/fileadmin/user_upload/contenu/documents/Fr__francais_/centredoc/rapports/ministere/RA_Piche_Ref_Action_coll_Qc.pdf).

[59] US Chamber Institute for Legal Reform, 'Response handed in to the call for public comment in relation to the Ministère de la Justice's review of the Québec class action regime' (consultation period 1 June to 31 July 2021) para 28.

IV. How to Do Better – Taking the Hodgian Perspective When Getting the Legislators on Board

Delivering redress is what Christopher Hodges has always strived to support and achieve.[60] His extensive research has shown that no class action in court can operate as quickly, effectively and at such low cost as regulatory redress and ombuds-based solutions. The often huge costs of the first instance in court, particularly those of the lawyers, have also been an important aspect in the reflections in Québec on potential reforms.[61]

Against the background of the Québec experience, putting collective court action into a subsidiary role should be an absolute 'must' for EU Member States as legislators when defining the requirements for admitting under their respective national laws of civil procedure the conduct of a representative action. Whether the criteria to do this will be called proportionality, preferability, desirability or superiority of a collective action does not matter – the important idea is that the collective court action as a very burdensome, slow, complicated and resource-intensive instrument will be used only as a last resort. And Member States can request this because defining the conditions for collective court action is their prerogative according to Article 7(3) of the Representative Actions Directive.

V. Conclusion for the EU and its Member States: What Should Be Done Now

The experience of Canada provides substantial evidence that can instruct us as we grapple in Europe with the issues that are the predictable result of badly thought-through legislation in Brussels. To attenuate the jurisdictional chaos and irresponsible delay in obtaining justice for the citizens concerned, urgent relief is required in national and finally EU legislative procedures. The individual Member States are hereby invited to make use of the transposition of the Representative Actions Directive in a forward-looking way, as follows:

- *Specialised courts* in all Member States need to be empowered to –
  - *authorise* representative actions *and coordinate* with the courts and administrative authorities of the same and other Member States on conflicting/overlapping representative actions, particularly on those with *cross-border* ambitions (see further below); and
  - coordinate on potential cross-border Settlement Approval hearings to permit all parties and all judges to participate in *joint hearings by video link* or other means. The 2018 reform in Québec instituted for the district of Montréal a group

[60] C Hodges and S Voet, *Delivering Collective Redress – New Technologies* (Hart Publishing, 2018) esp 281, 282, 301.

[61] Piché (n 58).

of 10 judges overseeing authorisation of class actions[62] – which looks like a sensible approach to follow.

- Clarification is needed in national Member State legislation that *no automatic recognition* will be granted to decisions in collective actions for redress from other Member States.
- Instead, recognition can only be granted against a defendant in the enforcement country if a specific kind of *exequatur* has been obtained, the Latin '*exequatur*' meaning 'it may be executed, enforced' – a decision in court to recognise the decision by a different (foreign) court.
- As a rule, such recognition should require that the foreign court procedure has previously been *declared acceptable by the NCP/Coordinating Court* in the enforcement country *under the future EU Protocol for the Management of Multi-Jurisdictional Representative Actions*. This Protocol should be created to coordinate within the EU along the lines of the Canadian Judicial Protocol for the Management of Multi-Jurisdictional Class Actions, that is, organising the coordination between NCPs/Coordinating Courts about conflicting/overlapping representative actions.
  - Each NCP/Coordinating Court that has been seised with an application for a representative action with *intended cross-border effects* (defendant cross-border; intended cross-border opt-ins; intended recognition of declaratory judgments) needs to ensure that the foreign action will adequately protect the rights and interests of the NCP's country's residents, and that the foreign qualified entity offering a cross-border opt-in is in a position to properly represent the NCP's country's residents (following the example of Article 577 CCP).
  - A *proportionality test* should be a further criterion for the recognition of a foreign representative action as acceptable: the qualified entity wishing to offer cross-border opt-in should *demonstrate* to the NCP/Coordinating Court that there is no other means available to potential beneficiaries in that NCP's country to obtain an economically reasonable outcome. This proportionality test should explicitly be required to strike a balance between speed, amount, cost and ease of truly receiving compensation rather than just getting a procedure running. And here is the integration of Christopher Hodges' thinking that is so urgently required: this comparison should explicitly include regulatory redress and ombuds/ADR solutions, both of which are bound to be quicker, cheaper and easier for consumers to obtain effective redress. The Coordinating Court should take its time while awaiting the results of such procedures and simply stay for that relatively short time the procedure for the recognition of a foreign representative action intending to take residents of the Coordinating Court's country on board.
- Particular attention will be required in drafting the *EU Protocol for the Management of Multi-Jurisdictional Representative Actions* regarding the contents of the notice to all potential beneficiaries for an *EU-wide settlement*, which could look like the description of what is required for that purpose in the section 'Settlement Approval'

[62] Zakaib and Saint-Onge (n 15) 9; Piché (n 58) 61: 'Projet-pilote du Groupe des 10 juges de la Cour, au sein d'une Chambre des actions collectives restructurée'.

of the Canadian Judicial Protocol for the Management of Multi-Jurisdictional Class Actions (paragraph no 8 lit a–j).

- As already mentioned (section II), any kind of efficient procedure to coordinate overlapping or conflicting representative actions requires *IT support* that truly empowers the EU's NCPs to communicate with the courts and administrative units involved regarding the plethora of information to be captured and processed in cross-border mass claims. The tool meant to fulfil this task in the future has been announced by the Commission as currently being developed under the name 'REACT' (Representative Actions Communication Tool).
- A final proposal, the second part of proposals made earlier, is repeated as follows:[63] the EU and Member States should quickly create in unison state-of-the-art *IT tools* to capture the data of *potential beneficiaries, including addresses and bank account numbers*. The nucleus for such IT support exists in the form of the so-called 'Self-Test' on the Commission website[64] for Online Dispute Resolution (ODR). And looking back to section III.B.i and Article 81(2)(g) TFEU, the EU does have a *particular legislative competence on which it could convincingly base such efforts*. The particular charm of this approach is that it embraces for a second time the results of the research conducted by Christopher Hodges: resolving conflicts, with a clear priority on quick, easy and cheap redress, should best be promoted by a single access point on the Internet from which an escalation to a mass claim in court would be possible, but possible only as a last resort if less expensive and quicker ways to provide redress have failed.

[63] See section II, n 13: 'Legal Tech for Justice, Not for Profit' (n 13) 9–11 and 12 (graphical presentation).

[64] See at https://ec.europa.eu/consumers/odr/main/?event=main.home.selfTest – also quoted and described in 'Legal Tech for Justice, Not for Profit' (n 13) 11.

12

Deadweight Loss and Collective Redress in Competition Law

FRANZISKA WEBER

It may not be necessary for us all to become comparative lawyers and to research unfamiliar disciplines, but some humility may help in recognising that answers can lie outside's one's experience, and that what is needed here is opportunities for free exchange of ideas, as long as someone is going to try to fit all the pieces together.

(C Hodges, 'Collective Redress in Europe: The New Model' (2000))

I. Introduction

This chapter combines two topics that lie at the heart of Chris's research topics: consumer compensation and collective redress. It furthermore ties into his time as a solicitor specialising in, amongst other things, competition law. In the light of Chris's continuously expressed dislike of the deterrence theory, this contribution argues from the compensation perspective, and remarks on deterrence are withheld until the conclusion. Competition law serves to prohibit and/or, if too late, compensate for harm resulting from behaviour that can be linked back to the availability of undesirable market power by a cartel or monopoly (for the remainder, this contribution will focus on the case example of a cartel). Market power leads to two effects: one distributional and the other allocative, if you wish a price and a quantity effect.[1] In other words, a cartel sells fewer units at higher prices than would be available in a competitive market. Consumers therefore first of all pay too much for the units they (still) purchase. Furthermore, a certain number of consumers who would have bought the product at the price but for the cartel no longer acquire the product. A so-called 'deadweight loss' (DWL) emerges. Traditionally, legal scholars are more concerned about redistribution than about the DWL, and many contributions focus on how consumers can obtain compensation for the cartel overcharge that they immediately suffered or that previous buyer levels suffered and passed on to them (for the remainder of the contribution, let us assume that the supply chain is

[1] M Motta, *Competition Policy – Theory and Practice* (Cambridge University Press, 2004) 40.

short and that the cartel sells directly to the final consumers).[2] Such compensation claims do not work perfectly yet. However, from a dogmatic legal point of view, approaching a quantification exercise for harm suffered due to a cartel overcharge is quite straightforward. This is very different when it comes to the second damage component that lies in the focus of this contribution: the DWL. For economists the major concern is the DWL, that is, the units that were not purchased due to the competition law infringement. Grasping this concept from a dogmatic legal point of view is far more challenging than ensuring compensation for payment of a price mark-up resulting from cartel activity. Competition law enforcement, if considerate of economic insights, needs to ensure that the tortfeasors also face liability for causing the DWL. Otherwise, full compensation as the overarching goal of European competition law enforcement is not achieved. This contribution will delve into the potential that collective redress has for this matter.

II. Claiming the Deadweight Loss by Way of Collective Redress

A. The Economic Importance of the Deadweight Loss

To explain the DWL, let us start by looking at the welfare situation of competitive markets. The simplified graph in Figure 12.1 displays the static outcome in a situation of perfect competition.

Figure 12.1 A market with perfect competition

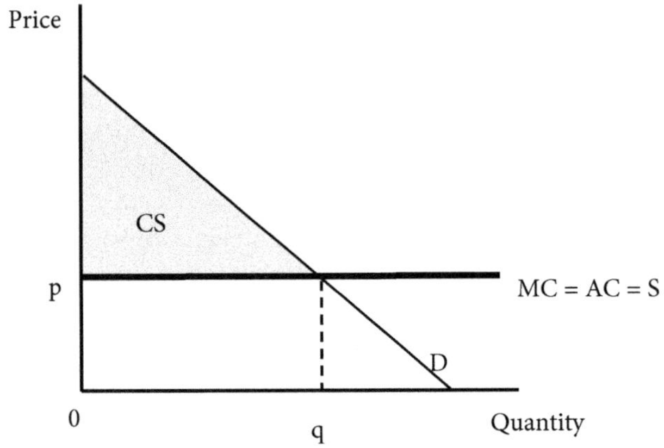

[2] R Van den Bergh, 'Private Enforcement of European Competition Law and the Persisting Collective Action Problem' (2013) 20(1) *Municipal Journal* 12; F Weber, 'A chain reaction – or the necessity of collective redress mechanisms for consumers in competition cases' (2018) 25(2) *Municipal Journal* 208; see, for an estimation, U Laitenberger and F Smuda, 'Estimating consumer damages in cartel cases' (2015) 11(4) *Journal of Competition Law & Economics* 955; G Gaudin and F Weber, 'Antitrust Damages, Consumer Harm, and Consumer Collective Redress' (2021) 12(5) *Journal of European Competition Law & Practice* 370. The latter article already touches upon the matter of the DWL as an additional argument to ensure compensation for the price effect. This contribution goes into more depth on the potential of collective redress to enable a remedy for the DWL as such.

In Figure 12.1,[3] each consumer is modelled as having a fixed reservation price for a certain product, that is, the highest price he or she is willing to pay.[4] This determines the shape of the demand curve (D). Those consumers whose reservation price equals the price at which a product is available in a given market are in principle indifferent as between buying and not buying. All the consumers whose reservation price is below that price do not buy. And, finally, all those consumers whose reservation price is above the price that emerges in a market are gaining in utility. They would have paid even more than the price at hand. Therefore, the so-called consumer surplus (CS) emerges. It is calculated in the following way, namely, by analysing the difference between the consumer's reservation price for a product and the actual price he or she paid. Now, what happens to overall welfare when a cartel is operating in a market?

For the sake of simplicity let us assume a market situation where a cartel sells a cartelised product directly to final consumers.[5] Hence, in this relationship there are only two layers (see Figure 12.2).

Figure 12.2 A cartelised market

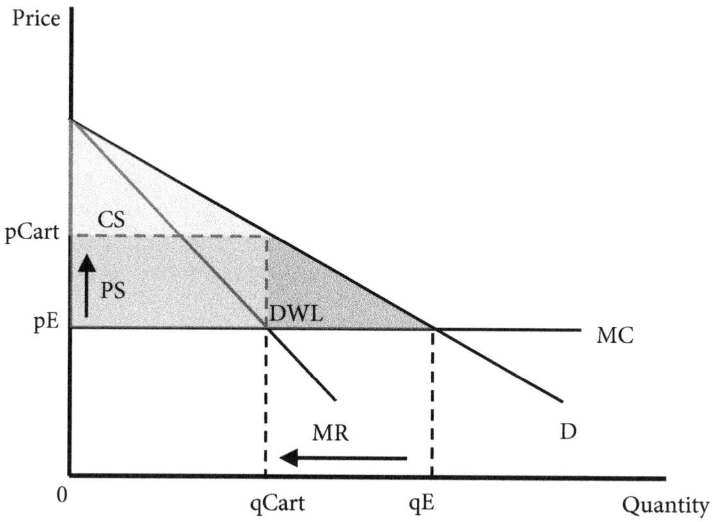

In Figure 12.2,[6] the outcome of a cartel's pricing behaviour is contrasted with the result obtained in a perfectly competitive market.[7] When optimising the price – just

[3] Own illustration of the static result of perfect competition, when producers face constant and identical marginal costs and no fixed costs. The supply curve (S) is horizontal and marginal costs (MC) equal average costs (AC).

[4] Obviously, there are a number of challenges regarding the quantification and the comparability of this reservation price but they lie beyond the scope of this contribution.

[5] It could likewise be a monopolist that sells a product directly to final consumers at the monopoly rather than the equilibrium price.

[6] Own illustration is based on M Motta, *Competition Policy – Theory and Practice* (Cambridge University Press, 2004) 40.

[7] In reality, markets in the absence of a cartel do not show all characteristics of perfect competition. However, this figure serves mainly to illustrate the emerging damage components.

as for a monopolist it pays off for the cartel to sell a lower quantity at a higher price – the equilibrium price (pE) does not emerge where demand D and the marginal cost curve MC intersect, but a cartelised price (pCart) emerges where MC and the marginal revenue curve MR intersect. This implies that a reduced quantity qCart is sold. This leads to two effects. A share of what would have been CS at an equilibrium price level is turned into producer surplus (PS). Furthermore, aside from this redistributive effect, the DWL emerges, which is an allocative effect: sales are lost. Buyers, who in this example are immediately the final consumers,[8] are, therefore, harmed in two ways by such an infringement of competition law. First, purchases that they made during the infringement period (eg, while a cartel was ongoing) were made at inflated prices. This shift from CS to PS is typically referred to as the 'cartel overcharge' in legal terminology. Second, the DWL captures the benefits (the utility) that buyers would have derived from all the purchases they did not undertake because of the infringement. This is also called the 'lost consumption effect'.[9] It captures the harm of those buyers who refrained from purchasing (or reduced their purchase volume) during the infringement period precisely due to the inflated prices, but who would have bought (more) without the infringement. Hence, as a group, consumers will typically reduce the quantity they purchase in the light of a price increase.[10] Some consumers would have bought the product or service in question at the non-cartelised price but, however, not at the cartelised price. This also negatively affects the size of the consumer surplus.[11] The cartel is, therefore, not only liable for the harm resulting from having overcharged consumers, that is, the price mark-up that consumers had to pay because of the cartel; it is also liable for the harm emerging from lost purchases. The DWL is not negligible in amount.[12] For consumers as a group it may even be the larger damage component compared to the harm resulting from the cartel overcharge.[13]

B. Quantification Challenges and their Negative Effect on Individual Cartel Damage Claims in the EU

At European level an important legislative initiative in the context of competition law concerned the EU Antitrust Damages Directive (Damages Directive), which was

[8] But a comparable effect emerges for final consumers if they are at the end of a long supply chain too.

[9] RBB Economics/Cuatrecasas Gonçalves Pereira, 'Study on the Passing-on of Overcharges', European Commission Pass-on Study 2016, 13.

[10] This is the classical output effect that comes with a price effect that is only missing if the price elasticity of demand is completely non-elastic (and hence no consumer, in the light of the price increase in question, would switch to a different product and/or stop buying).

[11] Comparing the extreme scenarios of Figure 12.1 and Figure 12.2: what is now CS, PS and DWL would have been all CS under perfect competition.

[12] MA Han, MP Schinkel and J Tuinstra, 'The Overcharge as a Measure for Antitrust Damages' (2008) Amsterdam Center for Law & Economics Working Paper 2008-08; CR Leslie, 'Antitrust Damages and Deadweight Loss' (2006) 51 *Antitrust Bulletin* 521.

[13] See G Gaudin and F Weber, 'Antitrust Damages, Consumer Harm, and Consumer Collective Redress' (2021) 12(5) *Journal of European Competition Law & Practice* 370, 373.

enacted in December 2014 after almost a decade of consultations, with an implementation period running until 27 December 2016.[14] The Damages Directive regulates a number of damage components in considerable detail (in particular the overcharge and pass-on), but makes no reference to the DWL for the (final) buyer level.[15] What about accompanying and preparatory documents? The Pass-on Study of 2016 deals with the 'lost consumption effect' on a very superficial level with reference to its missing importance in litigation.[16] The 2019 Guidelines do not explain it.[17] The explanations in the proposal for a Damages Directive mention the terms 'material' and 'immaterial' damage.[18] The DWL, as in the utility consumers never enjoyed, is typically classified as 'non-material' rather than 'material' damage. This category of harm is in general more challenging to compensate. Also, normative considerations as to whether non-material harm should be compensated at all are voiced more often.[19] The Damages Directive does not seem to preclude claiming compensation for the DWL; however, it also does not facilitate it by way of stipulating any provision that specifically deals with it. After all, it is also a general principle of European law that non-material damage can be claimed.[20] The Damages Directive puts special emphasis on the necessity to fully compensate consumers, to create neither over- nor under-compensation.[21] This can be linked back to question of whether the DWL should, therefore, receive compensation. As we have just seen in the economic explanation, strictly speaking, the attainment of full compensation can only be ensured for the consumer side if the consumers are compensated for the overcharge they paid and if their lost consumption finds some compensation. It is, furthermore, noteworthy that whereas the Damages Directive regulates some aspects of quantification in detail, for others the responsibility is left to the Member States. In general, the topic of 'causation' – and with that on questions of causation in law, like adequacy, etc – is to be handled according to national law.[22] Hence, to what

[14] Directive 2014/104/EU of 5 December 2014 of the European Parliament and of the Council of 26 November 2014 on certain rules governing actions for damages under national laws for infringements of the competition law provisions of the Member States and of the European Union [2014] OJ L349/1.

[15] However, the Directive does stipulate that anyone can claim compensation: see U Schwalbe, 'Lucrum Cessans und Schäden durch Kartelle bei Zulieferern, Herstellern von Komplementärgütern sowie weiteren Parteien' (2017) 5 *Neue Zeitschrift für Kartellrecht* 157, 163; C Heinze, *Schadensersatz im Unionsprivatrecht* (Mohr Siebeck, 2017) 218.

[16] Pass-on Study (n 9) 13.

[17] Communication from the Commission of 9 August 2019 – Guidelines for national courts on how to estimate the share of over-charge which was passed on to the indirect purchaser C/2019/4899 [2019] OJ C267/07.

[18] Proposal for a Directive of the European Parliament and of the Council on certain rules governing actions for damages under national law for infringements of the competition law provisions of the Member States and of the European Union, COM/2013/0404 final – 2013/0185 (COD) 13.

[19] C Alexander, *Schadensersatz und Abschöpfung im Lauterkeits- und Kartellrecht* (Mohr Siebeck, 2010) 171: 'das deutsche Recht ist "misstrauisch"' ('German law is sceptical').

[20] Heinze (n 15).

[21] Recital 3 et seq and Art 1(1) first sentence and Art 3, Damages Directive; the antitrust damages regimes in the European Member States were already geared towards this goal before the implementation of the Directive, see BJ Rodger, M Sousa Ferro, and F Marcos, 'A panacea for Competition Law damages actions in the EU? A comparative view of the implementation of the EU Antitrust Damages Directive in sixteen Member States' (2019) 26(4) *Municipal Journal* 480, 498.

[22] See recital 11, Damages Directive.

extent compensation claims concerning the DWL could ultimately pass the causation standard would, in any event, be for the Member States to determine. Obviously, the power of the Member States is limited by the boundaries set by the Damages Directive. In particular the effectiveness principle should be considered, but also more specifically for this case the full compensation principle. So far, compensating for the DWL is not a priority in the Member States. German law is, for instance, very hesitant to compensate for harm resulting from lost consumption in general.[23] Furthermore, there are specific challenges regarding standing and proof. After all we are discussing a transaction that has never occurred, but that would have occurred if not for the infringement. The challenges concern identifying consumers who would have bought, how much they would have bought and also what they actually did as an alternative. Furthermore, in the light of the principle of full compensation, consumers should only be put in the position they would have been in but for the infringement; they should not be worse off, but neither should they be better off. Hence, if they found a rather good substitute, this would also need to be considered in assessing their actual utility loss. In other words, under certain conditions, compensating consumers for their full utility loss would be over-compensation – for example if they bought the product at a higher price elsewhere, but not at as high a price as the cartelised product price. Did they switch to a product of lower quality? Did they buy a substitute product, and how much less utility did that mean for them? Here, the rules of damages law take effect in full. Indeed, Haucap and Stürmer propose differentiating between three situations when it comes to the allocation effect:

1. Could the consumer buy the goods from the cartel's competitors?
2. Could the consumer substitute the goods with a less preferred alternative?
3. Did the consumer completely forgo the purchases?[24]

Certainly, if there are no good alternatives available, the consumer's loss is likely to be adequately reflected by the full DWL triangle as exemplified in Figure 12.2.[25] The assessment is further complicated by the possible existence of umbrella effects. These are important in markets where the scope of the cartel is not total or over-arching. Competition research, but also litigation,[26] is indeed increasingly aware of the overall

[23] FW Bulst, *Schadensersatzansprüche der Marktgegenseite im Kartellrecht* (Nomos, 2006) 306; G Meessen, *Der Anspruch auf Schadensersatz bei Verstößen gegen EU-Kartellrecht* (Mohr Siebeck. 2011) 403; FW Bulst, 'Zum Problem der Schadensabwälzung und seiner Analyse durch das KG in "Transportbeton"' in W Möschel and F Bien (eds), *Kartellrechtsdurchsetzung durch private Schadensersatzklagen?* (Nomos, 2010) 225, 228: 'Zurückhaltung vieler europäischer Rechtsordnungen' ('hesitation of many European legal orders'); H Schweitzer, 'Kartellschadensersatz – rechtlicher Rahmen' in K Hüschelrath et al (eds), *Schadensermittlung und Schadensersatz bei Hardcore-Kartellen. Ökonomische Methoden und rechtlicher Rahmen* (Nomos, 2012) 39, 67; WH Roth '§ 33a' in W Jaeger et al, *Frankfurter Kommentar zum Kartellrecht* (Dr Otto Schmidt KG, 93 Lieferung 04.2019) para 68.

[24] J Haucap and T Stühmeier, 'Wie hoch sind durch Kartelle verursachte Schäden: Antworten aus Sicht der Wirtschaftstheorie' [2008] *Wirtschaft und Wettbewerb* 413, 421: 'Erstens kann der Konsument das Gut von Kartellaußenseitern beziehen, zweitens kann er das Gut durch eine weniger präferierte Alternative substituieren, und drittens kann er ganz auf den Kauf verzichten.'

[25] See on this Oxera (2009) *Quantifying antitrust damages: Towards non-binding guidance for courts* 100: 'When there are no second-best alternative products, or these products are substantially inferior to the cartelised product, customers bear a loss equal to, or close to, the triangle.' See https://ec.europa.eu/competition/antitrust/actionsdamages/quantification_study.pdf.

[26] See the exemplary cases of Judgment of the Court (Fifth Chamber), judgment of 5 June 2014; Case C-557/12 *Kone AG and Others v ÖBB-Infrastruktur AG* ECLI:EU:C:2014:1317.

dynamics of cartels in markets.[27] Umbrella effects concern the situation in which a cartel's remaining competitors also do not stick to the prices they were charging in the situation before the cartel was formed, but precisely because of the cartel – under the umbrella of the cartel – they also raise their prices above the previous level. Applying this back to the situation at hand, we can see that for consumers who purchased the goods from a competitor instead of from the cartel, yet again at elevated prices, there is additional harm.[28]

Hence, from a dogmatic legal point of view, the classification of harm resulting from the DWL is a major challenge in European and Member State law. Therefore, the actual quantification challenge has not really been embraced yet. Economics convey a rather optimistic picture when it comes to determining the quantity of the DWL: the mathematical tools, if certain parameters of a market are known, enable economists to determine how large the DWL is for a group of consumers.[29] But note the term 'group'. Whereas quantifying the overall DWL is regarded as feasible (based on a number of defensible assumptions), extrapolating the loss incurred by each individual consumer might be more difficult. This leads us on to exploring the link between compensating the DWL and collective redress enabling compensation for a group, rather than for an individual consumer, in more depth.

C. The Potential of Collective Redress

i. An Inspiring Example: Chile

In 2019, a Chilean court for the first time awarded compensation for the DWL.[30] This competition law case was concerned with collusion among pharmaceutical companies. The pharmacy chains Cruz Verde, Salcobrand and FASA had colluded between December 2007 and March 2008 to artificially increase the prices of at least 206 drugs, most of them requiring prescriptions. Among the motives for this artificial price increase by way of collusion was the desire to compensate the lost margins of a preceding price war. The Tribunal de Defensa de la Libre Competencia (TDLC) found this infringement and imposed the legal maximum in fines.[31] The duration of the cartel came to an end

[27] R Inderst, F Maier-Rigaud and U Schwalbe, 'Umbrella Effects' (2014) 10 *Journal of Competition Law & Economics* 739.

[28] R Inderst and S Thomas, *Schadensersatz bei Kartellverstößen* (Fachmedien Otto Schmidt KG, 2018) 34, 71 f: 'Es ist bedeutsam, inwieweit es Substitute gibt, wie die Wertschätzung der Nachfrager für diese ist und ob es bei Kartellaußenseitern zu Preisschirmeffekten kommt.' Haucap and Stühmeier (n 24) 421: 'Der allokative Effizienzverlust hängt auch hier wieder von der Anzahl der Kartellmitglieder und der Außenseiter ab, da den Nachfragern durch den sog. *Umbrella Effect* auch dadurch ein Schaden entstehen kann, dass die Kartellaußenseiter in Reaktion auf den höheren Kartellpreis auch ihren (nicht kartellierten) Preis erhöhen.'

[29] MW Havens, MF Koehn and MA Williams, 'Consumer Welfare Loss: The Unawarded Damages in Antitrust Suits' (1990) 15 *University of Dayton Law Review* 457, 463; DC Hjelmfelt and CD Strother Jr, 'Antitrust Damages for Consumer Welfare Loss' (1991) 39 *Cleveland State Law Review* 505, 510; see, for a calculation, MP Schinkel, 'Illegale winsten en efficiëntieschade als gevolg van kartelafspraken in de Nederlandse bouw: een toelichting op de Zembla-uitzending "Afrekenen met de bouw"', Amsterdam Center for Law & Economics (ACLE) (2006).

[30] See C-1940-2013, judgment of 17 December 2019, 10º Juzgado Civil de Santiago.

[31] See TDLC, Sentencia No 119/2012 of 31 January 2012.

precisely because of the investigations by the Chilean competition authority. Insights on damage quantification can be drawn from a Supreme Court judgment, which upheld TDLC's decision,[32] and follow-on damages litigation in the civil court.[33] Given that the medication was only available on prescription, substitute products were basically not available. Thinking in terms of the three categories of consumer behaviour identified earlier, this means that rather than buying a substitute or medication of lower quality, some consumers had to abstain from buying altogether. In terms of price elasticity of demand for this particular product we likewise see that there is a low elasticity. We could therefore expect that many consumers would indeed still buy this product at a cartelised price, leading to a high redistributive and a low allocative effect. The Supreme Court judgment indeed asserted the market power of the respective companies at 92 per cent and confirmed the existence of harm as such.[34] It referred to the overcharge.[35] The price increase partly went beyond 50 per cent. The additional gross benefit of the cartelists was calculated to be \$27,000,000,000 (€29,074,665[36]).[37] The Court, furthermore, recognised that despite the low price elasticity of demand, an undefined number of consumers had had to withdraw from buying the products due to the price increase. This effect necessarily accompanies every artificial price increase, in the Supreme Court's view. Hence, referring to the Supreme Court judgment of 2012, the claimants saw scope for claiming *damnum emergens*, the overcharge, and to claim compensation for the lost consumption effect.[38] In the judgment of 2019, the 10° Juzgado Civil de Santiago ultimately awarded both damage components.[39] To that end, the court determined two groups of consumers: Group 1 consisted of the consumers who had paid an increased price between 1 January 2007 and 31 March 2008; Group 2 consisted of the consumers who had abstained from buying the medication due to the price increase. The calculation resulted in the compensatory amount of \$1,736,961,314 (€1,895,570.87) for Group 1. For Group 2 the lost consumption effect amounted to \$284,916,956 (EUR 311,069.03). The court in essence followed an expert report submitted by the claimants' side. That expert report contained two calculations:[40] a conservative calculation, resulting in total damages of roughly 2,021 million pesos, which the court followed in its judgment; and a less conservative calculation, resulting in more extensive total harm of circa 6,945 million pesos. The difference between the two calculation methods boils down to the

[32] Supreme Court, Rol No 2578-2012, approved TDLS's decision on 7 September 2012.

[33] See C-1940-2013 (n 30).

[34] See Supreme Court judgment, septuagésimo sexto. On this TDLC, Sentencia No 119/2012, centésimo nonagésimo octavo: potentially the whole Chilean population is affected by this cartel.

[35] See Supreme Court judgment, considerando nonagésimo, párrafo décimo.

[36] See, for conversion ratio, www.xe.com/currencyconverter/convert/?Amount=27&From=CLP&To=EUR, accessed on 9 November 2021.

[37] Thanks to the low price elasticity of demand, see Supreme Court judgment, decimo octavo.

[38] See Demanda SERNAC (ie the writ of summons by the Servicio Nacional del Consumidor, the Chilean consumer agency acting on behalf of the consumers) as received by the court on 1 February 2013, para 34, paras 41 et seq specifically on the DWL.

[39] See C-1940-2013, judgment of 17 December 2019, 10° Juzgado Civil de Santiago, Cuadragésimo noveno and following.

[40] A Gonzalez, 'Estimación de Daños a Consumidores por Alza Coordinada de Precios de las Farmacias Ahumada, Cruz Verde y Salcobrand' (2015) available at https://centrocompetencia.com/wp-content/uploads/2020/12/InformeDa%C3%B1osFarmacias-SernacAldoGonzalez.pdf.

difference in counter-factuals applied. In the latter case, the counter-factual was situated in the period during which the heavy price war went on, which is why there is a larger difference between the counter-factual price and the cartelised price, and hence a higher damage amount. The more conservative estimation is based upon a counter-factual of average prices calculated over a longer period.

Now, what led to this remarkable judgment in the light of the quantification challenges, questions of causation and standing discussed earlier? To begin with, Chile has rather advanced legislation concerning consumer collective redress.[41] This consumer collective redress procedure can apply here despite the applicability of special legislation like competition law. Ley 19.496 sets out in general that consumers can claim compensation.[42] Importantly, there is a special procedure by way of a representative action available when the collective and/or diffuse consumer interests are hurt (see Article 51 of Ley 19.496). Article 50 of Ley 19.496 defines 'collective interests' and 'diffuse interests':

> interés colectivo se refiere a acciones que se promueven en defensa de derechos comunes a un conjunto determinado o determinable de consumidores, ligados con un proveedor por un vínculo contractual, en tanto el interés difuso se refiere a las acciones que se promueven en defensa de un conjunto indeterminado de consumidores afectados en sus derechos. [English translation: collective interest refers to actions that are promoted in defence of rights common to a determined or determinable group of consumers, linked to a supplier by a contractual bond, while diffuse interest refers to the actions that are promoted in defence of an indeterminate group of consumers affected in their rights.]

Chilean law thus does not insist on the requirement to link the harm very specifically to one consumer, by also allowing compensation in cases where 'diffuse consumer interests' are hurt and the group of consumers is 'indeterminate'. This gives considerable procedural flexibility to award damages for a non-material damage component such as the DWL that cannot easily be tied to the actual consumers. It should be further noted that in the case at hand, the allocative effect was rather low due to the high price inelasticity of demand. This may be different in other scenarios where the price elasticity of demand is greater.

ii. Developments at European Level

To foster compensation claims, from a scientific point of view collective redress is a powerful tool.[43] This is particularly the case if damage may be trifling but widespread –

[41] This is contained in Ley de Protección de los Derechos de los Consumidores (Consumer Rights Protection Law) (Ley 19.496).

[42] See in its Art 3e): 'El derecho a la reparación e indemnización adecuada y oportuna de todos los daños materiales y morales en caso de incumplimiento de cualquiera de las obligaciones contraídas por el proveedor, y el deber de accionar de acuerdo a los medios que la ley le franquea …' [English translation: 'The right to adequate and timely compensation and compensation for all material and moral damages in the event of non-compliance with any of the obligations contracted by the supplier, and the duty to act according to the means that the law allows …']

[43] C Hodges, *Multi-Party Actions* (Oxford University Press 2001); C Hodges (2008) *The Reform of Class and Representative Actions in European Legal Systems: A new framework for collective redress in Europe* (Hart Publishing, 2008); SE Keske, *Group Litigation in European Competition Law* (Intersentia, 2010)

a classical scenario regularly faced by the final consumers in competition law.[44] As elaborated upon before, if a feasible way to compensate the DWL is to be found, collective rather than individual redress seems to be a necessity in the light of the challenges in quantification. Despite these insights, the final text of the Damages Directive does not mention collective redress. In the discussions preceding the Damages Directive, collective redress was the first item of discussion in the Green Paper,[45] and it also figured in the White Paper.[46] The drafters explicitly refer to the possibility of ensuring that the goals of the Damages Directive are reached with either individual or collective litigation.[47] After all, for many years the most far-reaching EU policy document was a non-binding recommendation,[48] but finally a Collective Redress Directive to institutionalise EU-wide collective redress mechanisms was enacted in 2020.[49] Both national and cross-border infringements fall within the scope of the Collective Redress Directive (Article 2(1)). The European compromise puts special emphasis on a qualified entity, representing the collective interests of consumers, that may bring representative actions for the purpose of both injunction and redress measures against traders infringing certain provisions of EU law. This entity can be any organisation or a public body (Articles 3(4), 4). Design-wise, both opt-in or opt-out mechanisms are possible. The number of remedies is wide: the qualified entity may request the stopping or prohibition of an infringement, and seek redress, such as compensation, repair or price reduction.[50] Article 7(4) sets the minimum standard in terms of remedies for providing for injunctive measures and measures of redress. Given that it is a minimum standard, Member States could go further.[51] Importantly, the Directive does currently not apply to competition law.[52] However, Member States are free to extend the scope of application to competition law.[53] They may, furthermore, when keeping, designing or reforming their national systems of collective redress, find inspiration in the provisions of the Collective Redress Directive. For the European level it is also noteworthy that the fields of application are collected in Annex I – and to update an Annex does not require going through the whole legislative procedure at EU level.

To assess the power of these provisions with a view to enabling compensation for the DWL, the key is to look in more depth at the formulations as regards redress. Article 9

[44] Weber (n 2).

[45] See table of contents as an annex to the Green Paper, 'Damages Actions for breach of the EC Antitrust Rules' COM (2005) 672 final

[46] White Paper, 'Damages Actions for Breach of the EC anti-trust rules' COM (2008) 165 of 2 April 2008, 4.

[47] See recital 13, Damages Directive.

[48] Commission Recommendation of 11 June 2013 on common principles for injunctive and compensatory collective redress mechanisms in the Member States concerning violations of rights granted under Union law [2013] OJ L201/60.

[49] Directive of the European Parliament and of the Council of 25 November 2020 on representative actions for the protection of the collective interests of consumers and repealing Directive 2009/22/EC [2020] OJ L409/1 (Collective Redress Directive).

[50] For a definition of 'redress measure', see Art 3(10), Collective Redress Directive.

[51] Art 9(9), Collective Redress Directive fits into this.

[52] It is beyond the scope of this contribution to carefully analyse Member State law. Art 1(2), Collective Redress Directive furthermore makes it explicit that aside from the regime prescribed by European law, other national mechanisms may remain in place as well.

[53] To the best of my knowledge no Member State has explicitly done this.

concerns the redress measures, and Article 9(1) gives the options 'compensation, repair, replacement, price reduction, contract termination or reimbursement of the price paid'. Member States are free as regards the design choice when it comes to the question of when the individual consumers concerned explicitly or tacitly express their wish to be represented (Article 9(2)).[54] Importantly, Article 9(5) grants a certain flexibility regarding the degree to which the consumers have to be identified: 'Where a redress measure does not specify individual consumers entitled to benefit from remedies provided by the redress measure, it shall at least describe the group of consumers entitled to benefit from those remedies.'[55] Hence, describing a group of consumers suffices even in the context of a redress measure. Redress can then be claimed within a specified time; if, however, redress funds remain, Member States ex ante have to lay down the destination of such (Article 9(7)). For the purpose of claiming compensation for the DWL, Article 9(5) seems to be particularly interesting. Again, to a certain extent, as in Chilean law Ley 19.496, there is no necessity for there to be a concrete link to a specific consumer. Reading this in combination with the requirement that consumers do not need to explicitly express their wish to participate in the collective action in question but that a tacit expression suffices, it seems to give certain leeway to experiment. The Collective Redress Directive omits a definition of the 'tacit expression to be represented', which leads to some procedural uncertainty. In the competition law context, the Directive is currently only an inspiration, and European Member States are free to develop their own mechanisms by which compensation for the DWL can be facilitated. Also, for all fields of application that the Annex I does list, it is true that European Member States can continue to experiment with effective collective redress mechanisms within the scope of the Collective Redress Directive.

III. Conclusion

From an economic point of view, the allocative effect resulting from infringements of competition law is a major concern. It is a parameter that is, aside from the cartel overcharge, crucial when discussing whether the full compensation principle is adhered to. To be very clear: consumer harm consists of both the (passed on)[56] overcharge amount and the DWL. In the light of the legal and economic quantification challenges, the feasibility of also compensating consumers for the DWL depends on the existence of

[54] Different rules apply to consumers residing outside the Member State in question, see Art 9(3).

[55] The Directive has undergone quite a number of changes during the legislative procedure. This element, however, was already present in the Proposal for a Directive of the European Parliament and of the Council on representative actions for the protection of the collective interests of consumers, and repealing Directive 2009/22/EC, COM/2018/0184 final – 2018/089 (COD) (Proposal). This is in line with Art 5b(4) of the Proposal, which reads 'If the redress measure does not specify individual consumers entitled to benefit from remedies provided by the measure, it shall at least describe the group of consumers entitled to benefit from those remedies.'

[56] For the sake of this contribution, a direct cartelist-consumer relation was described. However, in reality the supply chains may be longer, and the final consumers would, hence, not be confronted with the overcharge directly but with that percentage of the overcharge that previous levels in the supply chain decided to pass on to them.

smart collective redress mechanisms. The Chilean example is proof that considering the DWL as a damage component in civil litigation is possible in principle. The European Collective Redress Directive seem to provide for a certain flexibility as well: Member States are free to experiment. A limitation of this contribution is a pure look at achieving full compensation for the final consumers by way of private (collective) enforcement. The real picture is more complex, and we need to fine-tune the compensation goal with the function of the fine in public enforcement, as cartel damages claims are typically follow-on litigation. Thinking the compensation perspective through in its entirety, we have not yet said anything about who actually obtains the damages paid for the emergence of the DWL. Aside from compensation, EU competition law considers deterrence a complementary goal.[57] The deterrence perspective is interesting, in that it places less emphasis on neatly compensating every consumer but looks at the overall deterrent value of the amount that can be claimed and the likelihood with which such a claim can be successful.

[57] Recital 5, Collective Redress Directive refers to the need to improve deterrence.

13

Third-Party Funding in Collective Redress

ASTRID STADLER

> Funding is essential for large cases and claimant lawyers have long argued that the absence of funding is the main problem in bringing mass litigation. The forensic reason is that, given the size of the required investment in costs and the size of the adverse costs risk, the total amount of funding required for a mass case of any size is significant and not easily available, and there is therefore considerable risk to funds invested, even without taking into account the 'adverse costs gamble'.
>
> (C Hodges, 'Settlement and Its Pitfalls in England and Wales' (2013))

I. Third-Party Funding – A Controversial Issue

Chris Hodges's 2013 estimation of the importance of third-party funding (TPF) remains valid, and it is true not only for the United Kingdom (UK) but also for other European jurisdictions. Despite the consensus among proceduralists and practitioners that TPF is essential for collective redress proceedings in Europe, particularly in jurisdictions that do not allow contingency fee arrangements with lawyers, rejection of commercial TPF has been articulated by some EU Member States and the European Parliament. In Germany, an often-repeated and widely accepted argument against collective redress is the risk of a 'litigation industry' and US-style 'lawyer-driven' group actions, which includes the likely alliance between law firms and funders. The German Federal High Court in 2018 and 2019 ruled that the use of TPF by a consumer association to bring a skimming-off action under section 10 of the German Unfair Competition Act was against public policy because of the risk that the funder's profit-seeking might trump consumer interests.[1]

Resistance against commercial litigation funding, which is still a rather new market in Europe, was also clearly articulated in the European Parliament during the deliberations on the representative actions Directive 2020/1828.[2] In June 2021, the conservative members of the European Parliament published a draft report with recommendations to the EU Commission on responsible private funding for litigation, the so-called Voss

[1] Bundesgerichtshof, I ZR 26/17 BeckRS 2018, 24788; Bundesgerichtshof, I ZR 205/17 BeckRS 2019, 12868.

[2] Council Directive 2020/1828 of 25 November 2020 on representative actions for the protection of the collective interests of consumers and repealing Directive 2009/22/EC [2020] OJ L409/1.

Report.[3] Although the authors want to make us believe that the Voss Report is a proposal for the *regulation* of TPF, it is actually a proposal to deter funders and to prevent the market from growing by implementing a strict supervisory scheme for funders.

The Voss Report is also a political attempt to regain control of collective redress actions by destroying the financial resources of potential claimants. The system suggested by the Report can be the death blow for collective redress, dealt through the back door. The Directive will have no practical significance if qualified entities do not have sufficient financial resources themselves, which is the case in almost all countries, and have no access to external funding because funders retreat from the European market or because national legislatures restrict TPF. This chapter analyses different political approaches to TPF and the implications of the Voss Report.

II. European Model Rules of Civil Procedure (ELI/UNIDROIT 2020)

In 2014, the European Law Institute (ELI) in Vienna and the International Institute for the Unification of Private Law (UNIDROIT) began a joint project on the development of European Rules of Civil Procedure (ERCP) and prepared a set of model rules based on the ALI[4] /UNIDROIT Principles of Transnational Civil Procedure, the European 'acquis' and comparative research. The ERCP, elaborated by eight working groups and an overarching structure group, were adopted by partner institutions in September 2020.[5] Part XI of the ERCP provides rules on collective proceedings in rules 204–238, including provisions on costs, expenses and funding in rules 237 and 238, which supplement the general provisions regarding costs in Part XII.

Following the policy set out in EU Recommendation 2013/396 and the European Commission's 2018 proposal for a directive on representative actions,[6] the ERCP explicitly state in rule 237(1) that claimants in collective redress actions should be allowed to use TPF. Rule 245 provides a general provision on TPF and success fees, and confirms that parties may enter into success-fee arrangements with counsel or third-party funders in a manner consistent with the applicable national law. No detailed suggestions are made regarding how to regulate TPF. The ERCP confine themselves to establishing a certain standard of transparency and permitting the court to consider funding arrangements when making a final cost order, as set out in rule 245(4), or when scrutinising a proposed settlement in a collective action, as set out in rule 224(d). Details on funding agreements and possible restrictions are left to national law.

The ERCP accept that in collective redress proceedings, qualified claimants must be in the position to make funding arrangements even without the explicit consent of

[3] European Parliament Committee on Legal Affairs, 'Draft Report with Recommendations to the Commission on Responsible Private Funding of Litigation' (2021) 2020/2130(INL).

[4] American Law Institute.

[5] ELI-UNIDROIT Model Rules on European Rules of Civil Procedure – From Transnational Principles to European Rules of Civil Procedure (Oxford University Press, 2021).

[6] Proposal for a Directive of the European Parliament and of the Council on representative actions for the protection of the collective interests of consumers, and repealing Directive 2009/22/EC, COM/2018/0184 final.

the individual group members, although a success fee may have to be paid in the end. Agreements with a funder are normally negotiated in a pre-litigation phase and often before the group of victims has been clearly identified. The ERCP provide no details on how such an agreement with the funder becomes binding for the whole group (although they perhaps should). One could think of the qualified claimant as acting as a representative of the group, but the basis for his or her power of attorney is unclear, particularly if arrangements are made before an action has been filed and before any opt-in or opt-out scheme may grant power to act on behalf of the group. A different approach often discussed now for the transposition of Directive 2020/1828 into national law is requiring court approval of funding arrangements at the beginning of a representative or collective action.[7] Courts would then be able to meet obligations under Article 10 of the Directive. Such a court decision may bind all group members joining the proceedings to the contract terms negotiated with the funder.

In any case, rule 238(3) of the ERCP provides that the qualified claimant's 'costs and expenses incurred in bringing the proceeding must be paid from the common fund before any distribution of compensation to the group members'. Rule 238(3) has relevance primarily regarding success fees to be paid to a lawyer or a funder, because all other costs will be subject to an adverse cost order against the defendant.[8] Apparently, the drafters had no doubts that the success fee has to be deducted from the compensation to be paid by the defendant, and that the principle of full compensation for breaches of EU law as established by the Court of Justice of the European Union (CJEU) must be modified in this respect.[9] One may, however, dispute whether it is actually a modification. The group members are awarded 'full compensation' by the court, but they have to pay the price for the funder's support and a risk-free enforcement of their claims from the compensation. Therefore, the ERCP cost rules also seem to take it for granted that success fees are not recoverable from the defendant without stating this explicitly[10] (details on the recoverability of success fees are discussed section III.B).

III. Directive 2020/1828 and Third-Party Funding

A. Does Directive 2020/1828 Allow Third-Party Funding?

Directive 2020/1828 takes a restrictive approach to legal standing in collective redress proceedings. Only qualified entities, which must be non-profit-oriented consumer associations, are allowed to bring representative actions according to Article 4(3). The European legislature did not impose an obligation on Member States to guarantee the adequate financial strength of consumer associations. Article 20(2) lists several possible supportive measures, but public funding is only one possibility. Consumer organisations

[7] M Voit, Sammelklagen und ihre Finanzierung (Nomos, 2021) 388 ff.

[8] Such a court order on cost may also include preparatory costs; ERCP (n 5) r 240.

[9] Eg Case C-295/04 Manfredi v Lloyd Adriatico Assicurazione SpA ECLI:EU:C:2006:461.

[10] In case of a mass settlement, such an arrangement is possible and common in practice. In these situations, the court has some influence on the amount of the success fees to be paid by the defendant due to its obligation to examine whether the settlement terms are fair and adequate; ERCP (n 5) r 224.

across Europe have limited budgets, and due to the 'loser pays' rule, as has been fixed in Article 12(1) of the Directive, qualified claimants must not only finance their own case but also cope with the risk of adverse cost orders. Furthermore, the Directive clearly states in Article 12(2) that consumers concerned with the representative action shall not pay the costs of the proceedings. At that point, the Directive becomes riddled with the drafter's position on TPF.

Article 10 presumes that representative actions can be third-party funded, albeit only in accordance with national law. Article 10(1) requires Member States to ensure that

> funding by third parties that have an economic interest in the bringing or the outcome of the representative action for redress measures does not divert the representative action away from the protection of the collective interests of consumers.

Courts will thus have to examine the funder's success fee and – according to paragraph 3 – ensure that funders do not unduly influence procedural decisions and do not interfere with settlement negotiations.

Funders normally claim success fees, varying in size and form depending on the individual case. A success fee can be a percentage of the amount paid by the defendant, but it can also be calculated by multiplying the amount of cost actually paid by the funder. Any form of success fee must be paid by the claimant's side, so the compensation finally distributed to consumers is reduced. Despite Article 10 of the Directive, national legislatures or courts may interpret Article 12(2) (costs not to be paid by individual consumers) and Article 20(3) (qualified entities may charge consumers only a modest entry fee or similar charge) as clear restrictions to make individual consumers pay the success fee.

B. Recoverability of Success Fees

i. *The Netherlands*

It is unlikely that the European legislature ignored the fact that success fees are a corollary of TPF. Even if national law provides for a cap on success fees, consumers participating in the funded action will not receive the full amount awarded by the court. The Directive does not ban TPF outright, and it might take the position that 'low compensation is better than no compensation'. One way of having full compensation and TPF at the same time could be by making success fees recoverable from the defendant under national 'loser pays' rules.[11] The Dutch Act on Collective Damage Claims (WAMCA),[12] which came into effect at the beginning of 2020, provides for such a rule in Article 1081(i)(2) of the Dutch Civil Procedure Code:

> A judgment under Article 1018i contains an order for costs, whereby the court may, insofar as necessary and in derogation from Book 1, Section 12, § 2, order the unsuccessful party to

[11] In international arbitration, the recoverability of the funder's fees can be subject to a 'test of reasonableness'; International Chamber of Commerce, 'ICC Commission Report: Decisions on Costs in International Arbitration' (2015) 2 *ICC Dispute Resolution Bulletin* 26; J von Goeler, *Third-Party Funding in International Arbitration and its Impact on Procedure* (Kluwer, 2016) 393.

[12] Wet Afwikkeling Massaschade in Collectieve Actie Art 3:305a Dutch Civil Code; Arts 118b-m Dutch Civil Procedure Code.

pay reasonable and proportionate legal costs and other costs incurred by the successful party, except where this would cause injustice.

Although the text does not refer explicitly to the recoverability of success fees, the Dutch legislature wanted the successful claimant organisation to be entitled to the full recovery of all costs by mentioning 'other costs'. The reason is that in case of mass settlements under the Dutch Mass Settlement Act of 2005 (WCAM),[13] costs including success fees are normally paid by the party liable for the mass tort. The WAMCA, which supplements the WCAM and allows for representative actions for damages, takes a similar approach. The irrecoverability of success fees in an action for damages would have provided the wrong incentives for the defendant's side to refuse settlement.[14]

ii. England and Wales

In the UK, the recoverability of lawyers' success fees has a meandering history. When legal aid had been largely abolished in 1995, conditional fee agreements (CFAs)[15] became the number one choice of private litigation funding, supplemented by after-the-event (ATE) insurance to cover the risk of adverse cost orders.[16] In 1999, the Access to Justice Act made ATE premiums and CFA success fees recoverable under the 'loser pays' rule.[17] Only 10 years later, the Jackson Report identified the recoverability of CFA success fees as a main reason for increasing litigation costs and as an extreme burden for defendants.[18] In particular, costs liabilities for defendants can become grossly disproportionate and drive defendants into early settlements.[19] Moreover, in January 2011, the European Court of Human Rights held that the recoverability of success fees can violate the freedom of the press rights guaranteed by Article 10 of the European Convention on Human Rights in a case in which the recoverable amount is excessively high and the claimant party is not in need of a CFA to have access to justice as set out in Article 6 of the Convention.[20] Therefore, the 2012 legal reform on litigation costs[21] abolished the recoverability of CFAs and ATE insurance premiums.

Following the recommendations of Lord Jackson and to mitigate the consequences of abolishing recoverability of success fees, in personal injury cases the level of general

[13] Wet Collectieve Afwikkeling Massaschade 2005.

[14] I Tzankova, 'Collective Actions in the Netherlands – A Step Forward?' [2020] *Zeitschrift für Zivilprozess International* 83, 95.

[15] Courts and Legal Services Act 1990, s 58.

[16] C Hodges, 'Settlement and Its Pitfalls in England and Wales' in C Hodges and A Stadler (eds), *Resolving Mass Disputes. ADR and Settlement of Mass Claims* (Edward Elgar, 2013) 122.

[17] ibid.

[18] R Jackson, Review of Civil Litigation Costs: Final Report (TSO, 2010) 109 et seq.

[19] ibid 111.

[20] *MGN v United Kingdom* 39041/04 [2011] ECHR 66, (2011) 53 EHRR 5; see also *Campbell v MGN* [2004] UKHL 22, [2004] AC 457. In 2015, the UK Supreme Court confirmed the legality of England's system of recoverable CFA success fees and held that as a matter of principle, the recoverability of CFA success fees does not violate the parties' right to access to justice and to a fair trial. The Court also emphasised that 'in the absence of widely accessible civil legal aid system … it is impossible to devise a fair scheme which promotes access to justice for all litigants'; *Coventry v Lawrence* [2015] UKSC 50, 72. The decision is critically reviewed by A Higgins, 'The Costs of Civil Justice and Who Pays' (2017) 37 *OJLS* 687.

[21] Legal Aid, Sentencing and Punishment of Offenders Act 2012 (LASPO).

damages for pain and suffering was increased by 10 per cent across the board.[22] Damages-based agreements (DBAs) were introduced in 2013,[23] but recoverability is limited by the courts[24] and the Legal Services Act of 1990, section 58AA(6A). In cartel damages cases before the Competition Appeal Tribunal, DBAs are not enforceable if they relate to opt-out collective proceedings.[25] In contrast to CFAs and DBAs, the Jackson reform did not touch upon litigation funding agreements, as set out in section 58B of the Courts and Legal Services Act of 1990. To this day, only a self-regulatory code exists, and success fees to be paid to a third-party funder are not recoverable.

iii. Germany

In Germany, the debate on how to handle TPF has only begun. Proposals on how to transpose Directive 2020/1828 into national law have considered the recoverability of a funder's remuneration but, so far, all have declined to accept it. Beate Gsell and Caroline Meller-Hannich, who, on behalf of the most important German consumer association (vzbv), developed a draft for a new representative action, emphasise that one should consider recoverability only if there is a cap on the funder's fee to protect defendants from excessively high extra costs.[26] The German legislature is unlikely to impose such a burden on defendants. Domestic trade and industry stakeholders will point out, not without good reason, that access to justice for qualified entities must be guaranteed by the state: if claimants lack the necessary resources, support must be provided, whether by legal aid, public subsidies for consumer associations, or a public fund to which qualified claimants can apply in individual cases. If a qualified claimant considers TPF a better option because it permits the claimant to shift the risk of an adverse cost order to the funder (which is, for example, normally not permitted in the case of legal aid), the consequences of such a decision should not be vested in the defendant. Consumers who benefit from the cost- and risk-free enforcement of their claims will have to pay the price for it.[27]

IV. Voss Report

The traditional reservations about third-party litigation funding in Europe are deeply rooted in the conviction that a third party should not advance funds and support the claim of another in return for a share of the proceeds, particularly in the form of an

[22] Jackson (n 18) 112. There is also a cap on success fees; see Courts and Legal Services Act 1990, s 58(4A)–(4B).

[23] Damages-Based Agreements Regulations 2013 (SI 2013/609).

[24] CPR Practice Direction 44.18.

[25] Competition Act 1998, s 47C(8).

[26] *Die Umsetzung der neuen EU-Verbandsklagerichtlinie* (2021) 49 available at www.vzbv.de/sites/default/files/downloads/2021/02/03/21-02-04_vzbv_verbandsklagen-rl_gutachten_gsell_meller-hannich.pdf.

[27] A Stadler, *Prozessfinanzierung und Kostenerstattung* (Liber Amicorum Becker-Eberhard 2022, forthcoming); Voit (n 7) 375, 414, 467. See also A Siebert-Reimer, *Der Anspruch auf Erstattung der Kosten der Prozessfinanzierung* (Duncker & Hublot, 2017), who rejects the recoverability of success fees under the procedural 'loser pays' principle but argues in favour of considering success fees as part of actual damages under substantive law.

assignment of claims.[28] Despite the medieval English rules against maintenance and champerty,[29] UK courts have by now accepted TPF.[30] Once litigation funding by lawyers through CFAs had been permitted by legislation in 1995,[31] TPF emerged, although it was initially met with concern.[32] In Continental Europe it is still 'in its childhood phase',[33] and the attitudes of courts vary from jurisdiction to jurisdiction. There are, however, no statutory rules on TPF.

In contrast to litigation funding by lawyers, most legislatures have not interfered with the growing commercial litigation funding market in recent years. In the UK, at least some soft law has been laid down in the Code of Conduct for Litigation Funders, which was developed in 2011 by the Association of Litigation Funders (ALF) and the Civil Justice Council.[34] The recently founded Association of European Litigation Funders (EALF) is still working on such a code and has not published one yet, which might be one reason why the European Parliament became active and proposed state regulation for litigation funding that suggests placing a tight rein on funders.

The draft parliamentary resolution on litigation funding addresses three basic points:

1. It proposes the establishment of a public law supervisory regime on funders similar to those for financial services provided by banking institutions and insurance companies, including, for example, capital adequacy requirements.[35]
2. It aims to establish transparency[36] and fairness requirements,[37] including a cap on the funder's remuneration,[38] and to impose a fiduciary duty on funders.[39]
3. It proposes safeguards to prevent undue influence by funders.[40]

[28] Some civil procedure codes (CPCs) explicitly require that parties to litigation must have an interest of their own in the subject matter of the case, eg, the French rule '*nul de plaide par procureur*' (Arts 31, 32 French Civil Procedure Code); in Germany, albeit not explicitly formulated, the clear intention of the CPC is that parties must litigate on their own behalf and in their own interest. Case law has accepted limited exceptions. There are, however, additional requirements in case of assignments if the assignor retains an economic interest in the outcome of the litigation, to protect the defendant from abuse. Assignees must, for example, have sufficient financial resources to meet an adverse cost order. For details see Bundesgerichtshof, VII ZR 337/84, *Neue Juristische Wochenschrift* 1986, 850.

[29] Criminal and tort liability for maintenance and champerty were abolished in 1967. Nevertheless, Lord Jackson emphasised in his report (n 18 123) that '[t]he uncertain ambit of the law of maintenance and champerty has on occasions caused doubt as to the precise boundaries of proper conduct in relation to litigation funding'.

[30] For an overview, see I Tilemma, *Entrepreneurial Mass Litigation – Balancing the Building Blocks* (Eleven International, 2019) 125–238.

[31] Courts and Legal Services Act 1990, s 58; Conditional Fee Agreement Regulations 1995 (SI 1995/1675); Conditional Fee Agreement Order 1995 (SI 1995/1674). For details, see C Hodges, 'England and Wales' in D Hensler, C Hodges and M Tulibacka (eds), *The Globalization of Class Actions* (SAGE, 2009) 110.

[32] Tilemma (n 30) 205. In 2005, the Court of Appeal accepted TPF in *Arkin v Borchard Lines* [2005] EWCA Civ 655, [2005] 1 WLR 3055 (CA).

[33] EALF, 'Welcome to the European Association of Litigation Funders' (nd) available at https://europeanlitigationfunders.com/.

[34] ALF, 'Code of Conduct' (2011) available at https://associationoflitigationfunders.com/code-of-conduct/.

[35] ibid Arts 4–10.

[36] ibid Art 15.

[37] ibid Arts 11–14.

[38] ibid Art 13(4).

[39] ibid Art 5(1)(c); Proposal's Introduction nos 4 & 5, p 5, recital 9.

[40] Draft Report (n 3) Art 13(2).

As a matter of principle, this is in line with Directive 2020/1828, but it goes beyond the Directive in many details, particularly by the imposition of fiduciary duties on the funder. The Voss Report addresses some core concerns, which Lord Jackson had already raised. First, funders may unduly influence proceedings by voting for early settlements once their return on investment is assured. Second, funding agreements may allow the funder to withdraw funding in circumstances that would be contrary to the client's interest or unreasonable. Finally, funders may become insolvent, causing problems for both the claimant and defendant if the funder had agreed to pay adverse costs.[41]

Although all these reservations carry some weight, an authorisation system and a close-meshed supervisory regime as envisaged by the Voss Report do not seem necessary to protect the parties.[42] Commercial litigation funders are neither banks nor insurance companies, which both offer long-term contracts requiring the trust of individuals and of capital markets in their solvability. In Australia, the country of origin of TPF, the question of whether funding arrangements fall within the regulatory provisions related to managed investment schemes has yielded different answers over the years. Whereas the Australian Federal Court and the then Labor Government exempted litigation funding from this regulatory framework in 2009, the Conservative Government that later came into office subjected litigation funding to a regulatory regime supervised by the Australian Securities and Investment Commission (ASIC). Since August 2020, litigation funding schemes have been considered to be 'financial products' that require an Australian Financial Services licence. The system has been heavily criticised by leading class action experts such as Peter Cashman[43] and by federal judges.[44] Since 2021, new reform proposals are being discussed and may pass Parliament in 2022.[45]

The European Commission is well advised to consider these developments, to assess the Voss Report critically and to consider other options. In particular, imposing fiduciary duties on funders goes too far and is unnecessary to protect clients appropriately. Unfair contract terms in funding arrangements (eg, with respect to the termination of the agreement) may be void according to existing contract law and regulations on terms and conditions, and funders must respect the professional duties of lawyers. Funded parties are typically companies, special purpose vehicles or consumer associations, but not individual consumers who might particularly need protection. The funding of collective actions involves special risks for group members and must meet special requirements, such as court approval of the arrangements made by the qualified claimant.

Capital adequacy requirements are proposed in Article 6 of the Voss Report, but can also be found in the ALF Code of Conduct.[46] The collapse of a funder may indeed have a considerable impact on both parties to the litigation. Nevertheless, the claimant party,

[41] Jackson (n 18) 118.

[42] For a detailed review of the Voss Report, see A Stadler, 'Die (Dritt-)Finanzierung von Klagen des kollektiven Rechtsschutzes' in M Reiffenstein and B Blaschek (eds), *Konsumentenpolitisches Jahrbuch 2021* (Verlag Österreich, 2021) 135, 162 et seq.

[43] P Cashman, 'Class Action and Litigation Funding Reform – Lessons from Down Under?' [2021] 2 *Mass Claims* 93, 99.

[44] Beach J in *Stanwell v LMC Funding* [2021] FCA 1430.

[45] A general overview of the development and recent debates is provided by Cashman (n 43).

[46] ALF (n 34).

particularly if it is not a consumer, does not need better protection for funding agreements than for any other economically important contracts, and most clients are in the position to assess the insolvency risk. Defendants, however, need to be protected with respect to the compensation of their litigation costs if the funded action is dismissed. Qualified claimants themselves will often not be able to pay, but funders might have agreed to do so. In both regular and collective proceedings, the best possible safeguard in this respect is security for cost orders, which the court can make on a case-by-case analysis, as described in rules 209 and 243 of the ERCP. The ERCP also provide guidelines for transparency requirements.

Moreover, a general cap on the funder's fees as proposed by the Report and as discussed in Australia now does not seem necessary. Clients are protected by contract law regulations against usury and violations of public policy, which allows consideration of the circumstances of each case – an individual and preferable approach. The remuneration of funders depends on many factors. It depends, among other things, on the complexity and the prospects of the case, and a general cap is at risk of being too low for a particular case. In collective actions, courts should therefore be given leeway when approving the funding arrangements of the qualified claimant.

V. Conclusions

Third-party funding does not require a strict regulatory regime in Europe, unless striking misuse or market failure becomes known – which has not occurred to date. Codes of conduct should be our first choice for the moment, and more experience with the TPF market is still need in Europe. For now, legislatures primarily need to address only some issues with respect to collective actions, such as transparency, security for costs and fairness requirements for the protection of group members who were not involved in negotiations with the funder. Legislatures must also offer alternative funding options by establishing access-to-justice funds for representative actions in consumer law. This is not only necessary with respect to redress actions that are not attractive for funders because they are not for monetary relief:[47] national legislatures must also provide ways to fund collective actions that do not reduce the compensation awarded to consumers through success fees.

[47] Directive 2020/1828 (n 2) Art 9.

14

Do Collective Redress Mechanisms Deliver Justice?

MARY E BARTKUS

> The issue, therefore, is to select a mechanism that delivers redress swiftly, effectively, efficiently, without false results or abuse, with no or minimal costs or barriers for claimants to access the procedure, without significant reduction in the redress paid to claimants through intermediaries' or transactional costs, and with proportionately low overall transactional cost for payers.
>
> (C Hodges, 'Collective Redress: The Need for New Technologies' (2019))

The European Representative Actions Directive[1] introduces a basic framework for consumer collective redress litigation,[2] which the 27 Member States must transpose into national law not later than 25 December 2022, for application from 25 June 2023. The Representative Actions Directive requires each Member State to enable nationally designated qualified entities to bring representative actions on behalf of classes of individual consumers of any Member State, in any Member State court, for injunctive relief and redress, including compensation, for infringements of any of the 66 European Union (EU) laws listed in the Annex to the Directive.[3]

I. National Approaches to Collective Redress Litigation

The new Representative Actions Directive does not harmonise class litigation procedure throughout the EU. It 'does not prevent' Member States from adopting or retaining

[1] Directive (EU) 2020/1828 of the European Parliament and of the Council of 25 November 2020 on Representative Actions for the Protection of the Collective Interests of Consumers and Repealing Directive 2009/22/EC [2020] OJ L409 (Text with EEA relevance) ('Representative Actions Directive' or 'RAD').

[2] This basic framework covers nationally designated qualified entities and the circumstances in which they may bring representative actions (RAD Arts 4–7); injunctive measures (RAD Art 8); redress, and measures including funding and settlement (RAD Arts 9–11); res judicata (RAD Art 15); suspension of limitations periods (RAD Art 16); procedural expediency (RAD Art 17); and disclosure of evidence (RAD Art 18).

[3] The Annex lists 29 Regulations and 37 Directives.

national rules and national procedural mechanisms enabling consumer class litigation.[4] It provides that qualified entities 'shall be free to choose any procedural means available to them under Union or national law'[5] in pursuing collective redress in any Member State court. The Directive also 'does not affect' rules under EU law or national law that provide consumers with contractual and non-contractual remedies for infringements of the laws listed in its Annex.[6]

The Representative Actions Directive thus encourages the continuing development of diverse Member State court-based procedural mechanisms for collective redress, amplified by principles of procedural autonomy that accept national differences in approaches to pleading, discovery, standards of proof, assessment of evidence, and financial incentives.[7] Interestingly, the Directive expressly states that it is 'without prejudice' to European Regulations on jurisdiction, enforcement of judgments, and the law applicable to contractual and non-contractual obligations in civil and commercial matters,[8] rules that were adopted when claimants in consumer redress litigation typically were natural persons bringing individual actions for redress in Member State courts.

It is too soon to tell whether this European model for consumer collective redress litigation will achieve its goal of delivering justice while avoiding US-style litigation abuse.[9] Practitioners, academics, regulators, and others continue to discuss the extent to which national differences in procedural law, substantive law, and the conduct and culture of litigation will lead to forum shopping, parallel litigation, inconsistent judgments, satellite litigation, and collateral attacks or appeals raising issues of jurisdiction, effective notice, rights to be heard, rights of defence, applicable law, and the recognition and enforcement of judgments. Claimants and respondents, and their advisors and investors, face new, unpredictable, and different, national approaches to the resolution of collective redress litigation, which may discourage settlements for lack of certainty or finality, and lead to litigation across jurisdictions to set aside, re-open, or amend court-approved settlements. If so, this would lead to wars of attrition and away from mechanisms for the efficient delivery of consumer redress for demonstrated wrongs.

[4] RAD Art 1(2).

[5] RAD Art 1(3).

[6] RAD Art 2(2).

[7] But see C Hodges and S Voet, *Delivering Collective Redress: New Technologies* (Hart Publishing, 2018) (recording 'major paradigm shift in debates on collective redress' and identifying, examining and comparing 'new techniques' in lieu of traditional civil procedure mechanisms, for effective, efficient delivery of collective redress).

[8] RAD Art 2(3). These are Regulation (EU) 1215/2012 of the European Parliament and of the Council of 12 December 2012 on jurisdiction and the recognition and enforcement of judgments in civil and commercial matters [2012] OJ L351; Regulation (EC) 593/2008 of the European Parliament and of the Council of 17 June 2008 on the law applicable to contractual obligations (Rome I) [2008] OJ L177; and Regulation (EC) 864/2007 of the European Parliament and of the Council of 11 July 2007 on the law applicable to non-contractual obligations (Rome II) [2007] OJ L199. See RAD recital 21: 'This Directive should not affect the application of rules of private international law regarding jurisdiction, the recognition and enforcement of judgments or applicable law, nor should it establish such rules. Existing instruments of Union law should apply to the procedural mechanism for representative actions required by this Directive. In particular, [the three Regulations] should apply to the procedural mechanism for representative actions required by this Directive.'

[9] The EU aspires to avoid US-style litigation abuse, characterised by large jury verdicts, punitive damages, the anonymity of opt-out class litigation, so-called blackmail settlements of class and complex multi-jurisdictional litigation, wide-ranging discovery, relaxed pleading, extensive motion practice, delays, and financial incentives encouraging speculative litigation, such as contingency fees, third-party funding and no cost-shifting.

II. Tribute

Now, this is a good place to stop and celebrate the many achievements of a great friend, Christopher Hodges OBE, whom I met nearly 20 years ago, during a discussion about whether compensation schemes, similar to those existing in Scandinavia, might be preferable, as a matter of policy, to personal injury pharmaceutical product litigation throughout Europe. At the time, having practised law in London, Chris was a professor at the University of Oxford concentrating on civil justice systems at the Centre for Socio-Legal Studies, and the author of many published works, based on extensive empirical research, addressing dispute resolution. Together with the late Malcolm Carlisle OBE, and many other interested colleagues, among them academics, practitioners and regulators, we discussed and debated, in many fora, existing, new, and potentially more sensible approaches to dispute avoidance and dispute resolution throughout Europe. Chris delivered a great many lectures and publications on this topic, among them books, chapters, articles, policy briefs, and white papers, and led many seminars and workshops, all based on his extensive empirical research, and all aimed at producing ethical, fair, safe, effective, and cooperative outcomes and systems. We listened, read, thought, continued to discuss and debate, and learned from this body of work and from one another. We became great friends.

Today, Chris is Emeritus Professor of Justice Systems, Centre for Socio-Legal Studies, University of Oxford, and a Supernumerary Fellow of Wolfson College Oxford. He has held chairs at Oxford and Erasmus Universities, and visiting chairs in China, Australia and Belgium. He co-founded the International Network for Delivery of Regulation (INDR). He advises governments, regulators and ombuds across the world, and is regarded as the leading European expert on consumer dispute resolution, ombuds, and alternative dispute resolution.

All this and more: Chris is optimistic, fair-minded, curious, joyful, a visionary, an explorer and, most importantly, a great fan of Fiona and the girls, music, the opera, gardens, a loyal friend and supporter, an excellent dinner-party host and a man of principle. Most appropriately, in a recent work, a short paper written during the pandemic, Chris posits 'a change is occurring in which pursuit of personal wealth and success at the expense of others is being replaced by recognition of the need to found society and commerce on interconnectedness'.[10]

To be effective, he writes, that change must be 'based on the human values of other-regarding and mutual support and solidarity based on a demonstrable commitment to ethical values in conduct'. He concludes that cooperation

> is facilitated where people place or share trust, and trust is based on evidence of trustworthiness. Accordingly, a society that wishes to do well should concentrate on enhancing the positive values of its members, and on mechanisms that build reliable evidence that people and organisations can be trusted. Structures and mechanisms that can deliver these functions will be needed. *They will be explored in further papers.*[11]

[10] C Hodges, 'Basing Action and Structures on Values in a Post-Corona World' Oxford Legal Studies Research Paper 18/2020 available at https://ssrn.com/abstract=3589690.

[11] ibid (emphasis added).

Chris, we look forward to your continuing explorations, to reading those further papers and many others, and to meeting soon in Oxford with you and our good friends and colleagues, to celebrate your many achievements and those yet to come.

III. Collective Redress Actions for Product Litigation?

We return to the Representative Actions Directive, which invites class litigation to resolve disputes arising under any of 66 EU laws, to focus on potential class litigation involving one of those laws, Directive 85/374/EEC, the European Product Liability Directive,[12] notified nearly 40 years ago, the foundation for product litigation throughout the Union.[13]

A. Background: The Product Liability Directive

The Product Liability Directive approximates, but does not completely harmonise, Member State laws on liability for defective products. Article 1 provides that 'The producer shall be liable for damage caused by a defect in [its] product.'[14] Article 4 provides that 'The injured person shall be required to prove the damage, the defect and the causal relationship between defect and damage.'[15] The Product Liability Directive defines two of these three elements: 'damage' and 'defect'. The first listed element, 'damage', in a personal injury case, is 'damage caused by death or by personal injuries … without prejudice to national provisions relating to non-material damage'.[16] For the second listed element, a product has a 'defect' or

> is defective when it does not provide the safety which a person is entitled to expect, taking all circumstances into account, including:
>
> (a) the presentation of the product;
> (b) the use to which it could reasonably be expected that the product would be put; [and]
> (c) the time when the product was put into circulation.[17]

As the Court of Justice of the European Union (CJEU) observed in *W and Others v Sanofi Pasteur MSD SNC*, the Product Liability Directive does not, however, define the third element listed in Article 4, 'causal relationship',[18] leaving that definition to national

[12] Council Directive 85/374/EEC of 25 July 1985 on the approximation of the laws, regulations and administrative provisions of the Member States concerning liability for defective products [1985] OJ1985 L210, as amended by Directive 1999/34/EC of the European Parliament and of the Council of 10 May 1999 [1999] OJ1999 L141 ('Product Liability Directive' or 'PLD'). The PLD was notified to the Member States then existing on July 30, 1985; the states notified were to transpose it into national legislation by 30 July 1988.

[13] The PLD has been the model for similar legislation in jurisdictions outside Europe, eg in Australia.

[14] PLD Art 1.

[15] PLD Art 4.

[16] PLD Art 9.

[17] PLD Art 6(1).

[18] Case C-621/15 *W and Others v Sanofi Pasteur MSD SNC* ECLI:EU:C:2017:484, para 22 (the PLD 'does not contain any definition of the concept of "causal relationship" within the meaning of Articles 1 and 4 thereof').

law. Compounding matters, while the 'injured person'[19] has the *burden* of proof, and must prove each of the three elements (ie damage, defect, and causation), national *standards* of proof differ, as do national methods of proof, rules for admissibility of evidence, procedures for hearing evidence and principles for the assessment of evidence.[20]

Among other references to national law, the Product Liability Directive does 'not affect' claimants' rights under national laws of contractual or non-contractual liability.[21] It does 'not affect' claimants' rights under Germany's 'special liability system'.[22] In most Member States, producers may prove the development risks defence,[23] but five Member States derogated from that defence: Finland; Luxembourg; France as to products of the human body; Hungary as to pharmaceutical products; and Spain as to medicinal products, foodstuffs and foods intended for human consumption.[24] Article 5 (joint and several liability) and Article 8(1) (act or omission of third party) are 'without prejudice' to national laws on rights of contribution or recourse,[25] and Article 9 (definition of damage) is 'without prejudice to national provisions relating to non-material damage'.[26] Claimants must bring 'proceedings for the recovery of damages' within a three-year limitation period,[27] subject to a 10-year long-stop provision,[28] but national laws 'regulating suspension or interruption of the limitation period shall not be affected'.[29]

The term 'caused by' is used in Arts 1 and 9, and the term 'causal relationship' is used in Art 4 in the English language version of the Product Liability Directive. References in this chapter are to the English language versions of the PLD, the RAD, Rome II and the judgments of the CJEU.

[19] The 'injured person' is the claimant in personal injury product litigation, who must prove each of these three elements to establish a claim under the PLD.

[20] *W and Others* (n 18) para 25 ('under the principle of procedural autonomy and subject to the principles of equivalency and effectiveness, it is for the national legal order of each Member State to establish the ways in which evidence is to be elicited, what evidence is to be admissible before the appropriate national court, or the principles governing that court's assessment of the probative value of the evidence adduced before it and also the level of proof required').

[21] For example, historically, some claimants seeking redress for personal injuries allegedly caused by a defective product have combined claims under their home country's national law implementing the PLD with claims under the national law of non-contractual liability.

[22] PLD Art 13 (the 'Directive shall not affect any rights which an injured person may have according to … a special liability system existing at the moment when this Directive is notified'). At the time, Germany was the only Member State with such a special liability system, a system of liability limited to pharmaceutical products. The CJEU has interpreted Art 13 to include within that system post-notification amendments that added claimants' rights, a presumption of causation, and a right to information. Case C-310/13 *Novo Nordisk Pharma GmbH v Corinna Silber* ECLI:EU:C:2014:2385, paras 12, 13, 22.

[23] PLD Art 7(e): 'The producer shall not be liable as a result of this Directive if [it] proves: … (e) that the state of scientific and technical knowledge at the time when [it] put the product into circulation was not such as to enable the existence of the defect to be discovered …'

[24] Commission, 'Report on the Application of the Council Directive on the approximation of the laws, regulations, and administrative provisions of the Member States concerning liability for defective products' COM (2018) 246. PLD Art 15(1)(b) allowed Member States to derogate from PLD Art 7(e) by maintaining legislation, or providing in legislation subject to a process outlined in PLD Art 15(2), that a producer would be liable even if it proved the development risks defence.

[25] PLD Arts 5, 8(1).

[26] PLD Art 9.

[27] PLD Art 10(1).

[28] PLD Art 11.

[29] PLD Art 10(2). For example, in some countries, sending a claim letter to a potential respondent may have the effect of suspending or interrupting the running of the applicable statute of limitations in some circumstances. See also RAD Art 11 (Member States to ensure a pending representative action 'has the effect of suspending or interrupting applicable limitation periods in respect of the consumers concerned by that representative action').

Although Member State courts have interpreted and applied national law implementing the Product Liability Directive for many years, the law in this field continues to develop across Europe. The CJEU has delivered only 17 judgments addressing the Product Liability Directive.[30] Six of those judgments were delivered in proceedings brought by the European Commission for a declaration that a Member State had failed to fulfil its obligations under the Directive and the Treaty by failing to transpose or by incorrectly transposing the Directive into national law. The remaining 11 judgments[31] were delivered in proceedings on references from Member States for preliminary rulings interpreting the Product Liability Directive.[32]

B. Hypothetical Collective Redress Actions and Questions for Consideration

Against this background, consider a hypothetical personal injury pharmaceutical product collective redress action brought by a qualified entity in one Member State, founded on that Member State's national law implementing the Representative Actions Directive, in which class members include, on an opt-out or opt-in basis, persons habitually resident in that Member State and, on an opt-in basis, members habitually resident in each of the 26 other Member States.[33] The qualified entity alleges that the pharmaceutical producer infringed national law implementing the Product Liability Directive by marketing a defective product in the 27 Member States, causing personal injuries to each of the class members.[34] In this simplified hypothetical, under Rome II, the applicable law is 'the law of the country in which the person sustaining the damage had his or her habitual residence when the damage occurred'.[35]

[30] According to the list found at https://eur-lex.europa.eu/legal-content/EN/ALL/?uri=CELEX:31985L0374 listing 17 judgments over a nearly 30-year period for this nearly 40-year old PLD. The first of these judgments was delivered in 1993.

[31] Three of these 11 judgments are among those most relevant to practitioners litigating personal injury product cases involving producers in life sciences industries: *Novo Nordisk* (n 22); Cases C-503/13 *Boston Scientific Medizintechnik GmbH v AOK Sachsen-Anhalt – Die Gesundheitskasse* and C-504/13 *Betriebskrankenkasse RWE* ECLI:EU:C:2015:148; and *W and Others* (n 18).

[32] The CJEU has jurisdiction to give preliminary rulings concerning the validity and interpretation of legislation of the EU. A Member State court or tribunal, where such question is raised before it, may, 'if it considers that a decision on the question is necessary to enable it to give judgment', refer the question to the CJEU for a ruling. See Art 267(b) TFEU (ex Art 234 TEC) for more information.

[33] The Representative Actions Directive requires Member States to have rules stating 'how and at which stage' of a pending representative action for redress the 'individual consumers concerned' by the action 'explicitly or tacitly express their wish within an appropriate time limit' to be included in the action 'and to be bound or not by the outcome' (RAD Art 9(2)). Member States, however, 'shall ensure that individual consumers … not habitually resident in the Member State [where the action is pending] have to explicitly express their wish to be represented in that representative action in order for those consumers to be bound by the outcome' (RAD Art 9(3)).

[34] For each of the 27 Member States, the producer and its subsidiary based in the country marketed the product in the country. All have been named respondents in the hypothetical action. In this simplified hypothetical, the qualified entity conservatively limits the collective action to national law implementing the PLD, and does not include claims arising under national law of contractual or non-contractual liability of the 27 Member States.

[35] Rome II Art 5(1)(a). Recall that the RAD is 'without prejudice' to the choice of law rules set forth in Rome II. To further simplify our hypothetical, we assume that no class member changed habitual residence after 'the damage occurred' within the meaning of Rome II Art 5(1)(a).

This means that the Member State court in our hypothetical will be asked to apply the laws of 27 Member States, that is, its own and those of 26 other countries, to the claims of class members. These laws include not only the national laws implementing the Product Liability Directive, but also all of the other national laws, for example on causation, that must be applied in order to adjudicate the claims. In concrete terms, the parties in this hypothetical action will ask the court to consider the following 'Factors for Consideration':

1. The laws of 27 Member States on causation.
2. Whether, in applying a particular jurisdiction's law of causation, or the law bearing on any other element of a claim or defence, the court should consider that other jurisdiction's different national standards and methods of proof.
3. Whether, given the need to consider and apply the laws of 27 Member States to the claims of class members, the court should decline to admit (certify)[36] the representative action as unmanageable.
4. Whether persons habitually resident in Germany, who are class members in the hypothetical action brought before a court in another Member State, may assert the rights afforded by Germany's special liability system.
5. Whether, if the action is pending in Germany, class members habitually resident in other Member States may assert the additional rights afforded by Germany's special liability system, that is in addition to those afforded by their own national laws.
6. Whether, in an action pending in a Member State that has not derogated from the development risks defence, the producer may assert the development risks defence regarding the claims of class members habitually resident in Member States that have derogated from that defence.
7. Whether, in an action pending in a Member State that has derogated from the development risks defence, the producer nevertheless may assert that defence regarding the claims of class members habitually resident in Member States that have not derogated from that defence.
8. Each class member's pharmacy, medical, hospital, work and related records;[37] the evidence of treating physicians and other fact witnesses; and the evidence of expert witnesses; all in order to establish whether or not:
   (a) the particular individual used the medication and is an 'injured person' who suffered 'damage' within the meaning of Articles 1 and 4 of the Product Liability Directive;
   (b) there is any causal relationship between the individual's alleged condition or disease and the medication;
   (c) there are explanations other than the medication for the individual's condition or disease; and
   (d) the individual is appropriately a member of the class represented in the action.

[36] RAD Art 7(3): 'The courts or administrative authorities shall assess the admissibility of a specific representative action in accordance with this Directive and national law.' See also RAD recital 11 (it is for Member States to lay down rules on admissibility).

[37] Presumably all of these records are in the language of the class member's home country.

9. For each of the 27 Member States:
   (a) the full regulatory history, including pharmacovigilance, of the medication;
   (b) for each of the periods during which class members used the medication, the presentations of the medication, including its Product Information and Patient Leaflets;
   (c) for each of the periods during which class members used the medication, all of the other information about the medication and its risks and benefits that was available to patients, their physicians or both;
   (d) evidence of any and all other 'circumstances' to be taken into account, 'having regard to the reasonable expectations of the public at large',[38] in establishing whether or not the medication was 'defective' at any time, including, without limitation, evidence of lay persons, regulators, and experts, all regarding the circumstances to be taken into account, plus such additional evidence as may be necessary to establish any development risks defence.
10. Whether, given the highly individualised nature of these personal injury claims, the voluminous evidence relating to each individual's medical history, and the detail and rigour with which each claim must be considered in order to adjudicate the claim, the court should decline to admit (certify) the representative action.
11. Whether, given the complex factual and legal matrices involved in a personal injury pharmaceutical product action, and the interrelatedness of the three elements of a claim made under the Product Liability Directive in this context, the court should:
    (a) decline any applications to bifurcate any of the elements for decision, also considering that litigation in stages, interlocutory appeals, and references to the Court of Justice would delay further the adjudication of the dispute; and
    (b) decline to admit (certify), in whole or in part, the representative action.
12. Whether, during what is certain to be a lengthy proceeding in this hypothetical representative action involving complex issues and many hearings, interlocutory appeals, and references to the Court of Justice, the court is required to consider, or should consider, any judgments more expeditiously delivered in parallel individual actions brought by persons alleging injuries caused by the same medication.

In a second hypothetical, qualified entities bring 'cookie-cutter' actions in each of 27 Member States. Class members in each action include, on an opt-out or opt-in basis, persons habitually resident in the Member State in which the action is filed and, on an opt-in basis, one or more members habitually resident in each of the 26 other Member States. In this second hypothetical, persons habitually resident in a given Member State may opt in to a representative action pending in any other Member State. As in the first hypothetical, the parties will present 27 Member State courts with the Factors for Consideration. This second hypothetical adds that each Member State court will 'compete', from the perspective of litigants, for opt-ins habitually resident in other Member States.[39] In addition, this model could drive opt-out activity by class members

[38] *Boston Scientific* (n 31) para 37, referencing PLD recital 6.
[39] These persons will have opted out of the representative actions pending in any opt-out home jurisdictions.

habitually resident in any Member State with an opt-out regime that is perceived as a 'less desirable' jurisdiction by these class members.

In a third hypothetical, one or more qualified entities bring 'cookie-cutter' actions in each of 27 Member States, but the class members in each action include, on an opt-out or opt-in basis, only those persons habitually resident in the Member State in which the action is brought. In this third hypothetical, the parties will present, to 27 Member State courts, Factors for Consideration 8–12. In other words, each court will apply the law of its own jurisdiction to the claims of class members habitually resident in its own Member State, taking into account Factors for Consideration 8–12.

Each of these hypotheticals raises for consideration whether the new European collective redress litigation model, or any class litigation model, is more appropriate for personal injury pharmaceutical product litigation than traditional or individual personal injury product litigation. Does this model efficiently deliver redress for demonstrated wrongs, or does it introduce additional complexity, unnecessary friction among Member State courts,[40] delay, and expense?

C. United States Experience

In United States (US) jurisdictions with a great deal of experience adjudicating cases in this field, federal judges regularly decline to certify classes of claimants in personal injury pharmaceutical product litigation,[41] citing (i) the need to apply the laws of many jurisdictions to the claims of proposed class members from different jurisdictions; (ii) independently, the need to examine highly individualised factual issues; and (iii) the availability of superior means of adjudicating these cases, that is, through centralised coordination of individual cases.

Instead, the US Judicial Panel on Multidistrict Litigation (JPML) transfers individual cases pending in federal court to a particular judicial district for centralised coordinated or consolidated pre-trial proceedings before a single federal judge. The JPML does so when it finds that the actions involve common questions of fact, and that centralisation will serve the convenience of the parties and witnesses, eliminate duplicative discovery, prevent inconsistent pretrial rulings, conserve the resources of the parties, their counsel and the judiciary, and promote the just and efficient resolution of the litigation.[42]

[40] See, eg, in Canada, *In Canada Post Corp v Lépine*, in which the Chief Justice of the Supreme Court of Canada observed 'the creation of national [Canada-wide] classes … raises the issue of relations between equal but different superior courts [in Canada's provinces] in a federal system in which civil procedure and the administration of justice are under provincial jurisdiction. This case shows that the decisions made may sometimes cause friction between courts in different provinces.' *Canada Post Corp v Lépine* [2009] SCC 16, para 57. See *Tiboni v Merck Frosst Canada Ltd* [2008] CanLII 37911 (ON SC).

[41] See, eg, *In re Vioxx Products Liability Litigation*, 239 FRD 450 (ED La 2006) and cases cited (choice-of-law analysis presents 'significant hurdles' to certification of nationwide class of medication users because application of laws of 51 jurisdictions to claims of proposed class creates problems for typicality, adequacy, predominance, and superiority requirements of Rule 23; even if one State's law could be applied to entire class, 'individualized factual issues concerning specific causation and damages dominate this litigation and create independent hurdles to certification.').

[42] See at www.jpml.uscourts.gov/ for more information on the Judicial Panel for Multidistrict Litigation. As of 15 February 2022, 424,720 active cases, down from 761,093, were pending on 185 MDL Dockets in 45 transferee districts before 149 transferee federal judges. US Judicial Panel on Multidistrict Litigation,

Nearly 30 years ago, in *Matter of Rhone-Poulenc Rorer Inc*,[43] the US Court of Appeals for the Seventh Circuit ordered a judge of the US District Court for the Northern District of Illinois to rescind a certification order in an action alleging that a defective blood product caused patients to contract HIV and AIDS.[44] At the time, the defendants already had prevailed in 12 of 13 individual cases tried to verdicts in different courts, and some 300 pending individual cases remained to be tried in federal and State courts around the country, one of which, in federal court, involved the certification order.[45] According to the Court of Appeals:

> A notable feature of this case … is the demonstrated great likelihood that the plaintiffs' claims, despite their human appeal, lack legal merit. This is the inference from the defendants' having won 92.3 percent (12/13) of the cases to have gone to judgment. Granted, thirteen is a small sample and further trials, if they are held, may alter the pattern that the sample reveals. But whether they do or not, the result will be robust if these further trials are permitted to go forward, because the pattern that results will reflect a consensus, or at least a pooling of judgment, of many different tribunals.[46]

In the circumstances, 'a sample of trials [made] more sense than entrusting the fate of an industry to a single jury'.[47] Had the Court of Appeals not rescinded the certification order, thousands more claims of unidentified persons, not previously brought in any court, regardless of legal merit, likely would have been included within the certified opt-out class. Among the concerns was the threat of what has become known as a form of 'judicial blackmail', that is that defendants would be forced to settle, even if they had no liability, even if they had meritorious defences, given 'the sheer *magnitude* of the risk to which the class action, in contrast to the individual actions pending or likely, exposes [defendants]',[48] and

> [the defendants] could not be confident that the [meritorious] defenses would prevail. They might, therefore, easily be facing $25 billion in potential liability (conceivably more), and with it bankruptcy. They may not wish to roll these dice. That is putting it mildly. They will be under intense pressure to settle.[49]

MDL Statistics Report – Distribution of Pending MDL Dockets by Actions Pending (15 February 2022). Most multijurisdictional mass torts include numerous State court actions, which may be centralised before a single State court judge. Best practice is that the federal MDL judge and the managing State court judges communicate and coordinate with one another for the benefit of the overall litigation.

[43] *Matter of Rhone-Poulenc Rorer Inc*, 51 F.3d 1293 (7th Cir 1995) ('*Rhone-Poulenc Rorer*').

[44] The Court of Appeals found the District Court's approach an abuse of discretion. The District Court had certified the class with respect to particular issues but had declined to certify a class as to the entire dispute, recognising that 'The differences in the date of infection alone of the thousands of potential class members would make such a procedure infeasible' (ibid 1296–97). The District Court instead decided to submit, to a single jury of six lay persons, particular issues, or a number of questions, concerning whether or not the defendants were negligent. If the jury found no negligence, the case would have been over. If, however, the jury found negligence, 'individual members of the class would then file individual tort suits in state and federal district courts around the nation and would use the [jury's] special verdict, in conjunction with the doctrine of collateral estoppel, to block relitigation of the issue of negligence' (ibid 1297). This approach was set aside by the Court of Appeals.

[45] The JPML previously had transferred the federal cases to the US District Court for the Northern District of Illinois for centralised pre-trial proceedings: ibid 1296.

[46] ibid 1299–1300.

[47] ibid 1304 (citations omitted).

[48] ibid 1297 (original emphasis).

[49] ibid 1298.

The Court of Appeals was concerned

> with forcing these defendants to stake their companies on the outcome of a single jury trial, or be forced by fear of the risk of bankruptcy to settle even if they have no legal liability, when it is entirely feasible to allow a final, authoritative determination of their liability for the colossal misfortune that has befallen the hemophiliac population to emerge from a decentralized process of multiple trials, involving different juries, and different standards of liability, in different jurisdictions; and when, in addition, the preliminary indications are that the defendants are not liable for the grievous harm that has befallen the members of the class.[50]

In *Castano v American Tobacco Co*,[51] decided one year later, the US Court of Appeals for the Fifth Circuit reversed a certification order in 'what may [then have been] the largest class action ever attempted in federal court'.[52] The Court of Appeals held the US District Court for the Eastern District of Louisiana abused its discretion by failing to consider how variations in State law in a proceeding involving class members from different States would affect the predominance and superiority requirements of the applicable Federal Rule of Procedure,[53] and how a trial on the merits would be conducted in this potentially massive proceeding.[54] The Court of Appeals concluded that '[t]he collective wisdom of individual juries is necessary before this court commits the fate of an entire industry or, indeed, the fate of a class of millions, to a single jury',[55] having observed in its analysis of superiority:

> In the context of mass tort class actions, certification dramatically affects the stakes for defendants. Class certification magnifies and strengthens the number of unmeritorious claims. Aggregation of claims also makes it more likely that a defendant will be found liable and results in significantly higher damage awards.
>
> In addition to skewing trial outcomes, class certification creates insurmountable pressure on defendants to settle, whereas individual trials would not. The risk of facing an all-or-nothing verdict presents too high a risk, even when the probability of an adverse judgment is low. These settlements have been referred to as judicial blackmail.[56]

In the course of its decision, the Court of Appeals observed that class proceedings very well could 'lengthen, not shorten, the time it takes for the plaintiffs to reach final judgment':

> In a complicated case involving multiple jurisdictions, the conflict of law question itself could take decades to work its way through the courts. Once that issue has been resolved, discovery, subclassing, and ultimately the class trial would take place. Next would come the appellate process. After the class trial, the individual trials and appeals on comparative negligence and

[50] ibid 1299.

[51] *Castano v American Tobacco Co*, 84 F.3d 734 (5th Cir 1996) ('*Castano*').

[52] ibid 737: 'All nicotine-dependent persons in the United States … who have purchased and smoked cigarettes manufactured by the defendants; … estates … and [dependent classes].'

[53] The Court of Appeals referenced the predominance and superiority requirements of Rule 23(b)(3) of the Federal Rules of Civil Procedure.

[54] *Castano* (n 51) 740–41. Finding the tort immature, the Court of Appeals also dismissed the complaint, as class certification would not be a superior method of adjudication: ibid 741.

[55] ibid 752.

[56] ibid 746 (internal citations and footnotes omitted).

> damages would have to take place. The net result could be that the class action device would lengthen, not shorten, the time it takes for the plaintiffs to reach final judgment.[57]

Today, in the United States, through the Multidistrict Litigation (MDL) process, individual personal injury pharmaceutical product cases are centrally coordinated, identified, examined and designated for bellwether trials. In this way, no defendant 'rolls the dice' on an outcome in a large class proceeding before a single decision-maker. Instead, both sides assess the strengths and weaknesses of the cases through an individual bellwether-case-by-bellwether-case pre-trial and trial process. In this way, all parties whose individual cases are pending in the MDL can move forward much more quickly towards resolution than they would in lengthy class litigation.

D. Canadian Experience

By contrast, in Canada, where the objectives of class proceedings legislation are access to justice, judicial economy and behaviour modification,[58] claimants historically have brought personal injury pharmaceutical product cases as large, multijurisdictional class proceedings, usually simultaneously in several, if not all, provinces having class legislation. Courts, historically, certified those class proceedings, which the parties settled, often without litigating their scope or testing the merits, to avoid the expense and uncertainty of class proceedings common issues trials over the course of a year or more before a single judge. That practice led to a belief, among some stakeholders, that certified class proceedings fulfilled the access to justice, judicial economy and behaviour modification objectives of the legislation, when a defendant with meritorious defences may have settled simply to avoid the proverbial 'roll of the dice' for reasons similar to those discussed by the US Court of Appeals in *Rhone-Poulenc Rorer*. When the parties litigated these proceedings, however, they proved to be lengthy, years-long proceedings involving, in several provinces, procedural issues such as whether or not class certification was appropriate, the propriety of competing provinces' having certified overlapping classes, and other procedural issues, litigated at trial and appellate levels through to the Supreme Court of Canada. It was by no means clear that the objectives of Canada's provincial class proceedings legislation were met in these litigated cases.

Several years ago, the Law Commission of Ontario, one of the Canadian provinces experiencing a great deal of class litigation, released a report assessing Ontario's Class Proceedings Act, with 47 recommendations for reform.[59] Among the findings were that class proceedings had 'grown dramatically in volume, complexity, and impact in Ontario and across Canada' in the nearly 30-year period since the legislation had been enacted, and an estimated 1,500 class proceedings had been launched in Ontario over a 20-year period, with about 100 per year having been launched in the most recent of those years. The Law Commission found that almost all whom it consulted for its assessment reported 'the enormous expense and slow pace of class actions'. Certification

[57] ibid 751 (footnote omitted).

[58] *Hollick v Toronto (City)* [2001] 3 SCR 158, para 15 (McLachlin CJC).

[59] Law Commission of Ontario, *Class Actions: Objectives, Experiences and Reforms: Final Report* (Toronto: July 2019) (the 'Ontario Report') available at www.lco-cdo.org/en/our-current-projects/class-actions/.

motions were 'often the epicentre of cost and delay complaints … lengthy, expensive and hard to manage'.[60] Based on a review of published court decisions, the Law Commission also reported, among many other findings, that 'approximately 73% of contested certification motions are successful, in whole or in part',[61] that is, decided for petitioners, in favour of certification.

The Law Commission discussed, and decided not to recommend, amending the language of section 5(1)(d) of the five-part certification test, which required the court to certify a class proceeding if it determined that a class proceeding would be the 'preferable procedure for the resolution of the common issues' assuming the four other parts of the five-part certification test had been satisfied. Instead, the Law Commission included among its 47 recommendations for reform, a recommendation that 'courts interpret the existing elements of s 5(1)(d) ("preferable procedure") of the certification test more rigorously'.[62]

Following a proposal from Ontario's Attorney-General, however, the Province of Ontario added the following new definitional language to section 5:

> a class proceeding is the preferable procedure for the resolution of common issues … only if, at a minimum,
>
> (a) it is superior to all reasonably available means of determining the entitlement of the class members to relief or addressing the impugned conduct of the defendant, including, as applicable, a quasi-judicial or administrative proceeding, the case management of individual claims in a civil proceeding, or any remedial scheme or program outside of a proceeding; and
>
> (b) the questions of fact or law common to the class members predominate over any questions affecting only individual class members.[63]

Section 5, as so amended, now includes predominance and superiority tests, such as those in the United States, and includes within its superiority test considerations as to whether alternative means to dispute resolution may be superior to class proceedings, such as quasi-judicial or administrative proceedings, case management of individual claims in a civil proceeding, or any remedial scheme or programme outside of a court-based proceeding. Time will tell whether courts examining contested motions for certification guided by these criteria regularly will decline to certify personal injury pharmaceutical product class proceedings, and whether practitioners turn to any of the listed alternative means of dispute resolution, as preferable to lengthy and complex class proceedings for the resolution of consumer and other disputes.

IV. Conclusion

Access to justice is a necessary, but not a sufficient, condition for the delivery of redress to consumers for demonstrated wrongs compensable at law. Consumers should be

[60] ibid 51.
[61] ibid 5–7.
[62] ibid 52.
[63] Class Proceedings Act, 1992, SO 1992, c 6, available at https://canlii.ca/t/553sl.

compensated for demonstrated wrongs compensable at law. They should neither be overcompensated nor undercompensated for such wrongs. Any system for the delivery of redress must ensure fair procedure for all parties[64] and deliver a just outcome in a cost-effective and efficient manner.

Will the European collective redress national court-based litigation model, applied to personal injury pharmaceutical or other product litigation, achieve these goals, or does it introduce additional complexity, unnecessary friction among Member State courts, delay, and expense?

[64] Ontario Report (n 59) 44: 'It goes without saying that access to justice includes fair procedure for both parties.'

PART III

Consumer Dispute Resolution

15

Does CDR 'Get It'?

LEWIS SHAND SMITH AND MATTHEW VICKERS

> One common language I'm afraid we'll never get
> Oh why can't the English learn to set
> A good example …
> 'Why Can't the English?', *My Fair Lady* (1964)[1]

'I've been to regulator A and they get it.'

'Department Y, hopeless, they just don't get it.'

'Government B really gets it and they want it now.'

'Sector Z, no use, they don't get it – but they will.'

Professor Christopher Hodges, feeding back on his many national and international encounters as he proclaims the benefits of consumer dispute resolution (CDR), ombud systems and ethics-based regulation. His enthusiasm and evangelical fervour never daunted by a 'not interested'. A 'just don't get it' is for Chris a battle lost, never a campaign ended.

What, though, of CDR itself. Does it 'get it', or rather has it got what it takes to deliver what is expected of it? Are those expectations reasonable or even sensible? Does it have a place in commerce and the service industries? What is its role in the wider social, economic and regulatory systems? What part might it play in the huge transitions that are taking place, for example the drive for decarbonisation and the balancing of innovation with consumer protection? Where does it fit with civil justice?

I. Introduction and Approach

We come to this subject as practitioners in dispute resolution, the current and previous Chief Ombuds at Ombudsman Services (OS).[2]

[1] Given that one of the authors is a Shetlander, we are acutely aware that English and British are not the same, but the lyric was too good not to use.

[2] OS is the UK Energy Ombuds, is one of two ADR providers in Telecommunications, has covered redress in part of the domestic property sector, runs an appeals service for parking on private land (POPLA) and created the UK Consumer Ombudsman.

Our approach has been to interview a number of those with a keen interest in dispute resolution and consumer trust, to reflect on their knowledge and understanding.[3] We did not ask them for a detailed thesis or analysis, rather we were seeking an informed perspective.

While Chris's expertise on CDR and regulation is international, for the purposes of this chapter we have largely confined ourselves to the United Kingdom (UK), although we are confident that the broad shape of our argument will resonate further afield.

Our contention is that terms such as ADR (alternative dispute resolution), and even Chris's preferred and more tightly defined term CDR, conceal and sometimes confound the very different functions that dispute resolution performs. Once we recognise this variety of functions and objectives, we are better able to understand some of the challenges, risks and opportunities involved in building consumer trust across a range of sectors.

In essential services and regulated sectors in particular, it is important to set dispute resolution in the context of concerns that are wider than the transactional and the contractual. Collective intelligence and enhanced execution build the capability needed to deliver trusted outcomes. Dispute resolution can play a significant role in bridging the gap between high-minded regulatory intent and trust and fairness as feelings rooted in personal experience.

Elsewhere in this book, others have written about Chris's radical approach to outcomes-based collective regulation (OBCR). It is a reforming call – a thesis both inspiring and practical enough to be nailed to a cathedral door. It requires an equally evangelical and vernacular response from those of us involved in dispute resolution, to create a closer communion between aspirations for a better and fairer world and seeing them come to pass.

The chapter is organised in the following three sections. First, the background of dispute resolution (section II). This section reviews the development of dispute resolution and, as part of the narrative, suggests three typologies and a four-box model as tools to assist in designing dispute resolution mechanisms. It suggests that a failure to recognise different objectives and to reflect them both in design and evaluation of dispute resolution presents a number of challenges. Second, the changing context (section III). These challenges are being intensified as civil society, regulators and markets must accommodate new expectations that could leave dispute resolution at risk of becoming a disconnected technique reduced to failure demand. Third, the conclusions (section IV). We conclude that by understanding the lessons of the first two sections and by restoring dispute resolution to its wider context, we can design and deliver better. By building collective capability to translate intent into outcomes, we can create trust as a common good and as a critical asset in a sustainable economy.

II. Background and Development of Dispute Resolution

In 1967, the first UK Ombudsman, the Parliamentary Commissioner for Administration, was appointed, introducing the concept of the ombudsman, well established in Scandinavian countries, to the UK. Other public sector ombudsman schemes followed,

[3] We would like to thank Nausicca Delfas (Financial Ombudsman Service), Elisabeth Davies (Legal Services Board), Rachel Fletcher (Octopus and ex Ofgem and Ofwat), Cathryn Ross (Thames Water and ex Ofwat and BT), Simon McDougall (Zoominfo and ex ICO), Jo Causon (Institute of Customer Service), Sally Berlin

in health, local government and public housing. The year 1989 saw an extension into the private sector, initially with the creation of the Insurance Ombudsman and what can be seen as the first infant steps of CDR. This was the genesis of what would become The Financial Ombudsman Service (FOS), created by the Financial Services and Markets Act 2000. The FOS celebrated its 20th anniversary in December 2021, having dealt with four million complaints from consumers and small businesses.

Further Acts of Parliament required the relevant Secretaries of State to ensure, through the regulators, that ADR was available first in Telecommunications and then in Energy. It is mandatory for communications providers and energy retailers and networks to be part of the ADR service. Interestingly, these ombudsman schemes are not created by statute, but statute requires that they are in place. The Legal Services Act 2007 established the Legal Services Board and placed on it the obligation to create an ombudsman scheme (LeO) to take complaints about certain types of lawyers.

In the UK, therefore, there were four schemes, working within statutory regulation, that had certain features in common with public services ombuds around a decade before the European Union (EU) Directive on Consumer ADR[4] was transposed into UK law. They were expressly designed to be accessible in reach and informal and inquisitorial in resolution approach. At the 'front end' they invest in outreach and prioritise ease of access, giving support and advice to would-be complainants and, where appropriate, helping them to formulate complaints. They seek to treat customers empathetically and to provide particular support for those who are identified as vulnerable.

Typically they use several different processes for finding a path to resolution, for example conciliation, mediation and investigative adjudication. All were set up with the intent of keeping processes informal, without the need for legal capability (although in the case of the FOS and LeO this intent was undercut in part by making the decisions subject to judicial review).

We have borrowed and adopted Dr Christof Berlin's description of this approach as a triangulation (see Figure 15.1).

Figure 15.1 Triangulation of expertise, efficiency and empathy

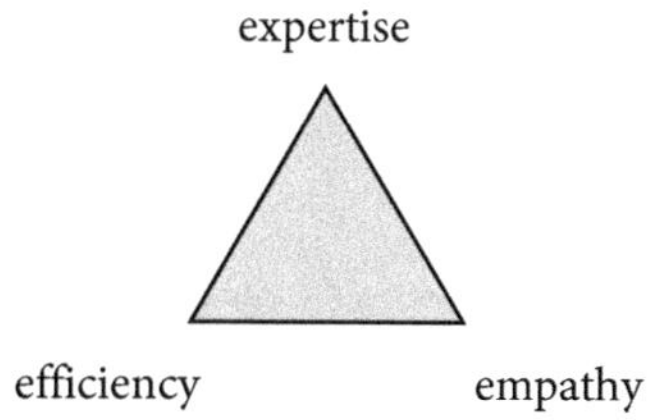

(British Banking Resolution Service), James South (Centre for Effective Dispute Resolution), Sam Ghibaldan (Consumer Scotland & Water Industry Commission for Scotland), Christof Berlin (Schlichtungsstelle fur den offentlich Personenverkehr e.V), John Walters (Citizens Advice) and Andy Allan (CTSI).

[4] Directive 2013/11/EU of the European Parliament and of the Council of 21 May 2013 on alternative dispute resolution for consumer disputes and amending Regulation (EC) No 2006/2004 and Directive 2009/22/EC (Directive on Consumer ADR) [2013] OJ L165/63.

In common with public sector ombuds, these private sector CDR bodies will look to see whether there has been maladministration. Additionally, where a contract for the supply of goods and services is in place, they will consider whether it has been fulfilled. They will question whether a customer has been treated fairly. Decisions are made on a basis of what is fair and reasonable in the circumstances, taking into account law, regulation, codes of conduct and standards of practice. When accepted by a complainant, ombuds requirements for redress are legally enforceable on the provider.

These ombuds are concerned with more than the individual complaint and its resolution. They feed learning back to businesses and sectors with suggestions for improvement, acting as an early-warning system when they spot emerging trends or areas of systemic failure leading to widespread consumer detriment. Complaints brought by some of the customer base of a business can therefore have a positive impact for a much larger group of clients. We will expand on this theme later in this chapter.

Operating within the regulatory framework, they engage with government departments, regulators and consumer organisations such as Citizens Advice, supplying data and offering insights to inform a context in which traders are encouraged and empowered to treat customers fairly in ways most appropriate to the circumstances, learn from mistakes, and are supported in getting policy and practice right in the first place. The unique insights an ombuds gains from considering complaints are invaluable in the development of regulation and standards, as well as service provision and attitudes towards the customer journey.

Ombudsman Services use a *four-box model* to describe the component parts of its work (see Figure 15.2).

Figure 15.2 Four-box model

1 *ACCESS* *Ease of use* *Focus on inclusion and vulnerability* *Delivering and signposting to advice and support*	*2* *RESOLUTION* *Informal* *Fair and reasonable test* *Designed to restore trust not only adjudicate*
3 *INSIGHT* *Collect quantitative and qualitative data* *Identify trust and execution gaps*	*4* *ENGAGEMENT* *Help businesses to improve execution* *Help regulators, consumer bodies and government with intelligence*

This is close to the five core functions of an ombuds described by Chris Hodges: Information, Advice and Assistance, Dispute Resolution Pathways, Collecting, Aggregating and Feeding Back Data, and Affecting Behaviour.[5]

[5] C Hodges, *Delivering Dispute Resolution* (Hart Publishing, 2019).

Alongside the development of these schemes with their origins in statute in regulated sectors, several voluntary CDR bodies were established to handle disputes between the suppliers of goods and services and their domestic customers. Generally, they were set up at the initiative of trade associations or professional bodies. Some, which met the criteria of the Ombudsman Association, were established as ombudsman, others were set up as adjudication or redress schemes.

The service offered by these bodies tended towards the transactional, looking first to see whether a contract was in place for the supply of goods and services and, if so, whether the contract been fulfilled. If not, then appropriate redress would be recommended. A number of these schemes offered complaint-handling or customer-service training, or accreditations as added value services for members.

During the first decade of the twenty-first century, ombuds and CDR schemes expanded rapidly and on an ad hoc basis; so much so that in 2008, the National Consumer Council (NCC) published a pamphlet calling for a strategic assessment as part of a root-and-branch review of consumer protection. It described gaps and overlaps, called for convergence and efficiency, a requirement for them to highlight systemic failure and to influence regulatory priorities.[6]

The patchy provision of CDR within the UK was reflected across the EU. Some Member States, such as the Netherlands and the Scandinavian countries, had comprehensive coverage, while others, like Germany, had little or none. In sectors like energy and finance, directives had placed a requirement on Member States to provide out-of-court dispute resolution for customers.

Disparities in coverage, quality and awareness were seen to constitute a barrier to the internal market and posited as a reason why customers might not shop, and traders be unwilling to sell, across national borders. A Directive introduced by Directorate General SANCO, the EU Directorate for Health and Consumer Protection, concluded in the Preamble that:

> In order for consumers to exploit fully the potential of the internal market, ADR should be available for all types of domestic and cross-border disputes covered by this Directive, ADR procedures should comply with consistent quality requirements that apply throughout the Union, and customers and traders should be aware of the existence of such procedures. …[7]

The Directive was published in the *Official Journal of the European Union* on 21 May 2013, 'for the out-of-court resolution of domestic and cross-border disputes concerning contractual obligations stemming from sales contracts or service contracts'.[8]

The Directive on Consumer ADR and Regulation on Consumer ODR[9] were transposed into the UK as the Alternative Dispute Resolution for Consumer Disputes (Competent Authorities and Information) Regulations 2015 (SI 2015/542). While it was mandatory for businesses to point to the existence of ADR, it was not mandatory for them to use it. The UK Government decided that markets should be left to supply the

[6] S Brooker, *Lessons from Ombudsmania* (National Consumer Council, 2008).
[7] Directive on Consumer ADR (n 4) Preamble, recital 7.
[8] ibid Art 2(1).
[9] Regulation (EU) No 524/2013 of the European Parliament and of the Council of 21 May 2013 on online dispute resolution for consumer disputes and amending Regulation (EC) No 2006/2004 and Directive 2009/22/EC (Regulation on Consumer ODR) [2013] OJ L165/1.

ADR bodies. Seven of the existing public regulators, for example the Gas and Electricity Markets Authority (Ofgem) and the Financial Conduct Authority (FCA), were approved as competent authorities for their sectors. The Chartered Training Standards Institute (CTSI) was appointed competent authority for all other areas. The Legal Services Board, the regulator for the Legal Ombudsman, was not appointed.

The regulators took different approaches; for example, Ofgem and the FCA approved the existing entities, Ombudsman Services: Energy (OS:E) and the Financial Ombudsman Service (FOS), as the only approved schemes in their sectors – sticking with the *four-box model*. By contrast, the Civil Aviation Authority and the Gambling Commission went out to the market and approved several ADR entities in their respective sectors. The CTSI has so far approved around 50 ADR entities.

The imperative for the Directive was to support the efficient functioning the internal market by increasing consumer confidence and participation, and the purpose of ADR was to ensure a high level of consumer protection by giving access to 'simple, efficient, fast and low-cost ways of resolving domestic and cross-border disputes which arise from sales or service contracts'.[10] Studies on the application of the subsequent ADR regulations within the UK have highlighted weaknesses in their implementation, with calls for major changes, comprehensive application and mandated engagement.

MoneySavingExpert cooperated with the All Party Parliamentary Group (APPG) on Consumer Protection to conduct a review of developments since the regulations came into force. In their Report published in 2019 they describe a broken and fragmented system, lacking in coherence;[11] one with competition between ADR bodies, resulting in gaps and overlaps and causing confusion for consumers. There was praise for ombuds schemes where they have statutory powers, compulsory membership in their sector and where they work alongside a strong regulator. The APPG's recommendation was for wholesale reform of the ombuds sector to deliver one ombuds per sector with compulsory membership, and to advance engagement with businesses to drive improvement.

More recently, in 2021, *Which?* published a report into ADR schemes.[12] It concluded that while there are some examples of good ADR practices in the UK, particularly in regulated sectors, too often the provision of ADR is not working for consumers. The Report found that many businesses refuse to participate, so there are significant gaps in coverage and awareness. It described an 'often chaotic patchwork of schemes' to be negotiated by consumers, and claimed that many schemes were themselves marked by delays and low levels of trust around expertise.

In addition, *Which?* highlights the failure of ADR bodies to collect data on consumer disputes that could be used to proactively 'promote improvements' or focus on 'prevention and culture change', and 'to inform businesses and regulators about recurring issues and help prevent complaints arising in the first place'. A central conclusion reached by *Which?* is that 'Consumers should have access to a single mandated Ombudsman service in key sectors.'

[10] Directive on Consumer ADR (n 4) Preamble, recital 4.

[11] APPG on Consumer Protection, *Report from the Ombudsman Enquiry*, vol 1 (January 2019).

[12] 'Are Alternative Dispute Resolution Schemes Working for Consumers' *Which?* (Policy Report, April 2021).

In 2021, the Department for Business, Energy and Industrial Strategy (BEIS) itself launched a consultation on ADR, in which it recognised

> inconsistent standards, a confusing landscape and insufficient incentives for businesses to participate. … [S]ome businesses see reputational benefit in ADR while others think it a marginal factor in consumer choice … [B]usiness participation in ADR will be unlikely to increase significantly without regulatory action.[13]

Two broad movements can thus be discerned in CDR. The first is of schemes (usually named ombudsman schemes) in some regulated sectors that were required by statute and of which membership is mandatory.[14] These drew heavily from the public ombudsman tradition in their ethos and objectives, and were conceived as part of a regulatory and consumer protection landscape. The second was of schemes that were more typically established by trade associations or professional bodies. While the position is not as clear-cut or binary as described above, the overall contours of the two movements are recognisable and serve a useful analytical purpose.

Consumer dispute resolution has a third objective. Linked to the courts as a means of settlement before a hearing, it is cheaper, faster and of less risk to the parties than going before a court. It is seen as an answer to the capacity crisis in the English civil jurisdiction, with CDR aligned to judicial processes. Alternative methods of dispute resolution are described as quasi-judicial, part of the justice system. Many of those we interviewed saw this as a disadvantage, in that some CDR bodies tend to use quasi-judicial language that creates a barrier to entry, and to use adversarial methods where the ability of the parties to frame and articulate their case effectively can confer a significant advantage in the process.

To add to the confusion, in courts and tribunals, as well as in government, the term 'mediation' is frequently used as a catch-all for CDR or ADR. Mediation is a facilitative rather than determinative technique; that is, the outcome is not binding until agreed by the parties. At the outset there is an agreement that what takes place in a mediation, and the evidence exchanged, will be completely confidential. There is no opportunity to collect and analyse data, nor to share with a business or sector to suggest improvements to practice. A recent report on mediation in civil justice in Scotland recommended that the basic data in relation to mediation should be collected, which might include geographical location, general sector of the dispute, duration of the mediation and the outcome.[15]

An international conference held in Oxford in 2016 concluded:

> CDR is distinct from civil litigation, and each should be valued for itself and not as substitutes for each other. Courts measure up well on quality criteria but poorly on other consumer principles of access, information, and value for money. In an expanding innovative universe, debate is to be expected, but a binary juxtaposition of courts and ADR is fallacious and polarizing.[16]

[13] Department for Business, Energy and Industrial Strategy, *Alternative Dispute Resolution – Impact Assessment* (June 2021).

[14] Albeit with a choice between an ombudsman and an adjudication scheme in telecoms.

[15] The Expert Group on Mediation in Civil Justice in Scotland (2019).

[16] C Hodges et al, *ADR and Consumer Disputes in the EU* (The Foundation for Law, Justice and Society, 2016).

Responding to a Civil Justice Council report on compulsory alternative dispute resolution, its Chair, Master of the Rolls Sir Geoffrey Vos, commented:

> ADR should no longer be viewed as 'alternative' but as an integral part of a dispute resolution process: that process should focus on 'resolution' rather than 'dispute'. This report opens the door to a significant shift towards earlier resolution.

In a speech given at the re-launch of Hull University's Mediation Centre, Sir Geoffrey outlined his vision for the integration of ADR into the dispute resolution process. He argued in favour of removing 'alternative' from ADR, that dispute resolution should be an 'integrated whole' and 'that there is nothing *alternative* about either mediation, early neutral evaluation or judge led resolution'.[17]

It can be seen that 'CDR' is used as a descriptor of systems with three distinct but related objectives:

- A mandatory process within regulated sectors that has a part to play in public policy and where the consumer is a citizen. Where information, advice and empathetic support are available for the individual, and data and insights are used to influence policy and stimulate improvement for a much larger group of citizens.
- A route to the resolution where a trader has failed to provide goods or services contracted for, where the consumer has a contract and a claim. Where the focus of dispute resolution is more individual and transactional.
- And a part of the judicial system where the claim is seen primarily as a legal dispute. Its value here is seen in terms of releasing court capacity and in widening access to justice.

In a particular context a dispute resolution scheme may aim to meet one or more of these objectives to different extents, and this should be reflected in the design and practice, in the culture and techniques adopted by the scheme.

While the elements of the Christof Berlin triangle – legal expertise, empathy, efficiency (see Figure 15.1) – may be there in each of the three CDR systems described above, their weighting may be different based on the particular objectives of the CDR process.

Chris Hodges and Stefaan Voet argued that there are fundamental overall goals for all consumer redress systems in their review of collective redress:

> We suggest that the fundamental objective of a redress system is not merely to deliver redress but to function as part of a wider market control system. The redress component should deliver at least the following functions:
>
> 1. To identify a mass problem;
> 2. To deliver appropriate redress or non-monetary compensation;
> 3. To provide feedback. Passing on information on the existence of a mass problem to independent authorities who do not have conflicts of interest for them to act in addressing the problem and obtaining collective redress. Hence, to contribute to affecting the future behaviour of a trader and of the market generally, and thereby ensure that an unbalanced market is rebalanced so as to be a level playing field;

[17] Speech by Sir Geoffrey Voss, MR: *The Relationship Between Formal and Informal Justice* (Hull University 26 March 2021).

4. To provide standing mechanisms to which consumers and traders can refer individual and collective issues and have them resolved efficiently and expeditiously. The traditional answer to that has been the courts, but the courts have proved to be far from ideal in handling both small value individual cases and aggregations of multiple cases. If that is so, alternative structures need to exist and to be readily and permanently accessible. The best structures are consumer ombudsmen;
5. To achieve both of these goals in the most efficient manner in terms of speed/duration, costs, and finality.[18]

In addition, however, Chris and Stefaan argue that there are connected, but not always identical, roles that redress performs in effective regulatory systems, which succeed through:

1. Establishing clear rules and their interpretation
2. Identification of individual and systemic problems
3. Decision on whether behaviour is illegal, unfair, or acceptable
4. Cessation of illegality
5. Identification of the root cause of the problem and why it occurs
6. Identification of which actions are needed to prevent the reoccurrence of the problematic behaviour, or reduction of the risk
7. Application of the actions (a) by identified actors (b) by other actors
8. Dissemination of information to all (a) firms, (b) consumers, (c) other markets
9. Redress
10. Sanctions
11. Ongoing monitoring, oversight, amendment of the rules.[19]

Their conclusion was that litigation primarily addresses objective 9 (redress) alone, while integrated regulatory and ombudsman systems are able to address all of the objectives. This provides instructive context for the *four-box model* (see Figure 15.2). Some dispute resolution schemes only look to deliver the second area – resolution. Even then, some may do this by more closely following adversarial or quasi-judicial processes such as paper-based adjudication or arbitration. In contrast, others seek to deliver less formal, more inquisitorial resolution techniques, or invest more heavily in data and insight capabilities or look to engage more fully with industry, consumer advocates and public policy formulation.

This is not to suggest that only those schemes that operate across all four dimensions are valuable or that they are always the optimal design choice, but rather to underline that not all ADR is the same – and nor should it be.

III. The Changing Context

Our review of the development of dispute resolution in section II indicates that ADR and indeed CDR do not conform to a single type. Different design considerations and objectives have been met in a range of ways that are not immediately obvious when we reduce the field to a single category.

[18] C Hodges and S Voet, *Delivering Collective Redress* (Hart Publishing, 2018) 308–309.
[19] ibid 301.

Insufficient attention has been paid by practitioners, policymakers and academics to the circumstances and objectives that should inform dispute resolution design. The elision of a wide range of structures and techniques into an ADR, or even CDR, catch-all has further obscured a disparate set of functions and outcomes. A number of shifts in the social, economic, political and technological context are likely to exacerbate these strains on dispute resolution, consumer protection and regulatory systems.

The Covid-19 pandemic has led to a more vulnerable consumer base, putting more pressure on front-line service and complaint-handling operations. In July 2020, the Institute of Customer Service launched its Service with Respect campaign, following research that 'showed a highly concerning rise in intolerant and abusive behaviour from customers towards front-line service staff during the pandemic'. Subsequent research indicated that 51 per cent of frontline staff believed customers were 'more intolerant now than they were six months ago'.[20]

Heightened emotions are with cause. Citizens Advice reported in November 2021 that one family in 10 (equivalent to 3.2 million households) was facing 'financial crisis' in the winter ahead.[21] In April 2022, the energy price cap increased by £693.[22] Ofcom's affordability report of February 2022 noted that 6.8 million households were on means-tested benefits, and commented that 'affordability pressures are likely to worsen in 2022 due to rising retail prices and wider pressures on the cost of living'.[23]

The consequences have been increased volumes and complexity for complaint handlers at both the first-tier (businesses) and the second-tier (ADR schemes and ombudsman organisations). Complaint handling is always emotionally intense work. The pandemic and the cost of living crisis have raised the stakes for consumers when complaint-handling agents themselves face the same pressures. Remote and hybrid working environments have made it more difficult to provide the tools and support to bolster their resilience. Practitioners of ADR recognise the need to focus on the person rather than just the complaint, to bring emotional intelligence to the conflict, and a sense of purpose, stability and calm.

In a 2018 paper for the Carnegie UK Trust, Julia Unwin argued for the importance of kindness in public policy and service delivery. She illustrated the tensions between 'impartiality and consistency, and intuition and empathy', arguing that balancing these imperatives was seen as a 'challenge for the front line … but never for the designers, evaluators, auditors and managers'.[24] We noted the interplay between efficiency, empathy and expertise in section II of this chapter.

[20] Institute of Customer Service, available at www.instituteofcustomerservice.com/service-with-respect-intolerance.

[21] Citizens Advice, 'Three million families facing crisis as cost of living crunch bites' (25 November 2021) available at www.citizensadvice.org.uk/about-us/about-us1/media/press-releases/three-million-families-facing-crisis-as-cost-of-living-crunch-bites/.

[22] Ofgem, 'Price cap to increase by £693 from April' (3 February 2022) available at hwww.ofgem.gov.uk/publications/price-cap-increase-ps693-april.

[23] Ofcom, 'Affordability of Communications Services' (15 February 2022) available at www.ofcom.org.uk/__data/assets/pdf_file/0016/232522/Affordability-of-Communications-Services.pdf.

[24] J Unwin, 'Kindness, emotions and human relationships: The blind spot in public policy' *Carnegie UK* (2018) available at www.carnegieuktrust.org.uk/publications/kindness-emotions-and-human-relationships-the-blind-spot-in-public-policy/.

Finding and maintaining an equilibrium is complicated, since trust and fairness cannot be reduced to questions of contractual rights and obligations. The past five years have seen prominent movements and momentum around diversity and inclusion, climate justice and intergenerational fairness, as a few examples. In addition there are expectations of companies to demonstrate their credentials on environmental, social and corporate governance (ESG) as commentators write of a 'crisis of capitalism'.

As we have already noted in section II, the EU Directive on Consumer ADR and Regulation on Consumer ODR of 2013 were designed to underpin the effective functioning of the internal market. The focus of the Directive was disputes between consumers and traders stemming from obligations under sales or services contracts, since this would build trust and confidence. However, over the intervening period it has become clear that contractual obligations do not encompass issues such as sustainability and social justice, which have become central to the legitimacy of the capitalist model. Asserting the 'here and now' claims of consumers may be at best insufficient and at worst inimical to the public good, since consumers are also citizens.

Dieter Helm's talk at the Oxford Martin School in 2022[25] challenged the hegemony of maximising utility, instead advancing a novel framework for the design and governance of a sustainable economy. Helm argued that the principal focus should be on assets, whether social, financial, ecological or physical, and that the test of a sustainable economy is whether a generation leaves a set of assets for the next generation at least as good as those they inherited themselves.

There is a risk of CDR mechanisms failing to address these claims, and concerns if they are narrowly focused on contract and consumer law. Evidently the level of risk varies across different sectors of the economy with the content and context of the dispute. The legitimacy and proportionality of taking such wider concerns into account mean that we should not approach designing mechanisms for disputes about a packet of crisps or a garage in the same way as we would for broadband or access to legal advice. Nor does it follow that all of these considerations and claims have to be resolved within an individual dispute.

As we will return to later in this chapter, however, it does suggest that care should be taken not to dislocate individual complaints and experiences from wider and longer-term considerations of fairness. Consumer dispute resolution does resolve volume, which would otherwise fall to an overburdened court system, and it plays a role in building confidence in a commercial transaction, but it also has a role in the regulatory landscape.

Regulators have recognised the importance of fairness as a consumer outcome, and have defined it more broadly than compliance with codes or consumer law. Ofcom's Fairness Framework[26] and the FCA's new consumer duty, with its aim to 'set a higher standard of conduct for firms in relation to their retail market activities', are two

[25] Professor Sir Dieter Helm, 'What would a sustainable economy look like?', talk at the Oxford Martin School, University of Oxford, 3 February 2022, available at www.oxfordmartin.ox.ac.uk/events/what-would-a-sustainable-economy-look-like/.

[26] Ofcom, 'Statement: Making communications markets work well for customers – a framework for assessing fairness in broadband, mobile, home phone and pay TV' (17 June 2019) available at www.ofcom.org.uk/consultations-and-statements/category-2/making-communications-markets-work-well-for-customers.

examples of where a focus on outcomes shifts regulatory expectations beyond meeting contractual obligations.[27]

As regulators have moved from detailed prescriptive rules towards regulation based on outcomes and on principles such as fairness, the role of ombudsman schemes in regulated markets has developed. In the absence of exhaustive rules, ombudsman schemes send signals to the market around behaviour, both through individual case decisions and through more general guidance.[28] The 'fair and reasonable' test usually applied by an ombudsman is informed by, but not limited to, industry codes or consumer law.[29] This affords greater flexibility in resolving disputes that emerge in novel fields, and offers a resolution philosophy that is more aligned with fairness principles, although it does pose challenges around consistency and legitimacy.

The FCA's consumer duty recognises the growing complexity of modern markets, with business models often based on disruption and disaggregation. The risks of consumer detriment frequently do not sit neatly within regulated entities or vertically integrated structures. Supply chains, trust chains and execution chains have become much more variegated and fragmented. The FCA intends its proposals to 'extend to firms that are involved in the manufacture or supply of products and services to retail clients, even if they do not have a direct relationship with the end customer'.[30]

For dispute resolution to fulfil its role as part of the wider regulatory landscape, there is a need to review its remit and to assess the capabilities and partnerships required accordingly. Consumer harms may stem from multiple sources and result from a confluence of factors – harms may sit across the intersection of a number of redress mechanisms. Connected homes, electric vehicles, online harms and greenwashing claims are examples of this increasing complexity.

This complexity becomes more commonplace as new products and services and new markets emerge. There are significant social, economic and environmental opportunities that penetration of low-carbon technologies and services and digital inclusion can deliver, which benefit wider society as well as individual consumers. Trust is an important system asset that can underpin the adoption of greener services, since there is a need to expand consumers' buying repertoires and to encourage participation. Rachel Botsman's definition of trust as 'a confident relationship with the unknown'[31] points to the value of trust in promoting changes of behaviour and of consumption patterns.

John Penrose MP highlighted in his report to the UK Government that high-trust economies perform better than low-trust economies. Individual transactions will tend to be faster and lower-cost; and on the broader scale, entire economies become more productive and competitive. For Penrose, 'customers need to have trust and confidence

[27] Financial Conduct Authority, 'CP21/13: A New Consumer Duty' (13 May 2021) available at www.fca.org.uk/publications/consultation-papers/cp21-13-new-consumer-duty.

[28] J Black, 'Making a Success of Principles Based Regulation' [2007] *Law and Financial Markets Review* 196.

[29] Financial Ombudsman Service, 'How we make decisions' available at www.financial-ombudsman.org.uk/who-we-are/make-decisions.

[30] 'CP21/13: A New Consumer Duty' (n 27).

[31] R Botsman, *Who Can You Trust?* (Penguin, 2017) 20.

in the legal and complaints system, so they know it is on their side and they can put things right if there's a problem.'[32]

Yet trust and fairness, as we have seen, are not comprehensively captured by contracts or consumer law. In 1999, Francis Fukuyama's paper to the International Monetary Fund emphasised that contracts cannot possibly specify every contingency that might arise, and that those that attempt to do so become very inflexible and costly to enforce. He predicted that 'coordination based on informal norms … becomes more important as the nature of economic activity becomes more complex and technologically sophisticated'.[33]

The growth of digital markets has been marked by the complexity and technological sophistication that Fukuyama foresaw. Consumer expectations around service delivery's being speedy and seamless have increased. At the same time there are growing concerns about privacy and the use of data. Ipsos MORI's Global Trustworthiness Monitor for 2022 reflects this, with the majority of survey respondents seeing the benefits of technological innovation while also believing that tech companies have too much power.[34]

Across a number of separate consultations by the UK Government on online harms, digital trust frameworks and data, is a connecting imperative to ensure that the protection consumers and citizens need to encourage participation in the digital economy is delivered without stifling innovation. As the foreword to the Online Harms White Paper stated, 'innovation and safety online are not mutually exclusive … [B]uilding trust in the digital economy and in new technologies … will build a firmer foundation for this vital sector.'[35]

In the late 1990s and early 2000s, redress in regulated sectors was conceived of in terms of independent second-tier complaint handling. Financial and legal services, energy and telecoms all saw the establishment of ombudsman schemes (although telecoms providers were also able to choose to work with an adjudication scheme). However, the history of the Information Commissioner's Office (ICO) demonstrates that in data and digital, the shape of second-tier complaint handling in redress is changing.

In 2009, one of the main objectives of the ICO's Corporate Plan was 'to provide an efficient and valued customer service that deals with all information rights complaints and enquiries'.[36] In the Foreword to the ICO's Regulatory Action Policy in 2018, the Commissioner described the core of her role as 'both an educator and an ombudsman'.[37]

[32] J Penrose, 'Power to the People' (16 February 2021) available at www.gov.uk/government/publications/power-to-the-people-independent-report-on-competition-policy.

[33] F Fukuyama, 'Social Capital and Civil Society', Paper prepared for the International Monetary Fund Conference on Second Generation Reforms (1 October 1999) available at www.imf.org/external/pubs/ft/seminar/1999/reforms/fukuyama.htm#II.

[34] Ipsos MORI Global Trustworthiness Monitor 2022 available at www.ipsos.com/sites/default/files/ct/news/documents/2022-01/ipsos-global-trustworthiness-monitor-is-trust-in-crisis.pdf 73, 74.

[35] Department for Digital, Culture, Media and Sport, *Online Harms* (CP No 57, April 2019) Joint Ministerial Foreword available at https://assets.publishing.service.gov.uk/government/uploads/system/uploads/attachment_data/file/973939/Online_Harms_White_Paper_V2.pdf.

[36] Information Commisioner's Office, Annual Report 2009/10.

[37] Information Commissioner's Office, 'Regulatory Action Policy' available at https://ico.org.uk/media/about-the-ico/documents/2259467/regulatory-action-policy.pdf.

Yet in contrast, the ICO's Service Standards are clear that 'our role is not to investigate or adjudicate on every individual complaint. We are not an ombudsman.'[38]

The vision that the UK Government has for the ICO, as set out in *Data: A New Direction* in 2021, is to refocus 'its statutory commitments away from handling a high volume of low-level complaints and towards addressing the most serious threats to public trust'.[39] The document argued that current legislation 'requires the ICO to allocate a significant amount of its resources to handling data protection complaints; some of this activity delivers low-value outcomes for data subjects and is poor value-for-money for data protection fee payers'.[40] The Government proposed to 'enable the ICO to take a risk-based approach, focusing on upstream activities in order to identify and address problems before they cause widespread harm'.[41]

To achieve this, a requirement for complaints to be raised directly with data controllers at the first tier would be introduced to 'reduce the number of vexatious complaints' and to 'encourage better explanation and more dialogue'. There would also be a requirement for data controllers to have 'a simple and transparent complaints handling process in place to deal with data subject complaints', which would allow the ICO to 'focus on complaints that carry a higher risk of harm to individuals … in a more agile, risk-based way'.[42]

These proposals, along with one to 'introduce a proportionate requirement for organisations to report on the nature and volume of complaints they receive',[43] were welcomed by the ICO in its response to the consultation, as 'ensuring efficient use of resources that deliver the best outcomes for people and businesses.

The data and digital sector provides an example of where increasing complaint volumes and the challenge of delivering trust without stifling innovation or increasing the burden of regulation are shaping the design of redress beyond the orthodox second-tier model. Redress in this landscape is tending towards better design and assurance of first-tier complaint handling, and to approaches centred on risk, intelligence and building capability and accountability.

The weakness of such an approach is that it is still likely to leave a large volume of cases unresolved after the first tier, which may not be taken up by the ICO. The definition of 'best outcomes' for users may look very different from the viewpoint of a regulator seeking efficiency and strategic clarity than from that of a user seeking individual assurance. Yet trust is embodied in the latter, not the former.

More established regulatory regimes have also seen questioned the effectiveness of current arrangements and paradigms. In 2019, following a review of regulation in energy, telecoms, water and financial services, the National Audit Office (NAO) concluded that

[38] Information Commissioner's Office, 'Our service standards' available at https://ico.org.uk/about-the-ico/our-information/our-service-standards/.

[39] Department for Digital, Culture, Media and Sport, *Data: A New Direction*, Consultation Document (10 September 2021) available at www.gov.uk/government/consultations/data-a-new-direction, 114.

[40] ibid 131.

[41] ibid 131.

[42] ibid 133.

[43] Information Commissioner's Office, 'ICO response to DCMS consultation "Data: a new direction"' (7 October 2021) available at https://ico.org.uk/about-the-ico/news-and-events/news-and-blogs/2021/10/response-to-dcms-consultation-foreword/, 17.

regulators should 'do more to translate their high-level intended consumer outcomes into what this means in practical terms'.[44] In some areas regulators were clear on what outcomes they wanted to see but lacked powers to achieve their aims. The NAO cited the energy sector as an example where Ofgem had limited powers over intermediaries between energy suppliers and consumers, and hence faced constraints on how it could act to improve consumer experience.

In a review of consumer protection, also carried out in 2019, the Public Account Committee noted that regulators

> need to be more specific on what exactly they are trying to achieve for consumers, and how they will measure and report on how well they are doing it. A huge part of the problem is that regulators have traditionally worked on the basis that competition will lead to the best outcomes for people.[45]

These reviews underlined the importance of connecting individual outcomes and experiences to regulatory strategy. The link between the macro level intent of regulatory design and the micro level execution of regulatory delivery was noted. Insights into and influence on supply and execution chains are of heightened importance to regulators. The Regulators' Code places a duty on regulators in the UK to ground their work 'in a way that supports those they regulate to comply and grow' and to 'base their regulatory activities on risk'.[46]

So whether across existing regulated sectors or in emerging markets such as the digital arena, execution is becoming more of a focus. First because good intent is only translated into good outcomes through execution. Trust and fairness are not simply lofty concepts; rather, they are experienced in individual lives. We have already noted the pressure on regulators to measure and deliver outcomes and to think more creatively around the regulatory toolkit. To the macro theories and interventions of economic regulation must be added attention to the micro level of individual outcomes. Detriment is unevenly distributed, and so the personal experiences that are sometimes dismissed as edge cases are not only where much of the harm may be embodied but crucially where claims to legitimacy and inclusion will need to be negotiated. Regulators cannot be seen to retreat to a strategic Macronesia inhabited by *Homo economicus*.

Second, for the economic and in some cases environmental benefits of new products and services to be realised, businesses have to focus on building and maintaining trust. In doing so business cannot rest on performative virtue or empty statements but must be able to execute and to deliver outcomes aligned with good intent. The Ipsos MORI Trustworthiness Monitor draws on the work of Phillip Pettit's model to 'ground an abstract concept – trustworthiness – on a very tangible and simple transaction'. The Monitor concluded that basic trust, framed as organisations doing what they say they

[44] National Audit Office, 'Regulating to Protect Consumers: Utilities, communications and financial services markets' (2019) available at www.nao.org.uk/report/regulating-to-protect-consumers-utilities-communications-and-financial-services-markets/.

[45] UK Parliament, 'Committee of Public Accounts, Consumer Protection Review' (2019) available at https://publications.parliament.uk/pa/cm201719/cmselect/cmpubacc/1752/175205.htm.

[46] Better Regulation Delivery Office, 'Department of Business, Innovation and Skills', Regulators' Code (2014).

will, and being open and transparent are 'globally the most important reasons given by the public for trusting different types of organisations or institutions'.[47]

When execution is becoming more complex and challenging, and is also seen as key to developing the social capital of trust, dispute resolution will be most effective where it can help to identify risks and opportunities to improve outcomes. On the *four-box model* set out earlier (see Figure 15.2), this involves effective delivery of the insight and engagement functions to build the bigger picture, and to actively engage with regulators and industry to improve intelligence and to add to capacity and capability in the system as a whole. Providing a definitive answer on an individual complaint is insufficient to restore and advance trust. Disconnecting dispute resolution from the intelligence and capability functions risks condemning it to meeting failure demand – sometimes on an overwhelming scale. The aim should be to build capability and confidence, not just to manage claims and conflict.

In 2015, Ofgem commissioned a review of the Energy Ombudsman, which offered a three-tier analysis of the role that dispute resolution can play in a regulated sector. The review recognised the core role of resolving individual complaints and emphasised two additional roles.

By engaging with industry and the regulator to make recommendations about complaint handling at individual firms (suppliers), the Energy Ombudsman would increase its impact and the value of the insight from the individual complaints. More broadly, by identifying wider systemic issues and opportunities across the sector, the work of the ombudsman 'benefits everyone, those who do complain, those who complain initially but do not pursue their claim further with the ombudsman, and the millions of people who do not. So it has the potential to deliver the greatest consumer benefit of all three roles.'[48]

The review recognised the risk of duplication or overlap between the roles of ombudsman and regulator, and recommended that Ofgem work with the Energy Ombudsman to clarify roles and responsibilities. Subsequent work on implementing the recommendations of the review incorporated the role of Citizens Advice as the statutory consumer advice body, resulting in a tripartite engagement format 'where the three organisations work together to identify key themes and issues to be tackled jointly, provide better information to consumers, and achieve a stronger impact through coordinated supplier engagement'.[49]

There have been similar initiatives in other sectors, such as the Wider Implications Framework established in 2021, where members of the financial services' 'regulatory family work with each other and other parties as appropriate on issues that could have a wider impact across the financial services industry'.[50] Where the turn of the millennium saw the establishment of large second-tier complaint handling mechanisms, two

[47] Ipsos MORI (n 34) 36.

[48] Ofgem, 'Review of Ombudsman Services: Energy' (23 September 2015) available at www.ofgem.gov.uk/publications/review-ombudsman-services-energy.

[49] Ofgem at www.ofgem.gov.uk/publications/tripartite-group-engagement-diagram (21 March 2019).

[50] Financial Ombudsman Service, available at www.financial-ombudsman.org.uk/who-we-are/work-other-organisations/wider-implications-framework.

decades on we find opportunities for data, intelligence and engagement if dispute resolution is better integrated into the market and regulatory ecosystem.

As Chris Hodges' work on outcomes-based collaborative regulation (OBCR) has argued, new possibilities open up with an focus on execution and outcomes, and on the connections in relationships and intelligence to track and manage risk more effectively. The four-box ombudsman model outlined earlier points to the importance of going beyond the individual dispute to invest in trust as a systemic and social asset.

IV. Conclusions

This is very far from the narrower and more atomised dispute resolution set out in the 2013 Directive on Consumer ADR, not least since the Directive had a more limited contractual and transactional scope primarily conceived in terms of stimulating commerce. Nor is it reduced to the role of volume management for the courts. Dispute resolution in regulated sectors is expected to play a broader role as part of a wider system with the regulator as convenor, connector and curator, rather than predominantly as a rule setter and enforcer.

For the last decade, Chris Hodges has been insistent on making a distinction between ADR and CDR, and this chapter recognises the wisdom of doing so. As we have argued here, there are at least three strands of dispute resolution work that are unhelpfully elided into the catch-all ADR chimera.

There are significant differences between essential services and other areas of consumer spending. Social, economic and environmental changes are driving different public expectations and functions in the regulatory landscape that go beyond supplying independent dispute resolution, however effective that may be. The dynamics of being a supplier of a service to an individual company or trade association looking to protect reputation and build confidence are not always the same as those of a sector ombudsman in a regulated sector. Similarly, the functions and objectives of an online court will not be those of regulatory redress, whether macro or micro. It is important to reflect those differences.

Principles and outcomes-focused approaches require dispute resolution to be designed as part of a wider system that can build capability and promote innovation through improved intelligence and execution. The role becomes one of cultural change, as well as of administrative justice.

The *four-box model* advanced in this chapter is offered as one way of approaching redress design. Wider access helps to deliver a more inclusive service and to ensure that data and intelligence on execution and trust gaps are as representative and insightful as possible. In turn, recognising and fulfilling all three roles identified in the Ofgem review means that the benefits of improved execution are translated into improved outcomes for all. The techniques and tests used to resolve disputes can also been designed to be less formal and legalistic, and more flexible than a focus on contracts and consumer law.

And it is in the other two areas of insights and engagement where Chris's work, both on regulatory and redress objectives and, more recently, on OBCR, is particularly valuable. Feedback from dispute resolution contributes to a more detailed and nuanced picture of risk. Insights and engagement can help to support industry capability and execution, leading to better outcomes. Outcomes-based collaborative regulation sites dispute resolution beyond the alternative and beyond even a consumerist frame into the broader opportunity of building trust. Chris challenges us to think about how functions, capabilities and intelligence can be developed, connected and integrated across an ecosystem. Increasingly, we are moving beyond the dispute and, at last, to trust.

Chris is more choral music than chorus lines and musicals, but we hope he may join with another esteemed professor in exclaiming 'By George [they've] got it! *By George [they've] got it*!'[51]

[51] Professor Henry Higgins, *My Fair Lady* (1964).

16

Consumer Dispute Resolution in the Digital Era: Access for All, Or Access for Some Consumers?

ELINE VERHAGE AND NAOMI CREUTZFELDT

> We are seeing new solutions emerging for old problems, since the old problems have not been solved by previous solutions. Some people may find the new solutions too revolutionary, but the new approaches have already spread widely, and are continuing to spread. … The real questions that need to be asked are: what solutions work? … Which options deliver best outcomes?
>
> (C Hodges, 'Modes of Redress for Consumers: ADR and Regulation' (2012))

I. Introduction

We have come together to write a chapter on our experience with, and study of, access to justice and consumer dispute resolution ('CDR' or 'consumer ADR'). We want to take this as an opportunity to thank Chris Hodges for bringing us to the distinct world of CDR. Both of us have benefitted greatly from his insights, contacts and enthusiasm for the topic. We have fond memories of our annual ADR conferences in Oxford, with fruitful exchanges between academics and practitioners followed by heated debates at a local pub.

We also spent time travelling through Europe and talking to people about CDR. Each of these adventures sharpened our minds, leaving us all the wiser, and, quite without our realising it, moulded us into true connoisseurs of Europe's rich selection of national, regional and local cheeses. Here we want to make clear that Fiona Hodges, in her wisdom, always saw right through her husband's officially banned cheese schemes. We tend to agree with Fiona that certain barriers excluding someone from access to a 'pasteurised' remedy can be just and reasonable. In the context of consumer redress schemes, however, barriers restricting access to court or CDR procedures are quite problematic, as these barriers tend to exclude not just one but often whole groups of consumers. One such barrier to consumer access to justice is digitalisation, which will be the focus of this chapter.

This chapter is divided into three sections. First, we describe our respective research trajectories in the field of CDR in the United Kingdom (UK) and the Netherlands, explaining the progression of our scholarly work on consumer access to justice. We then discuss a topical common theme in our trajectories: the impact of the digitalisation of access to justice on marginalised consumers. We will highlight how the Covid-19 pandemic has shown both the potential and the limitations of digitalised court and CDR procedures to effectively deliver access to justice to marginalised consumers in the UK and the Netherlands. Based on these events, we conclude by proposing three strategies in readying both CDR entities and courts for a more digitalised, post-pandemic future of consumer redress: to make online information and procedures more accessible; to strengthen offline variants for those consumers for whom improved online access does not suffice; and to prompt closer collaboration between public and private institutions to realise a more holistic approach to inclusive consumer access to justice.

II. Two Research Trajectories in Consumer Access to Justice

A. Who Can Use ADR and Who Cannot? Naomi's Trajectory

Naomi's research journey with the (non-) user of ADR in mind started 11 years ago, from being hired as a post-doc at the Centre for Socio-Legal Studies at the University of Oxford in January 2011, not knowing what consumer ADR was, to being a Professor of Socio-Legal Studies at the University of Westminster. She has developed her research interests, from ADR bodies and their procedures to empirically understanding the (non-) users of these systems with a wider focus on access to justice.

She was first introduced to ADR and consumer access to justice at the outset of her post-doc. During her post-doc she helped Chris Hodges to research and study for *Consumer ADR in Europe*, which outlined the *state of the art* of consumer ADR in selected European countries. Back then, the European consumer ADR Directive (2013/11/EU) and consumer ODR Regulation ((EU) 524/2013) were in the making, and everyone in the ADR community was anxiously watching how the European Union (EU) Member States would implement this new legislative framework.[1] The study provided an overview of the state of play of consumer ADR systems and concluded, without much of a surprise, that some Member States were doing better than others.[2] The material for the book was collected on many trips across Europe, conducting

[1] Directive 2013/11/EU of the European Parliament and of the Council of 21 May 2013 on alternative dispute resolution for consumer disputes and amending Regulation (EC) No 2006/2004 and Directive 2009/22/EC (Directive on consumer ADR) [2013] OJ L165/63; Regulation (EU) No 524/2013 of the European Parliament and of the Council of 21 May 2013 on online dispute resolution for consumer disputes and amending Regulation (EC) No 2006/2004 and Directive 2009/22/EC (Regulation on consumer ODR); A Biard, 'Impact of Directive 2013/11/EU on Consumer ADR Quality: Evidence from France and the UK' (2019) 42 *Journal of Consumer Policy* 109; N Creutzfeldt, 'Implementation of the Consumer ADR Directive' (2016) 5(4) *Journal of European Consumer and Market Law* 169.

[2] C Hodges, I Benöhr and N Creutzfeldt-Banda (eds), *Consumer ADR in Europe* (Hart Publishing, 2012).

interviews, observing consumer ADR bodies, holding conferences to test their findings and a lot of team discussions. The authors spoke to ADR bodies, ombuds, regulators, businesses, and EU officials who were responsible for the creation of the ADR Directive and ODR Regulation.

After subsequently studying the institutional framework and procedures necessary for the implementation of the EU legislation in the UK and other Member States, Naomi's interest turned to the people who (do not) access consumer ADR bodies. This led to her winning funding from the Economic and Social Research Council (ESRC) to study the impact and legitimacy of the 'middlemen' (ie ombudsmen) in Europe.[3] During this three-year project (2013–16), she compared levels of engagement and trust in ombuds in France, Germany and the UK. The main empirical findings were, among others, that a distinctive sociodemographic group uses ombuds (educated, middle-aged, *white* male) – which is the same group that is able to use ADR easily and navigate the court system. The study also found that the initial contact with users and the ombuds staff is especially important, because staff procedural justice – voice, being heard, treated respectfully and neutrality – promotes outcome acceptance. As a spin-off to this project, Naomi and Chris Gill won ESRC Impact Acceleration Account funding[4] from the University of Oxford, to delve into more detail about those people who access ADR and are unhappy with the outcome. They examined activist consumer groups who – based on their negative experience with ombuds – set up online protest groups to highlight their concerns about the operation of ombuds and campaign for change.[5]

The next step was an institutional change. In February 2016 Naomi got a permanent job at the University of Westminster. There, she built on her findings from her first ESRC grant, teamed up with Chris Gill, and won another ESRC grant to study access to justice for vulnerable and energy poor consumers in the European energy market.[6] This project investigated the users of ADR, asking the question how ordinary people do (and do not) access justice. Across the world, scholars have found that access to justice is highly constrained for ordinary citizens, and even more so for those who might be considered vulnerable.[7] Naomi and Chris Gill chose to investigate these issues in the context of the European energy sector. This sector features significant levels of consumer vulnerability,[8] and addressing this has been a prominent concern

[3] N Creutzfeldt, 'Impact and legitimacy of Ombudsmen in Europe' (2016) available at www.law.ox.ac.uk/trusting-middle-man-impact-and-legitimacy-ombudsmen-europe.

[4] Together with Chris Gill at www.law.ox.ac.uk/research-and-subject-groups/online-critics-ombudsmen.

[5] C Gill and N Creutzfeldt, 'The "Ombuds Watchers": Collective Dissent and Legal Protest Among Users of Public Services Ombuds' (2018) 27(3) *Social & Legal Studies* 367.

[6] Project website: N Creutzfeldt and C Gill, *Research on access to justice for vulnerable and energy poor consumers in the European energy market* (2017–20) available at https://esrcjustenergy.wordpress.com.

[7] eg L Ervo and A Nylund, *The Future of Civil Litigation. Access to Courts and Court-annexed Mediation in Nordic Countries* (Springer 2014); H Genn, 'What is civil justice for-reform, ADR, and access to justice' [2012] 24 Yale Journal of Law & the Humanities 397; S Wrbka, *European consumer access to justice revisited* (Cambridge University Press 2014)

[8] M Bartl 'The Affordability of Energy: How Much Protection for the Vulnerable Consumers?' (2010) 33 *Journal of Consumer Policy* 225; M George, C Graham and L Lennard, *The Energy Penalty: Disabled people and fuel poverty* (University of Leicester, 2013) available at www.fuelpovertylibrary.info/sites/default/files/EAGA31%20%282013%29%20REPORT%20The%20energy%20penalty%20-%20disabled%20people%20and%20fuel%20poverty.pdf.

of policymakers.[9] Lighting, powering and heating homes are essential to daily life, but increasing energy prices, decreasing incomes and the global financial crisis have left large numbers of consumers facing fuel poverty.[10]

A project that Naomi is currently (2022) involved in, funded by the Nuffield Foundation, is looking at the court reform programme and the response to the pandemic.[11] For this project she has teamed up with experts in procedural justice and ethnography. They aim to better understand the effect of rapid digitalisation on the advice and redress systems as well as its users; to identify the effects on access for marginalised groups; and to explore how trust can be built and sustained in specific parts of a justice system affected by the pandemic. They are looking at pathways to justice in the administrative justice system across two areas: *housing* (Property Chamber, Housing Ombudsman) and *special educational needs and disabilities* (Special Educational Needs and Disability Tribunal, Local Government and Social Care Ombudsman). Related to this project, Naomi is increasingly interested in joined-up partnership agreements that help people access justice, in particular health-justice partnerships (HJPs) in hospital settings.[12] Growing evidence shows the close connection between poor health and unmet social welfare legal needs, including inadequate welfare benefits, housing, debt and employment.[13] This new project seeks to address current and timely gaps in the evidence base about the value of integrating social welfare legal advice in healthcare settings. Cross-sector working has become a policy focus in both health and legal sectors, responding to rising levels of legal need and increasing pressures on healthcare services linked to social issues. The project will focus on NHS hospital settings, where little research on HJPs has been undertaken, and will explore outcomes where hardly any robust evidence exists.

At the time of writing this chapter (early 2022), the CDR landscape in the UK provides coverage for all consumer complaints through different types of ADR.[14] The Chartered Trading Standards Institute holds a list of just under 60 approved ADR bodies.[15] These bodies range from dispute resolution groups, associations, centres, redress schemes, ombuds, consumer codes, consumer protection schemes, adjudication services, to federations. Some have specific remits; others cover more than one sector. Here it is noted that after Brexit, the ADR Directive was amended by the Consumer

[9] European Commission 2016 available at https://energy-poverty.ec.europa.eu/energy-poverty-observatory_en; Ofgem 'Consumer Vulnerability Strategy Progress Report' (2015) available at www.ofgem.gov.uk/sites/default/files/docs/2015/09/cvs_progress_report_for_website_final.pdf.

[10] N Creutzfeldt et al, 'The social and local dimensions of governance of energy poverty: adaptive responses to state remoteness' (2020) 43 *Journal of Consumer Policy* 635; N Creutzfeldt et al, *Access to Justice for Vulnerable and Energy-Poor Consumers: Just Energy?* (Hart Publishing, 2021).

[11] N Creutzfeldt et al, 'Delivering administrative justice after the pandemic' (2021–23) available at www.nuffieldfoundation.org/project/delivering-administrative-justice-after-the-pandemic.

[12] N Creutzfeldt et al, 'Access to social welfare advice in a hospital settings: integration of services' (2021) available at https://ajc-justice.co.uk/wp-content/uploads/2021/06/AJC-Health-Justice-Report-Final.pdf.

[13] DH Genn and S Beardon, 'Law for health' (2021) available at www.ucl.ac.uk/health-of-public/sites/health_of_public/files/law_for_health_hjp_final.pdf; S Beardon et al, 'Social Welfare, Legal Services, Delivery of Health Care, Integrated, Social Determinants of Health' (2020) *Journal of Public Mental Health* available at https://discovery.ucl.ac.uk/id/eprint/10107428/1/Preprint_%20Beardon%20et%20al%20JPMH%2003.2020.pdf.

[14] C Gill et al, 'Confusion, Gaps, and Overlaps' (2017) available at www.citizensadvice.org.uk/Global/CitizensAdvice/Consumer%20publications/Confusiongapsandoverlaps-Original1.docx.pdf.

[15] Chartered Trading Standards Institute list of ADR providers in the UK (2021) available at www.tradingstandards.uk/consumer-help/adr-approved-bodies/.

Protection (Amendment) (EU Exit) Regulations 2018 (SI 2018/1326). One major change meant that from 1 January 2021, the UK Secretary of State for the Home Department became responsible for publishing the ADR provider list (rather than the EU). Also, UK-based ADR providers are no longer required to offer cross-border services to consumers in EU Member States, and traders are no longer able to offer their consumers non-UK ADR alternatives. Brexit also meant that the ODR Regulation was revoked, which occurred with the coming into force of the Consumer Protection (Amendment) (EU Exit) Regulations 2018. Hence, from 1 January 2021, consumer and businesses in the UK can no longer use the ODR platform.

Despite the existence of all these consumer ADR providers (for all types of consumer complaints except for education and health), it remains a challenge for most consumers to find them.[16] Consumer dispute resolution has not become the norm, or default go-to institution, as some of the advocates had promised and hoped. While the CDR landscape in the UK remains strong in its sectorial coverage, with many providers available, consumers do need to be made aware of the CDR pathway to be able to make use of its full potential.

B. Enhancing Effective Consumer Access to Justice: Eline's Trajectory

Eline is currently nearing her first decade in the field of CDR – first as a graduate student, then as a doctoral researcher and most recently as a consultant to CDR institutions. She was first introduced to consumer ADR in 2012 as a law student at her alma mater – Leiden University – familiarising herself with the various pathways to civil justice in the Netherlands. At the time, consumer ADR was about to go through significant transitions in light of the European legislative proposals for a consumer ADR Directive and consumer ODR Regulation. Eline decided to write her master's thesis on the subject of how the Dutch legislator would need to implement the proposed ADR Directive and ODR Regulation for the Dutch CDR landscape.

Then, in late 2014, Eline was appointed as PhD Fellow in Civil Procedure at Leiden University, expanding her research on the interaction between the EU legislative framework on CDR and the Dutch CDR landscape. Before the Dutch implementation of these instruments in 2015, Weber and Hodges described the Dutch CDR landscape as one of the most accomplished in Europe.[17] They particularly lauded the *Stichting Geschillencommissies voor Consumentenzaken* (SGC) (Foundation for Consumer Complaint Boards) for its ability to secure comprehensive sectoral coverage of CDR through a centralised, national, single framework.[18] The SGC was established in 1970 as an independent foundation to oversee, establish and administer

[16] M Loos, 'Consumer ADR after Implementation of the ADR Directive: Enforcing European Consumer Rights at the Detriment of European Consumer Law', Amsterdam Law School Research Paper 42/2015, available at http://papers.ssrn.com/sol3/papers.cfm?abstract_id=2685651.

[17] F Weber and C Hodges, 'The Netherlands' in Hodges et al (eds) (n 2) 129, 164.

[18] ibid 129.

sectoral CDR boards for a broad range of consumer markets.[19] Over half a century, around 50 sectoral CDR boards were established, primarily through self-regulatory initiatives in the marketplace, and embedded in the SGC framework.[20] Besides the SGC, in the mid-2000s, three sectoral CDR providers were established: for the financial sector (*Klachteninstitituut Financiele Dienstverlenening* (Kifid)), for the health insurance sector (*Stichting Klachten en Geschillen Zorgverzekeringen* (SKGZ)), and for public housing (*Huurcommissie* (DHC)). The SGC, Kifid, SKGZ and DHC are the only four approved CDR providers under the national legislation implementing the ADR Directive.[21] Generally, the SGC, Kifid, SKGZ, and DHC facilitate a multi-faceted toolkit of consumer ADR procedures. These range from (early) dispute settlement stages, such as information and advice, conciliation, ombuds and mediation, to the dispute resolution stages of binding advice and arbitration.[22] Binding advice is a typically Dutch ADR procedure, in which an independent third party gives a binding resolution to the dispute between two parties.[23]

Around the time that Eline commenced on her PhD research, she also started collaborating with Chris Hodges on a project mapping the implementation of the ADR Directive in 19 EU Member States. After discussing a variety of consumer ADR landscapes in the EU at their first meeting for this project, Chris – almost Dutch in his directness – asked the pressing question 'Clearly, these systems are interesting, but do they work?' Throughout the years, this question served as a *cantus firmus* in their collaborations, underlying the polyphonic composition of the answers they retrieved from a wide variety of ombuds and CDR practitioners in the Netherlands, Spain, Italy, the UK, Belgium and Austria. These various interactions, and the collaboration with Chris, shaped Eline's scholarly thinking and helped her observe the Dutch CDR landscape from a socio-legal angle.

The insights Eline gained from her work with Chris involved in essence the fundamental question 'Does CDR work in real life?' The focus that this question calls for influenced how Eline framed her doctoral research. In her thesis, she suggests how the Dutch implementation of the European legislative framework for CDR might be improved to ensure *effective* consumer access to justice. Her conceptual framework presents a matrix of policy objectives and regulatory techniques derived from the ADR Directive and ODR Regulation. First, as to the policy objectives, Eline argues that for these instruments to realise their objective of delivering 'a high level of consumer protection' and 'proper functioning of the Internal Market', they must achieve 'effective' consumer access to justice. That is to say, besides *de jure* redress, CDR procedures should enable consumers to obtain *de facto* redress; law in the books and law in action

[19] E Verhage, 'The Implementation of the Consumer ADR Directive in the Netherlands' in P Cortés (ed), *The New Regulatory Framework for Consumer Dispute Resolution* (Oxford University Press, 2016) 229.

[20] Weber and Hodges (n 17) 136.

[21] Implementatiewet buitengerechtelijke geschillenbeslechting consumenten, *Stb* 2015, 160.

[22] E Verhage, 'Een blik over de grens: CDR in Nederland' in S Voet (ed), *CDR in België* (Die Keure, 2018) 205.

[23] M Knigge and E Verhage, 'The impact of the ADR Directive on article 7:904 par. 1 DCC explored. What is "unacceptable according to standards of reasonableness and fairness" after the implementation of the Directive?' in CG Breedveld-de Voogd et al (eds), *Core Concepts in the Dutch Civil Code. Continuously in Motion* (Wolters Kluwer, 2016) 61; PE Ernste, *Bindend advies* (Kluwer, 2012).

should coincide. Second, as to the regulatory techniques, Eline distinguishes two types of rules by which the ADR Directive and ODR Regulation set out to reach their objectives: those setting institutional and those setting procedural requirements.

Through this lens, Eline's doctoral thesis examines how the institutional and procedural implementation of the two instruments in the Dutch CDR landscape can best meet the ultimate objective of effective access to justice for consumers. Here, Eline underscores two aspects by which the Dutch implementation falls short in realising effective access to justice for all consumers. First, regarding the 'access' component, the national legislation does not guarantee 'full coverage' (Article 5(1), ADR Directive) of procedures for all consumers due to the Netherlands' emphasis on voluntary business participation. In 2015, the Dutch legislator mended existing gaps in sectoral coverage by embedding a national residual CDR board with a general scope (*Geschillencommissie Algemeen*) in the SGC framework.[24] In practice, however, this residual board does not effectively mend existing gaps in coverage of CDR procedures.

Second, as to the 'justice' element, the Dutch implementation does not ensure the optimal substantive quality of CDR. The reason is a lack of interinstitutional mechanisms by which CDR institutions can secure uniform application of mandatory (EU) consumer law in their processes. The resulting legal uncertainty is particularly critical given the binding nature of decisions of the most commonly used types of ADR. Eline's thesis offers solutions to these specific shortcomings by advising which steps the legislature, courts, CDR institutions and businesses can take individually and jointly.

As Eline's doctoral thesis progressed, her continuing wish was to offer practice-based solutions to the shortcomings she addressed in her work. In late 2020, she was given the opportunity to complement her academic trajectory with a position as senior advisor of Strategy, Policy & Legal Affairs at the SGC. In this position, she had the opportunity to exchange views and collaborate with all the relevant stakeholders in the Dutch CDR landscape, from consumer and trade associations to policymakers at the Ministry of Security and Justice and Economic Affairs, and policy meetings with staff from Kifid, SKGZ and DHC.

Eline's position at the SGC led to her becoming an independent ADR consultant. At the SGC and then as a consultant, she has experienced first-hand the profound impact of the Covid-19 pandemic on consumer access to ADR and court procedures. For example, the impact of the rapid introduction and expanded use of virtual hearings on people who have difficulties navigating the digital space became apparent to her. In addition, she experienced the need to mitigate barriers in *offline* access to ADR procedures caused by the pandemic, particularly in-person hearings, to guarantee that the parties' fundamental procedural safeguards continued to be protected. In other words, Eline's experiences at the SGC helped her better recognise which consumers have difficulty accessing ADR processes and to think about how these hurdles might

[24] In 2019, another residual CDR board was established under the umbrella of the SGC. The *Geschillencommissie Algemeen* (2015) is the residual CDR board for consumer disputes against traders who do not participate in an existing sectoral CDR board within the SGC framework. The *Geschillencommissie voor Consumentenzaken* (2019) is the residual CDR board for consumer disputes against traders in market sectors where no sectoral CDR board has been established (yet).

be addressed. The combination of her academic research and experiences in the field gave further depth to the question she explored with Chris, that is, whether the systems work, namely: How do we shape and build consumer redress that delivers equal access to justice for all consumers in the digital era?

III. Digitalised Access to Justice and Marginalised Consumers

Our respective research trajectories have not only Chris's inspiration in common, but also a theme where our work intersects. Both of us have turned our attention to the role of digitalisation in realising consumer access to justice that is inclusive, meaning that is effective for *all* consumers. As the following study shows, the recent Covid-19 pandemic has spurred the digitisation of consumer redress. The way both CDR entities and courts have responded to this historic event illustrates that digital or online solutions can expand pathways to access to justice for some consumers, but also potentially diminish accessibility for others. Digitalisation of consumer redress risks marginalising people who are digitally illiterate. The policy challenge here, which we address next, is how both CDR entities as well as courts can use technical advances to improve consumer access to justice, not for some but for all consumers.

A. Digitisation of Consumer Redress Systems and the Impact of the Pandemic

i. Digitalisation of the Civil Justice System and the CDR Landscape

Since 2016, digitisation of the justice system has been a concerted effort in the UK.[25] The courts and tribunals' modernisation agenda aims to provide new and user-friendly digital services. As a by-product, an increase in efficiency is promised. Pilots have been underway since, and the pandemic fast-tracked and stress-tested the ongoing digitalisation process. Consumers always could access ombuds online, but they are also able to send a letter, call or visit the ombuds in person (although this is not common). The ADR Directive assisted in the default online access to consumer ADR. In other words, the digitalisation of the court system creates an interesting moment to reflect upon access to justice and the parallels with the consumer ADR/ombuds system.

In the Netherlands, the digitisation of the justice system gained political and legislative momentum in 2012. At the time, the Ministry of Justice and Security and the judiciary initiated the Quality and Innovation of the Judiciary (*Kwaliteit en Innovatie Rechtspraak (KEI)*) programmes, which aimed to modernise and digitise the civil and administrative justice systems.[26] Besides legislation modernising the codes of

[25] HM Courts & Tribunals Service, 'The HMCTS Reform Programme' (9 November 2018) available at www.gov.uk/guidance/the-hmcts-reform-programme#a-justice-system-for-those-who-need-it-most.

[26] *Kamerstukken II*, 2012/13, 29 279, nr 164 (Letter, Minister of Security and Justice, 11 June 2013).

Dutch civil and administrative procedure to fit an online context being adopted in 2016, an extensive digitisation process of the court infrastructure was part of the KEI innovations.[27] However, in 2018, the digitisation process proved too ambitious in terms of scale, governance and funding, and the judiciary opted for a 'reset' of this tier of KEI.[28] The judiciary eventually elaborated a more moderate approach towards digitalisation of the civil justice system in the Digital Accessibility project (*Digitale Toegankelijkheid* (DT)).[29] The latter relates to online submission and exchange of documents and digital communications between the courts and external parties (litigants, lawyers, bailiffs, etc). The judiciary's digitisation agenda generally did not aim to fully move oral hearings online.[30] Facilities to conduct hearings online were limited, and not available across the board. Hence, up until 2020, oral hearings at the court were in-person by default.

The Dutch CDR landscape was set up to provide consumers with an easy, cheap and informal pathway to justice alongside the courts. Compared to the civil justice system, digital access to consumer ADR procedures was already quite advanced in the Netherlands. From 2010, consumers could submit their complaints online at the SGC, with Kifid, SKGZ and DHC soon following suit and digitising access to their respective procedures in order to meet the standards set out in the ADR Directive and ODR Regulation.[31] The Directive merely seeks to enhance online accessibility of CDR procedures (Article 8(a)) and does not require CDR entities to facilitate hearings exclusively online. Prior to the pandemic, none of the CDR entities chose to introduce virtual hearings.

ii. Access to Digital Justice: Procedural Safeguards to Be Met Online and Offline

The various efforts moving the justice systems and CDR landscapes online in the UK and the Netherlands not only seek to keep these pathways on a par with the rapid digitalisation of society, but also aim to deliver better access to justice.[32] Online technology is supposed to keep simple claims out of court, to leave courts and judges for the most challenging cases. 'All of this helps some of the most vulnerable people facing difficult situations get justice as quickly as possible and supports litigants who do not have legal representation.'[33]

[27] E Bauw 'KEI, een gamechanger voor de civiele en bestuursrechtspraak?' (2016) 2 *Rechtsgeleerd Magazijn THEMIS* 55.

[28] *Kamerstukken II*, 2018/19, 29 279, nr 420, p 1 (attachment, Letter President of the Council of the Judiciary, 10 April 2018).

[29] *Kamerstukken II*, 2020/21, 29 279, nr 623 (Letter, Minister of Legal Protection, 29 October 2020).

[30] X Kramer, E Van Gelder and E Themeli, 'e-Justice in the Netherlands: the Rocky Road to Digitised Justice' in M Weller and M Wendland (eds), *Digital Single Market: Bausteine eines Rechts in der Digitalen Welt* (Mohr Siebeck 2018) para 3.2.5.

[31] Verhage (n 19) 235, 245.

[32] Bauw (n 27).

[33] HM Courts & Tribunals Service (n 25).

Here we will concentrate on the most fundamental requirements that access to justice imposes on a court and CDR provider, to discuss if these requirements are met by the digitalisation agenda and what the Covid-19 pandemic has shown us.

Achieving the promoted aim that consumer redress systems (courts and ADR) will enable better access to justice for all is an enormous challenge. Under English law, the documented irreducible minimum standards of 'access to justice' could serve as a starting point for this discussion. Byrom[34] set these out as a standard against which the court reform and its impact can be empirically assessed and held to account. There are four criteria: (i) access to the formal legal system; (ii) access to an effective hearing; (iii) access to a decision in accordance with substantive law; (iv) access to a remedy.

A similar access to justice 'reality check' needs to be undertaken in the consumer ADR context. In the UK, ombuds and ADR providers are set up to help people access alternative (to the courts) pathways to justice. These pathways to resolving a consumer dispute are supposed to be accessible, faster and free of charge (as a first step).[35] If we consider the four basic criteria for access to justice, they also need to hold true in relation to an ombud process. We might amend them to: (i) access to ADR; (ii) access to a fair and effective process; (iii) access to decision in accordance with what is fair and reasonable; (iv) access to a remedy (apology, financial, etc).

Under Dutch law, Article 6 of the European Convention on Human Rights (ECHR) and Article 47 of the EU Charter of Fundamental Rights (EU Charter) lay down irreducible standards of 'access to justice' against which the digitisation of the civil justice system can be assessed.[36] Similar to the standards applicable under English law, Article 6 of the ECHR and Article 47 of the EU Charter also safeguard parties' right to have: (i) access to a tribunal previously established by law; (ii) access to a fair and public hearing; (iii) access to a decision in accordance with substantive law (Article 121, Dutch Constitution); and (iv) access to a remedy.

The ADR Directive, and the Dutch implementation legislation, sets out minimum standards of 'access to justice' against which approved CDR procedures can be assessed. For every consumer dispute falling within the scope of the ADR Directive (Article 2), accredited CDR entities must ensure that consumers have: (i) *online* and *offline* access to a CDR procedure (Article 8(a)); (ii) access to a fair process (Article 9(1)(a)); (iii) access to a decision either in accordance to what is fair or reasonable, if a solution is proposed to the consumer (Article 9(2)), or in accordance with the protection of mandatory consumer law, if a solution is imposed on the consumer (Article 11); and (iv) access to a remedy.[37]

[34] N Byrom, 'Digital Justice: HMCTS data strategy and delivering access to justice' (2019) available at https://research.thelegaleducationfoundation.org/wp-content/uploads/2019/09/DigitalJusticeFINAL.pdf.

[35] Hodges et al (eds) (n 2).

[36] Bauw (n 27).

[37] Whether an ADR procedure provides access to a remedy depends on whether the result of the procedure is binding on the parties or not. In this regard, recital 45 of the ADR Directive stresses that parties cannot be deprived from their right to seek redress before a court if the ADR procedure does not result in an outcome which is binding. In such cases, parties should 'not be prevented from initiating judicial proceedings in relation to that dispute'. See also Art 9(2)(b)(ii): 'The parties, before agreeing or following a proposed solution, are informed that: … (ii) participation in the procedure does not preclude the possibility of seeking redress through court proceedings …'

In order to effectively deliver better access to consumer justice in the digital era, the four basic criteria of 'access to justice' distinguished for courts and consumer ADR procedures need to be met offline as well as online. The emergence of the Covid-19 pandemic brought to our attention the reality of access and the ability of the courts and CDR providers in the UK and the Netherlands. Essentially serving as a 'stress test', the pandemic forced a fast response from both the justice systems and the respective CDR landscapes, and made it evident what technology could, and could not, offer.

iii. Impact of the Covid-19 Pandemic 'Stress Test' on Consumer Access to Justice

In March 2020, both in the UK and the Netherlands, courthouses and CDR entities had to close their doors and bring all business to a halt as people were not connected remotely to their work computers or needed paperwork that had been left on their desks. It meant that all the usual pathways to advice, assistance and justice had to be brought to a (temporary) halt. The *typical* consumer journey, from experiencing a problem, seeking advice (friends, local advice providers), preparing to bring a claim to a court or to a CDR entity, was completely disrupted. The initial response of the courts and CDR entities to the stress test was to re-establish access to their pathways for consumers online.

In the UK, the pandemic forced the justice system to go fully online overnight. It was not ready for this transition; the courts had to deal with a lack of funding, as well as jump-starting online services where possible.[38] After a few months of total closure, slowly some of the buildings were being accessed by staff to collect the mail and to set up a remote working possibility. This happened to different degrees in both the justice system and the respective ombuds/CDR entities. Eventually a few people were let back into buildings to help set up connections between office computer systems/programs, so that people could access them from home in a secure manner. In most cases this meant investing in new devices, hardware and software, adding work telephone lines to home landlines – in short, it was a massive investment that some could afford more easily than others. Once the phone and online access was established, there remained the challenge of not being able to access physical documents that were locked up in the workplace.

It meant that some access to justice was available again, but solely online, which by default excluded those who were less able to access and navigate the online space. People could generally also reach these organisations via the phone, but due to staffing issues this involved waiting times and delays in progressing cases.

The ombuds, providing an online service in principle, also had some challenges to overcome during the pandemic. This was to do with staff not being able to access the building and connect remotely to the online and telephone systems. Here the question

[38] UK Parliament, 'Report published on the impact of COVID-19 on courts and tribunals in England and Wales' (30 March 2021) available at https://committees.parliament.uk/committee/172/constitution-committee/news/153596/report-published-on-the-impact-of-covid19-on-courts-and-tribunals-in-england-and-wales/.

of access and vulnerability is a slightly different one. For those people who have trouble accessing the ombuds online, the phone option exists as well as the possibility to send a letter. This last means of communication might slow down the process but it does enable access. Of course, this still excludes some groups. As this situation was caused by a global health crisis, there was a reasonable amount of acceptance and patience, allowing the processes to resume in a piecemeal fashion.

In the Netherlands, the first national lockdown completely halted access to the courts and CDR entities alike. While staff transitioned into remote working, in-writing procedures continued. As discussed above, oral hearings at the courts were in-person by default, and facilities for teleconferencing or telephone hearings were limited. As offline access to justice was not available, the pandemic forced courts to introduce virtual hearings overnight. In just a few months the IT infrastructure of the justice system was adjusted, and the use of virtual hearings was gradually expanded across the board. Simultaneously, temporary legislation amending the Dutch Code of Civil Procedure was enacted to legitimise the use of these technological innovations in court procedures.[39] The expanded use of technology meant that some access to the courts was re-established, namely *online*, but this only benefitted consumers who were able and inclined to use a digital pathway to justice. Once court procedures could be accessed online, the focus of the judiciary shifted towards re-establishing the *offline* availability of its procedures. Buildings were swiftly adjusted, and the judiciary could gradually accommodate in-person hearings again in selected cases. Criteria by which courts could determine whether a hearing would take place in person, virtually or in a hybrid manner, or whether the case could be resolved in writing, were laid down in temporary regulations for case management.[40] Consumers who relied on the offline pathway to access courts could also reach the courts by telephone, but initially only between specific times during the day. Courts soon expanded this option by adding time slots in the evenings.

Like the courts, CDR entities also swiftly introduced virtual hearings and adjusted their buildings to allow in-person hearings to re-establish consumer access to justice. Such entities do not have multiple offices and hearing rooms, unlike the justice system. Hence, their capacity to accommodate in-person hearings safely and in a timely matter was often restricted. In cases where an in-person hearing was indicated, delays in processing times could not be prevented. Throughout the pandemic, the CDR entities could generally facilitate online access to CDR procedures through the expanded use of virtual hearings. Still, the availability of their offline pathways, specifically the ability to accommodate in-person hearings, remained limited as the government restrictions on in-person gatherings continued. Consumers could always contact the CDR entities by telephone, but only during working hours.

[39] Art 2(1) Tijdelijke wet COVID-19 Justitie en Veiligheid (Temporary Act COVID-19 Justice and Security). Available in Dutch at https://wetten.overheid.nl/BWBR0043413/2020-12-17.

[40] Tijdelijke algemene regeling zaaksbehandeling Rechtspraak (Temporary general case-handling regulation judiciary) available at https://www.rechtspraak.nl/coronavirus-%28COVID-19%29/Paginas/COVID-19-Tijdelijke-algemene-regeling-zaaksbehandeling-Rechtspraak.aspx (5 November 2021); and specifically for small claims procedures, Tijdelijke regeling voor Kanton en Handel (Temporary case-handling regulation subdistrict and district courts) www.rechtspraak.nl/SiteCollectionDocuments/Tijdelijke-regeling-voor-handel-en-kantonzaken.pdf (30 November 2021).

iv. Upholding Procedural Safeguards Offline and Online

Courts and CDR entities in the UK and the Netherlands increasingly managed to re-establish online and offline access to their respective procedures and gradually expand the capacity of both pathways. However, both courts and CDR entities could not facilitate *offline* access to their processes at standard capacity during the pandemic. Consumers who depended on the offline pathways to courts and CDR entities were confronted with an increase in processing times due to adjournment of in-person hearings. One might argue that in some cases both the diminished offline accessibility and the delays resulted in consumers' fundamental procedural rights being compromised, as the irreducible standards of access to a court or CDR entity, a fair hearing and a remedy were de facto compromised, if not violated. However, unlike offline proceedings, online proceedings were by and large able to meet the procedural safeguards of access to justice. Disparities like these between offline and online procedures resulted from government health and safety regulations that limited in-person gatherings. Nevertheless, the uptake and expanded use of digital technologies in court and CDR procedures will be an intrinsic element of conventional consumer access to justice from now on. Before the pandemic, digitisation of access to justice was supplementary, but online procedures have now become more mainstream and are here to stay. Given this prospect, it is vital to make sure everyone is included. The next subsection will discuss this issue.

B. Access for Some in the Digital Era: Exclusion of Marginalised Consumers

Section III.A depicted the disruptive effect of the pandemic on access to formal and informal pathways to justice for consumers in the UK and the Netherlands. In the initial stages of the pandemic, access to justice was compromised temporarily for every consumer in both countries. Although the introduction and use of online technologies expanded the online pathways to access to the courts and CDR entities, the equally critical offline pathways to access both systems remained impaired throughout the pandemic.

The reduced access to offline procedures offered by both courts and CDR entities highlighted the divide between those who can engage with justice online through digital platforms and those who cannot.[41] Those who could navigate the Internet with ease and were used to carrying out their everyday transactions online had newfound access to the court process, the ombuds, CDR entities and the advice providers. Those people who were used to accessing support by walking into a building and talking to other humans face-to-face had an extremely hard time accessing justice during the pandemic.[42]

[41] Byrom (n 34).

[42] N Creutzfeldt and D Sechi, 'Social welfare [law] advice provision during the pandemic in England and Wales: a conceptual framework' (2021) 43(2) *Journal of Social Welfare and Family Law* 153 available at www.tandfonline.com/doi/full/10.1080/09649069.2021.1917707; M Ter Voert et al, 'Gevolgen van Covid-19 voor de rechtspraak en kwetsbare rechtzoekenden: een onderzoek naar de maatregelen en de positie van rechtzoekenden binnen het straf-, civiele jeugdbeschermings-, en vreemdelingenrecht' (2022) Nijmegen/Leiden/Utrecht: Radboud University/Leiden University/Utrecht University available at https://hdl.handle.net/2066/248272.

While a few still managed to seek help and access support, others were cut off from pathways to justice completely. That part of the population that was already disadvantaged was pushed aside and generally left without access.

The pandemic showed that marginalisation of consumer access to justice due to advanced digitalisation of court and CDR procedures should not be underestimated. Nor should the potential scope of this issue. Research shows that a significant segment of the populations of the UK and the Netherlands face digital exclusion from access to justice. In 2019, the Eurostat survey, measuring the level of digital competencies and skills in information-gathering, communication, problem-solving and software skills, indicated that 20 per cent of individuals aged 16–74 in the UK and 16 per cent of individuals in the Netherlands have low overall digital skills.[43] These individuals lack the basic digital skills necessary to successfully use and navigate the digital space in one to three of the four indicated domains.[44] If this group gets involved in a consumer dispute, the availability of offline pathways to courts and CDR entities is essential to their having access to justice.

As discussed, disparities in the availability of online and offline access to courts and CDR entities during the pandemic were caused by ongoing government measures restricting access to buildings and in-person gatherings. Courts and CDR bodies will likely be able to facilitate consumers to access their systems via both the offline and online pathways once the government regulations are fully lifted. Nevertheless, the stress test of the pandemic, although unique, brought to the fore the reality of the access to justice 'gap' digitally illiterate consumers face. Despite there being compelling arguments in favour of digitalisation of redress systems improving access to justice, it needs to happen in a measured way.[45] Attention needs to be paid to those left behind and measures put in place so that these groups can also access justice.

IV. Towards Inclusive Consumer Justice in the Digital Era

The need to take digital illiteracy into account raises the question of how, in practice, courts and CDR entities should tailor their online and offline procedures. The remainder of this chapter offers several strategies towards realising this post-pandemic, forward-looking take on digital and inclusive consumer access to justice.

We propose that this objective would entail at least three strategies: to make online information and procedures more accessible; to bolster offline variants for those for whom improved online access is not enough; and, lastly, to prompt all public and private institutions involved to work together more closely and thus realise a more holistic

[43] Eurostat, 'Individuals who have basic or above basic overall digital skills by sex' (*Eurostat*, 2019) available at https://ec.europa.eu/eurostat/cache/metadata/en/tepsr_sp410_esmsip2.htm.

[44] ibid.

[45] S Hynes, 'An online court has the potential to revolutionise access to justice but it should not be rushed' (LAG, March 2016) available at www.lag.org.uk/article/201991/an-online-court-has-the-potential-to-revolutionise-access-to-justice-but-it-should-not-be-rushed.

approach to inclusive justice. These strategies do not require a complete overhaul of the consumer redress systems, but instead should start from and improve current practices that already show great potential.

The following overview presents some of those existing practices to illustrate the starting point of more inclusive access to justice for all consumers.

A. Online Comprehensibility: Using Plain Language

One strategy toward improving inclusive digital consumer redress systems is for courts and CDR entities to use language online that is comprehensible to any consumer. In this regard, such an approach can begin with various projects that have recently commenced in both the Netherlands and the UK.

In the Netherlands, for example, courts and CDR entities are running various projects that enhance the accessibility and comprehensibility of their procedures. These projects are aimed at using 'plain language' for rules of procedure, decisions and external communication. They also include presenting key procedural steps on their websites, using infographics or animated instructional videos. To this end, courts and CDR entities actively seek to collaborate with various social partners, empowering vulnerable consumers, to ensure that their institutional response removes barriers to offline and online access to their systems. The collaborations range from courses on plain language in legal communication to focus groups that test the clarity of rewritten rules of procedure.

In the UK, similar to the Netherlands, efforts are underway to rephrase complex explanations about courts and ADR, processed into plain language for the public to access. Short informative videos that explain the court process and the ADR process can be usually found on the respective institutions' websites. These have the aim of explaining to people who seek access how best to go about achieving this.

B. Proximity: Bringing Courts and CDR Closer to People

A second strategy is to bring offline consumer redress pathways closer to the people and simplify access to the justice they provide. After all, one lesson the pandemic taught is that the digitisation of court and CDR procedures may offer an additional route to better access to justice, but not if this does not work in tandem with offline procedures. The reason is that there will always be consumers in need of an offline pathway to justice. Research shows that eradicating digital illiteracy is one of the biggest challenges of the digital era, and the issue will likely never be entirely resolved.[46] Hence, courts and CDR entities will need to tailor their procedures to the specific needs both of consumers who are digitally literate and of those who are not.

[46] M Non, M Dinkova and B Dahmen, 'Skill up or get left behind? Digital skills and labor market outcomes in the Netherlands' (*CPB* February 2021) available at www.cpb.nl/sites/default/files/omnidownload/CPB-Discussion-Paper-419-Skill-up-or-get-left-behind-Digital-skill-labor-market-outcomes-netherlands.pdf.

Various examples of current projects suggest promising ways of improving offline access to justice for consumers. In the Netherlands, most CDR entities operate an informal early dispute resolution phase characterised by information provision, conciliation and (referral to) mediation.[47] Those entities also enhance easier access to offline procedures at various physical locations. The SGC, for example, facilitates oral hearings at central locations in the Netherlands (eg, The Hague and Utrecht). Similarly, the courts establish the objective of simpler access to justice through various pilot projects under the umbrella of the Socially Effective Administration of Justice programme (*Maatschappelijk effectieve rechtspraak*).[48] One such pilot project introduced the concept of the 'proximity judge' (*nabijheidsrechter*), and another facilitated a 'community judge' (*wijkrechter*).[49] Some of these initiatives take civil procedure out of the physical courtroom and resolve disputes in a more informal manner at local community centres.[50] Similar to ADR processes, judges who take part in these pilots experiment with ADR techniques. In doing so, they untangle the various financial, social, emotional and legal aspects of disputes that keep parties divided.

Another way to bring courts or CDR entities closer to the people is to make information more readily available in various forms suited to a broader variety of consumers. For example, as already noted, in both the UK and the Netherlands, short informative videos that explain the court process and the ADR process can be usually found on the respective institutions' websites. Similarly, consumers in both countries can always reach both the courts and CDR entities by telephone for information, including how the procedure works and for non-legal advice. In addition, societal partners offer consumer support and advice by telephone, such as the Consumer Association (*Consumentenbond*) and the consumer regulator, the Authority for Consumers & Markets (*Autoriteit Consument & Markt*), in the Netherlands and Citizens Advice in the UK. These personal interactions with the institutions' staff can build trust that this pathway to justice is there for consumers and a sense of inclusion.

C. A Holistic and Collaborative Approach

Third, no matter what benefits the preceding two strategies may offer, the results will not be optimal if the public and private institutions involved do not work together to realise a more holistic or collaborative approach to offering access to justice that includes people who have difficulty accessing online dispute resolution systems. Such an integrated approach would entail that when different organisations independently aid the same consumers, all of these services may be more effective in helping those consumers, from the onset of a complaint till its resolution.

[47] Verhage (n 19) 233; Weber and Hodges (n 17).

[48] Raad voor de Rechtspraak, Agenda voor Onderzoek en Kennisdeling 2021–2022, available at www.rechtspraak.nl/SiteCollectionDocuments/agenda-voor-onderzoek-en-kennisdeling-2021–2022.pdf.

[49] E Bauw et al, 'De nabijheidsrechter en maatschappelijk effectieve rechtspraak' *Tijdschrift voor Civiele Rechtspleging* (2020) 1; E Bauw et al, *Naar een nabijheidsrechter? Een onderzoek naar de inpasbaarheid van de vrederechter in België en Frankrijk in het Nederlandse rechtsbestel* (Boom Juridisch, 2019) 139–40.

[50] Temporary legislation was put in place to legitimise these 'sandboxes' innovating civil court procedures. See *Stb* 2020, 223 ('Tijdelijke Experimentenwet rechtspleging') available at https://zoek.officielebekendmakingen.nl/stb-2020-223.html.

Such increased collaboration can begin with some of the dialogues and methods of coordination that have been emerging in recent years between various public and private institutions that aim to assist vulnerable consumers to find redress.

The energy sector in the UK offers an example of such a holistic approach. Several public and private actors assist vulnerable consumers at various stages in the resolution of a consumer complaint. First, energy companies are required by regulation to take additional steps to assist vulnerable customers and resolve their complaints. Second, Citizens Advice is a nationwide government advice service that runs an Extra Help Unit (EHU) in the energy sector.[51] The EHU is a consumer advocate[52] that supports people across Great Britain and acts on behalf of vulnerable consumers to help them with their energy problems. The EHU can make a claim on behalf of the citizen or give advice. Third, the Energy Ombudsman provides independent dispute resolution in, amongst others, the energy sector to resolve consumer complaints. Each quarter, the EHU, energy companies, the Ombudsman and other actors in the field convene in 'quarterly supplier liaison meetings' to discuss developments in relation to vulnerable consumers in the energy sector.

Similarly, in the Netherlands, the Consumer Association (*Consumentenbond*) offers its members access to legal advice, digital self-help tools and the option to ask legal staff to draft a personalised complaint letter.[53] However, the *Consumentenbond* does not assist consumers in bringing their case to the courts or CDR entities. The latter role is usually included in the services offered by a legal expenses insurance company. The insurance policy that these companies offer entails that once a dispute arises, the consumer is assigned a lawyer who then assesses the legal merits of the case and could decide to submit the case either to the court or to the CDR entity on behalf of the consumer. While these organisations work independently, the SGC has begun working with both the Consumer Association and insurance companies to streamline operations, for example towards establishing a fast-track procedure between the SGC and some legal expenses insurers.[54]

These examples show how different public and private actors aid vulnerable consumers in several ways at various stages in the life of a complaint. Increased cooperation and dialogue will increase the effectiveness and efficiency of getting the help to consumers who need it most.

D. Future Outlook

These examples show that the courts, CDR entities and societal partners in the UK and the Netherlands have started taking steps – individually or cooperatively – towards preparing the stage needed for a redress system that delivers inclusive digital access to justice for all consumers. These steps may be the beginning of a new model of access to

[51] See at https://ehu.org.uk.
[52] Creutzfeldt et al (n 10).
[53] See at www.consumentenbond.nl/service/abonnement/abonnementen-tarieven.
[54] SGC, 'Annual Plan 2021' (*De geschillencommissie*, 2021) available at https://www.degeschillencommissie.nl/wp-content/uploads/Jaarplan-DGC-2021.pdf.

justice through court and CDR procedures. That model is thus comprehensive in two respects. First, courts and CDR entities ensure consumers have unencumbered access to court and CDR procedures in both offline and online forms. Second, all public and private organisations involved take a broader, holistic, and collaborative approach that encompasses not only courts and CDR entities, but also consumer support and advocacy groups, trade associations and other societal partners.

V. Conclusion

This chapter has brought together our work and thoughts about consumer ADR in Europe and consumer access to justice. Based on our research interests, we identified challenges in a digital consumer redress system that the Covid-19 pandemic has brought to the fore: digital access to justice for marginalised consumers.

As we have outlined, the courts and CDR bodies in both the UK and the Netherlands have shown great resolve in dealing with the adverse effects of the pandemic on the accessibility of their dispute resolution systems. What the pandemic has shown us is that digitalisation can offer broader and more diverse access to justice, but that it also risks marginalising vulnerable consumers even further. The pandemic exposed, therefore, the stark divide between those who are able to access consumer redress systems online and those who are not. Hence, societies need to look out for people who are excluded from the online system and provide more resilient pathways to consumer justice.

We have proposed how courts, CDR entities and other stakeholders can take digital illiteracy into account and work toward inclusive access to justice in the post-pandemic era. The strategies that we suggest build on existing initiatives in the UK and the Netherlands, and aim to make online information and procedures more accessible; strengthen offline variants for those for whom improved online access is not enough; and call on all public and private institutions involved to collaborate to establish a more holistic approach to inclusive justice.

17

Rise and Fall of Traffic Accident ADR in Japan: The Cause and the Possible Remedy

TAKUYA HATTA

It 'did what it said on the tin'. But …
(C Hodges, *Delivering Dispute Resolution: A Holistic Review of Models in England and Wales* (2019))

I. Purpose of this Chapter

Although Japanese people are well known for their tendency to avoid bringing disputes before the courts and their preference for resolving them consensually,[1] alternative dispute resolution (ADR), especially by private organisations, is not so actively used by them.[2] Having said that, traffic accident ADR has been said to be one of the rare exceptions, being successful, with frequent use and a high settlement rate.[3]

However, more recently, the number of times traffic accident ADR has been used in Japan has been decreasing markedly, even as the number of traffic accident cases brought before the Summary Court (along with the appeal rate against the Summary Court judgments) has shown a tendency to increase.[4] The spread of legal expenses cover in car insurance is said to be the main reason for this phenomenon: because of the legal expenses cover in car insurance policies, victims of traffic accidents now do not hesitate to hire lawyers to file lawsuits instead of using traffic accident ADR, which is basically

[1] Including the analysis of its causes, see JM Ramseyer, 'Reluctant Litigant Revised: Rationality and Disputes in Japan' (1988) 14 *The Journal of Japanese Studies* 111 (English); T Tanase, 'The Management of Disputes: Automobile Accident Compensation in Japan' (1990) 24 *Law and Society Review* 651 (English); T Ginsburg and G Hoetker, 'The Unreluctant Litigant? An Empirical Analysis of Japan's Turn to Litigation' (2006) 35 *The Journal of Legal Studies* 31 (English).

[2] *See* T Hatta, 'ADR in Japan, Special Reference to Civil Mediation' in AI Blanco García (ed), *Tratado de Mediación, Tomo I: Mediación en Asuntos Civiles y Mercantiles* (Tirant lo Blanch, 2017) 70 (English); S Kakiuchi, 'Die Förderung der außergerichtlichen Konfliktlösung in Japan' (2014) 37 *Zeitschrift für Japanisches Recht* 17 (German).

[3] See section II.C.

[4] See section II.C.

free of charge, in low-value cases for which it would normally be economically unfeasible to hire a lawyer to file a lawsuit.[5] But there could be a deeper reason for the fall in use of the traffic accident ADR that could signify its malfunctioning and the need for change. The aim of this chapter is to analyse the reasons behind the decline in use of the traffic accident ADR and if there is any functional disorder causing it; and if there is, to identify the problem and seek its possible solution. The situation will be examined from the viewpoint of the purpose of this form of ADR.

This chapter starts with a brief overview of Japanese traffic accident ADR (section II), moving on to analyse the situation (section III) and ending with a summary of the outcome of the analysis (section IV).

The chapter is strongly inspired by the analysis of dispute resolution by the dedicatee of this book, the honourable Emeritus Professor Dr Christopher Hodges OBE.[6] First, Professor Hodges points to 'a slow evolution away from judicial contexts to other pathways'[7] in England and Wales. In Japan, in contrast, even though partially, a shift from ADR towards judicial resolution seems to be under way. This inevitably draws attention to what underlies the reason for this phenomenon in Japan. Second and more importantly, he emphasises

> a need, first, to map and evaluate the various sectoral developments so as to see if learning might be spread to other sectors, and, secondly, to carry out a holistic overview of the whole system to see if all the individual parts fit well together and how they might collectively be developed as part of a coherent whole.[8]

Unfortunately, the need to have a holistic view and to coordinate various pathways of dispute resolution is still not well perceived in Japan, and thus far there has basically been no attempt in such a direction (the author of this chapter is also not yet ready to embark on such a study); but to examine the reason for the rise and the fall of one example of seemingly successful ADR could serve as a preparatory work, even if a small one, with that aim in mind. With this contribution the author of this chapter would like to express his sincere gratitude for what he learned from Professor Hodges through his works and interactions with him. Especially in memory of the joint research trip to Seoul, Korea, and in Kobe and Tokyo, Japan, carried out in December 2018, and the reunion realised in Leuven, Belgium in February 2020.

II. Outlook of Japanese Traffic Accident ADR

A. The Underlying Judicial System

Before explaining the Japanese system of traffic accident ADR, a brief reference should be made to the basic judicial structure in Japan.[9]

[5] *The Yomiuri Shimbun* (25 October 2014) morning edition, 1 (Japanese). See also K Nakayama, 'Hajimeni – Kikakushushi Setsumei' (2020) 15 *Journal of Japanese Arbitration and ADR* 84, 85 (Japanese).

[6] C Hodges, *Delivering Dispute Resolution: A Holistic Review of Models in England and Wales* (Hart Publishing, 2019).

[7] ibid 16.

[8] ibid 1.

[9] Visit www.courts.go.jp/english/judicial_sys/index.html (English) for more information.

Japan has one Supreme Court, eight High Courts, 50 District Courts and Family Courts, and 438 Summary Courts (there are no special courts, such as Labour Courts or Commercial Courts). For monetary claims, the Summary Courts and District Courts have jurisdiction at the first instance. Monetary claims up to 1,400,000 yen (approx £9,000) are received by Summary Courts, and monetary claims above 1,400,000 yen are received by District Courts. Appeals against the judgments of Summary Courts go to District Courts. Self-representation by parties (litigants in person) is allowed, but if you want representation at District Courts and Family Courts and courts above them, you have to hire a lawyer. In Summary Courts you can be represented by non-lawyers if the court gives permission. No loser-pays principle applies to the attorneys' fees. So even if the claimant wins the lawsuit, he or she has to cover his or her lawyer's fees. The cost of bringing one's own case to court is therefore high, which forms the basis for the demand for legal expenses cover in car insurance policies.

B. Organisations Conducting Traffic Accident ADR

Japanese traffic accident ADR mainly consists of ADR conducted by the following organisations: (i) The Dispute Resolution Organisation for Compulsory Car Insurance and Mutual Aid (*Jibaiseki Hoken Kyosai Funsoshorikiko*); (ii) The Japan Centre for Settlement of Traffic Accident Disputes (*Kotsujiko Funsoshori Centre*); (iii) Nichibenren Traffic Accident Consultation Centre (*Nichibenren Kotsujiko Sodan Centre*).[10]

i. The Dispute Resolution Organisation for Compulsory Car Insurance and Mutual Aid

This organisation[11] has its headquarters in Tokyo and one branch in Osaka. It offers an adjudication procedure for disputes concerning the payment of compulsory car insurance between the victims and the insurance companies. The adjudication is binding for the insurance companies, but not for the victims (the victims are free to reject the adjudication and turn to resolution by the courts).

ii. The Japan Centre for Settlement of Traffic Accident Disputes

This organisation (JCSTAD[12]) consists of headquarters, seven branches (one in each city where the High Court is located) and three consultation centres. It is under the

[10] ADR of traffic accident disputes is also offered by Dispute Resolution Centres of each local Bar Association, Summary Courts (as civil conciliation proceedings), General Insurance Counselling and ADR Centre ('Sonpo ADR Centre'). But the percentage of cases resolved by these organisations is not as significant as those mentioned in the main text.

[11] For more details of this organisation, see K Kobue, 'Kotsujiko niokeru ADR' (2020) 15 *Journal of Japanese Arbitration and ADR* 86 (Japanese); K Kobue, 'Kotsujiko niokeru ADR no Genjo to Kadai' (2010) 1403 *Jurist* 70 (Japanese); Nihonbengoshirengokai ADR Centre (ed), *Kotsujiko no Songaibaisho to ADR* (Kobundo, 2010) 81 (Japanese).

[12] For more details of this organisation, see at www.jcstad.or.jp/wp/wp-content/uploads/2021/05/business-summary2020.pdf (English); Kobue, 'Kotsujiko niokeru ADR' (n 11) 87; Kobue, 'Kotsujiko niokeru ADR no Genjo to Kadai' (n 11) 71; Nihonbengoshirengokai ADR Centre (n 11) 114; A Takeuchi, 'Kotsujiko Funsoshori Centre no Gyomu' (2020) 15 *Journal of Japanese Arbitration and ADR* 49 (Japanese).

supervision of the Cabinet Office and its funding comes from the insurance companies. It basically offers mediation and adjudication of disputes between the victims and the insurance companies regarding disputes over car traffic accidents in general, concerning the payment of voluntary insurance. The procedure before JCSTAD starts with consultation by the victim. Following that, JCSTAD offers mediation; and if the mediation fails, it will then examine the case and offer a solution (adjudication). The Centre has agreements with most of the insurance companies that obligate these companies to respond to a call for mediation and to accept the Centre's adjudication.

The procedure is free of charge for the victim. It is said that the amount of compensation available through the court for a traffic accident is standardised,[13] and that the amount of compensation offered via the mediation and adjudication procedure by the Centre is based on this standard (the so-called 'court standard'). So, a victim using the JCSTAD procedure can expect to receive the same amount he or she would get following a lawsuit. The procedure takes three to five meetings over three to six months in total. Mediation is conducted by a lawyer, and the procedure for the adjudication is conducted by a panel of three (a lawyer, an ex-judge and a scholar specialising in law).

iii. Nichibenren Traffic Accident Consultation Centre

This organisation (NTACC[14]) consists of headquarters, 54 branches and 157 consultation centres. It is related to the Japan Federation of Bar Associations, and its funding comes from a government subsidy that is comprised of the investment profit of compulsory car insurance. It basically offers consultation, mediation and adjudication for disputes between the victim and the person who caused a traffic accident that involves personal injuries, including cases that are not covered by voluntary insurance. The procedure before NTACC starts with consultation by the victim, which is conducted by a lawyer. And if the lawyer in charge of the consultation sees fit, the case is then sent for mediation by a different lawyer. If the mediation fails, the procedure basically ends there; but when the claim is covered by an insurance company that has an agreement with the Centre,[15] the case is moved on to the adjudication procedure, in which a panel of three lawyers examines the case and offers a resolution. The resolution offered in the adjudication procedure is binding on the insurance company but not on the victim.

The procedure offered by this organisation is also free of charge for the victim. The resolution offered by the adjudication and the settlement proposal offered by the presiding lawyer are based on the court standard here as well. The Centre tries to close the mediation within three meetings, and the average number of meetings is 1.73.[16]

[13] There are books that aggregate the cases of traffic accident lawsuits and show the standard of compensation granted by court rulings according to the circumstances of the accidents. One of them is the so-called 'Red book' ('*Akai hon*' in Japanese). Its official title is *Minji Kotsujiko Sosho Songaibaishogaku Santei Kijun*. The book covers court rulings nationwide and is revised every other year. The other is the so-called 'Blue book' ('*Ao Hon*' in Japanese). Its official title is *Kotsujiko Songaigaku Santei Kijun*. The book treats rulings by the Tokyo District Court and is revised every year. They are both published by NTACC.

[14] Kobue, 'Kotsujiko niokeru ADR' (n 11) 89; Kobue, 'Kotsujiko niokeru ADR no Genjo to Kadai' (n 11) 72; Nihonbengoshirengokai ADR Centre (n 11) 99.

[15] Currently nine insurance companies have such agreements with NTACC.

[16] Figure from the website of NTACC at https://n-tacc.or.jp/.

C. Data

Of the three above-mentioned organisations for traffic accident ADR, JCSTAD and NTACC are of importance because they deal with cases of traffic accidents in general and not just the payment of compulsory insurance. From this point, this chapter will focus on the ADR provided by these two organisations; and when traffic accident ADR is referred to it means ADR provided by JCSTAD and NTACC.

Figure 17.1 Newly commenced cases each year

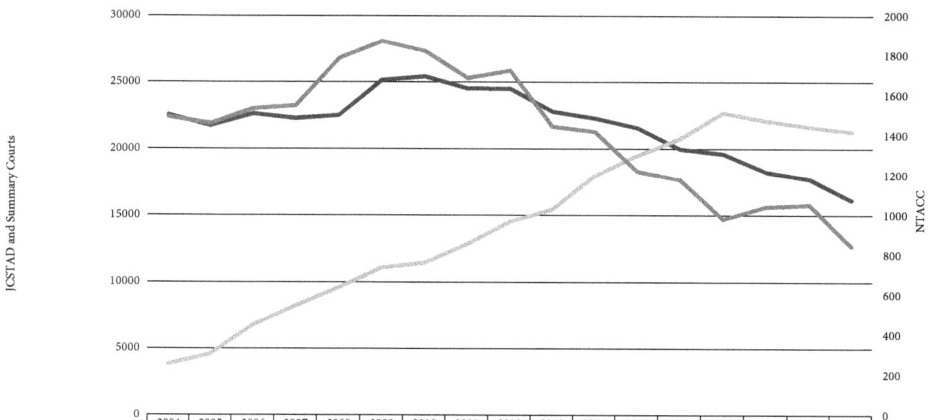

	2004	2005	2006	2007	2008	2009	2010	2011	2012	2013	2014	2015	2016	2017	2018	2019	2020
JCSTAD	22529	21718	22630	22271	22519	25164	25414	24524	24498	22811	22285	21571	19980	19620	18247	17742	16145
Summary Courts	3811	4582	6734	8182	9546	11070	11413	12813	14508	15428	17961	19473	20766	22719	22098	21655	21274
NTACC	1491	1459	1535	1549	1786	1871	1822	1687	1724	1445	1419	1221	1179	979	1043	1051	846

Figure 17.1 shows the number of newly commenced cases of mediation by JCSTAD and NTACC and lawsuits in the Summary Courts.[17] You will see that cases of mediation by JCSTAD and NTACC have shown a tendency to decline from the year 2010, whereas the number of lawsuits before the Summary Courts constantly increased until the year 2017. The statistics made public by the Legal Training and Research Institute of Japan[18] show that the number of cases in which an appeal was filed against the Summary Court's first instance judgment in traffic accident cases has also been constantly on the rise (from 48 in the year 1996 to over 253 in the year 2005 to 1,566 in the year 2015).

[17] The data for NTACC for 2004–10 are from direct inquiry to NTACC; for 2011–15 they are from the Japan Federation of Bar Associations, *White Paper on Attorneys 2016* (JFBA, 2016) 195 (Japanese); for 2016–20 they are from the Japan Federation of Bar Associations, *White Paper on Attorneys 2021* (JFBA, 2021) 217. The data for JCSTAD for 2004–14 are available at www.jcstad.or.jp/databank/; for 2015 they are from JCSTAD, *Business Summary 2020* (JCSTAD, 2020) (English) available at www.jcstad.or.jp/wp/wp-content/uploads/2021/05/business-summary2020.pdf; for 2016–20 they are from JCSTAD, *Business Summary 2021* (JCSTAD, 2021) available at www.jcstad.or.jp/wp/wp-content/uploads/2022/03/business-summary2021.pdf. The data for Summary Courts for 2004–17 are from Japan Federation of Bar Associations, *White Paper on Attorneys 2018* (JFBA, 2018) 118; for 2018–20 they are from Japan Federation of Bar Associations, *White Paper on Attorneys 2021* (JFBA, 2021) 117.

[18] Figure 3 in Shihokenshujo (ed), *Kannisaibansho niokeru Kotsusongaibaishososhojikenn no Shinri Hanketasu ni kannsuru Kenkyu* (Hosokai, 2016) 2 (Japanese).

Figure 17.2 Number of traffic accidents and the sales of insurance with legal expenses cover

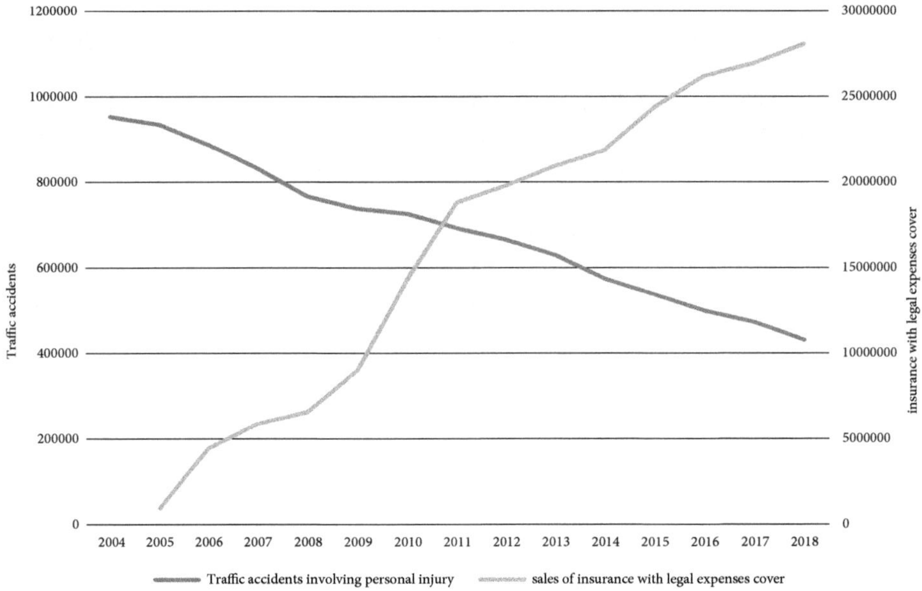

Figure 17.2 shows the number of traffic accidents involving personal injury[19] and the number of sales of insurance with legal expenses cover.[20] You can see that the number of traffic accidents involving personal injury is constantly decreasing, while the number of sales of insurance with legal expenses cover is constantly increasing.

Figure 17.3 Success rate of mediation

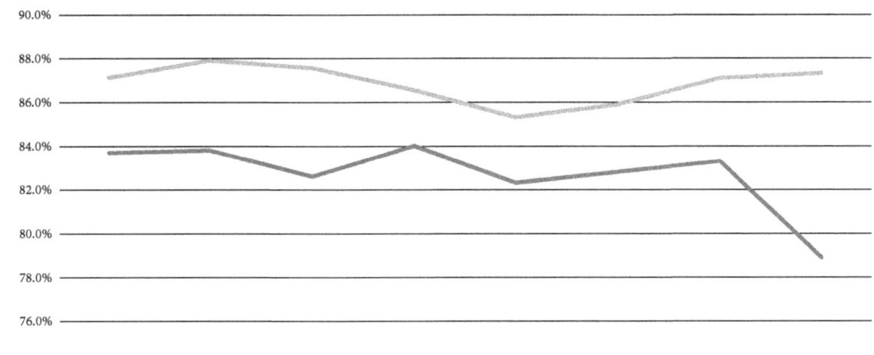

	2013	2014	2015	2016	2017	2018	2019	2020
NTACC	83.7%	83.8%	82.6%	84.0%	82.3%	82.8%	83.3%	78.9%
JCSTAD	87.1%	87.9%	87.6%	86.6%	85.3%	85.9%	87.1%	87.3%

[19] The data for the number of traffic accidents for 2004–17 are from Japan Federation of Bar Associations, *White Paper on Attorneys 2018* (JFBA, 2018), 118; the data for 2018 are from Japan Federation of Bar Associations, *White Paper on Attorneys 2021* (JFBA, 2021) 117.

[20] The data for the number of sales of insurance with legal expenses cover are from Japan Federation of Bar Associations, *White Paper on Attorneys 2021* (n 19) 231. Legal expenses coverage as part of car insurance has recently become very popular in Japan. Most insurance companies offer legal expenses cover, but as an option

Figure 17.3 shows the success rate of mediation by JCSTAD and NTACC.[21] You can see that the percentage reaching an agreement is basically constantly over 80 per cent for both.

Figure 17.4 Sales of insurance with legal expenses cover and percentage of lawyer representation

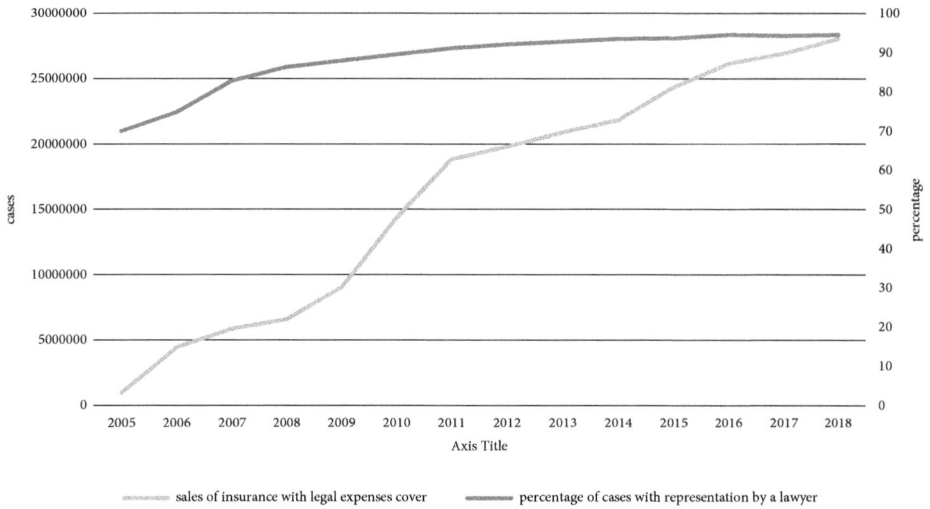

Figure 17.4 shows the number of the sales of insurance with legal expenses cover and the percentage of cases involving lawyer representation.[22] You can see that the rate of representation by lawyers increases in accordance with the rise of sales of insurance with legal expenses cover.

III. Analysis

As regards the purpose of traffic accident ADR, you might include: (i) reduction of the burden of the courts; (ii) proper resolution of the cases; and (iii) a policy purpose other than those set out in (i) and (ii).

within the main car insurance. If you chose legal expenses cover as an option, you are obligated to pay an additional insurance premium accordingly. Legal insurance started as an option in car insurance in Japan, and this remains the case in the majority of instances. Independent legal insurance, which covers legal disputes in general, has started to appear but is not so common. Within legal expenses coverage added to car insurance there are various ranges of cover: some policies only cover accidents involving cars, but some also cover accidents that happen in daily life, such as getting bitten by a dog.

[21] The data for NTACC for 2013–15 are from Japan Federation of Bar Associations, *White Paper on Attorneys 2016* (JFBA, 2016) 195; for 2016–20 they are from Japan Federation of Bar Associations, *White Paper on Attorneys 2021* (n 19). The data for JCSTAD for 2013–15 are based on the number of cases ending in settlement and the number of cases in total set out in Japan Federation of Bar Associations, *White Paper on Attorneys 2016* (JFBA, 2016) 197; for 2016–20 they are based on the numbers given in Japan Federation of Bar Associations, *White Paper on Attorneys 2021* (n 19) 220.

[22] The data for the number of traffic accidents for 2004–17 are from Japan Federation of Bar Associations, *White Paper on Attorneys 2018* (n 19), 118; for 2018 they are from Japan Federation of Bar Associations,

A. Reduction of the Burden on the Courts

From the viewpoint of reducing the burden on the courts, the increase in the number of traffic accident cases brought to the Summary Courts could be viewed as a problem. But if the burden on the courts gets too heavy, it should primarily be the matter for the courts to deal with themselves, and so the increase in the burden on the courts should not be viewed as a problem on the side of ADR.

B. Proper Resolution of the Cases

Here we should narrow down the meaning of the 'properness' of the resolution. As criteria for properness we might list: (i) cost; (ii) time; and (iii) the properness of the content of the resolution (ie the satisfaction of the parties concerned).

From the viewpoint of cost, it is true that lawsuits cost more than traffic accident ADR because ADR is free; but the fall in the number of traffic accident ADR cases and the rise in the number of lawsuits should not be a problem if this is the result of the increase in legal expenses cover in car insurance policies, since, thanks to this legal expenses cover, the victims will not have to pay the costs of the lawsuit.

But from the viewpoint of time and the properness of the content of the resolution (satisfaction of the parties concerned), the current phenomenon could be viewed as a problem.

It is said that mediation by JCSTAD takes three to six months,[23] and mediation by NTACC basically ends within three meetings[24] (average: 1.73[25]). First-instance traffic accident lawsuits in the Summary Courts take an average of 5.6 months.[26] If you compare the duration of traffic accident ADR and that of first-instance Summary Court cases, you cannot say for sure that lawsuits take longer than ADR. But if you take into account the fact that appeals against first-instance judgments are increasing,[27] you can certainly say that for those cases that are appealed, the court procedure takes more time than ADR.

Also, from the viewpoint of the content of the resolution or the satisfaction of the victim, the fact that appeals against first-instance judgments of the Summary Courts are increasing should indicate that the parties are not satisfied with the resolutions offered in the Summary Courts.

It could be argued, against such analysis, that the reason why appeals against Summary Court first-instance judgments are on the rise is that the cases newly brought to the Summary Courts are highly contentious and the parties are not likely to be satisfied with a solution offered by a third party anyway, and that therefore these cases will

White Paper on Attorneys 2021 (n 19) 117. The data for the percentage of lawyer representation are from Japan Federation of Bar Associations, *White Paper 2016* (2016) 103, *White Paper 2017* (2017) 103, *White Paper 2018* (2018) 118, *White Paper 2020* (2020) 126, *White Paper 2021* (2021) 117.

[23] Tochigiken Bengoshikai (ed), *Bunnyabetsu ADR Katsuyo no Jitsumu* (Gyosei, 2018) 30 (Japanese).

[24] ibid 35.

[25] See n 16.

[26] The figure in the year 2015. See Shihokenshujo (ed) (n 18) 4.

[27] See n 18.

not be able to be resolved through traffic accident ADR. But the lawyers in charge of mediation procedure offered by NTACC are well trained and have a thorough knowledge of the standards of resolution of traffic accident cases.[28] The Summary Court judges are not trained in any similar way, so they lack the expertise that the presiding lawyers in traffic accident ADR have. It is more probable that the lack of such expertise is the reason for the dissatisfaction of the parties with the resolutions offered by the Summary Court judges.

It could also be argued that the increase in the number of Summary Court cases is the result of the choice of the victims and therefore it should not be viewed as a problem. After all, the presiding principle of ADR is self-autonomy, so as long as turning to court is the free choice of the victims, there should be nothing wrong with that. It is said that the motive for establishing traffic accident ADR was to complement the lack of negotiation power on the side of the victims of traffic accidents against insurance companies that had come to be allowed to represent those who caused the accidents.[29] In light of that, if the victims' choice of lawsuit over ADR is the result of legal expenses cover in car insurance policies, it means that this is the result of the levelling up of negotiation power on the side of the victims through representation by lawyers, and that should be rather welcome.

But as a conclusion this should be viewed as problematic. There are two possible reasons for this. The first is that if a case of very low value ($100 to $200) is brought to court, this could be viewed as morally hazardous. It is said that the fee you must pay to the court in filing a lawsuit works as a deterrent against abusive lawsuits.[30] If plaintiffs do not have to pay anything as the court fee due to legal expenses cover in car insurance, this means that the court fee is not working as a deterrent, and so it could be possible to view this as a problem. As a countermeasure, it might be possible to charge victims a certain amount of money for filing a lawsuit in spite of their legal expenses cover.[31] But, as a conclusion, the fact that a case of very low value can be brought to court should not be viewed as a problem, and no countermeasures against abusive lawsuits should be taken so as to impose a certain cost on victims. First, such countermeasures would also be applied to contentious cases.[32] It is said that traffic accident ADR mainly deals with non-contentious cases.[33] Therefore, cases would appear for which filing a lawsuit is not economically reasonable for the victims because of the cost imposed on them, and at

[28] T Hatta, 'Tetsuzukiho Kenkyusha toshiteno Shiten' (2020) 15 *Journal of Japanese Arbitration and ADR* 98 (Japanese).

[29] M Yoshimura, 'Koekizaidanhojin Nichibenren Kotsujiko Sodan Centre' (2013) 41 *Kotsuho Kenkyu* 57 (Japanese); M Urakawa, 'Koekizaidanhojin Kotsujiko Funsoshori Centre' (2013) 41 *Kotsuho Kenkyu* 77 (Japanese).

[30] K Yamamoto, *Minjisoshoho no Kihonmondai* (Hanrei Times, 2002) 113 (Japanese).

[31] Or to set a minimum amount for the coverage by the legal expenses cover like in Germany. See A Oi, 'Bengoshi Hiyo Hoken wo meguru Shomondai' (2017) 636 *Journal of Insurance Science* 5, 8 (Japanese).

[32] 'Contentious cases' in this chapter means cases in which the parties to the accident disagree what happened. As opposed to that, 'non-contentious cases' here means cases in which there is no or little dispute between the parties as to what happened in the accident, and there is disagreement basically only over the evaluation of the damage caused to the victim.

[33] Tochigiken Bengoshikai (n 23) 29; S Kobayashi, 'Kekizaidanhojin Nichibenren Kotsujiko Sodan Centre no Jidan Assen' (2018) 13 *Journal of Japanese Arbitration and ADR* 61.

the same time there is no ADR available to cover the need for its resolution, if we were to take such countermeasures. Second, it is probable that the allegation of the victim is legitimate even in such low-value cases. So it does not make good sense to impose a burden on the victim in filing a lawsuit in order to prevent abusive suits.

But further, it is pointed out that some lawyers appointed by the victims charge them by the hour, and convince them to choose to file a lawsuit in order to prolong the resolution of the dispute and get more remuneration.[34] This indicates that the choice of lawsuit over ADR is not the result of the voluntary choice of the victims, which nullifies the basis of the above argument, because it is based on the self-autonomy of the victims. So as long as this assumption is true, the choice of lawsuit over ADR cannot be justified as the voluntary choice of the victims and must be viewed as a problem from the viewpoint of the time necessary for dispute resolution and the likely degree of satisfaction on the side of the victims. As a solution to the distorted choice of lawsuits over ADR, it is recommended that the lawyer's fee system, which makes it profitable for the representing lawyers to prolong the resolution of the dispute, be banned.

C. Other Policy Purposes

Traffic accident ADR can be useful for policy purposes other than those examined so far. One such purpose is to change the behaviour of insurance companies if there is anything wrong with it. And there has been something wrong with the behaviour of insurance companies up until now. It is quite likely that success of traffic accident ADR so far has actually been the result of an unjustifiable practice of insurance companies.

It is said that the traffic accident ADR mainly deals with non-contentious cases, where there is basically no discrepancy among the parties to the case with respect to the facts and the dispute is solely over the evaluation of the damage caused to the victims.[35] It is also said that in such cases the amount of compensation insurance companies offer in the bilateral negotiations with victims is lower than the appropriate amount according to the court standard.[36] Those victims who are dissatisfied with such offers turn to traffic accident ADR. And because the resolution offered by traffic accident ADR is based on the court standard,[37] which results in higher amounts of compensation than

[34] *The Yomiuri Shimbun* (25 October 2014) morning edition, 39 (Japanese). See also K Naito, 'Wagakuni niokeru Kenrihogohoken no Kino to Kadai' (2016) 634 *Journal of Insurance Science* 87, 108 (Japanese); S Kano and M Sase, 'Genjo no Mondaiten (Kenrihogohoken no Kadai to Kongo no Tembo)' (2013) 775 *Jiyu to Seigi* 33, 36 (Japanese). When a person who has car insurance with legal expenses cover gets involved in an accident and wants to hire a lawyer, he or she can turn to the insurance company that insures him or her, which in turn will call an intermediary called Nichibenren Legal Access Centre (LAC) to appoint a lawyer. LAC sets a guideline for the attorney fee to be paid by the insurance, and the lawyer appointed through LAC basically follows the guideline in charging its clients. This guideline allows time-charging, but stipulates that the maximum time-charge shall basically be 600,000 yen (approx £4,000), which corresponds to 30 hours. This guideline prevents unlimited time-charging, but the lawyers still have incentives to rack up time at least to 30 hours.

[35] See n 33.

[36] The standard of payment at the negotiation stage is called 'voluntary standard': Kobue, 'Kotsujiko niokeru ADR no Genjo to Kadai' (n 11) 74. See also Tochigiken Bengoshikai (n 23) 29. For the meaning of 'court standard', see section II.B.ii.

[37] See section II.B.ii and section II.B.iii. See also Urakawa (n 29) 83; K Fujimura et al (eds), *Jitsumu Kotsujiko Sosho Taikei* vol 1 (Gyosei, 2017) 310, 314.

offered by the insurance companies in the negotiations, most victims accept the resolution, which leads to a high success rate for mediation and high levels of satisfaction for the victims.

It may be argued that this practice of insurance companies is reasonable because it simply involves negotiation, and insurance companies as parties of interest in the case have the legitimate right to take a position favourable to them.[38] But victims of traffic accidents are given the right to make a claim directly against insurance companies under insurance contracts concluded by the companies themselves. The other parties to the contracts are the persons who caused the traffic accidents, but the contracts have a binding effect between the insurance companies and the victims as well, since insurance contracts have the character of contracts for the benefit of a third person and the victims are the beneficiaries of them. Thus, the insurance companies are obligated to pay to the victims an amount of compensation that coincides with the court standard, according to the insurance contracts that they themselves have concluded. It should be viewed against their contractual obligation to offer an amount less than what they are required to pay according to the court standard. It should also be pointed out that the reason for the insurance companies' practice of not offering the amount of appropriate compensation according to the court standard can also be attributed to the fact that the victims do not know the amount of compensation due to them according to the court standard. The insurance companies are taking advantage of victims' ignorance.

Some argue, in support of the above-mentioned practice of the insurance companies, that it should be reasonable to reach an agreement in negotiations for an amount lower than the court standard in exchange for avoiding the risks that a lawsuit entails, such as the uncertainty of the outcome of examination of evidence.[39] But there is basically no dispute over the facts of the accidents in non-contentious cases; and in such cases, thanks to the 'red books' and 'blue books', it is possible to foresee with high probability the amount you could be awarded in a lawsuit.[40] So there is no uncertainty to form the basis of the above-mentioned argument for the insurance companies.[41]

It is also argued that the so-called 'court standard' is too abstract, and therefore it is impossible to assume the amount the victims could get if they went to court in each individual case, which makes it impossible to compare the amount of money offered by the insurance companies at the stage of negotiation and the amount awarded to the victim in traffic accident ADR.[42] But this argument goes against the widely accepted notion that there does in fact exist an approximation of the amount you could be awarded from a lawsuit (which corresponds with the above-mentioned 'court standard'), and even taking the unique situation of each individual case into account you cannot deny the difference in the 'level' of the amount of money awarded in bilateral negotiations and in ADR/court proceedings.

[38] Hatta (n 28) 99.

[39] Kobue, 'Kotsujiko niokeru ADR no Genjo to Kadai' (n 11) 75.

[40] Nihonbengoshirengokai ADR Centre (n 11) 109 points out the patterned nature of traffic accident disputes and the existence of the standard for payment as the reason for success of the ADR by NTACC.

[41] Hatta (n 28) 99.

[42] Kobue, 'Kotsujiko niokeru ADR' (n 11) 101–02; Kobue, 'Kotsujiko niokeru ADR no Genjo to Kadai' (n 11) 74.

Therefore the practice of the insurance companies should be diagnosed as unreasonable and in need of correction. Alternative dispute resolution could be an effective means to achieve this by publicising the data accumulated in the traffic accident ADR: the general features of the case, without specifics that could lead to the identification of the victims; the name of the insurance company; the amount offered by the insurance company at the bilateral negotiation stage; the amount offered in the course of mediation by the presiding lawyer; and the amount with which settlement is achieved if a settlement is achieved. Through such publication it would be revealed to the public whether insurance companies stick to the practice of offering amounts lower than the court standard, and this should function to correct the practice.

It should be noted that if and when this practice of insurance companies changes and they start to offer amounts that are proper according to the court standard at the stage of negotiation with the victims, that should reduce the need and demand for traffic accident ADR in non-contentious cases.[43]

From this point of view, it should also be noted that there is high possibility that the above-mentioned practice of insurance companies is already currently being forced to change by the spread of legal expenses cover in car insurance policies. That is, it is quite likely that with the involvement of lawyers on the side of the victims even at the negotiation stage, which is realised through legal expenses cover, the negotiating power of the victims is enhanced and the standard of resolution at the negotiation stage (the voluntary standard) reaches the standard required in court (the court standard), which is causing the decline of the use of traffic accident ADR. This signifies that the need for traffic accident ADR is already disappearing in non-contentious cases. On the other hand, increasingly, some of the traffic accident disputes brought to the Summary Courts are contentious cases, for which it used to be economically unreasonable to file a lawsuit because the value at stake was low, but which became economically viable thanks to the inclusion of legal expenses cover in car insurance policies. Therefore, there should be some decrease in the number of cases using traffic accident ADR and an increase in the number of cases brought to the Summary Courts even where the two phenomena bear no relation to each other. This analysis signifies that there is increased need for dispute resolution in contentious cases, which traffic accident ADR has failed to cover till now.

IV. Summary

There are two possible causes of the decrease in traffic accident ADR and the increase in the bringing of lawsuits to the Summary Courts. The first is that lawyers are charging their clients an hourly rate, and since an increase in the lawyers' fees does not directly

[43] But the role of traffic accident ADR will not disappear completely. Since each case is unique, and even though there exists the court standard, it is impossible to draw out a resolution to each case through automatic application of such a standard, traffic accident ADR will still have a role to play in that, when disputes over the uniqueness of each case occur, they can be resolved by ADR faster than by a lawsuit. the accumulation of the resolution of such individual uniqueness of each case through ADR can be evaluated positively as the speciality of traffic accident ADR.

harm their clients, thanks to legal expenses cover in car insurance policies, lawyers prefer to prolong the resolution of the case. The second is that the power of negotiation of victims has been enhanced by legal expenses cover, and therefore victims have started to be able to get compensation in accordance with the court standard without the help of traffic accident ADR in non-contentious cases, which works to decrease the number of cases brought to ADR; on the other hand, contentious cases of low value, for which filing a lawsuit used to be too expensive, have started to be brought to court because filing a lawsuit has become economically reasonable thanks to the presence of legal expenses cover.

The first cause should be viewed as a problem, and measures should be taken to change the lawyers' fee system so that prolonging the resolution of the case will not benefit them. Here it should be noted that because of legal expenses cover, the clients' eyes will not work as a deterrent because there is no visible damage on the clients' side.

The second cause should not be viewed as a problem in itself. It is a good thing that the negotiation power of victims has been enhanced. It is also a good thing that cases that used not to be able to be brought to court for economic reasons can now be brought to court. But these two reasons signify the need for traffic accident ADR to change if it wants to attract more users, since the need for dispute resolution in the non-contentious cases, which the traffic accident ADR has been covering, is disappearing, although not completely, and a new demand is starting to surface with respect to the contentious cases, which traffic accident ADR has failed to cover so far. The change required here is in the direction of covering contentious cases. In order to do so, the organisations responsible for traffic accident ADR must equip themselves with the ability to examine evidence, which is beginning to be less difficult with the spread of objective-proof materials such as dashboard cameras.

Also, there has been a practice by insurance companies of offering less than they actually should according to the court standard in negotiations with the victims. The spread of representation of victims by lawyers, thanks to legal expenses cover, seems to be weakening this practice, but as long as it remains, traffic accident ADR can be used as a means to correct it. In order to do so the organisations carrying out traffic accident ADR should publicise the data of the cases they treat, such as the difference in the amount offered by the insurance companies at the negotiation stage and the amount achieved via mediation, along with the name of the insurance companies concerned.

The author of this article is aware that many of the analyses carried out here are not backed up with enough empirical evidence. But the examination presented in this chapter should at least work to show the need to dig more deeply into the reasons behind the seemingly successful situations of ADR in order to determine the future direction of its steering.

18

CDR: Catalyst for China's E-Commerce

YING YU AND ALEX CHUNG

> Colleagues and I have previously called Consumer ADR 'CADR', but I now think, as suggested by Dr Ying Yu of Wuhan University in a conversation in 2012, that 'CDR' is a better acronym.
>
> (C Hodges, 'Unlocking Justice and Markets: The Promise of Consumer ADR' (2014))

I. Introduction: The Context

During a work trip Professor Christopher Hodges undertook with Dr Ying Yu in 2013 to Shenzhen city, China, they met with Chinese consumer authorities, consumer agencies and academics, and gave lectures on the topic of consumer dispute resolution (CDR). After being introduced to the city, Professor Hodges noted that as the centre of Guangdong Province – the most vibrant region in China – Shenzhen's regional administration prided itself on being both the hub of innovation in modern market government and the home to then four of the world's top 500 businesses and half of Chinese cross-border e-commerce.

Professor Hodges was particularly and deeply impressed by Shenzhen's online dispute resolution (ODR) platform for consumer complaints and disputes, operated by Shenzhen's Consumer Council under the municipal State Administration for Market Regulation (SAMR). The platform was also linked up with ODR bodies in the United States, the European Union, Singapore and Japan.

Today, China's CDR landscape is drastically different from what it was 10 years ago. In the context of this landscape, this chapter explores the role CDR played in the rapid rise of e-commerce in China, as well as the latest state of CDR development.

A. China's Rapidly Expanding E-Commerce

As an 'exemplary for the world',[1] e-commerce in China has undergone the fastest growth globally. By 2018, online retail sales in China had reached over $1.3 trillion USD,

[1] UNCTAD (2022), 'China's structural transformation what can developing countries learn?' available at https://unctad.org/webflyer/chinas-structural-transformation-what-can-developing-countries-learn.

which accounted for 46.6 per cent of the global online retail sales.[2] In 2021, China accounted for more than half of all e-commerce retail sales worldwide, with total online sales passing $2 trillion USD. China also has the highest number of digital buyers globally; estimates have ranged between 780 million to 825 million people, representing up to 38 per cent of the global total.[3]

Within global e-commerce sectors, China also dominates the business-to-consumer (B2C) e-commerce sector and cross-border e-commerce (CBEC) sector. On the one hand, according to the UNCTAD B2C E-commerce Index (2020), China ranked tenth among global economies and second among global developing economies.[4] Further, four Chinese online platforms are ranked first (Alibaba), third (JD.com), fourth (Pingduoduo) and seventh (Meituan) among global B2C e-commerce companies by gross merchandise value.[5] Notably, Alibaba is still and has been the leading online platform in China since e-commerce began there just before the year 2000. On the other hand, the rapid expansion of China's cross-border e-commerce (CBEC) can be attributed to supportive state policies that have been launched by the Chinese Government since 2013. China's CBEC grew nearly ten-fold between 2016 and 2021, and continues to maintain its double-digit growth.[6] By 2018, China's CBEC became the world's largest economy, which accounted for just over a quarter of all global transactions and reached over 740 million buyers. Its annual compound growth rate was 96 per cent, which greatly outpaced the global CBEC growth rate of 54.1 per cent.[7] In 2021, China's imports and exports from CBEC totalled $311.3 billion USD, which increased by 15 per cent from the previous year.[8]

B. More E-Shopping and More Disputes: Mobile Payment and Covid-19

Two important enablers that contributed to the rapid rise of e-commerce in China are third-party e-payment systems and, in recent years, mobile technologies. As the first leading third-party e-payment system in China established in 2004, Alipay, a subsidiary company of Alibaba, paved the way for the e-commerce revolution in China.[9]

[2] ibid.

[3] 'E-commerce in China – statistics & facts' (1 February 2022) available at www.statista.com/topics/1007/e-commerce-in-china/; 'Global Ecommerce Explained: Stats and Trends to Watch in 2022' (16 February 2022) available at www.shopify.ca/enterprise/global-ecommerce-statistics.

[4] Includes Hong Kong SAR, 'THE UNCTAD B2C E-COMMERCE INDEX 2020: Spotlight on Latin America and the Caribbean' available at https://unctad.org/system/files/official-document/tn_unctad_ict4d17_en.pdf.

[5] 'Global E-Commerce Jumps to $26.7 Trillion, Covid-19 Boosts Online Retail Sales' (3 May 2021) available at https://unctad.org/press-material/global-e-commerce-jumps-267-trillion-covid-19-boosts-online-retail-sales.

[6] Zhonghongwang.com (2022), '中国外贸出口动能强劲，跨境电商或成"时代洪流' (16 March 2022) available at http://gd.zhonghongwang.com/show-168-9293-1.html.

[7] UNCTAD (2022) (n 1) 6; 'China remains world's largest B2C cross-border e-commerce market' *People's Daily Online* (13 July 2020) available at http://en.people.cn/n3/2021/0713/c90000–9871373.html

[8] Zhonghongwang.com (2022) (n 6).

[9] See at www.alibaba.com/ and https://global.alipay.com/platform/site/ihome.

Since 2011, WeChat has become a dominant player in the field of e-payment solutions once mobile technology further matured.[10] As of 2020, Alipay had captured over 90 per cent of the domestic consumer digital payment market and WeChat accounted for over 70 per cent.[11] The fact that 'Chinese consumers are unique in their high confidence in third-party payment systems'[12] has important implications for how CDR and ODR gave rise to the spurt in China's e-commerce growth. This is elaborated in section III.

Despite a generally high level of consumer trust in China's e-commerce, Chinese regulators have been struggling to efficiently handle the increasing number of online consumer disputes. To illustrate the scale of such challenges, one issue that Chinese regulators have been finding especially challenging to tackle in recent years is attributed to live e-shopping events.[13] These popular 'infomercial-like' events, hosted online by celebrities and influencers who often endorse or advertise the goods being sold, create large volumes of purchases within a short span of time. At times, they can reach more than half a million purchases per second and over 370 billion purchases a day.[14] Yet many of the purchases have resulted in complaints and disputes due to issues related to delivery or product quality and safety.[15]

As global retail e-commerce sales grew more than 25 per cent in 2020 during the Covid-19 pandemic,[16] owing in a large part to lockdown measures implemented by governments worldwide, online consumer disputes significantly increased in many countries. In China, while its 2020 annual e-commerce sales grew by 4.5 per cent and e-commerce retail sales grew by 10.9 per cent,[17] the daily average caseload recorded by SAMR's national ODR platform also saw a ten-fold increase in consumer disputes as compared to pre-pandemic figures.[18] Most of those cases were related to Covid-19 products purchased online, including disputes over low product quality, business non-compliance with regulations, poor customer services or logistics failure.[19]

[10] See at https://pay.weixin.qq.com/index.php/public/wechatpay.

[11] Compared to the use of online bank transfer at 27%; see 'Covid-19 and E-Commerce: Findings from a survey of online consumers in 9 countries', UNCTAD Survey (October 2020) available at https://unctad.org/system/files/official-document/dtlstictinf2020d1_en.pdf.

[12] 'The truth about online consumers', *KPMG Global Online Consumer Report 2017*, available at https://assets.kpmg/content/dam/kpmg/xx/pdf/2017/01/the-truth-about-online-consumers.pdf.

[13] '直播带货问题频出，消费者该找谁?' (20 January 2021) available at www.sohu.com/a/445676766_118778; '直播带货"的坑，该如何填？' (17 March 2021) available at www.sohu.com/a/456111522_141588.

[14] 'China e-shopping event rings in 580,000 sales per second' *Asia Financial* (11 November 2020) available at www.asiafinancial.com/china-e-shopping-event-rings-in-580000-sales-per-second.

[15] To address this, the International Consumer Protection and Enforcement Network (ICPEN) released guidance documents in 2016 related to online reviews and endorsements for review administrators, for traders and marketing professionals and for digital influencers. Disputes regarding education and training are another type of dispute that accounted for a large proportion of all recorded consumer disputes in 2021. This was perhaps an anomaly due to the sudden change in China's state policy banning privately-owned and -operated tutoring schools in 2021. As a result, many of the schools have had to close down and were not able to offer a refund, which led to an eight-fold increase in related disputes. '教育培训退费成痛点，2021年投诉量暴增超八成' (22 March 2022) available at https://mp.weixin.qq.com/s/2bOYhe6yiW0NdsLdD9IkVA.

[16] 'E-commerce worldwide – statistics & facts' (23 February 2022) available at www.statista.com/topics/871/online-shopping/#dossier-chapter1.

[17] '国家统计局统计科学研究所所长闾海琪解读2020年我国经济发展新动能指数' (July 26 2021) available at www.stats.gov.cn/tjsj/sjjd/202107/t20210726_1819836.html.

[18] '市场监管总局举办2021年第一季度例行新闻发布会' (22 March 2021) available at www.samr.gov.cn/xw/xwfbt/202103/t20210322_327136.html.

[19] '2020年上半年全国消协组织受理投诉情况分析' (5 August 2020) available at www.cca.cn/tsdh/detail/29727.html.

As China's advanced state of e-commerce development shows, Chinese consumers have relatively high confidence in the online shopping experience, mainly driven by the ability to make quick, easy and secure mobile purchases and payment. However, the technological innovations that enabled such convenience can also lead to mass-volume consumer disputes instigated by the likes of live e-shopping trends and pandemic-induced lockdown measures. To prevent the regulators and the judicial system from being inundated by the ever-increasing and sudden flux of consumer disputes, the Chinese Government has created a robust CDR ecosystem by continually improving policy, legal and regulatory frameworks; nationwide ODR platforms and e-courts for e-commerce; and public-private partnerships with e-commerce platforms and e-businesses.

The remainder of this chapter explores how China's CDR ecosystem has developed into its current form. Against this current state of play, this chapter also examines some of the present challenges and opportunities facing CDR in China.

II. Legal Approaches to CDR in China

A note of clarification before moving to the discussion on the five legal approaches to CDR in China: in the discourse on CDR, which mainly refers to alternative dispute resolution (ADR) and ODR, judicial avenues for dispute resolution are not normally considered viable and practical ways for consumers to obtain compensation and redress efficiently, particularly for low-value disputes. This is due to the relatively expensive, complicated and lengthy litigation processes involved. However, recent reforms of China's CDR ecosystem saw the development of novel and innovative e-courts that are specifically designed to reduce costs and barriers for consumers and businesses, which can feasibly be deployed at scale nationwide and even for cross-border cases. To contextualise these aspects within China's CDR ecosystem, but also because the judicial option is one of the five legal approaches to CDR stipulated by China's consumer protection law as shown in section II.A, the following discussion includes e-litigation and e-courts.

A. The Consumer Rights and Interests Protection Law

The legal basis of the avenues for and operationalisation of CDR in China is derived from the main statute concerning consumer protection – the Consumer Rights and Interests Protection Law.[20] Adopted in 1993 and amended in 2009 and 2013, the statute covers areas ranging from general principles concerning the protection of the legal rights and interests of consumers and the obligations of business operations, to the role of consumer organisations and legal liability. In addition, and importantly, it includes a

[20] Full title: Law of the People's Republic of China on the Protection of the Rights and Interests of Consumers. See at https://gkml.samr.gov.cn/nsjg/fgs/201906/t20190625_302783.html.

chapter on 'dispute resolution' (Chapter 6), Article 39 of which defines the five options for CDR as follows:[21]

1. negotiate and settle with the business directly;[22]
2. request mediation through a consumer association or other organisations established in accordance with the law;
3. lodge a complaint with the relevant administrative department;
4. seek arbitration based on the arbitration organisation specified in the contract agreement;
5. bring a lawsuit before a people's court.

While no explicit hierarchical or sequential order on how these five CDR routes should be implemented is specified in this statute or elsewhere, there are norms that consumers tend to follow in practice when they seek redress.

Compared to options 2 to 5, option 1 is the most common approach taken by consumers due to the popularity of top e-marketplaces and mature domestic e-commerce, as noted previously. As part of the mobile shopping experience, consumers can easily raise transactional disputes through the in-house ODR systems of the online platforms.

If option 1 is not readily available for the business with which a consumer is transacting, or if the first attempt at direct negotiation between the consumer and the business has failed, that is when the consumer would normally decide to pursue options 2 or 3. Currently, outside of option 1, the most common CDR approach is option 3, the well-known national '12315' consumer complaints hotline system that has been in existence since 1999 (see further section IV.A).

Options 4 and 5 are not considered very practical or feasible for low-value consumer disputes due to the inherent obstacles, such as the burden of proof for some types of consumer disputes, the lack of competency or jurisdiction of a court over certain types of disputes, and the prohibitive costs involved in the processes, the last of these including the time, energy and money required of the consumer.[23] Notwithstanding this, the launch of Internet courts, or option 5, in recent years as part of wider efforts to reform litigation and advance e-justice has led to an increase in their adoption and use for consumer disputes. In a recent promotional campaign by Chinese courts, judges have suggested that consumers can pursue e-litigation (option 5) as an alternative if they fail in attempting resolving their dispute directly with the business (option 1).[24]

B. The E-Commerce Law

The E-Commerce Law is another piece of legislation relevant to CDR in China. Adopted at the Fifth Session of the Standing Committee of the 13th National People's Congress

[21] The Law was adopted on 31 October 1993, with its first amendment adopted on 27 August 2009 and its second amendment and the current version adopted on 25 October 2013.

[22] Also known as conciliation.

[23] '别讓「過程複雜」成消費維權痛點-新華網' (17 March 2020) available at http://big5.xinhuanet.com/gate/big5/www.xinhuanet.com/comments/2020-03/17/c_1125722433.htm.

[24] '网络消费遇到问题怎么办？莫慌，成都互联网法庭这个视频告诉你' (15 March 2022) available at http://k.sina.com.cn/article_1887538377_v70818cc902000xafq.html (embedded video).

in 2018, China's E-Commerce Law complements the Consumer Rights and Interests Protection Law (see section II.A) but with a specific focus on e-commerce.[25] Articles 58 to 63 in Chapter IV of the Law contain provisions that cover 'E-commerce Dispute Resolution', reinforcing the various options for CDR as specified in the Consumer Rights and Interests Protection Law, including through the processes of negotiation, mediation, arbitration and litigation. In addition, the Law highlights the Government's position on encouraging e-commerce platforms to establish 'goods and service quality guarantee mechanisms', which includes providing 'convenient and effective' mechanisms for resolving disputes and reporting complaints in a timely way. Further, e-commerce platforms and businesses operating on the platforms are required to proactively and jointly assist consumers to protect their rights and interests.

* * *

The following sections of this chapter examine the ADR systems and ODR platforms in China, based on the laws discussed in this section, which together form China's CDR ecosystem. This includes a brief overview of CDR and ADR developments in recent years, how ODR platforms have been implemented and are functioning, as well as some thoughts on related challenges and opportunities.

III. In-House ODR of B2C E-Commerce Platforms

A. In-House ODRs Dominating the CDR Landscape

As noted previously, the rates of domestic mobile Internet adoption and third-party digital payment systems (as well as public confidence in such systems as Alipay and WeChat Pay) are peculiarly high in China, reaching close to 100 per cent.[26] These factors, coupled with market dominance by several e-marketplace platforms, have led to the consumer practice of heavily relying on e-commerce platforms and payment systems as means of resolving online disputes.

While the complaint- and dispute-handling procedures, workflows and technologies of these proprietary in-house ODRs may vary, what they do have in common is their user-friendly design and their ability to process large volumes of disputes with high efficiency. They also exhibit high levels of interoperability with some national ODR systems, to be discussed in section III.B. For these reasons, most consumers tend to initiate complaints through in-house ODR mechanisms in the first instance and reserve the option of using national ODR mainly for escalating disputes that cannot be resolved, or for purchases or payments that are made outside of major platforms.[27] Thus, national ODR platforms handle significantly fewer complaints by volume compared to e-commerce platforms.

[25] 'E-Commerce Law of the People's Republic of China, 2018', available at https://ipkey.eu/sites/default/files/documents/resources/PRC_E-Commerce_Law.pdf.

[26] UNCTAD Digital Economy Report (2019), 'Value creation and capture – implications for developing countries' available at https://unctad.org/webflyer/digital-economy-report-2019, xvii, 82.

[27] Yu Y, 'Hybrid approach to protect distance consumers' PhD Thesis, Wuhan University (2012) 156–59.

B. Consumer Trust and E-Commerce Ignited: The Case of Alipay

Past research has shown how some of the prominent in-house ODR systems operate.[28] To avoid repetition, a selected example of Taobao and Alipay is provided here to briefly illustrate how they became one of the most successful in-house ODR and e-payment systems in China.

During the budding years of e-commerce development in China, one of the main challenges Alibaba faced was a severe lack of trust between sellers and buyers that threatened to hinder the growth of e-commerce. To overcome this hurdle, Alibaba launched Alipay through Taobao e-marketplace in 2004, both of which quickly dominated e-commerce by the late 2000s and remain the leading players in e-commerce.[29]

One of the Alipay features that makes it appealing to consumers as a trustworthy and effective e-payment system is the way it acts as a third-party payment guarantor to help minimise transactional risks for the consumer. When a buyer on Taobao makes a payment, Alipay holds the funds until it can confirm that the goods have been received in a satisfactory condition, when Alipay releases the funds to the seller. Ostensibly, this method of safeguarding the payment appears similar to the way PayPal functions. However, the difference is that PayPal forwards the payment to the seller before receiving confirmation that the goods have been successfully delivered with satisfaction, which does not offer consumers the same peace of mind that Alipay does. In this regard, whereas PayPal acts as an agent of the seller, Alipay resembles escrow from a legal perspective.[30]

In addition to the escrow-like feature noted above, Alibaba has also launched Ali Wangwang,[31] an instant messaging service that allows buyers to engage with sellers directly to resolve any transactional issues or complaints during or after purchase, before they turn into full-blown disputes.[32] In other words, this ODR feature can be regarded as the in-house negotiation approach as detailed by option 1 of the Consumer Rights and Interests Protection Law (see section II.A).

[28] ibid; Yu Y, 'Contemporary Lex Mercatoria in China', Working Paper of Consumer Rights in China Programme, Oxford University (2015), available at https://papers.ssrn.com/sol3/papers.cfm?abstract_id=2590350; Yu Y and Shen M, 'Consumer protection as the 'Open Sesame' that allows Alibaba to crush the forty thieves' (2015) 3(1) *Journal of Antitrust Enforcement* 228; UNCTAD (2022) (n 1); Zheng J, 'The Role of ODR in Resolving Electronic Commerce Disputes in China.' (2016) 3(1) *International Journal of Online Dispute Resolution* 41; Zheng J, 'The Development of ODR in E-Commerce Transactions' in Zheng, J, *Online Resolution of E-commerce Disputes: Perspectives from the European Union, the UK, and China* (Springer, 2020) 33. These papers contain more information about how some of the e-commerce platforms and third-party payment systems work, including the complaints procedures and their impact on e-commerce.

[29] UNCTAD (2022) (n 1) 62–66.

[30] Yu Y, Presentation at the 13th International Conference on Consumer Law, organised by the International Association of Consumer Law (www.iaclaw.org), London (27–29 June 2011).

[31] See at https://wangwang.taobao.com/.

[32] UNCTAD (2022) (n 1) 62–66. This is partly facilitated by Cainiao Logistics, a data-driven intelligent logistics service founded in 2013 by Alibaba that handles inventory and parcel deliveries for third-party merchants on Alibaba. It analyses data from orders during every step of the logistics chain, thereby enhancing logistics services through efficient monitoring and reporting for its sellers and buyers (ibid).

IV. From the National 12315 Consumer Hotline to the National 12315 ODR Platform

A. The Rapidly Evolving CDR Landscape

China's CDR landscape has undergone a series of governance reforms over a period of more than two decades. In 1999, China's State Administration for Industry and Commerce (SAIC), the predecessor of SAMR and former competent authority in charge of market regulation,[33] related administrative law enforcement and protecting the legitimate rights and interests of consumers, launched a consumer complaints and disputes hotline known as 12315.[34] The 12315 system comprised a nationwide telephone hotline and a network of branch offices, phone centres and personnel for handling consumer disputes across China. Initially, the phone centres offered services in languages of ethnic minorities in China, as well as in English, Korean and Russian. By 2007, over 6,000 telephone centres had been established.[35]

The tremendous growth of China's e-commerce since the late 2000s has been accompanied by a steadily rising volume of consumer disputes. To address the demand for effective and efficient ODR services, China developed a strategy to modernise its national 12315 hotline into a nationwide ODR ecosystem. The led to the creation of the national 12315 ODR platform, which is rooted in China's existing CDR legal framework and ADR landscape. As the platform is funded and operated by SAMR, this CDR route reflects option 3 of the Consumer Rights and Interests Protection Law discussed in section II.A.

The first and second phases of the platform were officially launched on 15 March 2017 and 15 March 2018, respectively. The dates were deliberately chosen to coincide with and signify the World Consumer Rights Day.[36] In 2018, the then newly formed SAMR started consolidating four other national sectorial complaints hotlines into the 12315 ODR platform, following reform initiative orders from the central Government.[37] The five-digit hotlines that were eventually replaced by 12315 were quality control (12365); food and drugs (12331); product pricing (12358); and intellectual property rights (12330). This initiative was gradually implemented in various provinces across China over time.[38]

[33] SAIC was merged into SAMR in 2018.

[34] 'Buyers Need to Beware' *China Through a Lens* (27 October 2004) available at www.china.org.cn/english/2004/Oct/110523.htm.

[35] 'Safeguard Consumer Rights and Interests' (13 June 2007) available at http://www.china.org.cn/e-news/news070612-2.htm. By 2006, 12315 had received 4,682,000 enquiries and complaints from consumers, settled 722,000 cases, recovered 780 million RMB for consumers, and investigated and settled 156,000 infringement cases totalling 920 million RMB in value.

[36] '全國12315互聯網平臺今日正式上線' (15 March 2017) available at www.gov.cn/xinwen/2017-03/15/content_5177612.htm; '全國12315互聯網平臺二期上線' (16 March 2018) available at www.gov.cn/fuwu/2018-03/16/content_5274615.htm.

[37] SAMR 2021, '2020年全國市場監管部門為消費者挽回經濟損失44億元' (15 March 2021) available at www.samr.gov.cn/xw/zj/202103/t20210312_326825.html.

[38] '福州實現消費維權"五線合一"' (22 March 2018) available at http://m.icn.cn/xiaozhi/20180322/1019.html; '質檢12365、食藥12331等五條投訴舉報熱線統一為12315' (2 September 2019) available at www.sohu.com/a/338042907_115423.

China's financial sector, however, is absent from the 12315 ODR platform, despite being a mainstay of consumer activities and part of CDR generally speaking. A separate and soon-to-be-launched ODR platform for the financial sector has been established by the China Banking and Insurance Regulatory Commission, following the existing litigation and mediation mechanism laid out by the Chinese Supreme People's Court. Similar to the 12315, this forthcoming ODR platform aims to help consumers resolve disputes online in the comfort of their home. Reported statistics show that in 2020, even before the planned launch of the financial sector ODR platform, China's banking and insurance industries have successfully resolved more than 150,000 disputes, which amounted to around 21 billion RMB in recovered losses for consumers.

B. The National 12315 ODR Platform: Functioning, Procedure and Statistics

The national 12315 ODR platform[39] is available free of charge to consumers 24 hours a day. It is a fully-fledged ODR platform in the sense that it offers a nationwide single access point for raising complaints and disputes, online negotiation between business and consumer (the 12315 ODR platform is interlinked with e-businesses), and online mediation that leads to a binding decision for the business (if the decision is accepted by the consumer). The platform uses big data to conduct real-time monitoring and supervision of the dispute-handling processes. This helps the regulators to better develop consumer policies. Some of the big data features include dynamic analysis of consumer-demand hotspots, automated recommendation of regional SAMR branch units for redirecting disputes, sensitive word filtering, identification of repeat complaints and timely analysis of the market situation.[40]

The platform is staffed by around 92,000 SAMR employees, based centrally and regionally, who ensure that cases are processed under a standardised procedure. Alternative dispute resolution still operates in parallel to the ODR platform and is available to consumers by telephone, fax and in person through a branch visit. When consumers reach the call centre by telephone, they are encouraged to use the platform. Whether a case is processed via the platform or by telephone, it is redirected to a regional centre. There is a total of 286 regional centres across the country, staffed with 5,225 responders.[41]

There are regional differences among the 12315 network of ODR branch offices in terms of their focus and their services. For example, the Fujian branch puts an emphasis on information campaigns to publicise its ODR services, while the Hainan branch strongly promotes its ODR system's focus on disputes arising from duty-free products and airport-related issues.[42] Among the regional branches, the 12315 Shanghai ODR

[39] Available at www.12315.cn.
[40] Gov.cn 2018, '全國12315互聯網平臺二期上線' (16 March 2018) available at www.gov.cn/fuwu/2018-03/16/content_5274615.htm.
[41] SAMR 2021 (n 37) 15 March.
[42] SAMR 2020, '市場監管部門推進消費糾紛在線和解機制初見成效' (12 November 2020) available at www.samr.gov.cn/xw/sj/202011/t20201112_323411.html.

operations stand out due to its high efficiency and collaborative nature. In addition, the Shanghai branch of SAMR and 12315 have implemented multilingual services in 13 languages, catering to foreign consumers and tourists as well as to facilitate cross-border disputes.[43] This is part of a wider effort by China to promote dispute resolution services that are commensurate with Shanghai city's status as a 'modern international metropolis'.[44] Many of the disputes received at the Shanghai branch in 2020 were related to travel and airlines, personal services such as hair salons, and personal protective equipment – in other words, industries heavily impacted by the pandemic.[45]

Most consumers log onto the platform using their mobile phone app, which is interoperable with WeChat Pay, Alipay and Baidu App, though it is also accessible from laptop.[46] The interactive platform uses smart technologies to answer consumers' queries through automated responses. To search for the business they wish to complain about, consumers can choose the business by its registered company name or, if they do not know it, identify the business using the digital map embedded in the app. The system can use big data to facilitate the search by automatically matching the geographical location of the business with the regional SAMR authority, in order to determine the jurisdiction under which the case should be forwarded and processed.[47]

Once the regional 12315 personnel receive the case, they have seven days to determine whether the complaint falls within its competency and whether the business involved is registered. If the case is accepted, the case officer will forward the complaint to the business. Within 10 working days of receiving the request from the case officer, the business is required to proactively attempt to resolve the dispute through direct negotiation with the consumer. This increases the possibility of reaching a mutual agreement between business and consumer at the early stage, which saves costs for the business, consumer and 12315.[48] However, if the dispute cannot be settled, the consumer can escalate it further by requesting 12315 to intervene through mediation by a trained mediator.[49]

If the mediation result in an agreement, the outcome is binding for the business. The business has 15 working days to take redress action based on the terms of the agreement. If it does not, SAMR can take enforcement and/or disciplinary action against the business, based on the provisions of the Consumer Rights and Interests Protection Law. If the mediation does not result in an agreement, the consumer reserves the right to bring the case before an arbitration hearing or a court.[50]

In 2020, the platform handled 17.3 million disputes against 2,878,600 businesses, with an average processing time of 8.7 days per case. Compared to 2019, 2020 saw an

[43] The 13 languages are English, Japanese, French, Russian, Deutsch, Korean, Spanish, Portuguese, Turkish, Arabic, Malay, Indonesian and Kazakh.

[44] SAMR 2020, '上海市市場監管局投訴舉報中心聚焦「四單式服務」創新投訴舉報多語種服務機制.' (15 October 2020) available at www.samr.gov.cn/wljys/hjjs/202010/t20201015_322355.html.

[45] ibid.

[46] SAMR 2020, '14萬人的維權首選！ 你還不知道？(ODR教程)' (16 November 2020) available at www.samr.gov.cn/wljys/hjjs/202011/t20201116_323486.html.

[47] Gov.cn 2018 (n 40).

[48] SAMR 2020 (n 46) 16 November.

[49] Gov.cn 2018 (n 40).

[50] '市場監督管理投訴與舉報處理辦法（徵求意見稿)' (10 May 2019) available at www.moj.gov.cn/pub/sfbgw/lfyjzj/lflfyjzj/201905/t20190509_150597.html.

increase of 566.6 per cent in the number of cases.[51] Of the 17.3 million cases, 192,200 were resolved on the platform through negotiations between businesses and consumers. Most of the disputes were filed against businesses operating in the following sectors: gaming and entertainment, online education, smart manufacturing, housing rental, and medical and health. Notably, 1,547,900 out of the 17.3 million cases were related to the pandemic. Overall, the platform helped consumers to recover RMB 4.4 billion in economic losses in 2020, with a consumer satisfaction rate of over 80 per cent.[52]

C. The 12315 Green Channel Feature and its Umbrella ODR Network Function

The 12315 national ODR platform has a feature known as 'Green Channel', which enables e-businesses that have in-house ODR systems to join the platform. It provides interoperability between proprietary ODR systems of e-businesses and the 12315 ODR platform, so that disputes can be transferred and processed seamlessly between the two systems and allow for direct negotiation between the businesses and the consumer.[53]

In addition to its role as the national ODR platform, 12315 also acts as a national ODR umbrella system that oversees a satellite network of privately-owned ODR entities, under the purview of SAMR. This allows SAMR to supervise, monitor and support their ODR functions to better protect consumers. To increase the network coverage of the satellite ODRs, SAMR actively encourages interested online businesses to apply to become a SAMR-supervised ODR enterprise.[54] The applicant business should be a customer service-oriented online operator that is keen on consumer rights protection and willing to collaborate with SAMR. In addition, it needs to meet the following requirements: have access to a venue for dispute resolution; be able to employ responders and mediators; have access to information technology equipment for operating an ODR platform; and have a customer service contact telephone number. Once its application is approved, the business can register an account with 12315 to become a member ODR enterprise.[55]

Since 12315 was launched in 2017, the number of ODR enterprises have increased almost five-fold.[56] By the first half of 2021, there were 25,500 SAMR-supervised ODR enterprises participating in the nationally coordinated 12315 ODR network.[57] To incentivise business participation, the Government offers support to qualifying businesses. This includes assisting them to build private ODR platforms and to use big data gathered

[51] SAMR 2021 (n 37) 15 March.
[52] ibid.
[53] '12315互联网平台"ODR"缩短维权路' (23 August 2021) available at http://m.zjknews.com/e/action/ShowInfo.php?classid=78&id=335835.
[54] Gov.cn 2018 (n 40).
[55] SAMR 2020 (n 46) 16 November.
[56] SAMR 2020 (n 42) 12 November.
[57] SAMR 2021 (n 37) 15 March.

from the ODR; the latter includes using big data to identify common causes of disputes and to improve business management.[58]

V. China Consumers Association's ODR Platform

The China Consumers Association (CCA), a subsidiary agency of and funded by SAMR, offers another route for consumers to file complaints and disputes online.[59] Among its missions, the CCA aims to promote the use of CDR. Based on its institutional designation and mandates, the ODR services provided by the CCA[60] fall under option 2 of the Consumer Rights and Interests Protection Law (see section II.A).[61]

The CCA's ODR platform is accessible to consumers free of charge via its official website. Unlike the 12315 ODR platform, it does not offer a mobile version or support connections through a third-party app. Initially developed in 2008 as the CCA's Complaint and Consulting Information System, it was upgraded into an ODR platform in 2015 using cloud computing technologies. Akin to 12315, the CCA's ODR platform is national in scope and collaboratively handles consumer disputes with its 696 subsidiary consumer associations, which are distributed throughout 32 provinces and administrative regions.[62] In addition to enabling inter-agency case transfer, its functions also include mediation, case filing and automated statistical analysis of data gathered through the platform. The types of data gathered include the businesses involved in the disputes, the types of complaints and risks facing consumers.

Upon entering the CCA's ODR platform, the consumer is prompted to register the complaint either as an 'ordinary' complaint case or as a Green Channel case – the latter is a feature that is specific to the CCA's ODR platform, but it operates in a similar way to the Green Channel embedded within the national 12315 ODR platform. Currently, 25 e-companies, including some of the top-ranked B2C e-commerce platforms, such as JD.com, Taobao and Vipshop, have joined the CCA's Green Channel on its ODR platform. Launched on World Consumer Rights Day on 15 March 2016, this feature not only helps to transfer consumer dispute cases seamlessly and quickly to CCA-affiliated e-businesses, but it also leads to early resolution more frequently without the need for mediation, thereby greatly reducing costs for consumers.[63]

[58] SAMR 2020 (n 46) 16 November.

[59] See at cca.org.cn (2022).

[60] The CCA also aims to increase consumer satisfaction by performing statutory duties according to the law. These include enhancing the supervision of the quality and standard of goods and services, and increasing the integrity and legal awareness of the operators. It also supports economic and social development by lodging public interest litigation, carrying out product recalls, advancing legislative regulations, settling collective complaints, addressing consumption hotspot issues and providing guidance on dealing with pandemic-related complaints. See the official website of the CCA at cca.org.cn.

[61] Option 2 also includes 'other organisations established in accordance with the law'. Two examples of privately-owned ODR entities that offer nationwide services include Dian Su Bao ('E-Commerce Consumer Dispute ODR and Mediation Platform' at www.100ec.cn/Index/complain.html) and Xiao Fei Bao ('Consumer Service Protection Platform' at https://www.xfb315.com/).

[62] This includes autonomous regions and municipalities that are under the purview of the central Government.

[63] SAMR 2020 (n 46) 16 November. Official figures ending in early June 2021 showed that the Green Channel had handled 10,657 cases during the first half of 2021.

In terms of the ODR procedure, the CCA has up to 10 working days to decide whether to accept a case.[64] If the case is accepted, it is redirected to a case handler at the appropriate regional consumer association for processing. The entire process of case investigation, all the way up to mediation, can take up to 50 working days.[65] If a resolution is not reached through mediation[66] facilitated by a trained mediator, the CCA can pursue several options to obtain redress for the consumer. These include seeking assistance from the following authorities and bodies: industry authorities regarding quality issues; administrative authorities regarding business-related and administrative issues;[67] judicial authorities for legality issues;[68] and news media to publicise and shame the business for bad behaviour or practice.[69]

During 2021, the CCA processed 1,044,0861 cases, of which 836,072 were settled with a resolution rate of 80 per cent. Approximately 1.5 billion RMB in losses for consumers were recovered during this period.[70] In 2020, the CCA received a total of 982,249 complaints, of which 749,317 were settled with a resolution rate of 76.3 per cent. Approximately 1.5 billion RMB in losses were recovered for consumers.[71]

VI. E-Litigation for E-Commerce Disputes

A. Three E-Courts in Hangzhou, Beijing and Guangzhou

In recent years, three Internet courts have been established in Hangzhou (August 2017) and in Beijing and Guangzhou (September 2018).[72] They are primary courts with designated jurisdiction over 11 types of Internet-related cases, both non-consumer and consumer, including disputes arising from online sales, service contracts, online loans and intellectual property.[73] The choices of the cities for establishing these Internet

[64] If it involves special circumstances that require additional time for consideration, this can be extended by another 10 working days.

[65] Or an additional 20 working days for complex cases.

[66] Including complex cases where it is difficult to determine whether the business is responsible, such as when a low-quality product has caused physical injury to the consumer.

[67] Which has the power to fine or penalise the business by revoking its operating licence or rejecting an application for licence renewal.

[68] Shandong Province, for instance, has implemented the Consumer Rights and Interests Protection Law in such a way as to reverse the burden of proof to level the power asymmetry in favour of the consumer. Instead of placing the onus on the consumer to show evidence that the business is at fault, the business is required to show evidence that the consumer should be the one to bear responsibility. If the business cannot do so, it is deemed liable for any adverse event that occurred and is required to provide redress. '消費者協會對消費投訴的處理_河南消費維權資訊網' (7 February 2021) available at www.hnxw315.com/newsshow.asp?id=1706.

[69] ibid.

[70] '2021年全国消协组织受理投诉情况分析' (28 January 2022) available at www.cca.cn/zxsd/detail/30345.html

[71] '中消協發布2020年全國消協組織受理投訴情況' (4 February 2021) available at http://consume.people.com.cn/BIG5/n1/2021/0204/c425315-32022795.html

[72] See at www.netcourt.gov.cn/?lang=En; https://english.bjinternetcourt.gov.cn/; and https://ols.gzinternet-court.gov.cn/?lang=en-US.

[73] Supreme People's Court of China (2019). See at https://drive.google.com/file/d/1T8i303Czq1GV3RAbJc7tHXpSPxT2nv-5/view.

courts bear great significance to the primacy of the locations for trade and e-commerce. For example, Beijing is the capital of China, Guangzhou is one of the largest trade and port cities in China, and Hangzhou is home to China's largest e-commerce company Alibaba.[74]

While this e-litigation route, which falls under option 5 of the Consumer Rights and Interests Protection Law (see section II.A), is not considered ADR (or ODR, which is normally regarded as the online version of ADR) as previously noted, it nevertheless serves as a good example that illustrates efficient and user-friendly CDR systems that capitalise on the use of smart technologies for case handling. Moreover, in light of the White Paper issued by China's Supreme Court in December 2019 outlining the Government's strategy to comprehensively develop the 'Internet judiciary',[75] and the subsequent guidelines issued by the Ministry of Justice in March 2020 to accelerate this development, major advancements are expected in the years to come.[76]

The online courts are designed to be a 'one-stop online dispute resolution service, including mediation, case-filing, fee-payment, hearings, and e-delivery',[77] where the entire process is paperless and carried out from a laptop or smartphone. The Internet court platforms are connected to several dominant e-commerce platforms, such as Taobao and Tmall, thus enabling the e-court to obtain the necessary data for adjudication. The e-courts are also connected to other institutional platforms that commonly facilitate supplying electronic evidence (financial institutions, notary institutions and third-party evidence preservation agencies). In addition, the Hangzhou Internet Court uses blockchain technology to enhance its evidence verification capabilities.[78] On average, it takes this court five minutes to file a case and 28 minutes to conduct an e-hearing.[79] For these reasons, e-litigation is regarded as a convenient and efficient way for delivering e-justice for consumers. However, as the user needs to pay a fee to file an e-court case, it is still less efficient than the 12315 ODR platform (see section IV.B), which is free of charge to consumers.

By October 2019, the three above-mentioned Internet courts handled 118,764 cases and concluded 88,401; 80,819 cases were entirely conducted online from beginning to end. On average, it took 38 days to conclude a case. First-instance judgments were accepted in around 98 per cent of the cases without further appeals.[80]

[74] 'It's time to settle cross-border e-commerce disputes in China's Internet Courts' *China Justice Observer* (26 July 2020) available at www.chinajusticeobserver.com/a/its-time-to-settle-cross-border-e-commerce-disputes-in-chinas-internet-courts.

[75] Supreme People's Court of China (2019) (n 73).

[76] 'China Pushes for Increase in Online Dispute Resolution as It Reboots Economy' (19 March 2020) available at www.law.com/international-edition/2020/03/19/china-pushes-for-increase-in-online-dispute-resolution-as-it-reboots-economy/.

[77] Supreme People's Court of China (2019) (n 73) 61.

[78] 'A close look at Hangzhou Internet Court' *China Justice Observer* (3 November 2019) available at www.chinajusticeobserver.com/a/a-close-look-at-hangzhou-internet-court.

[79] 'China's Internet Courts are adapting to a new era' (7 March 2021) available at https://news.cgtn.com/news/2021-03-07/How-China-s-Internet-Courts-are-adapting-to-a-new-era-YqTdsiEcVy/index.html.

[80] Supreme People's Court of China (2019) (n 73) 61.

B. The China Mobile MiniCourt App for E-Litigation Nationwide

Following the launch of the Internet courts, one of the latest developments in this field is the introduction of a 'mobile micro court'.[81] Launched by the regional Ning Bo Intermediate People's Court in Zhejiang Province in January 2018 as a mobile app for online court, this innovation helped to improve e-litigation. The success of this app led to the development of a national version called the 'China Mobile MiniCourt', launched by the Supreme Court of China in August 2018. It has more than 30 functions, including online case filing, case inquiries, online delivery, WeChat payment, mobile phone file checking, legal inquiry, court navigation and enforcement application.

Similar to the three Internet courts, the Mobile MiniCourt App is mainly used for Internet-related cases, including consumer disputes,[82] that involve the use of electronic evidence. It is not suitable for cases that involve multiple parties, complex case facts or personal rights. Despite these limitations and by the end of 2020, the app had a total of 522 million visitors, 3,275,300 users and handled more than 2.2 million cases involving more than 2.1 million litigants. This may be partly due to its interoperability with WeChat app, as it is hosted on the latter (the app has 1.2 billion users in China). In the month of March 2020 alone, the app saw 390,000 new registered users with 437,000 new cases filed.[83] Of these, 72.6 per cent took less than 15 minutes for the litigants to file. The app has become particularly useful during the Covid-19 pandemic due to the restrictive measures around physical distancing and lockdowns.[84] It also helps to significantly reduce barriers in cross-border e-litigation through its WeChat-enabled identity verification processes, overcoming a procedural obstacle with which the Guangzhou Internet Court has been struggling.[85]

VII. Conclusion

The digital economy of China, and its e-commerce in particular, has witnessed unparalleled growth in recent decades. This is manifested through its lion's share of global e-commerce, including the B2C segment and the e-retail sector. In addition, China's

[81] C Shi, T Sourdin and B Li, 'The Smart Court – A New Pathway to Justice in China?' (2021) 12(1) *International Journal for Court Administration* 4.

[82] '湖南高院依法惩治侵害消费者权益犯罪去年共惩处犯罪分子1393人' (21 March 2022) available at www.court.gov.cn/fabu-xiangqing-351861.html.

[83] These figures do not distinguish between consumer cases and non-consumer cases.

[84] 'Chinese courts on smart phones' *China Justice Observer* (5 June 2021) available at www.chinajusticeobserver.com/a/chinese-courts-on-smart-phones.

[85] 'Filing lawsuits while living abroad: China's new policy' *China Justice Observer* (7 March 2021) available at www.chinajusticeobserver.com/a/filing-lawsuits-while-living-abroad-china-s-new-policy; 'How to sue in Chinese court online while living abroad' *China Justice Observer* (14 March 2021) available at www.chinajusticeobserver.com/a/how-to-sue-in-chinese-court-online-while-living-abroad. For procedures for registering and using the China Mobile MiniCourt App, see ibid.

cross-border B2C trade, and indeed global trade as well, holds vast untapped potential that is just beginning to be realised. This immense growth has led to an insurmountable volume of consumer disputes, not least according to the experiences of certain sectoral regulators in China. In addition, Covid-19 further unleashed B2C e-commerce trade, but also opened the floodgates to associated consumer grievances.

Against this backdrop, the Chinese Government has formulated laws and regulations to define five legal pathways that consumers can use to pursue justice and obtain redress, and policies that aim to help to build a robust CDR ecosystem based on these legal approaches. These include the creation of a nationally supervised and coordinated administrative ODR platform; initiatives that incentivise public-private ODR partnerships; e-court scheme pilots that have led to the deployment of national e-litigation apps; and policies that encourage consumer awareness of redress options and promote a culture of consumer protection.

These recent developments, largely supported by the widespread adoption of the mobile Internet and emerging digital technologies, have further advanced the transformation of China's CDR landscape from one that was dominated by a few large e-commerce players in the 2000s to a modernised and diversified field of national administrative bodies, private-sector players and e-courts. This focus on providing comprehensive coverage for CDR in the domestic sphere appears to be functioning relatively well, based on the statistics and Chinese consumers' confidence in the online shopping experience overall. Since consumer trust is vital for the health of digital economy and CDR is an indispensable tool for building and sustaining consumer trust,[86] these government strategies and positive developments appear to be setting China's e-commerce down the path of further expansion in the longer term.

Despite this, given that global cross-border e-trade, including China, is only beginning to burgeon, more can be done to fully seize opportunities by establishing effective CBEC CDR mechanisms. Apart from in-house ODR platforms and e-courts, the latter of which still encounter significant obstacles in respect of cross-border consumer disputes,[87] it is fair to say that China does not yet have effective or efficient CDR mechanisms for CBEC. However, there are promising developments currently with regards to the Regional Comprehensive Economic Partnership (RCEP) – the largest free-trade agreement in history, ratified in January 2022, consisting of 15 countries that include China[88] – that will see Guangzhou become the first Chinese city to develop a CBEC

[86] 'Consumer Trust in the Digital Economy: The Case for Online Dispute Resolution' UNCTAD Research Paper No 72 (11 November 2021) available at https://unctad.org/system/files/official-document/ser-rp-2021d15_en.pdf.

[87] 'Can I resolve cross-border online shopping disputes through the Chinese Internet Court: Inside China's Internet Courts Series -03' *China Justice Observer* (6 April 2019) available at www.chinajusticeobserver.com/a/can-i-resolve-cross-border-online-shopping-disputes-through-the-chinese-internet-court.

[88] In addition to China, RCEP includes the 10 Member States of the Association of Southeast Asian Nations (ASEAN), Japan, South Korea, Australia and New Zealand.

ODR platform for the economic bloc via the implementation of a special RCEP-focused policy.[89] Although it is unclear whether this ODR platform will be available to consumers (or only for B2B e-commerce), it can potentially inform future development of a consumer-focused CBEC ODR platform in China, just as inspirations may be drawn from other forthcoming systems and potentially effective functioning platforms around the world.[90]

[89] 'China and the RCEP: Guangzhou Becomes First City to Issue Special Cross-Border E-Commerce Measures' (16 April 2021) available at www.china-briefing.com/news/guangzhou-cross-border-e-commerce-china-rcep-special-measures/china-and-the-rcep-guangzhou-becomes-first-city-to-issue-special-cross-border-e-commerce-measures/. In March 2021, the Guangzhou Municipal Bureau of Commerce published '*Several Measures for Guangzhou to Grasp the Opportunity of Regional Comprehensive Economic Partnership (RCEP) to Promote the Innovative Development of Cross-Border E-Commerce (CBEC) (the Several Measures)*'. Policy 6 of '*Several Measures*' entails dispute resolution: 'Guangzhou will establish an online dispute resolution (ODR) platform for CBEC related disputes. The ODR platform will follow the rules set out in the Cooperation Framework for APEC Enterprises for Online Settlement of Cross-border Commercial Disputes and provide rapid electronic solutions and enforcement mechanisms for disputes across borders, languages, and different legal jurisdictions.' See at www.china-briefing.com/news/guangzhou-cross-border-e-commerce-china-rcep-special-measures/.

[90] ASEAN, for example, is developing a regional cross-border consumer ODR platform for Southeast Asian countries. 'Feasibility Study: ASEAN Online Dispute Resolution (ODR) Network' (November 2020) available at https://aseanconsumer.org/file/post_image/Feasibility%20Study%20ASEAN%20ODR.pdf.

PART IV

Court System Reform and New Technologies

19

Digital Technology and the Development of Holistic Dispute Resolution

SIR GEOFFREY VOS AND JOHN SORABJI

The idea of selecting the right pathway [to justice] for the right problem is fundamental ... [and the] fundamental question ... is how all of the various pathways and options are integrated into a coherent, effective, responsive, efficient national matrix.

(C Hodges, *Delivering Dispute Resolution. A Holistic Review of Models in England and Wales* (2019))

Preamble

Truly fundamental reform of our civil justice system is a rare occurrence. Historically, it has resulted from wider societal changes that rendered the system unable to deliver justice in a timely, efficient manner to those who needed to rely upon the courts to vindicate their rights. The last such reform occurred in England and Wales in the 1870s and 1880s, and resulted in the creation of the High Court, Court of Appeal and the Rules of the Supreme Court.[1] The need for those reforms, which transformed a justice system that had evolved to meet the requirements of a primarily agrarian society, stemmed from the Industrial Revolution. The late twentieth century and early twenty-first century have brought with them the Fourth Industrial Revolution: the digital revolution. Just as societal changes in the nineteenth century following from the Industrial Revolution exposed the fact that the justice system then was in need of systematic reform, the digital revolution has exposed a similar need today.

Since 2015, the civil justice system in England and Wales has been subject to reform, aimed at ensuring that it can meet the needs of today's digital society. One novel aspect of that reform, or modernisation, programme has been the aim of integrating various forms of what have traditionally been called 'alternative dispute resolution' with the formal court process. Digitisation has been, and is, the medium through which this

[1] The Judicature Acts 1873–1875.

is being achieved. In this chapter, two different perspectives on modernisation are developed. In section I, 'Reform from a Judicial Perspective', Sir Geoffrey Vos MR and Head of Civil Justice for England and Wales develops his perspective on reform. It is a perspective drawn from his experience of reform, which he currently leads on behalf of the judiciary. In section II, 'Reform from an Academic Perspective', John Sorabji offers an academic perspective on reform and the potential to develop aspects of it further than it is currently being taken. Both perspectives view the development of, as Hodges would see it, an integrated, holistic dispute resolution system as the goal of reform. They differ, in part, on where integration may ultimately lead.

I. Reform from a Judicial Perspective

A. Introduction

The starting point for court system reform is the starting point for the reform of all dispute resolution. Historically, there has been almost nothing joined up about dispute resolution. Commentators make the mistake of thinking that effective dispute resolution is a function of the distinction between civil and common law systems. It is nothing of the sort.

My thesis in this chapter is that every country has the need for a holistic and integrated approach to dispute resolution. The tail has too often been allowed in the past to wag the dog. The 'tail' is the tiny number of huge commercial cases dealt with in international arbitration, by domestic court systems or even by the growing number of international commercial courts. The 'dog' is the vast number of disputes that arise every year in every country between consumers and utility and other major companies, between spouses and partners, between citizens and the state, between citizens, between employers and employees, and between small and medium-sized entities (SMEs).

In short, we cannot successfully adapt centuries-old legal systems, whether civil or common law, that were designed to resolve major disputes between wealthy parties to resolve the vast bulk of low-value modern disputes.

We can and should, however, make the maximum use of modern technologies to create integrated dispute resolution systems that have four main guiding principles. First, they should be available to all, whether legally represented or not. Second, they should be able to provide resolution at a cost that is proportionate to what is at stake in every case. Third, they should provide final resolution without delays. Fourth, the dispute resolution systems must command the trust and confidence of the individuals, businesses and the state that they serve.

It is not easy to take the high-level overview of dispute resolution that is suggested in this chapter, because national approaches to the subject have been so disjointed and patchy over so many years. But technology gives us the opportunity to set a new path.

In England and Wales, the court-based legal system derives from a reform in 1883. Since then, successive enactments have overlaid a byzantine structure of tribunals to determine various specific kinds of disputes, for example between citizens and the state, and employees and employers. On top of that, hundreds of thousands of disputes arising in specific economic sectors are resolved by ombuds without the need for court or tribunal proceedings. At the far end of the scale, millions more disputes are resolved every year on Amazon and eBay.

An approach like that described in the last paragraph causes confusion. It leaves the average individual consumer, SME, spouse and employee unsure how to vindicate the claim they have or think they have.

The solution is to create an integrated online structure that allows anyone, whether represented or not, to follow a clearly signposted online path towards the effective, affordable and speedy resolution of their dispute.

There can be three basic tiers to the integrated digital justice system, the tiers together characterising dispute resolution as a funnel or inverted pyramid. The first tier is an authoritative, properly regulated website and online app that provides guidance to any person or business wishing to make any type of claim against any other person, business or the state. The first tier directs the would-be claimant to the second-tier online dispute resolution (ODR) service most suitable to the kind of right that is being asserted. The second tier, in the context of England and Wales, would be a range of pre-action portals, ombuds services and other dispute resolution platforms sponsored by government or particular industrial sectors. The vast bulk of disputes would be resolved at the second-tier stage, as is already happening in the present fragmented system. If, however, any claim is not resolved by a second-tier pre-action portal or ombuds service or platform, the data set created by that process would be transmitted by an application programming interface (API) to the third-tier online court-based dispute resolution service, where online judicial dispute resolution would finally resolve any intractable dispute that got that far.

The approach just described is a parochial one. The designers of these systems should realise too that many, if not most, disputes of the future will be cross-border, if only because so much data will be recorded on-chain; blockchain technologies being entirely borderless. Online digital dispute resolution systems should be designed to integrate with other such national systems, even if a single global system is beyond imagination.

Against that background, section I of this chapter now deals with the following aspects of the development of such a holistic and integrated digital dispute resolution service: (i) integrating the pre-action portals; (ii) creating an integrated online digital court-based dispute resolution service; (iii) integrating mediation into the dispute resolution processes; (iv) digital disadvantage and ensuring that parties, where necessary, have access to appropriate levels of legal advice; and (v) the cross-border element.

B. Integrating Pre-Action Portals

As already mentioned, the problem is in one sense the fragmented nature of what is already on offer. Integration requires coordination and cooperation. In England and Wales, it is hoped that new legislation currently going through the legislature will allow an Online Procedure Rule Committee to coordinate the pre-action space. Such coordination is essential if there is to be one holistic dispute resolution service avoiding confusion to users.

There will, for example, inevitably be some types of disputes that can only be resolved in court. Those disputes would by-pass the second tier of pre-action portals and be directed straight to the online court-based process. Examples might include patent cases, competition cases, and major corporate and commercial disputes. But these types of claims are, as said, a tiny minority. By far the majority of disputes fall into particular bulk categories. Without attempting any comprehensive categorisation, pre-action portals and ombuds services currently deal in England and Wales with personal injury and road traffic claims, employment disputes, some types of family disputes, financial services, insurance and banking claims, and most claims by consumers against utility and other large companies in the energy, telecoms, pharmaceuticals and retail sectors.

Ombuds services are entirely focused on resolution, suggesting settlement options at different stages of the process. Similarly, pre-action personal injury portals are directed at persuading insurers to offer a settlement sum that is acceptable to the claimant, once appropriate medical evidence has been provided. There are, however, always some claims that are not amenable, at least not immediately, to resolution. I will say something more about that in section I.D on integrating mediation into the dispute resolution process.

It is not necessary or desirable for all pre-action portals to adopt the same approach to achieving resolution. Indeed, the most appropriate approach will depend on the type of dispute, the nature of the parties and the complexity of the issues raised. For example, an employment dispute between an employee and employee would be likely to require different interventions than a financial services dispute between bank and customer. There will, however, be some common features. The pre-action process ought to be directed at identifying the issue that divides the parties. In a personal injury claim, it might, for example, be whether the claimant has a lasting injury or one that will clear up in a discernible period of time. In an employment claim, the issue might be whether the employer was entitled to terminate an employee's employment for non-attendance.

Every dispute is more easily amenable to resolution when the issue dividing the parties is properly understood. Fortunately, technology now allows issues to be identified more quickly and efficiently than was the case when the only possibility was the exchange of lengthy pleaded statements of case by each party. Online platforms can make use of decision trees that identify the issue by asking the parties a series of questions. It needs also to be remembered that many disputes can be resolved without fully identifying every issue that divides the parties. An element of pragmatism is required on both sides, but many, if not most, disputants are reasonably pragmatic.

The mistake in the past has been to assume that every party to every dispute wants or expects the perfectly just outcome. Apart from such an outcome being an aspiration rather than reality, most disputants actually want speedy, even rough and ready, resolution more than anything else. The most important things are trust and confidence in the process and freely informed consent being provided to the resolution. That is what all pre-action portals and ombuds processes are aimed at.

Of course, perfectly just outcomes must ultimately be available by judicial resolution, but they are not the purpose of the pre-action portal second-tier process, which is to achieve resolution for the vast majority of parties, who simply want to reach a reasonable compromise and get on with their lives and businesses.

The integration of pre-action portals and ombuds processes can be achieved over time by making high-level rules for their governance. They would not be required to adopt any particular process, but they would be required, for example, to adhere to the rules of natural justice, to hear both sides and not to set unreasonably short timescales for agreement to a suggested solution. In some types of cases, such as matrimonial financial remedies, spouses might be required to have legal or accountancy advice as to their entitlements before being permitted to agree a compromise. It would all depend on the nature of the dispute.

Another essential prerequisite for pre-action portals is the use of simple and accessible language. Experience has shown that lawyers tend to use over-complex language that is unintelligible to ordinary citizens. Pre-action portals, and indeed every stage of the online process of dispute resolution, should use the simplest possible language.

It is inevitable that many pre-actions portals and ombuds processes will (and already do) make use of artificial intelligence (AI). There is nothing wrong with doing so, provided some basic precautions are observed. No party should be required to agree to any solution without a proper opportunity to consider the consequences. Artificial intelligence should be directed at a clear set of objectives for the portal in question, such as identifying the issues on which the parties cannot agree, or suggesting resolutions for the consideration of the parties.

C. Creating an Integrated Online Digital Court-Based Dispute Resolution Service

Court processes in many countries within Europe and beyond remain entirely analogue and paper-based. Such systems require urgent reform. Citizens and businesses of the twenty-first century cannot be expected to have confidence in a system that fails to make use of the same technologies that those citizens and businesses use in every other aspect of their private and personal lives.

Digital justice systems should not be confused with analogue systems using electronic filing. The digital systems this chapter is talking about are smart systems that employ digital machine-readable information, enabling the system to take steps to remind parties of what needs to be done and then to enforce the orders that have been made. It is of limited value to allow parties to upload Word or other text documents that the system cannot itself understand. That is why digital ODR systems have to be built to receive information in machine-readable format. The addiction of many lawyers to non-smart Word or text documents cannot be carried forward into digital justice systems.

In the work that is being done in England and Wales to create online court-based dispute resolution systems, it was quickly realised that the various types of disputes have more in common than lawyers practising in particular or specialist fields would wish to think. Every dispute has claimants and defendants. They each have contact details and, in some cases, legal representatives. All parties may, in some cases, be required to pay fees. All parties may be required by the court to meet deadlines. Ultimately, the court may need to enforce its orders in all types of case. From the point of view of judges deciding cases within a digital justice system, they need to have the relevant cases allocated to them, and to know what their schedule requires them to decide when.

Accordingly, every part of a digital justice system must be integrated and accessible to parties, lawyers, witnesses and judges alike. The different components of a digital justice system must be able to talk to each other. The programs must be intuitive and simple to operate. They must not be labour-intensive for any of the participants.

It is even more important for a digital justice system quickly and efficiently to identify the issues that divide the parties (in so far as those issues have not been determined within a pre-action portal). This is done by the use of decision trees. Ultimately, in the more complex cases, the identification of the issues may require judicial intervention. But, in either case, the process must be directed towards that objective, because it is only once the issues have been identified that judicial dispute resolution can begin.

In every court-based dispute resolution system, there needs to be flexibility in relation to how decisions are reached. The simplest and least consequential decisions can be made by AI (for example, whether a party should respond to a request by 6pm on Tuesday or Wednesday), or by administrators or, in slightly more important matters, by lawyers, leaving the most significant decisions to be taken by judges. The process would, of course, ultimately allow the parties the right to have every decision reviewed by a judge.

The method of decision-making is also important. Not every interim decision needs a hearing; far from it. Many decisions can be taken online after the parties have stated their positions asynchronously in response to programmed questions. Once the issue between the parties has been identified, however, the decision can be taken by a judge either after asynchronous online representations have been received from the parties, or at a remote video hearing or, in some cases, at a physical hearing. In this context, the very low number of physical hearings that are actually needed in current analogue justice systems should guide us to deciding the kinds of disputes for which remote or in-person hearings are likely to be necessary.

Many of those who have no experience of online justice systems think, mistakenly, that the process is no more than a data-filing program into which the parties will upload the same old analogue documents that were used in legacy systems. Court pleadings, statements of witnesses and lengthy written submissions will, in most cases, be things of the past, save in the most complex and high-value cases. In the vast run of cases, the issues will be identified by decision trees. Evidence of both factual and expert witnesses will be provided digitally in smart format or in answer to questions posed online. To take an example, detailed experts' reports will only be required if the system identifies an issue that divides the parties which is a matter of expert opinion – such as, for example, how fast a car was travelling if it left a 10-metre skid mark on the road.

In this connection, it is worth noting that such matters of expert evidence are unlikely to be required for long. Digital on-chain recording devices are likely to become ubiquitous in motor vehicles. It will be unnecessary once that is the case to decide questions that are now commonplace, like the speed of a vehicle at the time of a collision. Such facts will be immutably recorded in every case on the blockchain.

Once an integrated set of online pre-action portals and ombuds services is established, the basic case data will be transmitted electronically to the appropriate part of the online justice system. This will occur once it becomes clear that resolution cannot be achieved within the pre-action portals. The parties will not, therefore, be required to give the same information more than once. That is an important system-wide improvement. One of the greatest causes of intransigence in the current arrangements is the need for the parties continually to repeat their case in different forms in different documents. This creates the opportunity, often taken, for elaboration. It also entrenches the positions of the parties, who become ever more convinced, by repetition, of the justice of their case.

D. Integrating Mediation into the Dispute Resolution Processes

Another of the advantages of ODR is the ability to integrate mediated solutions into the process itself. The pre-action and ombuds portals that I have been describing have, as I have said, always been directed at reaching resolution. Conversely, however, analogue court-based dispute resolution systems tend to exacerbate, rather than narrow, the conflict. This is partly because of the continuous repetition of each party's argument, but also because there is no part of the process that is directed specifically at finding common ground.

In recent years, some domestic court systems have tried to persuade the parties to litigation to stay their proceedings to attempt formal or informal mediation. This has, in many systems, been hit and miss for a number of connected reasons. First, mediation providers do not often attract as much confidence as the court-based processes. Second, parties are often implacably opposed to compromise, thinking they have paid a court fee and are entitled to a judicial resolution. Third, whilst almost every case has a sweet spot at which it is amenable to settlement, it is hard for a remote judge to know when that might be. Fourth, in most systems, mediation cannot be mandated by the court.

A digital online court-based dispute resolution system has the advantage that the system can itself repeatedly suggest mediated interventions and solutions to the parties. Cases do not always require formal mediations to settle. They often just need a trigger at the right time for the parties to consider compromising what may, for extraneous reasons, have become an unwelcome loadstone around the parties' necks.

The digital world is infinitely flexible. As court-based dispute resolution processes develop and improve, there will be many different ways in which the platforms will be able to direct the parties towards resolution rather than continued dispute. Judges will be able to suggest solutions, as will artificially intelligent bots, and the parties or their lawyers will be able to engage, as they can now, but online, in private negotiation.

E. Digital Disadvantage and Ensuring That Parties, Where Necessary, Have Access to Appropriate Levels of Legal Advice

I have already mentioned one type of case in which it is undesirable to allow an unrepresented party to settle without access to adequate legal advice. In matrimonial financial settlement cases, unrepresented spouses can sometimes be pressured into giving up their entitlement in order to bring finality to the dispute. This is just one situation in which parties to disputes may be disadvantaged by a digital system. Other examples include situations where vulnerable parties are unable to make proper use of digital systems or do not have access to the Internet.

First, the existence of vulnerable parties is not a good reason to abort a project to build an accessible digital justice system of the kind that this chapter contemplates. Such vulnerability is, however, a good reason to build safeguards into the system to ensure that it does not create injustices and exacerbate inequalities.

It is obviously important that assistance is available so that the digitally disadvantaged can have ways to access the system. In a sense, that is the easy part. It is probably more difficult to spot those able to access the system who are being harmed or discriminated against by some aspect of its operation. It is perhaps most important to be aware of the possible ways in which such harm can occur. It is beyond the scope of this chapter to identify all the desirable protections. That said, I would repeat that the need for such protections is not a reason not to create a digital justice system that improves access to justice for the vast majority of society.

F. The Cross-Border Element

I have now described the essential elements of an integrated and holistic online digital system of justice. Up to now, our discussion has assumed that every domestic legal system in every country will need to build or buy such a system for itself to cater for its own specific national needs. It may be thought that there is no alternative to the multiple municipal justice systems that are history's legacy. Indeed, the different approaches of civil and common law epitomised by the distinction between the inquisitorial and adversarial systems that underlie them, may be thought to reinforce that point of view. I beg to differ.

The European Law Institute and UNIDROIT approved in 2020 the ELI/UNIDROIT model rules of European Civil Procedure (the ELI-UNIDROIT Rules), which successfully adopted a holistic approach to civil procedure rules across civil and common law systems. By so doing it demonstrated, outside the digital environment, that there were essential features of all civil dispute resolution that transcended those distinctions. I believe that it would be worth exploring a similar approach within the environment of the digital justice system.

First, the disputes of the future are unlikely to resemble the disputes of the past. In the future, as I have already mentioned, factual disputes will be significantly reduced by the existence of far more extensive data and the digital recording of many, if not most, events in the lives of individuals and businesses. Blockchain technology, the internet of things and their successor technologies are likely to lead to an immutable and undeniable factual foundation to every dispute. Just as the speed of every moving vehicle (whether automated or driven by human beings) when every accident occurs will be known, almost every other fact will be recorded and indisputable.

Second, the blockchain technologies that underlie this data revolution are, as I have said, entirely borderless. Disputes are more likely to relate to cross-border supplies and technology than to the kinds of things we argue about today. Data relating to transportation, insurance, energy and telecoms, to name but a few sectors, will be recorded on-chain.

Third, despite the current international trend towards rather than against nationalism, pendulums swing. There will be nothing to stop a national of one country accessing the digital online justice system of another country except an inhibition on those with foreign addresses making claims. The systems will undoubtedly need to expand to encompass cross-border claims and to resolve them in pre-action portals as much as they resolve domestic disputes. Indeed, the conflict of laws is likely to become a more important part of the lawyer's armoury as cross-border technologies take hold.

It may be considered absurd to suggest that any digital dispute resolution system could ever operate globally. The underlying reason why such a suggestion is potentially problematic is, of course, that ultimately domestic justice systems derive their coercive powers from the national state.

Nonetheless, I believe that those considering the design and implementation of digital dispute resolution systems should be considering their interaction with similar systems in other countries. Legal systems have much more in common than that which divides them. At the very least, it should eventually be possible for the systems themselves to deal with cross-border disputes and cross-border issues.

G. Conclusions

The development of a holistic, integrated, digital dispute resolution system for all types of disputes is in progress in England and Wales and in some other national systems. Developments in digital technology are unlikely to slow down. Lawyers and courts are not exempt. Generally, too many lawyers hope that they will be able to retire before any of these developments take effect.

The legal community owes it to future generations to think beyond the way that disputes have historically been resolved. It is necessary now to be supremely inventive and imaginative in the use of developing technologies. In that way, disputes in all fields will be resolved more quickly and efficiently, at lower cost and with better outcomes. The systems that can achieve that kind of resolution must be integrated and accessible to all. The guiding light is access to justice.

II. Reform from an Academic Perspective

A. Introduction

The reforms outlined in section I of this chapter will, undoubtedly, if carried through, improve access to justice in England and Wales and provide it with, as Hodges has argued, an effective means to provide different pathways to dispute resolution. In three areas, I suggest in this Part of the chapter that more could be done to fully realise Hodges' vision and provide England and Wales for the first time with a coherent, integrated approach to dispute resolution. I focus specifically on the nature of the integrated online digital court-based dispute resolution service, the integration of mediation and the scope for cross-border coherence.

B. Creating an Integrated Online Digital Court-Based Dispute Resolution Service

Civil justice reform is rarely radical. On the contrary, it is generally ad hoc and evolutionary. The development, for instance, of the tribunals justice system over the course of the twentieth century is a case in point. Reactive developments with no overarching structure or coherence introduced a patchwork of tribunals dealing with different civil disputes between individuals and the state.[2] Equally, the singularly poor track record of the decennial reforms to civil procedure in the courts over the last 150 years tells its own story. It is only in the past 20 years that there has been any real movement towards the type of coherent, integrated reforms outlined in section I of this chapter. The rationalisation of the tribunals in 2007 is illustrative of this trend, as – of course – is the detailed work carried out by Hodges.[3]

Digitisation provides the means by which radical and coherent reform could be delivered. And from a practical perspective, the development of pre-action portals does, as Vos MR suggests, provide a realistic starting point for the introduction of an integrated three-tier system. It does, however, also carry with it a significant risk: design and implementation failure.[4] The track record of government information technology (IT) projects is a desultory one. Steps will need to be taken to ensure that the design and implementation of tier two, the pre-action portals, is achieved in a way that is consistent with, and capable of, integration with tiers one and three. Steps will also need to be taken to ensure that the system as a whole is able to meet the demands of the digital age and the sheer volume and nature of digital disputes that it is likely to need to resolve. One way in which these potential problems could be avoided would be to ensure that all three tiers of the new system were designed at the same time, as part of a coherent whole, with implementation running in tandem. As a consequence of this, more emphasis needs to be given now to the design and development of tier one as part of the integrated online court-based dispute resolution service; one that is properly a partnership between the state, individuals and private enterprise.

[2] G Drewry, *The Judicialisation of the 'Administrative' Tribunals in the UK: From Hewart to Leggatt*, Transylvanian Review of Administrative Sciences, No 28 E SI/2009 45.

[3] C Hodges, *Delivering Dispute Resolution. A Holistic Review of Models in England and Wales* (Hart Publishing, 2019).

[4] See, for instance, Thomson Reuters Court Management Solutions, C-Track® – Lessons learned in courts digitisation – A white paper, 7, available at http://legalsolutions.thomsonreuters.co.uk/content/dam/openweb/documents/pdf/legal/white-paper/2460102A%20C-Track%20Lessons%20learned%20in%20courts%20digitisation.pdf. The failure to implement an effective IT system in the NHS is the paradigm case in the UK of such failure: see A Maughan, *Six reasons why the NHS National Programme for IT failed* (September 2010) available at www.computerweekly.com/opinion/Six-reasons-why-the-NHS-National-Programme-for-IT-failed;

In terms of tier one, the starting point ought to be that facet of dispute resolution that has been most significantly under-emphasised historically: preventive justice. Sander alluded to it in his seminal paper, 'Varieties of Dispute Processing' in 1976.[5] It is also inherent in the development of the concept of the 'shadow of the law', developed slightly later by Mnookin and Kornhauser.[6] Most recently, its importance has been stressed by the UK Supreme Court and Susskind.[7] The former highlighted preventive justice by reference to the effect that court judgments have on the ability of individuals and businesses to order their affairs in ways to minimise the prospect of disputes arising, that is, by ordering them consistently within the law and by providing an effective framework for minimising the prospect that disputes could arise, that is through enabling prospective disputants to determine the nature of their potential dispute and its merits and through the existence of access to justice. The latter highlighted it through the idea of 'legal health promotion', a concept that in essence combines the shadow of the law and public legal education, and in doing so emphasises their importance to effective preventive dispute resolution.

Tier one ought properly, then, to promote preventive justice. There are multiple ways in which it could do so. The extended court portal could integrate access to legislation and court judgments online by, for instance, linking to The National Archives website, where both will be available by the middle of 2022. It could additionally provide guidance to lay persons on how to identify relevant legislation and judgments, and how to navigate within them to identify material relevant to the individual accessing them. Access is more than simply the ability to obtain such documents easily. Digital access to judgments does not, for instance, in and of itself amount to effective access. A lay person given access to a database of thousands of judgments may well not be able to identify the key judgments or determine their ratio. Tier one could and should properly provide means, perhaps AI-assisted means, for lay persons to identify relevant judgments and dicta from within them.

An effective tier one should also enhance the state's ability to provide free legal advice and assistance. Again, this could be achieved through integrating Citizens Advice into the system, or, at the least, through providing the ability to easily access advice from that organisation and other pro bono advice bodies. Tier one could thus operate as part of a one-stop shop for public legal education and advice. The advantage of tier one should not, however, end there. As a one-stop shop, it should also – inherent in holistic design – provide a readily accessible means for an individual or a business to access tier two of the system, where necessary, after having taken advantage of tier one. It is here that the particular importance of integrating pre-action portals into the system arises. Currently, the landscape of pre-action dispute resolution is, as Vos MR highlighted, fragmented. He is not the first to raise the point; similar complaints have, for instance, been made concerning the fragmentation to the public detriment of the landscape of ombuds

[5] F Sander, 'Varieties of Dispute Processing' (1976) 70 FRD 111, 112.

[6] R Mnookin and L Kornhauser, 'Bargaining in the shadow of the law' (1978–1979) 88 *Yale Law Journal* 950.

[7] *R (UNISON) v Lord Chancellor* [2017] UKSC 51, [2017] 3 WLR 409; R Susskind, *Online Courts and the Future of Justice* (Oxford University Press, 2019) 69, 116–88.

schemes[8] and consumer complaints mechanisms.[9] Further fragmentation is also, to a certain degree, inherent in the existence of various different pre-action protocols, which incorporate both best practice mechanisms and quasi-legislative, quasi-mandatory forms of pre-litigation requirements for certain types of litigation.[10]

Developing tier one does not, however, mean that the courts would take on responsibility for the provision of citizens advice and pro bono services. Responsibility for ensuring effective coordination and coherence in tier one, just as Vos MR suggests for tier two, ought to reside with the Online Procedure Rule Committee.[11] In respect of both these tiers, it ought to provide a means to promote the growth, as well as rationalisation, of actors in those fields through the development of minimum standards, which they then need to meet in order to be approved for incorporation into the online court website and app. In this way the Rule Committee could ensure that individuals and businesses have appropriate access to a cohesive and simplified pre-litigation landscape.

If we take tier two as an example, the Rule Committee could enhance coherence and simplicity in a number of ways. First, in order for an ombuds scheme or other resolution mechanism, whether private or public, to be certified and integrated into the system, it could be required to adopt common process features, with departures from the common approach only where justified by reference to specific features of the types of disputes on which they are focused. Second, and again as a function of simplicity, only those schemes that meet pre-determined accessibility criteria should be certified by the Rule Committee. Thus, it should set standards that promote ease of access, and particularly ease of access for the vulnerable. Third, it should actively promote the use of AI. Not just as Vos MR suggests, to identify issues on which parties cannot agree or to suggest solutions, but also to identify the most appropriate next step for the parties to take. One of the flaws of the initial approach to digitisation reform in England and Wales was the suggestion in the Civil Courts Structure Review that its own three-tier system, which would incorporate negotiation and mediation into a digital case management process, was sequential; that, broadly, parties would move through each stage of the digital process in turn – negotiation, then mediation, then adjudication – a model derived from the Civil Resolution Tribunal in British Columbia. The incorporation of AI into tier two could assist parties initially to determine the most appropriate dispute resolution mechanism, and if that fails could be used to determine the next most appropriate mechanism. Rather than progress from tier two to tier three in a sequential pattern, AI could help promote the effective use of multiple forms of dispute resolution

[8] All-Party Parliamentary Group on Consumer Protection, Report from the Ombudsman Inquiry (January 2019), at 14: '[T]he current system is little more than a consumer maze … fragmented and lacking in coherence,' caused by the fact that 'the ombudsman sector has tended to be developed in an incremental and ad-hoc fashion, rather than informed by principle … [with a] combination of … multiple competing redress schemes whilst at the same time having gaps in coverage'.

[9] As Hodges rightly outlines the position; see Hodges (n 3) chs 9–15.

[10] See *Practice Direction – Pre-Action Conduct and Protocols*, para 18, for a list of the current pre-action protocols, which encompass some pre-action portals, eg for public liability, employer's liability, holiday claims and some road traffic claims. Civil Justice Council, *Interim Report on Pre-Action Protocols* (2021) 76–89 available at www.judiciary.uk/wp-content/uploads/2021/11/CJC-PAP-Interim-Report.pdf.

[11] Judicial Review and Courts Bill 2021, ss 19–32. For previous attempts to introduce such a Rule Committee, see the Courts and Tribunals (Online Procedure) Bill 2019 and the Prison and Courts Bill 2017.

mechanism. Equally, and importantly, its continued use in tier three could also help parties identify, during pre-trial case management, whether an issue, issues or the whole claim are suitable to 'loop back' to tier two or to one of the non-adjudicative dispute resolution mechanisms available in tier three. In that way, an implicit feature of effective dispute systems design will be incorporated into the new system.[12]

C. Integrating Mediation into the Dispute Resolution Processes

The Rule Committee's role ought to be important in two other areas, both of which go beyond the necessary integration of mediation into the dispute resolution process. First, to embed effective feedback loops in the three tiers. Second, to ensure that design moves beyond mediation as the alternative pathway to dispute resolution in tier three, particularly as Vos MR properly notes in section I that digital world is infinitely flexible.

First, feedback loops. The promotion of pre-action portals and the use of ombuds schemes in tier two, as Vos MR describes, is intended to focus on the resolution of individual disputes. Some ombuds schemes look at disputes through a wider lens, using the individual dispute as a basis for carrying out a systemic appraisal of the sector for which they have responsibility.[13] Such appraisals can lead to recommendations for sectoral reform. Such reform can include changes in the law or organisational changes such that the potential for future disputes is reduced. By providing a single portal through which disputes are managed, the online court portal and app will provide a basis by which the materials for such systemic appraisals, and hence reforms, could be enhanced. Data, suitably anonymised where necessary, could be provided from all tiers and to appropriate ombuds schemes, to enable them to carry out their systems-review functions more effectively. In that way the entire system can be restructured around two clear purposes: the promotion of preventive justice so as to reduce the possibility of future disputes in so far as possible, particularly through tier two's links to ombuds schemes; and early individual dispute resolution through tiers one to three.

It is in respect of early individual dispute resolution that the second point arises. Vos MR, consistently with the approach taken by the judiciary generally[14] and governments across the world, focuses on the incorporation of mediation into tier three. Tier three would thus become a binary system promoting mediation and adjudication. In doing so, it fails to take proper account of the plethora of dispute resolution processes that could beneficially be applied to individual disputes. A better, more holistic approach would be to utilise the benefits of AI to enable tier three to match individual disputes to the most appropriate form of dispute resolution process for that dispute, whether that be negotiation, mediation, collaborative law, early neutral evaluation, arbitration or a hybrid process, such as arb-med or med-arb. Any assumption that mediation is the, or

[12] W Ury, J Brett and S Goldberg, *Getting Disputes Resolved* (PON, 1993) 62.

[13] C Gill, *The Evolving Role of the Ombudsman: a conceptual and constitutional analysis of the "Scottish solution" to administrative justice* (Public Law, Oct 2014) 662.

[14] As evident from Dyson LJ's dicta in *Halsey v Milton Keynes General NHS Trust* [2004] 1 WLR 3002 [5].

should be the only, alternative form of dispute resolution process in tier three would fail to learn the lessons of research in the United States or empirical evidence that supports the view that for some disputes other forms of dispute resolution process are more effective than mediation. Such an approach also fails to give proper weight to the facilitative role that the new integrated, holistic court could play in promoting individual responsibility. It is obvious that the state is under a duty to provide effective access to justice, and that that has traditionally focused on access to the court. Equally, though, the state has a duty to promote the public interest. Crucially, individuals have, or ought properly to be understood to have, a duty or responsibility to seek to resolve their own disputes consensually and, in doing so, to ensure that they only call upon the state to assist them when necessary. Providing in tier three a range of dispute resolution pathways is not just a matter of accepting that different disputes call for different routes to resolution; it also – consistently with the approaches that should be taken in tiers one and two – accepts that dispute resolution is a partnership between the individual and the state, each of whom have their own, complementary responsibilities. If the Rule Committee can ensure that tier three goes further than simply mediation and adjudication, it will go a long way to giving effect to this partnership of responsibility. In doing so it will properly promote effective access to justice.

D. The Cross-Border Element

It is a truism that civil justice systems derive their ultimate authority from the state. State power or sovereignty provides the basis on which parties and witnesses can, ultimately and if necessary, be compelled to take part in civil process. It is the basis on which orders are capable of enforcement against recalcitrant parties. It is equally the basis on which effective alternative and ODR rests. Without state power, for instance, arbitral processes would lack the means to compel witnesses to give evidence, and mediated agreements would not be capable of enforcement. There is currently little, if any, evidence that states are willing to pool or transfer their sovereignty over dispute resolution to international bodies. There is, for instance, no civil court for the European Union (EU) capable of dealing with EU cross-border disputes. Nor does one seem a likely development in the near to mid-term future. Nor is there likely to be an international civil court at any time in the foreseeable future.[15] That does not mean that harmonisation and integration of different national, municipal approaches to civil dispute resolution are not real possibilities.

The first and arguably fundamental reason why future harmonisation may occur is that, whatever the recent trends be in other areas, the overarching and continuing trend in the evolution of civil justice systems is towards harmonisation. As noted by Stürner,[16]

[15] Although see, M Steinitz, *The Case for an International Court of Civil Justice* (Cambridge University Press, 2019).

[16] R Stürner, 'Anglo-American and Continental Civil Procedure' in M Andenæs, N Andrews and R Nazzini (eds), *The Future of Transnational Civil Litigation* (BICCL, 2004) 9, 11. Also see G Canivet, *The Interrelationship Between Common Law and Civil Law* (2003) 63 *Louisiana Law Review* 937; G Seidman, 'The New Comparative Civil Procedure' in C Picker and G Seidman (eds), *The Dynamism of Civil Procedure – Global Trends and Developments* (Springer, 2016) 19, 23 ff.

amongst others, recent decades have seen the differences between common law and civil law systems lessen. From an English and Welsh perspective, the introduction of active case management via the Woolf reforms incorporated into the Civil Procedure Rules an approach analogous to judicial power that exists in, for instance, Austria and Germany, to supervise case management effectively (general *Prozessleitungspflicht*).[17] Equally, differences between civil law systems have also lessened over the same period due to the influence of EU legislation.[18] These trends are likely to continue in the future due to the influence that the ELI-UNIDROIT Rules could have on future developments. This influence ought to go beyond the point suggested in section I of this chapter, which sees the process by which the Rules were devised as a template for drafting a potentially harmonised approach for the future development of civil dispute resolution. It should appear clear, however, that the working practices and approach adopted by the project team does present a model for designers of future digital-based dispute resolution systems, not least through drawing on a wide range of expertise from lawyers, academics, the judiciary and policymakers from an equally wide range of jurisdictions.[19]

There are two fundamental ways in which the ELI-UNIDROIT Rules could influence the design of a harmonised approach to the design of digital dispute resolution systems in the future: tier two and tier three harmonisation. Taking tier three first, a reasonable assumption, and perhaps an assumption under section I of this chapter, is that different countries will create different digital civil procedure codes; that they will automate what they currently do. In that way we shall see the development of multiple, divergent, municipal justice systems. The ELI-UNIDROIT Rules provide, however, a template for the development of multiple, common, municipal justice systems. They provide a common framework for the digitisation of civil procedure across Europe. There is no reason, in principle, why European countries should encode the historic approaches to civil procedure digitally. On the contrary, digitisation should provide the spur to fundamentally rethink past approaches. The ELI-UNIDROIT Rules provide a framework for future design that could see the development of a common, municipal approach across jurisdictions. Such a common approach could form the basis for interoperable European cross-border systems, which could serve the digital, blockchain-based, economy. Such commonality of approach could, with further work, be adopted more broadly. There is in principle no reason why other regional model rules similar to the ELI-UNIDROIT Rules could not be developed, which could then form the basis of, for instance, greater harmonisation across South American jurisdictions, Africa jurisdictions and so on. Such regional developments could then themselves form the basis of future global harmonisation, or, at the least, they could provide the basis for greater convergence between systems than there is at the present time.

In essence, the ELI-UNIDROIT Rules could provide the basis for an integrated digital cross-border approach to the adjudicative aspect of the third tier of the holistic

[17] See, eg, S Nieuwendijk et al, 'The Paradox of Access to Justice – Empirical Research into the Attitude of the Cantonal Judge towards Unrepresented Parties in Dutch Civil Procedure' in A Uzelac and CH van Rhee (eds), *Revisiting Procedural Human Rights* (Intersentia, 2017) 287.

[18] See F Gascón Inchausti and B Hess (eds), *The Future of the European Law of Civil Procedure* (Intersentia, 2020).

[19] On the methodological approach adopted in devising the rules see, ELI-UNIDROIT Model European Rules of Civil Procedure (Oxford University Press, 2021) at 3 ff.

model outlined in this chapter. Such an approach would on the one hand obviate the need to consider and avoid the problems of designing and promoting regional or international courts for civil disputes, and the problems they would raise concerning national sovereignty. It could, however, have a further effect. Harmonisation is a design principle. Were countries to adopt an approach, based on the ELI-UNIDROIT Rules, that focused on designing digital civil procedure rules that were consistent with those in other countries, that could itself lead to a broader adoption of commonality in design. It could, for instance, lead to harmonisation of other elements of tier three, for example court-integrated ODR could be harmonised across borders in the same way that civil procedure rules could be harmonised.

Precedent for a degree of harmonisation lies in the EU Mediation Directive.[20] Work could properly be carried out to devise a model European code for court-based ODR, which could incorporate e-negotiation, e-mediation, etc.[21] Such developments are as consistent with Hodges' approach as they are with the ELI-UNIDROIT approach. And both are consistent with the need for countries to provide an effective means to resolve disputes of the digital future. Moreover, there is no reason why common approaches to tiers one and two could not be developed, and at least across EU jurisdictions steps taken to devise common digital platforms that could be integrated into the various national approaches to tier three. Equally, there is no reason – in principle – why non-EU, whether EFTA or otherwise, states could not contribute to devising, and then using, common digital tiers two. There could, for instance, be common standard setting for pre-action portals across countries so as to promote the development of a harmonised tier two. That might well be thought to be an important development given the likely prominence of private sector pre-action portals, and that they are likely to seek approval in, and be incorporated into, different municipal tiers two. And if, for instance, there is a growth of one-stop shop approaches to disputes in specific sectors, such as there were in cross-border disputes that involve consumers in multiple jurisdictions, the need for common standards and common approaches will be all the more important, not least to preclude the development of tier two forum-shopping across jurisdictions. Taken together, the ELI-UNIDROIT Rules and digitisation could then provide a template for harmonisation not just across tier three, but also tier two of future integrated, holistic digital systems.

E. Conclusion

Civil justice systems have been seriously engaged in digitisation, in one form or another, since at least the 1990s. It is only in the last decade, however, that there has been a step-change in approach; one that has called into question how states deliver dispute

[20] Directive 2008/52/EC of the European Parliament and of the Council of 21 May 2008 on certain aspects of mediation in civil and commercial matters [2008] OJ L136/3.

[21] Such an approach could build on the initial work carried out by ELI and the European Network of the Council of Judiciaries, see ELI-ENCJ, *The Relationship between Formal and Informal Justice: the Courts and Alternative Dispute Resolution* (2018) available at www.europeanlawinstitute.eu/fileadmin/user_upload/p_eli/Publications/ADR_Statement.pdf.

resolution through and outside their courts. Policymakers, judges and court administrations will continue to grapple with that question over the next decade as they continue to redesign and digitally re-engineer their civil courts. In doing so they will undoubtedly be influenced by the continued growth in digital disputes, the ubiquity of the data revolution, and the need to provide effective means to deliver justice for their citizens and citizens of other countries who are engaged in borderless, digitalised disputes. In the light of this, the transformation of civil dispute resolution ought not properly be left to ad hoc evolution but – on the contrary – should, as suggested both in section I and section II of this chapter, be the product of considered development; development that ought to see the creation of an integrated, holistic dispute resolution system that is able to place each dispute on the most appropriate of many different pathways to justice. Vos MR's vision in section I of this chapter is a crucial step forward in that direction. It could and should, however, be the first step in a broader journey to improve access to justice.

20

The Evolution of No-Fault Compensation Schemes for Personal Injuries

SONIA MACLEOD

> From the mid-1980s on, one of us (Hodges) was involved as a practitioner in, or close to, a series of large product liability cases, the majority of which failed to establish liability on the part of the defendant but left both parties and manufacturers unsatisfied, whilst conferring substantial benefits on the intermediaries in the legal transaction, the lawyers. This prompted the notion that there must be a better way of processing compensation claims, screening those that are valid and invalid, and generally caring for those who suffer misfortune.
>
> (S Macleod and C Hodges, *Redress Schemes for Personal Injuries* (2017))

No-fault compensation schemes have been surprisingly prevalent in providing redress for personal injuries, where they have been used in a variety of circumstances. These schemes range from providing a jurisdiction-wide alternative to tort litigation, to tailored responses to injuries caused by specific events, processes or circumstances. The development of vaccines for Covid-19 has led to a renewed interest in no-fault compensation schemes and the worldwide proliferation of such schemes to provide redress for adverse events following vaccination. This chapter will explore how such schemes are developed, their function, advantages and disadvantages, and how they fit within a wider legal and social context.

I. Introduction

I have been fortunate enough to work with Chris Hodges for many years, including co-authoring *Redress Schemes for Personal Injuries*.[1] Working with Chris has been interesting, intellectually challenging and a huge amount of fun. *Redress Schemes* in particular was a joy to work on. Chris's background as a successful common law product

[1] S Macleod and C Hodges, *Redress Schemes for Personal Injuries* (Hart Publishing, 2017).

liability solicitor makes his contribution to the field of no-fault compensation schemes quite remarkable; few people are willing, or able, to move away from the familiar and to countenance innovation and change in the way Chris has.

I continue to work on no-fault compensation with a new research programme on Covid-19 Vaccine no-fault compensation schemes, as outlined in Lorenz Ködderitzsch's contribution, 'No-Fault Compensation Systems in the Pandemic Context', in chapter 21. I am delighted that Chris has agreed to be an advisor on my Covid-19 Vaccine no-fault compensation schemes research programme; I could not think of anyone better suited to this role; Chris's experience and expertise will be invaluable.

II. Background

No-fault compensation has a long, and sometimes surprising, history. Workers' compensation schemes, the largest sub-group of no-fault compensations, can be seen way back in the seventeenth century, when pirates formalised their solidarity for injured comrades by setting up compensation tariffs for specific injuries.[2] These arrangements pre-date the introduction of statutory schemes that developed in Europe, starting with Germany, from the 1880s.[3] The workers' compensation movement started in the civil law jurisdictions, but was readily taken up in common law jurisdictions, and workers' compensation schemes are now found across both civil and common law jurisdictions.

It is worth considering how and why these workers' compensation schemes came into existence, as it contextualises no-fault compensation more generally. From the outside, the creation of the pirates' code initially seems a counter-intuitive for an occupation that was defined by its disregard for the law.[4] However, piracy was a collective (and dangerous) endeavour with no recourse to any other source of restitution following injury that required a solution. As pirates sat outside all the usual legal and societal structures, there was no option other than developing a *de novo* no-fault scheme. This set of rules, including predefined compensation tariffs, provided a degree of security and social cohesion within the group of pirates.

If you compare this to the evolution of workers' compensation in the United States (US) between 1910 and 1920, there are some parallels but also some key differences.[5]

[2] For an interesting comparison on the relative value of injuries under the pirates code and the 2005 Connecticut workers' compensation tariffs, see S Dubner, 'The Economics of Piracy (the real kind, with peglegs and pieces of Eight' (17 September 2007) available at https://freakonomics.com/2007/09/the-economics-of-piracy-the-real-kind-with-peglegs-and-pieces-of-eight/

[3] SB Horovitz, 'Worldwide Workmen's Compensation Trends' (1970) 59 *Kentucky Law Journal* 37 available at https://uknowledge.uky.edu/klj/vol59/iss1/6 describes schemes in Germany in 1871 and 1884; Austria in 1887; Norway in 1894; Finland in 1895; England in 1897; Denmark, France and Italy in 1898; Greece in 1901; and Belgium and Russia in 1903.

[4] Particularly as various different versions of the code contained a requirement that pirates were tucked up in their beds by 8pm!

[5] The development of workers' compensation in the US has a substantial body of literature; RL Rabin, 'Some Reflections on the Process of Tort Reform' (1988) 25(1) *San Diego Law Review* 13 (available at https://digital.sandiego.edu/sdlr/vol25/iss1/3/) provides a concise summary.

Workers' compensation in the US arose against the social, health and safety reforms seen during the Progressive Era, which prompted a re-evaluation of the existing tort liability frameworks. Injured workers had very few realistic options to deliver compensation after a workplace injury due to a lack of first-party insurance and defences that enabled employers to avoid liability for the majority of workplace injuries.[6] Nominally, injured US workers at the turn of the twentieth century could obtain compensation through litigation; in practice this was not an effective means to restitution for the majority. In this context workers' compensation was a replacement for litigation, rather than a *de novo* solution, and was a compromise for both workers and employers. Workers received the benefit of no-fault payments following injury in exchange for the right to sue their employers in tort for their injuries. Employers obtained immunity from negligence suits in exchange for giving up their right to raise defences to liability. Workers' compensation spread across the US on a State by State basis in the 1910s and 1920s. In some ways this was a radical departure, as the threshold to determine compensation had shifted away from blame-based liability and the associated arguments around moral hazard and deterrence (perceived as an integral part of tort-based compensation). In other ways this shift was far less radical. Workers' compensation schemes retained structures (courts) and processes (hearings, the potential for representation by a lawyer) that mirrored the tort system they had replaced. Workers' compensation is the largest sub-group of no-fault compensation. It has remained in place for over a century, with some expansions and retractions. From its inception, workers' compensation has had its critics;[7] but it is so well established that it remains a stable component of the compensation landscape.

III. No-Fault Schemes as a Replacement for Litigation

Workers' compensation is an example of a situation where a scheme replaced a pre-existing compensatory framework of tort litigation for a defined group of individuals. Replacing a right to litigation with a no-fault compensation scheme can take many forms. It could be a replacement for certain categories of claimants, workers in this case, or it could be a total replacement of litigation for accidents leading to personal injuries, as is seen in New Zealand. This raises a question as to what drives these replacements.

A. Total Replacement – New Zealand

The Accident Compensation Corporation (ACC) New Zealand is probably the best known of all the no-fault schemes, and has effectively decoupled compensation

[6] These were often referred to as the 'unholy trinity' and comprised contributory negligence, voluntary assumption of risk and the fellow-servant defence (an employer could not be held liable for injuries caused by actions of a fellow employee). See PV Fishback and SE Kantor *A Prelude to the Welfare State: The Origins of Workers' Compensation* (Chicago University Press, 2000)

[7] For a history, see E Spieler, '(Re)Assessing the Grand Bargain: Compensation for Work Injuries in the United States, 1900–2017' (2017) 69(3) *Rutgers University Law Review* 891; Northeastern University School of Law Research Paper No 306-2017, available at https://ssrn.com/abstract=3079871.

for injuries from litigation in New Zealand. This is one of the most comprehensive replacements of tort litigation, but it is important to remember that it was achieved incrementally. New Zealand was in the vanguard of the workers' compensation movement, enacting The Worker's Compensation for Accidents Act in 1900.[8] This was in part driven by the high level of workplace accidents in New Zealand arising from the disproportionate number of dangerous activities and industries, including seafaring, mining, whaling and logging, and industrial accidents in factories such as woollen mills. Starting in the 1870s, a series of Acts[9] gave injured workers the right to sue their employer for compensation, but litigation was expensive and the outcome was not guaranteed, so this was not a viable option for the majority of individuals. Even where compensation was provided, for example by the Mine Workers Levy established in 1891, it was often inadequate.[10] It was against this backdrop that the 1900 Act was developed. This Act established a no-fault principle and removed the need for injured employees or their representatives to demonstrate negligence; and while it provided compensation payments, these were modest and were paid for six years at most.

In the 1930s the welfare state was created in New Zealand. An extension of this safety-net approach can be seen in the creation of the Workers' Compensation Board in 1950, which protected employees whose employer had failed to comply with its statutory responsibility to take out insurance against workplace accidents. This was the beginnings of the assumption by the state of responsibility for compensation and rehabilitation.

From 1928, parallel developments under the Motor-Vehicles Insurance (Third-Party Risks) Act 1928[11] required all motor vehicle owners to take out insurance in respect of their liabilities arising from any accidents.

Despite discontent with the level of benefits for injured workers, the 1900 Act remained in force for six decades. It was widely acknowledged that employers and/or insurers often disputed their obligations to pay, making it difficult for injured workers to obtain compensation. In 1966, a Royal Commission was established on Compensation for Personal Injury, chaired by Chief Justice Owen Woodhouse. His seminal report, the Woodhouse Report,[12] recommended a unified approach to all personal injuries occurring in New Zealand on a no-blame basis. In exchange, New Zealanders would lose the right to sue for damages for personal injuries. This Report received cross-party political support and was given effect in the Accident Compensation Act 1972,[13] which provided cover for injuries to employees and the self-employed, and for motor vehicle-related injuries. Funding for the scheme, mandated under the Act, derived from levies that all

[8] Workers' Compensation for Accidents Act 1900 (64 Vict 1900 No 43) available at www.nzlii.org/nz/legis/hist_act/wcfaa190064v1900n43437/.

[9] For example, the Regulation of Mines Act 1874 (38 Vict 1874 No 60); the Employers' Liability Act 1882 (46 Vict 1882 No 20); the Factories Act 1891 (54 & 55 Vict 1891 No 32).

[10] See at https://teara.govt.nz/mi/workplace-safety-and-accident-compensation/page-2.

[11] Motor-Vehicles Insurance (Third-Party Risks Act 1928 (19 Geo V 1928 No 52) available at www.nzlii.org/nz/legis/hist_act/mira192819gv1928n52539/

[12] *Compensation for Personal Injury in New Zealand: Report of the Royal Commission of Inquiry* (Royal Commission of Inquiry into Compensation for Personal Injury 1967) available at https://gg.govt.nz/sites/default/files/2021-06/RC%20119%20Compensation%20for%20Personal%20Injury.pdf.

[13] Accident Compensation Act 1972 (1972 No 43) available at www.nzlii.org/nz/legis/hist_act/aca19721972n43231/.

taxpayers, self-employed individuals and motor vehicle owners were required to pay to the Accident Compensation Commission (later renamed the Accident Compensation Corporation (ACC)).

In 1973 an amendment[14] to the 1972 Act was passed that expanded the scope to include students, people who were not working and those visiting New Zealand. Three schemes were established:

- The earners scheme, funded by levies from employed and self-employed people.
- The motor vehicles accident scheme, funded by levies from motor vehicle owners.
- The supplementary scheme, which covered those not in work, students and visitors, funded by the government.

In 1974, ACC was created to administer the compensation programmes. It is a crown entity, which was formed with five guiding principles: community responsibility; comprehensive entitlement; complete rehabilitation; real compensation; and administrative efficiency. Various reforms to ACC occurred in the decade or so after its creation, including joining the three schemes listed above into one in 1982.

In a 1988 Law Commission Report,[15] major changes to eligibility were recommended, including the addition of coverage for sickness and changes to the thresholds used to determine cover after medical accidents. Other changes included increasing the time before ACC started to make payments for an injury from one week to two weeks (and for employees shifting the responsibility for paying compensation for the first two weeks onto the employer); making a Minister responsible for promoting safety and rehabilitation; and creating special conditions for victims of sexual violence. The 1992 Accident Rehabilitation and Compensation Insurance Act[16] enacted some of the 1988 Law Commission recommendations, including shifting the financial responsibility for paying for accidents that occurred out of work away from employers by creating a levy on earners collected by the Inland Revenue; splitting the scheme into the five accounts that exist today;[17] the introduction of risk-based levies for employers, determined using their claims history; and codifying the definition of 'medical misadventure'. Further reforms followed in 1996.[18]

[14] Accident Compensation Amendment Act 1973 (1973 No 112) available at www.nzlii.org/nz/legis/hist_act/acaa19731973n112311/.

[15] Law Commission, *Personal Injury: Prevention and Recovery: Report on the Accident Compensation Scheme* (9 May 1988) available at www.lawcom.govt.nz/our-projects/accident-compensation.

[16] Accident Rehabilitation and Compensation Insurance Act 1992 (1992 No 13) available at www.nzlii.org/nz/legis/hist_act/aracia19921992n13471/.

[17] These are: the Work Account funded by levies from employers and self-employed individuals, covering work-related injuries; the Motor Vehicle Account funded by motor vehicle licence fees, a motorcycle safety levy and a petrol levy, covering motor vehicle injuries occurring on public roads; the Earners' Account financed by levies from earners collected by the Inland Revenue and covering injuries that occur outside of work; the Non-Earners' Account, funded by appropriations made by parliament, covering injuries to non-earners' (minors, students, retired people, those on social security benefits, etc) for all injuries other than motor injuries or treatment injuries; and the Treatment Injuries Account funded by contributions from the Earners' and Non-Earners' accounts and covering treatment injuries.

[18] The Accident Rehabilitation and Compensation Insurance Amendment Act 1996 contained provisions for an increase in benefit levels for permanent injuries; an assessment pathway for ACC to determine if an injured employee can return to work; and reforms to enable ACC to purchase health and rehabilitation services to reduce treatment waiting times.

One of the most significant shifts was contained in the Injury Prevention, Rehabilitation and Compensation Amendment Act 2005,[19] which changed the test used for injuries occurring during healthcare from 'medical misadventure' to 'treatment injury'. While 'medical, surgical, dental or first aid misadventure' had been included from the outset of ACC, medical misadventure was an anomaly, as it was the only aspect to have retained a fault-based assessment. In part this was because the initial statutory definition was not well defined, so judicial interpretation stepped into the breach and shaped the definition of 'medical misadventure'.[20] Two categories of medical misadventure were covered:

(a) either an adverse consequence of treatment that was either totally unforeseen (medical mishap); or
(b) if an adverse event occurred that was outside the normal range of medical failure for that treatment or procedure (medical error).

Section 5 of the 1992 Act had codified the definition of 'medical error'[21] as follows:

> (1) For the purposes of this Act,—
>
> 'Medical error' means the failure of a registered health professional to observe the standard of care and skill reasonably to be expected in the circumstances. It is not medical error solely because desired results are not achieved or because subsequent events show that different decisions might have produced better results …

This was a fault-based test. There was a clear inconsistency between the fault-based assessment used for compensating injuries occurring in a healthcare context and those in all other contexts, where no fault or blame was sought. This was largely resolved by the shift to the no-fault threshold of 'treatment injury' contained in the 2005 Act,[22] though some definitional issues persisted.[23]

As this brief description demonstrates, the journey towards comprehensive no-fault coverage in New Zealand has been achieved in phases, including a hybrid stage where both no-fault and fault-based thresholds were used within the same administrative model. Given that the original intentions of the Woodhouse Report were clear, it is potentially surprising that this hybrid model arose at all. As the provisions of the Act were ambiguous, judicial interpretation was required, and that interpretation appears to have drawn on traditional concepts derived from tort litigation that would have been more familiar to the judges, rather than the no-fault intentions of the statute. It took just over 40 years for ACC to adopt no-fault thresholds across all five different accounts.

[19] Injury Prevention, Rehabilitation and Compensation Amendment Act (No 2) 2005 (2005, No 45) available at www.legislation.govt.nz/act/public/2005/0045/latest/DLM347050.html.

[20] *Accident Compensation Corporation v Auckland Hospital Board* [1980] 2 NZLR 748 (HC); *Viggars v Accident Compensation Corporation* [1986] 6 NZAR 235 (HC); *Bridgeman v Accident Compensation Corporation* [1993] NZAR 199 (HC); *Childs v Hillock* [1994] 2 NZLR 65 at 72 (CA).

[21] Accident Rehabilitation and Compensation Insurance Act 1992 (1992 No 13), s 5 available at www.nzlii.org/nz/legis/hist_act/aracia19921992n13471/.

[22] Injury Prevention, Rehabilitation and Compensation Amendment Act (No 2) 2005 (2005, No 45), s 32 available at www.legislation.govt.nz/act/public/2005/0045/latest/DLM347050.html

[23] For a more detailed description, see R Upperton, 'A Truly No-Fault Approach to Treatment Injury Cover in Accident Compensation', Thesis, Faculty of Law, Victoria University of Wellington (2013) available at https://core.ac.uk/download/pdf/41338608.pdf.

A significant portion of ACC's portfolio is on injury prevention, which included a broad range of themes from road safety and reducing sporting injuries, to making treatment safer, including preventing falls and pressure sores. The Corporation's position as the sole data repository for claims information provides it with a unique insight into how and where accidents occur, enabling the development of evidence-based policy on how best to prevent them.

Concerns about the efficiency and performance of ACC, and the fact it is a state-owned monopoly, have led to amendment of the governing provisions over the years. For one year from July 1999, New Zealand permitted private insurance for work-related accidents, to encourage open market competition, but this was a brief shift that was then reversed. When compared to a 'non-ACC' scenario, a 2008 review by Price Waterhouse Coopers found ACC was estimated as $190 million more expensive than tort-based systems in 2006/07, but this overspend is more than compensated for by the value added by ACC, for example the total increased workforce participation due to workforce participation in ACC's injury management was estimated at $315 million per annum. Further, ACC was found to be performing well, with a high proportion of spending being on claimant benefits and a wider range of claimants covered than would be the case under a tort-based system.[24]

B. 'Carve Out' Schemes – US Birth Injuries

In practice, all no-fault schemes are likely to be driven by a variety of factors. In some cases there are obvious economic drivers. For example, the cost of malpractice insurance is often cited as the primary driver of the birth-injury schemes seen in Virginia and Florida.[25] The first medical malpractice crisis in the US was in the 1970s, and as a result of that many States adopted changes to their tort systems, including Virginia, which placed a cap on the damages available in medical malpractice lawsuits. The second medical malpractice crisis struck in the mid-1980s, with higher numbers of lawsuits leading to increased medical malpractice insurance premiums and decreased availability of medical malpractice insurance.

Medical malpractice insurance is needed for all areas of practice, so why was a scheme created that only compensated birth injuries? The rationale was that obstetrics

[24] PWC Australia, *Accident Compensation Corporation New Zealand: Scheme Review* (March 2008) 20:

> However, achieving this extra 'value' must also be considered in the context of the cost of the ACC scheme compared to the cost of the alternative 'no-ACC' scenario. Total ACC contributions (excluding pre-1999 residual funding) for 2006/07 were $2,620 million. Over the same period we estimate the cost of the alternative scenario (including premiums workers' compensation premium costs, premiums for motor injury and other fault-based insurances, and additional health expenditure and increased social transfers) to be around $2,430 million. This gives an estimate of net additional ACC costs of $190 million. Importantly, this is less than our estimate of the value added by ACC, even if we consider only those values which are measurable.
>
> Further, we note that far more people are covered under the ACC scheme compared to the 'no-ACC' scenario. In the 'no-ACC' scenario, over half (56%) of current 'other benefits' claimants in the ACC scheme would not receive any compensation or social security support except for medical treatment and would need to meet a significant portion of the cost of their injury through their own resources.

[25] See at www.nica.com and www.vabirthinjury.com.

claims are particularly expensive due to the high costs associated with lifelong injuries and a high propensity to claim for compensation following an adverse event to enable a family to provide for the injured child. As a result, several insurers in Virginia put a moratorium on providing medical malpractice insurance for obstetrics, and physicians stopped providing obstetric care. This created a signific problem for some rural areas of Virginia; in some counties there was no obstetric provision available. The earlier reforms in the 1970s had not resolved the issues, and in response to this a more radical solution was proposed in Virginia – to remove the most expensive cases, birth injuries, from the tort system. Shortly afterwards Florida followed suit and created a birth-injuries compensation programme, the Florida Birth-Related Neurological Injury Compensation Association (NICA). Prior to creating the scheme, Florida had the highest medical malpractice insurance premiums of all US States. Although the malpractice crisis was US-wide, it did not affect all States equally; these two States were more heavily affected and in response enacted more radical change.[26]

The Virginia and Florida birth-injury programmes are broadly similar, though with some differences. Both schemes determine eligibility based on factual criteria, hinging on whether the injury occurred during labour, delivery or in the immediate post-delivery/resuscitation period. Admittance to each programme requires that the healthcare was provided by a participating healthcare professional or at a participating hospital. There are exclusions in both schemes for congenital and genetic disorders; and in Florida, babies under 2,500g (2,000g for a multiple birth) are excluded. These schemes are exclusive remedies; the right to litigate is foreclosed if the delivery is carried out by a participating healthcare professional and/or occurs at a participating hospital. However, participation in both schemes is voluntary for doctors/hospitals, so coverage is not universal and does vary geographically through each State.

Interestingly, for most of their existence, both schemes have been payers of last resort, though cases brought in 2018 in Virginia and in 2020 in Florida have asserted that the birth-injury schemes are primary to payments by Medicaid.[27] At first glance this would suggest that payments under these schemes would compare very unfavourably with the full compensation available under tort. This has not been the case in Virginia, where payments under the birth injury programme are comparable to those available under the capped tort system. In Florida a cap on damages in medical malpractice litigation was not introduced until 2003, which historically has led to greater disparity between NICA payments and what would be available under a tort settlement, though more recent reports have found there is now parity.[28]

[26] From 1 April 2011, New York has operated a Medical Indemnity Fund for those suffering birth injuries, but the threshold for admission is that the plaintiff suffered medical malpractice, so it is not a no-blame scheme.

[27] *US ex rel Arven v The Virginia Birth-Related Neurological Injury Compensation Program* No 1: 15-cv-00870 (ED VA 7 July, 2015) (complaint); *US ex rel Arven v The Florida Birth-Related Neurological Compensation Association* No: 19-cv-61053 (SD Fla 9 Sept, 2019) (amended complaint);

[28] A-M Farrell, S Devaney and A Dar, *No Fault Compensation Schemes for Medical Injury: A Review* (Scottish Government Social Research, 2010) available at www.gov.scot/binaries/content/documents/govscot/publications/consultation-paper/2012/08/consultation-recommendations-fault-compensation-scotland-injuries-resulting-clinical-treatment/documents/volume-2-fault-compensation-schemes-medical-injury-review/volume-2-fault-compensation-schemes-medical-injury-review/govscot:document/00403703.pdf

In its 2003 Review, the Virginia Joint Legislative Audit & Review Commission of the Virginia General Assembly[29] found that the birth-injuries scheme had alleviated the lack of availability of malpractice insurance, and in fact the creation of the scheme had led to lower malpractice insurance premiums for doctors in Virginia compared to other States. The Commission concluded that, overall, the benefits offered by the scheme were more advantageous and more children were compensated than would have been the case under tort. It identified a lack of provision for injured mothers under the Program, and on occasion an inability by the Program to meet the unique needs of individual children. The scheme offered clear advantages for individual beneficiaries and individual doctors; what were less clear were the wider societal benefits. Part of the rationale for the inception of the Virginia scheme had been to improve the provision of obstetric services in rural areas, but there was little evidence that the Program had had a significant impact on the provision of rural obstetrics. Another area of concern when the Program was commenced was the provision of obstetric services to indigent women in Virginia. The Department of Health implemented plans in 1988 for ensuring indigent women had access to obstetric services; but given there was no indication that the plans had been updated or were in effect in 2002, it is difficult to attribute the improvements seen in care provision to the provisions in the birth-injury act related to indigent care provision.

The cost of the Virginia scheme has been called into question, as it has been estimated that it is higher than the cost of tort litigation would have been. This is a difficult comparison, as the vast majority of the children under the Program are cared for at home, with the Program funding the home nursing. If the Program did not exist then the families who do not have the means to fund home-nursing care would have to institutionalise their children. This would be a particular issue in Virginia, where tort awards are capped at a level that is often insufficient to provide lifetime care. In such cases, the cost of institutionalisation is usually covered by Medicaid. Given that the cost of home nursing consistently makes up over 60 per cent of the payments made by the Program, the comparison between the value of tort-based awards and the Program is complex because it is not comparing like with like since the provision offered by these two systems differs.

Another area of concern is the actuarial soundness of the fund; in the early years assessments were reduced, leading to insufficient funds and projections of significant deficits in the Program. It is difficult at the outset to predict the required level of funding; with the benefit of hindsight, reducing the assessments was not the best course of action. The 2020 Actuarial Assessment[30] indicated that the fund remained actuarially unsound, but that the deficit was considerably smaller than had been predicted by previous actuarial assessments.

What these two 'carve out' schemes show is that it is possible to create a niche scheme that deals with a subset of claims and to remove these claims from the tort system.

[29] Virginia Joint Legislative Audit & Review Commission of the Virginia General Assembly, 'Review of the Virginia Birth-Related Neurological Injury Compensation Program' (2003) available at https://vabirthinjury.com/wp-content/uploads/2012/08/rpt2841.pdf.

[30] Commonwealth of Virginia State Corporation Commission – Bureau of Insurance 2020 Analysis of the Virginia Birth-Related Neurological Injury Compensation Program (21 December 2020) available at www.vabirthinjury.com/2020-actuarial-analysis-from-scc-scan/.

The choice of the types of claims to 'carve out' was primarily economic; the life-long consequences of severe birth injuries mean they are by far and away the most expensive claims. Both the US schemes are now well established, and provide both positive and negative elements that can be used to inform design of any future similar schemes.

C. Alternatives to Litigation – Patient Injury in Sweden

All of the Scandinavian countries have administrative schemes to compensate following a range of injury types. This section will focus on patient injury in Sweden, as it has the largest of the patient injury schemes.

During the early 1970s, Sweden's mechanism to compensate for medical injuries was a fairly standard civil law tort liability system. The debate around the merits of this system crystallised after the 1972 Tort Damages Act was brought in, with its emphasis on the use of tort both to deliver compensation and to deter future malfeasance, a view that remains popular in certain jurisdictions such as the US. It was clear that this system did not serve injured patients well, and very few obtained any compensation, as described by Dr Pelle Gustafson:

> I was not around as a practitioner in the late 1960s and early 1970s when the Swedish and Nordic schemes were introduced. I have spoken to those who were there, and from what I have heard, there was practically no opposition at all because we had nothing. What we had then was a bad conscience about the fact that perhaps 50, 70 or 100 people managed to get some kind of compensation for avoidable injuries. The major thing was that we had to fix it.[31]

In 1975 a voluntary insurance scheme commenced, formed around the Swedish notion that compensation should be decoupled from regulatory sanction and any attempt to deter or punish healthcare providers. This scheme was a voluntary collective, the patient insurance collective, which was operated by a variety of companies for many years. In 1992 a review of these arrangements recommended that the requirement on healthcare providers to provide compensation should be formalised. Sweden acceded to the European Union (EU) on 1 January 1995 and it was realised that the legitimacy of the Patient Insurance Collective under EU law was questionable. As a result, the Patient Injury Act 1996[32] created a statutory framework for patient compensation that operated from 1 January 1997. This statutory framework mirrored the previous voluntary arrangements, and codified the rights of patients to receive compensation for avoidable injuries and the obligation on healthcare providers to carry patient injury insurance.

The move away from a negligence threshold has been hailed as providing a system that makes it easier for clinicians to be open with patients when a mistake has occurred, as the compensation process does not require them to be found negligent or blamed for what has occurred:

> I have myself, as a practising orthopaedic surgeon, helped two separate patients to file claims. I must say that I felt relief in being able to mention to them that we had a compensation

[31] Dr Pelle Gustafson, Health and Social Care Select Committee Oral Evidence: NHS Litigation Reform, HC 740 (11 January 2022) available at https://committees.parliament.uk/oralevidence/3255/pdf/.

[32] *Patientskadelagen* 1996:799.

> system … You can expect that a number of physicians are happy at being able to compensate patients or other individuals. They know that they have done something that was not supposed to happen. The issue at the systemic level is to separate compensation from supervision, and not having leakage between those two systems.[33]

The vast majority of healthcare provided in Sweden is state-funded and provided by county councils and regions, all of whom use a common mutual insurer, Landstingens Ömesesidiga Försäkringsbolag (LÖF) jointly owned by the county councils and regions. It is funded by a combination of levies from the county councils paid on a per capita basis and patient payments. The patient payments comprise a fixed low tariff for outpatient appointments and a low daily payment for inpatient care, irrespective of the nature of the procedure. LÖF covers well over 90 per cent of the patient injury claims in Sweden. The remainder, which arise from privately funded care, are managed by the Patient Insurance Association, to which all patient insurance providers belong, so there is consistency of provision. If a healthcare provider does not have the required statutory patient insurance, the Patient Insurance Association will investigate and provide compensation, so it also acts as a safety net.

Injuries are compensated when they are avoidable, with an investigation carried out by the insurer to establish a causal relationship, based on preponderant probability, that the action or inaction led to the injury. Technically the burden to establish causation falls on the patient, but in reality the insurer investigates this, and it is only when the insurer cannot establish causation that the patient's burden comes into play. The use of an avoidable harm threshold[34] has shifted the focus from looking for individual blame under negligence to encompassing system-wide issues that have led to the adverse outcome.

In analysis of the Swedish system, much has been made about the generous nature of the social security system, which has been used to suggest that LÖF is a particularly Swedish solution that could not be applied in other national contexts. This fundamentally misunderstands the context in which LÖF operates. The Swedish Social Insurance system covers on-going needs, such as live-in carers and house modifications. The patient insurance covers economic losses (loss of income and costs incurred as a result of the injury) and non-economic losses (pain, suffering, loss of amenity, disability and inconvenience). There is a clear interdependence between these systems. This interdependence also exists in tort litigation in Sweden; the benefits available from LÖF largely mirror those available to successful litigants. Use of LÖF is entirely voluntary and patients can choose to litigate instead; the vast majority opt to use LÖF, as it provides the same compensation via a faster, non-adversarial route. The success of LÖF as a replacement for litigation is not driven by the social security provision available in Sweden; rather, it is contingent on there being parity between the compensation available from LÖF and the compensation available from litigation.

This scheme, in both the voluntary and the statutory forms, has always co-existed alongside the option to litigate, but it is the preferred option for virtually all claims given its speed. The centralisation of the patient injury claims data at LÖF provides

[33] Dr Pelle Gustafson (n 31).

[34] There are actually six different thresholds, all focused around whether an injury could have been avoided; see Macleod and Hodges (n 1) 177.

an opportunity for monitoring and improving medical practice. LÖF's work on safety improvement has led to considerable learning and improvement in areas as diverse as birth-related brain injuries and wound complication and infection rates after joint replacements.

Patient injury in Sweden (and other Scandinavian countries) sit within a wider social context of injury compensation, with parallel national schemes for workers' compensation, pharmaceutical insurance and third-party road-traffic schemes. This provides injury compensation coverage that is not as comprehensive as New Zealand's, but which is broader than examination of any individual scheme would suggest.

D. Adjuncts to Litigation – Coal Health Schemes

Historically, there have been schemes that are not intended to replace litigation but which are adjuncts to it. For example, the UK Coal Health Schemes were developed after successful test cases, where liability had been determined, and the intention was to administer claims outside of the court system. These schemes did not require individual claimants to demonstrate any proof of blame or proof of liability; instead eligibility was determined on factual criteria.

The schemes for mining-related health issues suffered by former coal miners and their families were the largest personal injury schemes in British legal history. Two schemes were set up for respiratory disease (chronic obstructive pulmonary disease (COPD)) and vibration white finger (VWF). They followed group actions, where British Coal was found liable for VWF in 1997 and lung diseases in 1998.[35] In order to keep the individual claims out of the court system, two schemes were devised, each with a claims-handling agreement detailing how claims would be processed and the associated legal fees.

Under the COPD scheme, claim applications included a work history to establish potential exposure, a medical assessment to establish severity of damage, a determination of contributory negligence from smoking, if appropriate, and, if eligibility had been established, a 'full and final' offer of compensation. There were various routes for claimants:

(a) the main scheme described above;
(b) an 'opt in' expedited option, which allowed for faster payment as it was based on a spirometer reading rather than a full medical assessment, but the compensation offered was lower;
(c) from 2005, optional risk offer schemes, which were akin to the expedited scheme, but claimants were automatically included and had to opt out if they did not want to take this route; and
(d) the entry of judgment/unaccepted offers scheme, to enable a final tranche of claims to be closed and the scheme to be wound up.

[35] *Armstrong and Others v British Coal Corporation* [1996] EWCA Civ 1049; and *Armstrong and Others v British Coal Corporation* [1998] EWCA Civ 1359.

Under the VWF claims-handling agreement, claimants were divided into three categories, depending on whether they had commenced legal proceedings and, if so, whether a medical report had been provided. The category in which a claimant was placed determined the route to be used to handle their claim. All claimants had to demonstrate potential exposure on the basis of belonging to a defined occupational group. The medical assessment process involved at least three different tests carried out by a trained technician in a controlled environment, followed by an assessment by a doctor.

This *ex post* scheme was intended to prevent the UK civil courts from being overwhelmed by mining-related claims. It was therefore time-limited and only designed for this specific reason. The claims-handling agreements were drawn up between claimant solicitors and the Department of Trade and Industry (DTI), who had taken over the responsibility for compensation from British Coal. The DTI had not sought any actuarial advice prior to entering into these agreements, and had estimated that there would be around 173,500 COPD claims. In fact, the various COPD schemes handled almost 592,000 claims, triple the original estimate. In part this was because the DTI had not made any provision for claims made by the estates of deceased miners, and since 44 per cent of the COPD claims were estate claims this was a significant omission. Similarly, the DTI seriously underestimated the number of VWF claims, predicting there would be around 45,000 when just under 169,000 VWF claims were actually made.

Another area where the Government was heavily criticised was as regards the fees agreed in the claims-handling agreements. These were flat fees, with annual inflationary increases and no option to review. This flat-fee structure meant that solicitors were paid even if they obtained very minimal payments for their clients; there was a COPD case where the compensation awarded was 50 pence but the associated legal fees were £1,974. This disproportionality in COPD payments was addressed from November 2006, when a minimum compensation payment of £500 was introduced, with solicitors required to make up any shortfall from their own funds if the compensation offered by the scheme was under £500. Payments for VWF were on average much higher, so the disparity was not so great.

There was significant criticism of these schemes.[36] In particular, a Senior Costs Judge assessed that the costs payable under the COPD claims-handling agreement were higher than the cost of an assessment by a senior costs judge would have been.[37] These schemes did achieve their primary objective, to keep cases out of the courts, but it is clear that there were significant issues in their administration. These schemes show that it is essential to design a scheme carefully, and to base it on actuarial input.

IV. Conclusions

Schemes that are adjuncts to litigation usually have a defined function. This may be based on an assessment of liability by the courts, or it may be that the scheme is

[36] National Audit Office Report, *Coal Health Compensation Schemes* (July 2007) HC 608 Session 2006–07.

[37] *Griffiths & Others v British Coal Corporation* [2007] EWHC (QB) 960177 available at www.bailii.org/ew/cases/EWHC/QB/2007/672.html.

a mechanism to administer a without liability settlement fund. These schemes are relatively self-contained. They are valuable in terms of lessons on the more mechanistic elements of how schemes can and should be administered and run, but they do not invoke a wider debate.

Schemes that are replacements for or alternatives to litigation are more interesting in many ways, as they need to be contextualised in the social and legal environment in which they operate. This brief analysis demonstrates that such schemes are evolved, they do not emerge fully formed, as ACC demonstrates. What is interesting is that a large number of countries have some form of no-fault compensation, often workers' compensation, but very few countries have a more comprehensive no-fault coverage. There are clearly significant hurdles that need to be overcome when moving from a fault-based tort framework to no-fault, but once a no-fault scheme is established it is seldom revoked.[38] Drivers for scheme creations are varied, cost is a clear incentive, as the US birth-injuries schemes demonstrate, but there are also wider social factors, as outlined by Professor Rabin:

> If the workers' compensation movement is at all suggestive, it intimates that the fundamental structure of rights to reparation and responsibilities for harm is likely to be altered only when tort reform rides on the coattails of a more powerful ideological impulse.[39]

As well as a positive driving ideology, any reforms also need to overcome barriers to their implementation, including the self-interest of some very powerful lobbies. In their 2002 paper, Mello and Brennan[40] describe how their attempts to encourage the replacement of medical malpractice litigation with no-fault in Utah and Colorado 'crumbled against the strength of the lobby of the American Trial Lawyers Association (ATLA) and the general lack of interest on the part of malpractice insurance companies'.

That is not to say that the development of new no-fault compensation schemes is impossible. In chapter 21 of this volume Lorenz Ködderitzsch outlines how the Covid-19 pandemic has impacted no-fault vaccine compensation. The pandemic clearly creates a unique set of drivers for vaccine compensation. The key question is whether the combination of the pandemic and the creation of a large number of no-fault vaccine compensation schemes will, in time, be the catalyst for wider reforms to injury compensation.

[38] Some US automobile schemes have been; see Macleod and Hodges (n 1) 308.

[39] RL Rabin, 'Some Reflections on the Process of Tort Reform' (1988) 25 *San Diego Law Review* 13 available at https://digital.sandiego.edu/sdlr/vol25/iss1/3.

[40] MM Mello and TA Brennan, 'Deterrence of Medical Errors: Theory and Evidence for Malpractice Reform' (2002) 80(7) *Texas Law Review* 1595.

21

No-Fault Compensation Systems in the Pandemic Context

LORENZ KÖDDERITZSCH*

> Covax [COVID-19 Vaccines Global Access] has already passed on a sizable legacy to planners of the next pandemic response in the form of universal no-fault compensation schemes, standardized indemnity and liability, pandemic labelling, delivery financing and a host of other innovations.
>
> (Seth Berkley, MD, CEO GAVI, The Vaccine Alliance)

I. Introduction

In chapter 20 of this volume, Sonia Macleod has outlined the long history of compensation systems. Regarding the compensation of vaccine injuries, the first system was created in Germany in 1961. The broader discussion on the merits of such an approach took off in the United States (US) in the 1980s, leading to the enactment of the National Childhood Vaccine Injury Act in 1986, which was expanded into the still existing Vaccine Injury Compensation Program (VICP). The debate was shaped by both academics and leading practitioners such as Richard Kingham.[1] In a 2017 publication, Chris Hodges and Sonia Macleod further expanded the research on redress schemes for personal injury.[2] This study influenced the debate in Europe and beyond. While the debate is still ongoing, on whether and which elements of redress systems might generally be applied to personal injury in the context of medical care, the study proved to be prescient of things to come a few years later with the Coronavirus 19 pandemic. The personal injury redress scheme study is a perfect example of the tremendous impact Hodges has on academic research and legal policy. He combines his intellectual curiosity and experience as an academic

* This contribution in honour of Chris Hodges reflects the personal views of the author and does not engage Johnson & Johnson.

[1] National Research Council, Vaccine Supply and Innovation, 1985; R Kingham, 'Compensation for Vaccine-Related Injuries' in JB Robbins, *Bacterial Vaccines* (Greenwood Press, 1987).

[2] S Macleod and C Hodges (eds), *Redress Schemes for Personal Injuries* (Bloomsbury Publishing, 2017).

and a practitioner to examine and develop different approaches across the world to a fundamental question: Are there human activities or specific situations where personal injury ought to be compensated although no liability can (reasonably) be established and, if so, by whom and for what reason?

The above-mentioned 600-page study reviews diverse areas of activity, ranging from New Zealand's Accident Compensation Scheme to the Nordic pharmaceutical compensation approach, including injuries arising in the automotive sector, clinical trials, industrial activities, mining, neonatal injuries, nuclear accidents, terrorist attacks and many other fields. As diverse as these areas are, so are the reasons for and approaches to creating compensation systems that put aside the question of liability. This can range from an *ex ante* risk allocation for innovation that benefits society as a whole but may impact a limited number of citizens in a severe manner (drug development in clinical trials) to an *ex post* political solution to a crisis that emerged where liability either cannot be established in a meaningful manner (medical treatment with unclear causality), or where the liable party is bankrupt or unavailable (some asbestos cases, the 9/11 terrorist attacks).[3] The analysis of some of the vaccines injury compensation systems existing around the world as of 2017 constitutes an important focus of the work by Macleod and Hodges.[4]

II. Pre-Pandemic Situation of No-Fault Compensation System

According to a survey in 2018 by Mungwira et al,[5] 25[6] of the 194 member states of the World Health Organisation had implemented some form of *ex ante* compensation system for vaccine-related injuries on a no-fault basis. Mungwira et al[7] followed up with a more systematic review of these systems before the outbreak of the Covid-19 pandemic, with a broad range of policy options and features.

Germany was the first country to introduce in 1961 a no-fault compensation system for vaccines, which is administered within the social affairs departments at a state level. The key rationale for setting up this system is encapsulated in the concept of 'special sacrifice' (in German: *Sonderopfer* and *Aufopferungsgedanke*).[8] Vaccination is pursued

[3] For an interesting typology of compensation systems, see J Knetsch, *Haftungsrecht und Entschädigungsfonds* (Mohr Siebeck, 2012).

[4] S Macleod, 'Vaccine Injury Compensation Schemes' in Macleod and Hodges (eds) (n 2) ch 15.

[5] RG Mungwira, C Guillard Maure and P Zuber, 'Economic and immunization safety surveillance characteristics of countries implementing no-fault compensation programmes for vaccine injuries' (2019) 37 *Vaccine* 4370 available at https://doi.org/10.1016/j.vaccine.201906.018.

[6] Americas: Quebec, USA; Asia-Pacific: China, Japan, Nepal, New Zealand, Republic of Korea, Thailand, Viet Nam; Europe: Austria, Denmark, Finland, France, Germany, Hungary, Iceland, Italy, Latvia, Luxembourg, Norway, Russia, Slovenia, Sweden, Switzerland and the UK.

[7] RG Mungwira et al, 'Global landscape analysis of no-fault compensation programmes for vaccine injuries: A review and survey of implementing countries' *PLOS ONE* (2020) 15(5): e0233334 available at https://doi.org/10.1371/journal.pone.0233334.

[8] Kümper in Kießling, Infektionsschutzgesetz – Impfschadensrecht, 2021; H Plagemann and K Baumann, Corona-Impfschäden – 'Soziale Entschädigung in Zeiten der Pandemie', *COVuR*, 9/2021, 514.

as a matter of public health policy, with the Government nudging for vaccination (in some cases making it mandatory) in the interest of society and only in an ancillary manner for the individual benefit. In such circumstances, any risk of damage caused by vaccination must be borne by society, ensuring adequate compensation of the unlucky few who suffer severe adverse events from vaccination. It also follows from this premise that the conditions for compensation are reviewed by the public administration and compensation is publicly funded.

The decade before the Covid-19 pandemic saw public-health emergencies such as influenza (H1N1), Ebola and Zika. This led manufacturers to work on novel approaches to vaccine development that would significantly advance the technology required to accelerate the development of vaccine candidates for Covid-19. This period also saw legal scholars arguing for no-fault compensation of vaccine injuries. Halabi and Omer[9] succinctly recap three alternatives (in short: (i) bad luck/no redress; (ii) litigate and try your luck second time round; and (iii) mutualisation of damage by publicly enabled no-fault compensation) and the respective ethical underpinnings in dealing with vaccine injuries. Freckelton[10] emphasises vaccine confidence as a further rationale beyond the societal fairness of no-fault compensation. Attwell et al[11] analyse no-fault compensation as a corollary to justifying mandatory vaccination and explore the different approaches that countries have put into practice.

III. Developments in the Pandemic Context

However, just as a multitude of other aspects of our lives have been impacted and change has been accelerated by the Covid-19 pandemic, so has the discourse, in both academia and public policy, gained speed with regard to the introduction of no-fault compensation for vaccine injuries.

Hodges[12] further develops the rationale for no-fault compensation systems for vaccine injuries in general and the even more compelling reasons for them in the pandemic context with the urgent need to develop, manufacture and deploy vaccines to contain the coronavirus. Halabi et al,[13] as well Hodges, review key design elements such as eligibility, elements of compensation, administration and funding.

[9] S Halabi and S Omer, 'A Global Vaccine Injury Compensation System' *JAMA* (23 January 2017) available at https://doi:10.1001/jama.2016.19492.

[10] I Freckelton, 'Vaccination Litigation: The Need for Rethinking Compensation for Victims of Vaccination Injury' (2018) 25(2) *Journal of Law and Medicine* 293.

[11] K Attwell, S Drislane and J Leask, 'Mandatory vaccination and no-fault vaccine injury compensation schemes: An identification on country-level policies' (2019) 37 *Vaccine* 2843 available at https://doi.org/10.1016/j.vaccine.2019.03.065.

[12] C Hodges, 'Covid-19 Vaccines: Injury Compensation Issues' (9 July 2020) University of Oxford Legal Research Papers Series, 2020, available at http://ssrn.com/abstract=3647042.

[13] S Halabi, A Heinrich and S Omer, 'No-Fault Compensation for Vaccine Injury – The Other Side of Equitable Access to Covid-19 Vaccines' (2020) 23 *The New England Journal of Medicine* 383.

Based on this academic research and related policy papers, a working group of practising lawyers under the auspices of the International Federation of Pharmaceutical Manufacturers and Associations (IFPMA)[14] developed a list of criteria that constitute important elements to further evaluate, develop and improve no-fault compensation systems for vaccine injuries (see Table 21.1).

Table 21.1 Structural building blocks for Covid-19 vaccine-related no-fault compensation systems

Structural Building Blocks
1. No-fault system: (a) Victims should only be required to demonstrate a causal link between the vaccine and the relevant damages, without the need to prove negligence, fault, or product defect. (b) Victims should be required to demonstrate causation by a preponderance of the evidence (or a similarly reasonable evidentiary standard).
2. Administrative structure: (a) Systems should be administered by a public administrative body. (b) Systems should include an adequate public-funding mechanism, with an option to add additional financing sources if necessary.
3. Governance structure: (a) Administrative bodies should include representation from diverse stakeholders. (b) Decision-making panels should be composed of experts with clearly defined requirements (medical, legal).
4. Covered vaccines: (a) Systems should cover injuries resulting from Covid-19 vaccines. Systems may cover injuries from other classes of vaccines as well, but the funding needs to be separate for Covid-19 vaccines. (b) Applicants can be anyone who has been administered a Covid-19 vaccine in [relevant territory].
5. Covered damages: (a) Systems should cover a reasonably broad class of damages, including death, injury, disability, pain and suffering, and other forms of economic and non-economic loss resulting from the injury. (b) Minor injury and resulting damages should not be covered.
6. Compensation: (a) The level of compensation offered by the system, as supplemented by other governmental arrangements (eg, social security programmes), should be sufficient to provide long-term relief to victims. (b) Compensation could be tariff-based, consistent with the level of compensation as per 6(a).

(continued)

[14] The author chaired the working group of IFPMA on No-Fault Compensation Systems. This list contains elements that Macleod and Hodges identified in their 'Outline of a Model for Personal Injury Compensation Schemes' in *Redress Schemes for Personal Injury* (n 2) 648.

Table 21.1 ***(Continued)***

Structural Building Blocks
7. Accessible and efficient procedures: (a) Systems should use simple and easily available intake forms. (b) Bringing claims should not require legal assistance. (c) Bringing claims should be free of charge. (d) The review and decision-making process should be well-defined and easily understood by potential users. (e) Systems should have reasonably efficient timelines for processing claims and rendering decisions. (f) Systems should allow victims to appeal decisions within the compensation system and finally through a court system (adequate legal remedies), with such appeal being directed against the compensation system (not against the manufacturer or any other party). (g) Jurisdictions should implement strategies to ensure broad public awareness of their compensation system. (h) Systems need to be properly resourced (personnel, funding, organisation) and have the proper infrastructure, in particular IT, to handle the case load.
8. Transparency: Systems should include formal, well-defined transparency measures, such as mandatory annual reports and/or requirements to regularly provide public access to system information (eg, claims received, claims excepted and compensation amounts) as well as transparency to individual claimants on the status of their claims.

Further to an exchange of views with numerous governments and multilateral organisations, with advocacy by Johnson & Johnson and other members of IFPMA, the number of countries covered by no-fault compensation systems for Covid-19 vaccine-related injuries went from 25 to 147[15] countries administered by 56 systems, with a world première of two regional systems, one set up by the World Health Organisation (WHO)[16] covering 92 Low/Middle Low Income Countries (LMIC)[17] and the other system set up by the African Union/African Vaccine Acquisition Trust (AVAT)[18] covering 54 countries (mainly Member States of the African Union and some Caribbean countries).

To see more than three-quarters of the WHO Member States covered by such systems is an extraordinary contribution to legal fairness and safety. Yet it may be premature to cry success, as an in-depth analysis of the design features of existing and new no-fault compensation systems for Covid-19 vaccine injuries is necessary, as well as an empirical survey of how these systems are operated. Some preliminary observations on design features may be in order.

[15] Compilation by the author as of 14 January 2022, to be validated by independent research, as suggested in section V.

[16] A Mazur et al, 'COVAX no fault compensation program for COVID-19 vaccine injuries in 92 low and middle income countries' (28 October 2021) available at www.sciencedirect.com/science/article/pii/S0264410X21013803?via%3Dihub.

[17] See at www.who.int/initiatives/act-accelerator/covax/no-fault-compensation#:~:text=It%20provides%20fair%2C%20no%2Dfault,Facility%20until%2030%20June%202022.

[18] Available at https://avatclaims.com/.

A. Damages Covered

Most systems, appropriately, limit compensation to serious adverse events following vaccination. Some of the newer systems, including WHO,[19] however, limit compensation to permanent damage. This is a missed opportunity, as it will unduly restrict the damage that requires compensation: Except for death following vaccination, which is a very rare outcome, the vast majority of serious adverse events, such as anaphylaxis or Guillain–Barré syndrome, are usually resolved within weeks or months. Though limited in time, such medical conditions can have significant impact on the livelihood of the person vaccinated and his or her family.

B. Compensation

As set out in Table 21.1 under point 6, compensation should be sufficient to provide long-term relief to victims. Levels of compensation should be in line with the socio-economic situation of each country, taking into account contributions to and the level of pay-outs by insurance and social security. Further in-depth analysis of compensation levels is warranted, but it is fair to say that some systems (eg, Russia[20] with a pay-out of RUB 10,000 = €100) are so low as not to be meaningful, or are capped at a level (UK at £130,000) that may provide initial relief but in case of a lifelong disability may prove to be insufficient.

C. Administration

Designing and enacting no-fault compensation systems is an important first step, but it is essential that such systems be properly managed, with appropriate processes, resources and IT support. Experience in Belgium[21] and France[22] has shown that systems can be overwhelmed and require significant re-adjustment to reach their stated aims.

D. Funding

Funding and appropriate resources are, as for any endeavour, crucial for the success of the no-fault compensation systems. A number of questions arise: who is to (co-) fund; what is the right level; and how are funds to be administered? In theory one can

[19] For instance the no-fault compensation systems set up by AVAT (ibid), Canada and WHO (n 16 and n 17).

[20] See at https://cms.law/en/int/expert-guides/cms-expert-guide-to-vaccine-compensation-regimes-in-the-cee/russia.

[21] W Buelens, *Het medisch ongeval zonder aansprakelijkheid* (Intersentia, 2019). The Belgian system 'Fonds Medische Ongevallen/Fond des accidents médicaux' covers medical treatment issues but not medicinal products.

[22] Cour des comptes, *Rapport public annuel 2017 – L'indemnisation amiable des victimes d'accidents médicaux: une mise en œuvre dévoyée, une remise en ordre impérative.*

envisage three different types of funders: public, private and a combination thereof. In practice one can observe each of these permutations. Vaccination as a matter of public health would indicate that this ought to be publicly funded, but the funding source is ultimately a matter of policy choice within each national context. The question of appropriate funding of a no-fault compensation system is somewhat more complicated and requires assumptions on (i) compensable adverse event incidence rates (eg, one or two cases in a million vaccinated persons?), (ii) the amount of compensation and (iii) costs to run the system. The uncertainty around these parameters and finite resources may have led some of the newer systems to suffer design limitations in terms of the damage to be compensated (permanent versus transient) and the duration of applicability.[23]

Linked to the first two questions of who funds and at what level is the question of administration of funds and adjustments in case of under- or over-funding of the system. Given the demands for compensation, the latter would appear to be unlikely, but there are systems, such as the Vaccine Injury Compensation Program in the US and the Pharmapool in Germany (which is strictly speaking not a fund but more a reinsurance system[24]), that are over-funded,[25] with no clear mechanism to adjust the levies that finance the systems. A similar concern arises in current draft legislation submitted to the Polish Parliament, which foresees a levy similar to a sales tax in the amount of 1.5 per cent on supply of vaccines to the Polish healthcare system: the basis for the amount of the levy is not explained in the legislative documents, nor is there a mechanism to adjust the levy.[26] Finland, Norway and Sweden operate no-fault compensation systems for pharmaceutical products that are set up by the pharmaceutical trade associations in these countries, operated by an organisationally separate claims handler and with annual levies on respective turnover of member companies of these trade associations based on actuarial calculations. Where vaccine manufacturers are expected to (co-) fund, it is reasonable that the funding companies have a defined role in the administration of the funds. Interestingly, the Finnish Government has agreed to contribute to the pharmaceutical no-fault compensation system for Covid-19-related vaccines, as it views this as a public health measure, with related damage compensation to be publicly funded.[27]

E. Role of the Courts

Under regional conventions such as Article 6 of the European Convention on Human Rights, and pursuant to constitutional rights of access to the courts, most jurisdictions will create a no-fault compensation system for vaccine injuries as an option for

[23] See n 18.

[24] H Woopen and C Hodges, 'Germany' in Macleod and Hodges (eds) (n 2) ch 22.

[25] See, eg, at www.usaspending.gov/federal_account/075-8175.

[26] Polish Act on Prevention and Control of Human Infections and Communicable Diseases, as amended on 27 January 2022; pursuant to its Art 17 c), the financial provisions will only enter into force on 1 January 2023.

[27] Presentation by Jaakko Laurila on 20 December 2020 to Vaccines Europe on the Finnish Mutual Insurance Company for Pharmaceutical Injury Indemnities.

claimants in addition to court proceedings. In most jurisdictions, even where strict liability standards are applied, such as in product liability laws, the claimant in court will bear the burden of proof of damage and causation, and will often be confronted with risk defence[28] remedies of defending parties. The inherent risk, cost and duration of litigation makes it impractical in many cases to pursue vaccine injury claims in court. Hence the advantage of the no-fault compensation systems with their administrative rather than adversarial approach to establishing the facts. This being said, there is a role for courts to play, first, as a review mechanism to ensure that the no-fault compensation system has properly discharged its duties of review. Second, one might foresee that the no-fault compensation system would want to submit a question to a court for clarification.[29] Finally, one should consider no-fault compensation systems as having the right to seek compensation from parties involved in the development, manufacturing and administration of the vaccine ('vaccine providers', which goes beyond the pharmaceutical manufacturer) in cases of wilful misconduct. This specific and exceptional constellation should warrant against the 'moral hazard' of vaccine providers, remove the risk of having to go to court from those injured by vaccinations, and lead to a more rational dispute in court between the no-fault compensation system and the vaccine provider. Such an approach can be seen in the recourse rights of ONIAM in France[30] or in Germany,[31] where any compensation via the no-fault system to a person injured by vaccination is conditioned upon the claimant's assigning by way of law his or her compensation entitlement to the public body providing the no-fault remedy. This mechanism also ensures that there is no double compensation via the courts and the no-fault compensation system. This should be a basic feature of all systems.

IV. Need for More Legal-Empirical Research as Basis for Pandemic Preparedness

The increase in numbers and regional coverage of no-fault compensation systems for vaccine injury is an impressive achievement. There are great variations in design and implementation of the systems, and has yet to be seen which systems will live up to their stated aim, namely, to provide redress in an efficient, fair and equitable manner where a Covid-19 vaccine has likely caused serious injury. It is fortuitous that the Centre for Socio-Legal Studies at Oxford University (CSLS) has agreed to conduct a systematic review under the leadership of Dr Sonia Macleod, with advice by Professor Hodges. In an initial phase, a publicly accessible electronic repository of all available materials (legislation, implementation decrees, guidelines, literature) will be constituted to create

[28] Such as the development risk defence pursuant to Art 7(e) of Council Directive 85/374/EEC of 25 July 1985 on the approximation of the laws, regulations and administrative provisions of the Member States concerning liability for defective products [1985] OJ L210/29 (the EU Product Liability Directive).

[29] Proceedings similar to preliminary ruling requests to the Court of Justice of the European Union pursuant to Art 267 TFEU.

[30] See n 22.

[31] See n 8.

a resource to research all Covid-19-related no-fault compensation systems. The plan is then to develop review criteria, for instance those listed above in Table 21.1 or similar/additional ones, to analyse the possible gap between design and implementation of the no-fault compensation systems. To that end, ongoing monitoring of case handling, funding and administration is envisaged to identify best practices and develop system recommendations.

V. Conclusion

Different situations of societal interactions require different redress schemes:[32] for example, invoice overcharging in telecom services, utility contracts or banking can be dealt with in a very effective way by the ombuds system/regulatory schemes that would not be applicable to other situations, where the commonality of legal question, the determination of quantum and the consumers to be compensated may not be easily determined. Courts have an important role to play, in particular in deciding questions of law, for instance by way of preliminary ruling, but are not necessarily well suited to achieving redress in a timely and cost-effective manner in small-value but repetitive consumer disputes where 'alternative' dispute resolution systems have become mainstream. Thus, there is the need to identify the right tool in the 'redress toolbox'.

Hodges and other authors[33] have persuasively made the case for no-fault compensation systems for vaccine injuries as the most fair and effective approach to redressing vaccine-related injuries, in particular when vaccination is a public rather than strictly individual good. The current pandemic has pushed numerous governments and multilateral organisations to adopt such systems, however, with much variation in design and implementation.

Fundamental issues of justice and the need to encourage vaccine uptake require that we analyse no-fault compensation systems, and in a broader sense issues of liability of actors responding to future health crises, to identify characteristics impacting their efficacy, not least in the service of pandemic preparedness.

Although it is still early for the identification, much less resolution, of compensation claims for Covid-19 vaccines, it is now an ideal moment to take stock of the numerous no-fault compensation systems for vaccine injuries that existed or have been created for Covid-19 vaccines, to make these systems publicly available for research, and to rigorously evaluate them based on transparent criteria in order to develop best practices and ultimately improve compensation redress systems, in particular for vaccines in public-health crises.

[32] C Hodges and S Voet, *Delivering Collective Redress – New Technologies* (Hart Publishing, 2018).
[33] See n 12 and n 13.

PART V

Ethical Business Regulation, Corporate Behaviour and Regulatory Delivery

22

Ethical Business Practice and Regulation and Beyond: Challenging Traditional Approaches to Compliance and Enforcement

RUTH N STEINHOLTZ AND SRIKANTH MANGALAM

> This book sets itself the ambitious goal of analysing what ethical businesses look like and how they behave. It doesn't dodge the hard questions or promise simplistic solutions but dares to look fearlessly at the most important questions of our age.
>
> (M Heffernan, *Willful Blindness: Why We Ignore the Obvious at Our Peril*, reviewing C Hodges and R Steinholtz, *Ethical Business Practice and Regulation. A Behavioural and Values-Based Approach to Compliance and Enforcement* (2017))

I. From Ruth Steinholtz's Perspective

The origins of *Ethical Business Practice and Regulation: A Behavioural and Values-Based Approach to Compliance and Enforcement*[1] could be traced back to our respective early lives, but I will spare the reader that much detail, beginning instead when Chris and I were already established legal professionals.

We have known each other since we were both practising lawyers in the 1990s. I cannot recall exactly when we first met, but it was almost certainly during my years in the pharmaceutical and medical device industry.

A. My Legal Career and its Profound Influence on My Ideas

What little you need to know about me is that I spent the first decade of my career in private practice in corporate law, starting in San Francisco and then in Milan and Cairo

[1] C Hodges and R Steinholtz, *Ethical Business Practice and Regulation. A Behavioural and Values-Based Approach to Compliance and Enforcement* (Bloomsbury Publishing, 2017) (hereinafter 'EBP&R').

(long story). After a decade of private practice, I moved to Barcelona and went in-house. I was soon transferred to the United Kingdom (UK) and worked my way into increasing responsibility in different industries, from food and drink (Cadbury Schweppes), to pharmaceuticals and medical devices (Allergan, Inc) to petrochemicals (Borealis A/S and AG).

I joined management and added other related functions over time, notably security, crisis management preparation and business ethics. The six years I spent as General Counsel at Borealis, working from their headquarters in the Nordics and then Austria, brought a new perspective. Throughout my legal career, I worked on cases involving corruption or alleged corruption in a variety of settings and from a variety of perspectives. Working in satellite offices of large law firms and in-house meant that I became a generalist. In later years, when asked my specialism I would say that I specialised in being a generalist. My three decades of immersion in culturally diverse organisations shaped my approach to values, ethics and compliance.

B. A Great Synthesiser of Diverse Material

What sets Chris Hodges apart from most lawyer/academics is the breadth of his knowledge and his ability to integrate material from many different fields, sectors and disciplines – and to make the connections between them. His ability to read and digest vast quantities of information and to see the big picture while still diving into the detail is unusual to say the least. On a different and more modest level, being a generalist means I can see the practical connections, and my predilection has been to wander across cultures, disciplines and organisational functions looking for commonality rather than division. The result is a partnership in writing EBP&R that has great depth of field, focusing in on the role of the individual and moving outwards through the organisation to wider institutions of society. It is a holistic approach applicable to both regulators and business, and the interaction between the two.

It was an honour and a pleasure to write a book with Chris. As this *Liber Amicorum* testifies, he has published numerous important works on many different subjects. And, in the unlikely event that no one else has said this, he is a generous and caring person. One of the themes of EBP&R is the importance of working together in an atmosphere of collaboration, openness and challenge to produce better results; and that is what we did. I soon lost track of the amount of red ink and the number of drafts that passed between us, with no defensiveness in sight.

I am also grateful to have been able to realise a long-standing ambition to write a book that offered an alternative to the traditional compliance approach to anti-corruption. I abhor the word 'compliance', meaning 'the act of obeying an order, a rule or request'.[2] To me, it suggests unquestioning obedience to authority, which as we know too often can lead to unethical behaviour. As a lawyer in industry engaged with the subject of business ethics and integrity, it was clear to me that simply creating policies and procedures, even if accompanied by (often especially in the early days mind-numbingly dull) training, was not only ineffective, but counterproductive. If you want to influence people's

[2] See at https://dictionary.cambridge.org/dictionary/english/compliance.

behaviour engage them, inspire them, provide values-based material to guide them and then empower them.

Despite having written articles for legal and compliance publications and speaking regularly at practitioner conferences, I had not found a way to pull together the various strands of my eclectic approach to anti-corruption. How do you wrestle such diverse topics as organisational culture measurement and change; behavioural ethics and psychology, values, leadership and effective business ethics approaches into a single publication? Then a mutual friend came to the rescue. David Marks was matchmaker, telling me that I really must get in touch with Chris Hodges, because 'you are converging on the same subject', and telling Chris the same. At that time, Chris was writing *Law and Corporate Behaviour*,[3] the necessary precursor to EBP&R and a tour de force that deserves far more attention.

Law and Corporate Behaviour laid the foundation, inter alia, by undermining the foundations of deterrence theory:

> What is the goal of deterrence? Deterrence refers to an intention to prevent future offence. The objective is the prevention of future non-compliance especially by those who have been found to have committed an infringement or, to put the objective more positively, to induce future compliance.[4]

If this is the intention, is it always the result, Hodges asks? It is impossible to set out here his detailed analysis of deterrence from so many perspectives. Suffice it to say, Chris found it wanting:

> Any justification for deterrence as a policy of enforcement of law needs to be founded on the fact that it actually works – or, at least, works in a sufficient number of instances and works in ways that are fair and do not produce an unacceptable incidence of undesirable effects. In short, there needs to be robust evidence that deterrence affects future behaviour. … On the evidence assembled in this Part [Part B], such evidence is simply not convincing. Furthermore, as chapter one shows, there are far better explanations of what does affect human behaviour.[5]

The problems with the theory of deterrence are explored in a more concise form in chapter 3 of EBP&R.

Our discussions during that period led directly to the writing of EBP&R because we wanted to connect to a wider audience. Our purpose was to reach and influence those who could bring about change: regulators and the businesses they regulate, and we knew an 800-page book was not the vehicle for doing that.

C. A Better Approach

As long as legislation, regulations and enforcement policies and practices rely on deterrence and punishment, businesses will have no choice but to create complicated

[3] C Hodges, *Law and Corporate Behaviour: Integrating Theories of Regulation, Enforcement, Compliance and Ethics* (Hart Publishing, 2015).

[4] ibid 48.

[5] ibid 153.

tick-the-box compliance programmes. The result is a large amount of activity, but these programmes rarely provide the outcomes society desires. Regulation must encourage business to focus on organisational culture, based on genuine ethical values. The notion that 'culture eats strategy for breakfast', widely attributed to management guru Peter Drucker, applies to compliance too. Leaders must engage the entire organisation by focusing on leadership, culture and values – factors that do influence behaviour rather than creating a paper trail for reporting purposes. And conveniently, there is now a mountain of evidence to support Richard Barrett's assertion that 'Values-driven organizations are the most successful organizations on the planet.'[6]

What sets Ethical Business Practice apart perhaps is the focus on human risk and culture risk, and on the utility of measuring culture, based upon values.

The method of measuring and making sense of culture that we recommend, and which I have used for over 10 years with a variety of organisations, is the Barrett Cultural Values Assessment, created by Richard Barrett in the mid-1990s and based on his Seven Levels of Consciousness Model. The Seven Levels Model was inspired by Abraham Maslow's well-known Hierarchy of Needs, which held that people must first satisfy their 'deficiency needs' relating to survival, belonging and self-esteem, before being able to focus on their growth needs and become 'self-actualised'.[7] Barrett applied the concept beyond the individual to organisations and society. He also expanded the concept of self-actualisation, breaking it down into three levels, 5, 6 and 7 – Alignment, Collaboration and Contribution – which were originally called Internal Cohesion, Making a Difference and Service.

In simple terms, in order to reach its full potential, an organisation would experience 'full spectrum' consciousness, meaning it would consciously live values at all levels. It is perhaps easier to think of consciousness in terms of focus or awareness. Organisations that focus on all of these areas of their functioning, and that have a balance between the foundational levels 1–3 (Viability, Relationships, Performance) and levels 5–7 related to purpose, will be more successful. It is easy to see why. An imbalance, for example caring only about Collaboration or Making a Difference, while admirable, would not be sustainable without also paying attention to financial wellbeing, relationships between employees and with strategic partners, having effective systems and processes, consciously evolving and cultivating internal cohesion through a shared vision and shared values.

Once Barrett had the concept of the Seven Levels, he worked to allocate values to the level they were related to, and it then became clear that it would be possible to measure the values (and behaviours) that were being experienced in the current culture of the organisation, and also to inquire as to the values and behaviours that would, in the opinion of the members of the organisation, help the organisation reach its highest potential. The resulting Cultural Values Assessment (or CVA, as it is called), is easy to administer, and was one of the original Cultural Transformation Tools (CTT™). The methodology

[6] R Barrett, *The Values-Driven Organization: Unleashing Human Potential for Performance and Profit* (Routledge, 2013).

[7] AH Maslow, 'A Theory of Human Motivation' (1943) 50 *Psychological Review* 370; and AH Maslow, *Towards a Psychology of Being* (D Van Nostrand, 1962).

involves providing a long list of values for participants to pick from (both positive and 'potentially limiting') and asking three questions:

- What are your (top 10) personal values?
- What (top 10) values and behaviours are you experiencing currently in your team/department/business unit/organisation?
- What (top 10) values and behaviours do you believe would drive your team/department/business unit/organisation to reach its highest potential?

The questions can be asked regarding any unit in the organisation, and the results can be analysed by any number of factors, such as location, position or seniority, depending on how the CVA has been set up. The results are processed by the Barrett Values Centre (BVC) and used by a certified consultant to work with the organisation in a variety of ways, depending on its needs and goals.

Thousands of organisations of all types globally have used CVAs to measure, understand and make sense of their cultures. They have used them to identify their core values, to check whether the values they espouse are actually living in the organisation, to plan and implement cultural change programmes, to diagnose issues blocking the organisation from achieving its goals and for many other purposes.

From the point of view of Ethical Business Practice, one of the most interesting data points that results is the percentage of potentially limiting values that are chosen in relation to the total. In the Barrett lexicon, this is called Cultural Entropy. We think of it as culture risk. Potentially limiting values or behaviours, such as information hoarding, silo mentality, bureaucracy and hierarchy, confusion, corruption, exploitation, greed or manipulation, only appear in levels 1, 2 and 3, and represent such factors as fear, dysfunction, inefficiency and wasted energy in the system. If these limiting values represent a significant percentage, they will likely cause disengagement among employees, or worse. Disengaged employees or employees who feel they have been treated unfairly are more likely to behave unethically and less likely to report unethical behaviour in others when they observe it.

Disengagement is also a factor in Professor Dan Ariely's so-called 'fudge factor',[8] which is the notion that we human beings are inclined to cheat in order to gain an advantage for ourselves or others we care about, but only to the extent that we can continue to think of ourselves in a positive light. It is an elastic concept, and is one of the explanations for the fact that many unethical or even illegal acts are committed by essentially good people with positive values who find themselves in organisations where the culture accepts a high degree of deviance from the norms of ethical behaviour. In those situations, it is easier to do wrong while continuing to think of oneself as a good person, because 'everyone is doing it'.

I was inspired to create the Seven Levels of Ethical Business Practice, based upon the Barrett Model and our book. I worked with Phil Clothier, former President of the BVC. Certain values are potentially limiting and could lead to unethical behaviour;[9] and

[8] D Ariely, *The Honest Truth About Dishonesty: How We Lie to Everyone, Especially Ourselves* (Harper Collins, 2012).

[9] Available at www.valuescentre.com/resource-library/ethical-business-practice.

others, although usually positive, could lead one to behave unethically, depending on the circumstances. For example, loyalty to a friend might lead one to lie to protect that friend. In an article on the BVC website, there are questions that can be asked in order to help managers understand how aspects of their culture might be causing unethical behaviour.

There is a great deal more one could say about cultural measurement, and it is indeed a somewhat contentious topic; however, in practice the Barrett method provides the means for senior executives to understand the culture(s) of their organisation and to create strategies to bring about the effective ethical culture that we believe underpins Ethical Business Practice. It is an excellent way to pinpoint the areas that might be creating culture risk, and those where good practice has created a healthy culture. Sharing the results of a CVA with one's regulator could also be a powerful way to increase transparency and trust. Indeed, we advocate that regulatory organisations themselves utilise CVAs to evolve their own cultures, and many have done so over the years.

D. A Reminder That a Healthy Culture is an Advantage

An article by Emma Seppälä and Kim Cameron entitled 'Proof That Positive Work Cultures Are More Productive'[10] refers to 'positive cultures'; but as the authors indicate with the word 'virtuous', ethics is one important element of a positive culture:

> In sum, a positive workplace is more successful over time because it increases positive emotions and well-being. This, in turn, improves people's relationships with each other and amplifies their abilities and their creativity. It buffers against negative experiences such as stress, thus improving employees' ability to bounce back from challenges and difficulties while bolstering their health. And, it attracts employees, making them more loyal to the leader and to the organization as well as bringing out their best strengths. When organizations develop positive, virtuous cultures they achieve significantly higher levels of organizational effectiveness – including financial performance, customer satisfaction, productivity, and employee engagement.[11]

A detailed and interesting study reported in the *Journal of Financial Economics* stated:

> [We] study whether, on average, a culture of integrity adds value and whether, on average, this culture is weaker among publicly traded companies. We find both these statements to be true. Integrity is positively correlated with financial performance …[12]

So, no need to sacrifice profits in the pursuit of Ethical Business Practice.

People are far more likely to 'do the right thing' when motivated by intrinsic values or peer pressure than by rules. That is one of the reasons why my team created a network

[10] E Seppälä and K Cameron, 'Proof That Positive Work Cultures Are More Productive' *Harvard Business Review* (1 December 2015) available at https://hbr.org/2015/12/proof-that-positive-work-cultures-are-more-productive.

[11] ibid.

[12] L Guiso, P Sapienza and L Zingales, 'The value of corporate culture' (2015) 117 *Journal of Financial Economics* 60.

of 'ethics ambassadors' at Borealis in 2004, and empowered them to help educate their peers on the importance of integrity and to ensure that our anti-corruption approach was relevant and effective. Ethics is everyone's responsibility. A large central compliance department is therefore counterproductive. Compliance is the outcome of a strong ethical culture, or, put another way, compliance is an outcome, not an approach.

E. Learning from Safety Culture

Separately, Chris Hodges and I were both learning lessons from pioneers in the field of safety. Safety was the number one item on the agenda from my first day at Borealis in Copenhagen. It became clear to me that one could use some of the same safety-related principles and activities to nurture an ethical culture. The subsequent ethics excellence programme we developed and implemented, called *A Question of Ethics*, benefitted from this insight.

Meanwhile, Chris studied the evolving aviation safety approach of the Civil Aviation Agency (CAA) in the UK. Modern aviation safety is about creating a 'just culture' where mistakes or failures are viewed as learning opportunities and punishment is only meted out for gross negligence, wilful violations and destructive acts. Accurate root-cause analysis and the implementation of improvements can only occur in this environment. This experience and these principles became part of the foundation of Ethical Business Practice.

F. Psychological Safety

Reinforcement for these ideas comes from the work done on psychological safety by Edgar Schein and Warren Bennis in 1965[13] and brought up to date by Amy Edmondson and others.[14]

A psychologically safe environment is essentially one where people can express themselves in an open and honest way, and in which robust conversations can occur without fear of retaliation. In the work I have done with organisations since the publication of EBP&R, I have come to see these concepts of just culture and psychological safety as the cornerstones of Ethical Business Practice. Without them, leaders are unlikely to know what is actually going on. What is sometimes less discussed is the need for leaders themselves to feel psychologically safe in order to be open with their regulators, and for regulators to feel psychologically safe engaging with the businesses they regulate in this way.

[13] EH Schein, *Personal and Organizational Change Through Group Methods: The Laboratory Approach* (Wiley, 1965).

[14] AC Edmondson, *The Fearless Organization: Creating Psychological Safety in the Workplace for Learning, Innovation, and Growth* (Wiley, 2018).

Just in case, Figure 22.1 contains the briefest introduction to Ethical Business Practice and Regulation as we saw it at the time of publication.[15] In addition, we stated that 'To achieve EBR, both regulators and businesses need to adopt ethical practice.'[16] It has since become clear just how important this is in order to create the trust required for a business to be open and transparent with its regulator; and just how difficult.

Figure 22.1

The Essence of Ethical Business Practice

An organisation in which the leaders consciously and consistently strive to create an effective ethical culture where employees do the right thing, based upon ethical values and supported by cultural norms and formal institutions. … Engagement with EBR then requires the organisation to be open with its regulators and provide evidence of EBP.

Ethical Business Regulation

A relationship between a business, or a group of businesses, and a regulator or group of regulators, in which the business produces evidence of its ongoing commitment to EBP and the regulator recognises and encourages that commitment.

G. The Counterintuitive Problem

Unless one understands the limited effectiveness of punishment and deterrence, it may seem counterintuitive not to advocate blame and/or punishment for someone who is failing to live up to the expectations of the organisation, or for making a mistake that has serious consequences. However, fear of punishment drives useful information underground – energy will be wasted trying to hide the problem or finding a way to blame someone else. The real lessons may never be learned and any remedial measures will likely fail. Figure 22.2 demonstrates how we illustrated the concepts.[17]

[15] EBP&R (n 1) xxiii.
[16] ibid.
[17] EBP&R (n 1) Fig 7.1 (colour not reproduced).

Figure 22.2 Open, just culture versus blame cultures

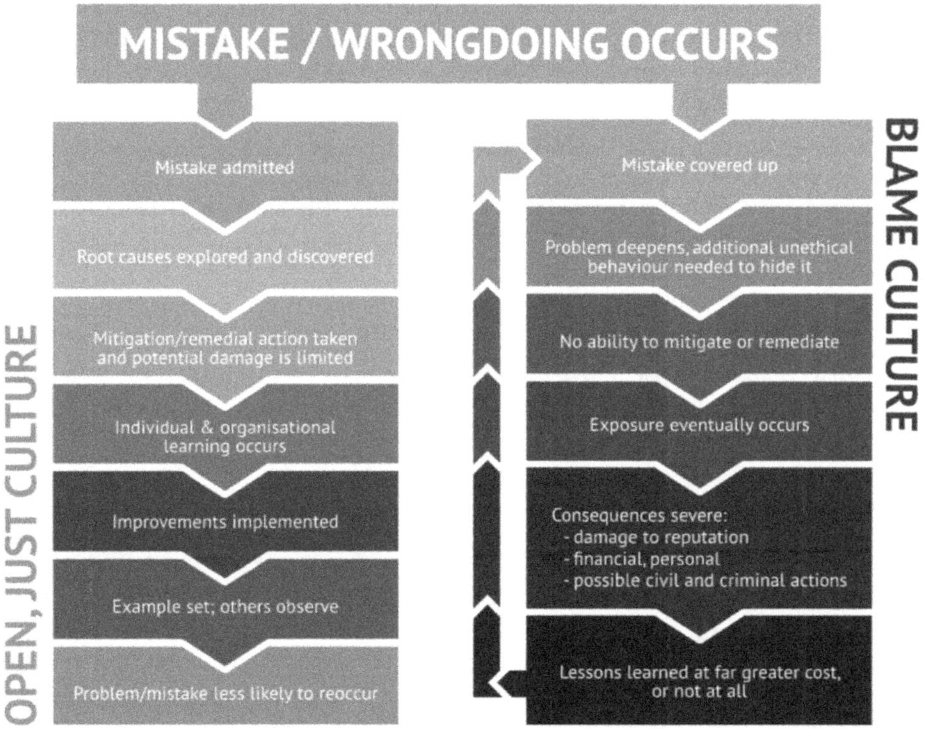

Unfortunately, when something goes wrong the media, politicians and the public often appear to be looking for someone to blame and to scapegoat as a way of showing that action has been taken. Regulators themselves are often blamed when a business they regulate behaves unethically. And while Ethical Business Regulation does not mean failing to hold people accountable for their acts (on the contrary), it does recognise that multiple contributing factors are common and that sometimes good people do bad things. Regulators should be able to consider the attitude of the business and its efforts to prevent bad things from happening when deciding how to intervene. Not every bad outcome deserves the same regulatory response. Pressure on a regulator to act may paradoxically cause it to do so in a counterproductive way.

This tendency to blame rather than to promote learning from mistakes seems even more dysfunctional when you talk to the people most closely affected by serious errors or failings. They will often say they it is not the money; they just do not want anyone else to have to go through what they did; lessons must be learned. In order for them to achieve this, the institution must come to understand the many factors that contributed to the final tragic outcome and learn all the relevant lessons to be able to implement the necessary changes. Firing one person is rarely likely to achieve that result.

Why have I raised this here? It is one of the challenges to the acceptance of the concepts of Ethical Business Regulation by regulators themselves. At a time when corporate misbehaviour is very much in the news, regulators are understandably concerned that they not appear to be 'soft on business' and criticised for failing to do their job. So, we are faced with a vicious circle of enforcement actions that do not achieve the expected result; the imposition of fines that do little to change behaviour and may even worsen it. Probably the most often-cited research on this is that described by Gneezy and Rustichini. The authors summarise it bluntly like this:

> The deterrence hypothesis predicts that the introduction of a penalty that leaves everything else unchanged will reduce the occurrence of the behavior subject to the fine. We present the result of a field study in a group of day-care centers that contradicts this prediction. Parents used to arrive late to collect their children, forcing a teacher to stay after closing time. We introduced a monetary fine for late-coming parents. As a result, the number of late-coming parents increased significantly.[18]

There is plenty of evidence from other settings. As well as being ineffective, fines divert funds that could otherwise have been used to fix the issues that caused the behaviour. In state-owned industries, fines just move money from one pocket to the other, and are therefore particularly ineffective.

H. A Change is Needed

So, for Ethical Business Practice and Regulation to become accepted practice, policymakers, politicians, the public and, crucially, the media must grasp the underlying concepts. In 2017 we said, 'We think that broad political approval for EBR will be essential if it is to be fully implemented by all regulators and businesses, and accepted by the public.'[19] I am hopeful this can occur, although realistically it will most likely be sector by sector. I am hopeful for the simple reason that one rarely hears serious criticism of the core principles of aviation safety *when they are working*. Indeed, the saga of Boeing and its 737 Max aircraft is a poignant example of a company who had long since drifted away from being a just culture, and 346 passengers and crew paid the ultimate price.

Our 2017 book is one of many pointing to the contributing factors leading to unethical behaviour, often with tragic consequences. It is important to recognise that not all of the people whose behaviour contributed to terrible outcomes were evil – in fact many of them thought they were doing the right thing. Others knew that something was wrong and said nothing for fear of losing their jobs. And some tried to speak out but were ignored or even threatened.

This is why in EBP&R we examine the evidence from behavioural science and related fields regarding the myriad of factors influencing human behaviour individually and in groups. It is this latter that is particularly important in organisations. Good people with positive ethical values may still be drawn into unethical behaviour, and the reasons for this are varied and numerous.

[18] U Gneezy and A Rustichini, 'A Fine is a Price' (2000) 29 *The Journal of Legal Studies* 1.
[19] EBP&R (n 1) xxix.

I. More Challenges

Perhaps the next challenge is the use of the word 'ethical'. Sometimes people's reaction when they hear the terms 'ethical business practice' or 'ethical business regulation' is to become defensive, saying, 'Are you insinuating that we are not already ethical?' That is of course not the intent. It is important that the terminology should not prevent engagement with the concepts in EBP&R.

It is important to focus on the underlying concepts, as Chris is increasingly doing, such as those introduced in chapter 5 of EBP&R, entitled 'The Need for Cooperation'. Others, such as the Water Industry Commission for Scotland (WICS) and Scottish Water, focus on trust and confidence. The concept of Outcome Based Cooperation (OBC) has matured in Hodges' recent writing as a wider concept applicable in various circumstances, including communities, organisations and commerce, regulation and dispute resolution. In the regulatory context, Outcome Based Cooperative Regulation (OBCR) encompasses Ethical Business Practice and Ethical Business Regulation, and continues to contain those elements intact and as fully relevant.

Chris Hodges explains how it all fits together as follows:

> Everything in EBP and EBR remain fully valid and relevant. OBCR can be seen as viewing a regulatory system as a whole, rather than the issues of how an organisation should operate (EBP) or (how) a regulator should operate (EBP and the Regulatory Delivery Model), or (how) the relationship between regulator and regulatees should ideally be (EBR). All of these elements fit together in a coherent whole.[20]

There are other challenges to implementing the principles of Ethical Business Practice and Regulation, and they lie mainly with the cultures and hierarchies of businesses and regulators alike, and in the capability of their leaders and managers. The components of 'The Cultural and Leadership Framework for Ethical Business Practice in Organisations' (chapter 13) point to the importance of the quality of leadership and its ability to nurture a consistently effective ethical culture. It is an overused, variously stated and dubiously attributed quotation, but in fact, 'we cannot solve problems with the same thinking that created them' (Einstein), so we need to help people widen their perspectives and seek new solutions.

J. Where is This Work Going?

i. Application to the Water Industry in Scotland

Since EBP&R was published at the end of 2017, it has been read in 104 countries, included in university anti-corruption courses, and cited in numerous academic papers and books in a wide variety of sectors.[21]

[20] Personal correspondence with Chris Hodges (on file with author).

[21] M De Benedetto, N Lupo and N Rangone (eds), *The Crisis of Confidence in Legislation* (Nomos/Hart, 2021); M De Benedetto, *Corruption from a Regulatory Perspective* (Hart Publishing, 2021); M De Benedetto, 'Effective Law from a Regulatory and Administrative Law Perspective' (2018) 9 *European Journal of Risk*

In Scotland, Ethical Business Regulation has even become official government policy, in particular in the water sector, with the economic regulator, WICS (or 'the Commission'), leading the way. In looking for ways to meet the growing challenges of the sector, WICS states:

> Meeting these targets will require Scottish Water to transform its business, ensuring it delivers best value in all that it does. In tandem, we are transforming how we regulate – to a model based on the principles of 'Ethical Business Regulation' (EBR) …[22]

One aspect of this is illustrated in the outcome of the Strategic Review process, where transparency, trust and cooperation were emphasised:

> Ensuring a Transparent Process This final determination has been the result of our most open and collaborative Strategic Review process to date. Stakeholders were consulted at every stage and this engagement was underpinned by robust analysis and by an extensive programme of customer research overseen by the Research Co-ordination Group (which comprised representatives from the key sector stakeholders including Scottish Government, Customer Forum, Scottish Water, Consumer Advice Scotland (CAS), the Scottish Environment Protection Agency (SEPA) and the Drinking Water Quality Regulator (DWQR)).
>
> This consultative approach has, we believe, resulted in a significantly better outcome for customers and communities.[23]

It is worth setting out in detail WICS' perspective on Ethical Business Practice and Regulation, as it illustrates how the Commission sees it functioning in practice:

> This approach is very different from that of previous regulatory control periods in that our expectation is that Scottish Water will evidence its progress on an ongoing basis to the customers and communities that it serves, and our reporting of their performance will reflect their success in doing so. This is at the heart of Ethical Business Practice (EBP).
>
> Our Decision Papers and draft determination explained the approach that underpins Ethical Business Regulation (EBR) and set out our expectations of the EBP that is expected of Scottish Water. In summary, we expect Scottish Water to:
>
> - take full ownership of enduring relationships with the customers and communities it serves;
> - promote an open discussion of its purpose, aspirations and values;

Regulation 391; H Hijmans, 'How to Enforce the GDPR in a Strategic, Consistent and Ethical Manner?' (2018) 4 *European Data Protection Law Review* 80; A Kasdorp and J van Erp, 'Supervision Practice in the Face of Emerging Health Risks: How Market Dynamics Are Forcing Enforcement Officials to Stretch Their Mandate' (2019) 15 *Utrecht Law Review* 99; B Fisse, 'Penal Designs and Corporate Conduct: Test Results from Fault and Sanctions in Australian Cartel Law' (2019) 40 *Adelaide Law Review* 285; C Walker, 'The Role of the Board of Financial Services Firms in Improving Their Firm's Culture' (2020) 43 *Seattle University Law Review* 723; B Clarke, 'Individual Accountability in Irish Credit Institutions. Lessons to Be Learned from the United Kingdom's Senior Manager's Regime' (2018) 47 *Common Law World Review* 35; C Hodges, R Steinholtz and A Salles, '"The future of regulation is culture": opportunities to change unethical behaviour in business and public administration in Brazil' (2020) 279 *Revista De Direito Administrativo* 79; C Robinson, 'Regulation of Insolvency Practitioners in a Pandemic' (2020) 28 *Insolvency Law Journal* 181; J Woodlock and H Hydén, '(f) Lex avionica; How soft law serves as an instrumental mediator between professional norms and the hard law regulation of European civil aviation maintenance' (2020) 121 *Safety Science* 54.

[22] Water Industry Commission for Scotland, *Final Determination. Strategic Review of Charges 2021–27*, available at https://wics.scot/system/files/publications/2021-27%20Final%20Determination.pdf 4.

[23] ibid 7.

- set out clearly – and in a way that is accessible to all – its current performance and plans for improvement;
- engage in regular and frank discussion of performance, recognising that performance expectations will always change and become more demanding;
- adopt a collaborative, timely and pro-active approach to meeting the needs and aspirations of its regulators, aiming to address their concerns even before they have had to ask; and
- embrace these challenges as an opportunity –and be seen to do so in a positive and constructive way.[24]

And finally, according to WICS:

> There are already signs that Scottish Water, the Commission and other stakeholders are benefiting from the opportunities that EBR and EBP provide, and we look forward to continuing to support Scottish Water as it seeks to make the necessary transformation within its organisation over the coming months and years.[25]

Since the end of the Strategic Review, work has continued to embody Ethical Business Practice and Regulation, manifesting itself in work related to trust and confidence and wider participation of stakeholders in the retail market as well.

K. Widespread Interest and Application

Through presentations and discussions at conferences from Australia to Singapore, London, Brussels, Amsterdam, Rome and beyond, Chris and I have presented and debated these concepts. A conference of the International Network for the Delivery of Regulation (INDR) illustrated how various aspects are being taken forward in countries around the world, including Australia and Finland.

For my part, I see it as my purpose to increase the adoption of the various strands of Ethical Business Practice, many of which were first proposed by others, into an holistic approach, creating organisations where employees' sense of pride and their collective positive values enable them to resist the many forces, whether part of the human psyche or external, that may try to drag them off course.

If we are going to tackle the many existential challenges we are facing, we must evolve the kind of organisations that are capable of cooperating effectively and with a sense of urgency. We have a long way to go and a short time horizon; however, the change of mind set and approach proposed in EBP&R, and its evolution, could provide the incentive to get on with it.

II. From Srikanth Mangalam's Perspective

My journey with Chris Hodges began in the early part of 2016 while I was working as Director for Risk Management at the Ontario Technical Standards and Safety Authority

[24] ibid 16.
[25] ibid 17.

(TSSA), a regulatory agency responsible for the safety of technical devices and equipment. In my role then, as science-based advisor to decision makers, I was particularly interested in understanding the root causes for the prevalence of non-compliance in the sectors that we regulated and their potential impact on causing harm to the public. My team of intelligent analysts were finding through their analysis that root causes were largely pointing to the underlying culture and motivations of the regulated organisations. Our set of compliance enforcement tools did not seem to include (or at least as to what we thought then) the necessary mechanisms to influence change in culture and behaviour, especially when we knew that most instances of non-compliance were not intentional but due to lack of understanding and appreciation of their significance.

My research in trying to identify literature for guidance in this regard led to a report that Chris had published for the UK's Department for Business, Innovation and Skills Better Regulation Delivery Office, entitled *Ethical Business Regulation: Understanding the Evidence*.[26] Everything that Chris wrote in that report made sense to me. His research on how people made decisions based on their intrinsic values and morals, the benefits of promoting an open culture, the need for fair and proportionate responses using a collaborative approach, all seemed to be precisely what we needed to consider in our regulatory environment.

I attempted to connect with Chris multiple times, but it was extremely hard to get in touch. I persisted and finally got him on the phone one day; but, without going into detail, it was not the most memorable of calls. I was nervous (talking to a professor at Oxford) and he was matter-of-fact. I must have said something smart that got his attention, and the rest, as they say, is history. I managed to invite myself, thanks to Chris, to Graham Russell's international conference in London that year, and made an adequate enough impression on both of them to bring them over to Canada the following year. We have not stopped since.

I left TSSA in August 2016 and began the PRISM Institute, with the objective of assisting regulatory institutions worldwide in modernising their regulatory systems to become more risk-based and to look at alternative approaches, largely advocating for Ethical Business Regulation and now outcome-based cooperative models. The two books, the one on Ethical Business Practice/Ethical Business Regulation that he co-wrote with Ruth Steinholtz,[27] and the one on the Regulatory Delivery Model that he co-edited with Graham Russell,[28] have become foundational pieces for the advocacy efforts that Chris and I decided to jointly pursue. I have been fortunate enough to have been working with Chris (and Ruth in some instances) in full earnest since 2018, work that has taken me to several parts of the world, including Australia, Malaysia, Canada, Finland and Africa.

I am a big believer in applying a systems approach to addressing challenges with regulatory systems. Our paths had another reason to cross. Chris's more recent extensive

[26] C Hodges, *Ethical Business Regulation: Understanding the Evidence* available at https://assets.publishing.service.gov.uk/government/uploads/system/uploads/attachment_data/file/497539/16-113-ethical-business-regulation.pdf.

[27] EBP&R (n 1).

[28] G Russell and C Hodges, *Regulatory Delivery: Introducing the Regulatory Delivery Model* (Hart Publishing, 2019).

research has led to very interesting thinking on the advantages of using a cooperative (as opposed to a competitive) approach to meeting a common purpose and achieving the desired outcomes. Systems approaches are largely built on setting clear expectations of desired outcomes, recognising the various interconnected pathways towards those outcomes and ensuring that those pathways are operated in an optimal manner. My understanding of what is currently called Outcome Based Cooperative Regulation (OBCR) is ideally suited for systems-based thinking. I was particularly excited to hear from Chris on the evolution of his thinking (and we have had several hours of conversations on this topic) on cooperative models, and inspired to bring the two aspects of systems-based thinking and cooperation together. We have since been testing these ideas out in different contexts: global food safety, weights and measures, protection of seniors and, more recently, in circular economy.

This new approach I believe is what truly brings Ethical Business Practice/Ethical Business Regulation and the Regulatory Delivery Model together and more. Take food safety as an example. Societal expectations from food systems are wide-ranging: access to food, food safety, food quality, nutrition, food security, equity, climate adjusted, etc. Many of these expectations are handled and delivered using regulations, albeit independently. Businesses, as a result, have to deal with multiple regulatory systems with potentially overlapping or conflicting expectations. Society may have different thresholds and levels of tolerance for acceptance. Supply chains operate in a global context and are therefore dealing with additional regulatory systems. The most effective and efficient means of meeting societal expectations would be using a cooperative approach, applying a systems view, setting standards that encourage stakeholders to 'doing the right thing', and establishing an evidence base that helps to build and maintain trust in the systems. I believe this is what Chris's research points to as a recipe for success, and it has been a privilege working with him, especially in the last three years or so in building these case studies.

The journey continues and I look forward to Chris's forthcoming book, which I believe will be path-breaking, revolutionary in its ideas, and yet simple and logical in its comprehension. I am convinced by this approach, and would expect many to follow and lead in the future.

23

The Evolution of INDR 2017–2022

HILARY EVANS AND GRAHAM RUSSELL

Humans achieve more when we cooperate.
(C Hodges, 'Supporting Cooperative Behaviour' (2022))

Complicated situations sometimes give rise to the best of ideas. And so it has been with the International Network for the Delivery of Regulation (INDR).

The subject of how regulation is delivered, as opposed to the policy that formulates regulations, had been under-researched for many years when Chris Hodges entered the arena. As a lawyer with a particular interest in product liability, regulation was not unknown to him, but it was his report with Chris Decker for the British Retail Consortium (BRC), *Government-sponsored voluntary regulation*,[1] and his book *Law and Corporate Behaviour*[2] that brought him directly into the field of combat. Through this work, in which he integrated theories of regulation, enforcement, compliance and ethics, he provided a fresh perspective and much-needed academic rigour. Assumptions and shibboleths were prevalent and awaiting challenge – including the efficacy of inspection and deterrence, the value of transparency and trust, and the potential for cooperation. In his charming yet determined manner, Chris arrived to unsettle and re-order existing conveniences.

The United Kingdom (UK) had for some years led the way with international exchanges between regulators, including the Inspection Reform conferences organised by Graham Russell and his team at the Office for Product Safety and Standards (OPSS) in the UK's Department for Business, Energy and Industrial Strategy (BEIS). With support from Florentin Blanc (now of the Organisation for Economic Cooperation and Development (OECD)) and from his then colleagues at the World Bank, these conferences have, since 2012, drawn together around 400 delegates from 50 countries and been highly regarded by all participants as a forum for learning and knowledge exchange.

[1] C Hodges and C Decker, *Government-sponsored voluntary regulation* available at www.law.ox.ac.uk/research-subject-groups/research-index/impact-index/government-sponsored-voluntary-regulation.
[2] C Hodges, *Law and Corporate Behaviour: Integrating Theories of Regulation, Enforcement, Compliance and Ethics* (Hart Publishing, 2015).

The World Bank's practices team was already supporting reform in a range of partner countries, and the OECD's Regulatory Policy Committee, under Nick Malyshev, had begun to extend its sphere of interest into regulatory delivery, bringing interested member states together. The confluence of these streams led to a rich and diverse dialogue about the capacity of regulatory reform to drive a range of ancillary outcomes – from post-conflict stabilisation and poverty relief to community engagement, small business growth and productivity. Outcomes that now stand in sharper relief for regulators since the global financial crisis of 2008 initiated what Mark Carney has come to call the three global threats of our century – Credit, Coronavirus and Climate.[3]

The engagement between Chris and Graham, which had commenced when they met during his work for the BRC, led to conferences for Canadian regulators facilitated by Srikanth Mangalam of the PRISM Institute. And it was a conversation in an Ontario coffee-shop that led to cooperation over a ground-breaking textbook on the topic[4] and to the idea of establishing an international hub for the sharing of information and experience in relation to regulation.

By July 2017 this idea had evolved as follows, with Chris as ever holding the pen during drafting:

> It is proposed to establish the International Network for Delivery of Regulation (INDR), to be based for a trial period at the Centre for Socio-Legal Studies, University of Oxford.
>
> The initial purposes of INDR will be to provide:
>
> 1. a Centre of Excellence in a world class university to support improvement in the way regulation is delivered, namely how regulations are received and applied by businesses and others whose behaviour they seek to control, and the manner in which they are enforced.
> 2. an international hub for the sharing of information on regulation and enforcement models, approaches and techniques, which brings together governmental policy and regulatory practitioners with academic support, to support strong practical applications of best regulatory delivery practice.
> 3. coordination of further research and experience on regulatory delivery issues.[5]

As well as detailing the involvement of Chris, Graham Russell and Hilary Reid Evans, this initial document set out the immediate objectives of INDR as:

- To contact key regulatory experts around the world and engage them in INDR.
- To produce an edited book on INDR with contributions from selected key experts.
- To host a meeting of the key experts in Oxford in autumn 2017 to agree on the future development of INDR. It is likely that this will involve around 10 such people, forming a Steering Committee.
- To host a follow-up meeting in Oxford in spring 2018.
- Subject to agreement, to contribute an event to HMG/RD's International Conference on regulatory delivery in autumn 2018.
- To plan ongoing action, such as establishment of a subscription structure for INDR.[6]

[3] M Carney, *Value(s): Climate, Credit, Covid and How We Focus on What Matters* (William Collins, 2021).
[4] G Russell and C Hodges, *Regulatory Delivery* (Bloomsbury Publishing, 2019).
[5] INDR internal strategy document, June 2018.
[6] ibid.

At the same time as giving birth to INDR, ever busy, Chris was working with Graham Russell on the drafting of the book that detailed the Regulatory Delivery Model (RDM).

This book (*Regulatory Delivery*) explains the model and records and evaluates innovative regulatory delivery initiatives from around the world. These cover key issues, including the importance of designing good regulatory 'delivery' mechanisms (enforcement) into the process of securing desired regulatory outcomes, including how regulations are received and applied by businesses and others whose behaviour they seek to control, and the manner in which they are enforced. It focuses on the relationship between the major players in the regulatory landscape, regulated entities, beneficiaries and regulators (see Figure 23.1).

Figure 23.1 Relationships between parties in the regulatory landscape

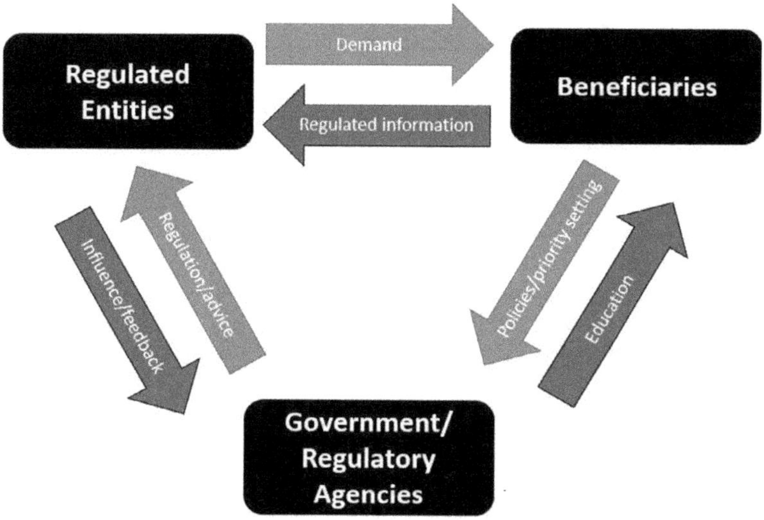

The RDM sets out a map for how any regulator can assess its position and chart the path forward. It does this by establishing the prerequisites (Governance, Accountability and Culture – see Figure 23.2) and the three practices (Outcome Measurement, Risk-based Prioritisation and Intervention Choices) that determine whether a regulator can succeed. This provides a framework within which concepts such as Responsive Regulation, business engagement, trust-based relationships and community engagement can be understood and adopted by regulators.

With an emerging body of thinking (see chapter 22 of this volume, 'Ethical Business Practice and Regulation and Beyond'), it became increasingly important to turn the INDR concept into reality and provide a forum for debate and dissemination. This began with the circulation in 2017 of an initial strategic plan for INDR, amongst invited participants, while much of the thinking behind INDR was introduced to an international audience by Chris during the Inspection Reform Conference hosted by Graham in London in October 2018:

> **'The Initial International Network for Delivery of Regulation Outline Strategic Plan' (October 2017)**

Figure 23.2 Prerequisites in the RDM

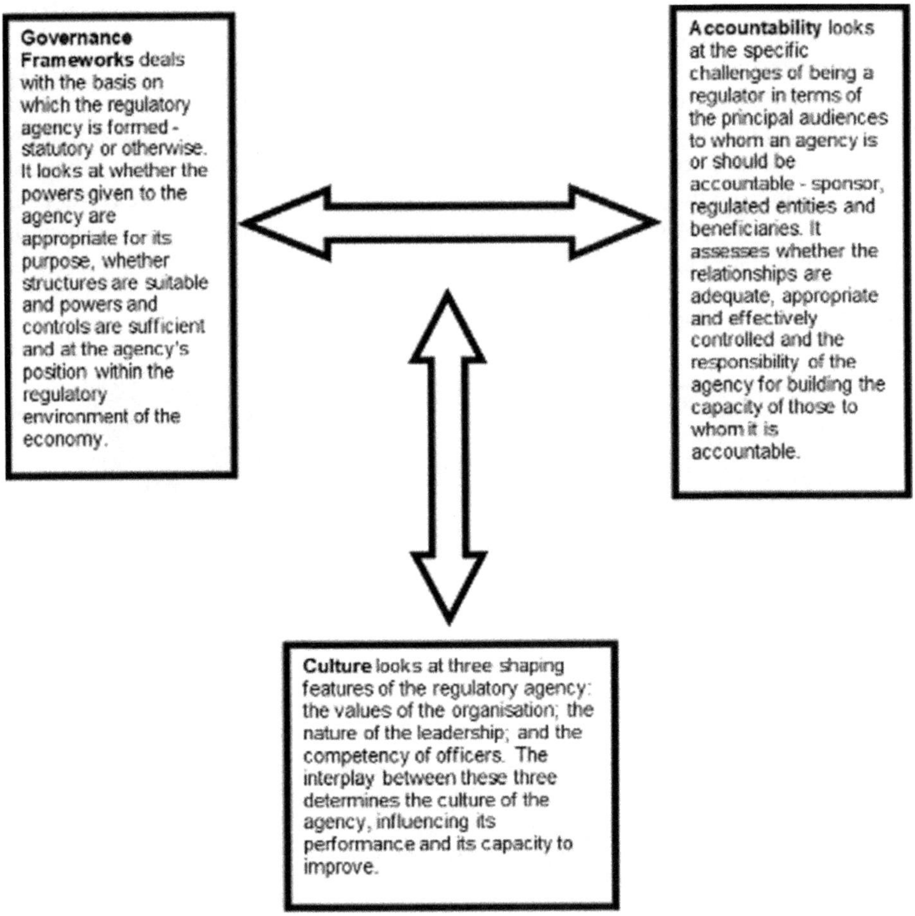

Background

The concept of 'regulatory delivery' is new in regulatory theory and practice. It might be defined as the art and science of ensuring that regulatory rules are effectively applied and observed in practice. Regulatory delivery looks beyond the traditional assumption that because a rule exists it will be observed. It engages with how rules are received and applied by businesses and others whose behaviour those regulations control, and hence the manner in which they are enforced so as to achieve maximum compliance and performance with minimal cost to the state and the regulated.

With decreasing budgets and increasing expectations, governments around the world are looking for ways of delivering better regulatory outcomes. Some transformative developments are currently occurring, and there is a wide demand for identifying reliable evidence and sharing knowledge on best practice. However, few governments have coordinating bodies that bring together experience and expertise in regulation and little academic attention has been devoted to regulatory delivery worldwide. Academic literature tends to lag behind what is actually occurring on the ground, while more theoretical approaches present problems of implementation for regulators and governments.

Figure 23.3 Practices in the RDM

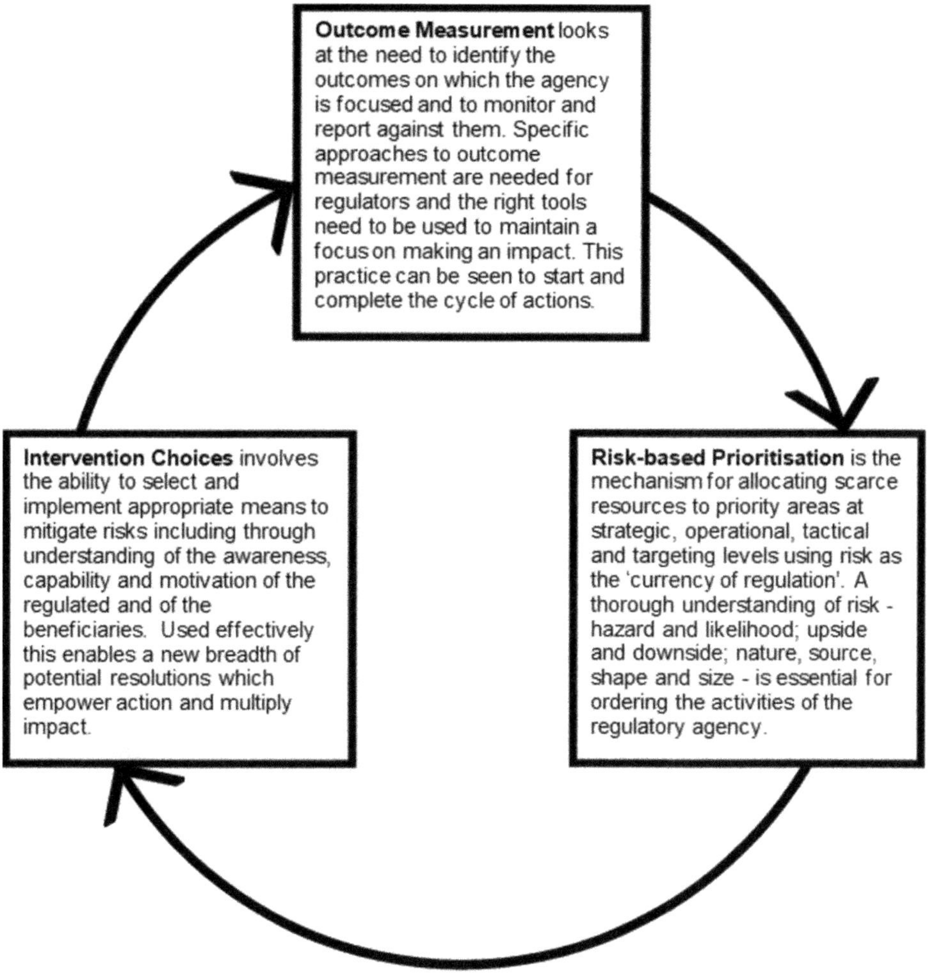

Purpose of an international network

The purpose of INDR is to bring together leading experts from across the world to record current practices, analyse different approaches, and develop a sound theoretical base on which policy makers may proceed to spread best practice.

By bringing together those engaged in shaping and delivering regulatory outcomes, leading edge academic research and commercial experience, INDR aims to provide a knowledge network, a forum for experience sharing and a problem-solving mechanism.

The global nature of INDR ensures that key government regulatory decision makers have access to a growing global knowledge base. Although political objectives may and will vary, the use of a common understanding regarding the delivery of regulation should lead to a greater commonality of approach and an improved competitive environment and act as a language set for trade negotiations, since all parties will have access to the latest thinking and lessons learned.

Objectives

The objectives of INDR are:

To provide an international hub to support improvement in the way regulation is delivered by bringing together governmental policy and regulatory practitioners with academic support and business insight, to support implementation of good regulatory delivery practice.

To provide thought leadership in the area of regulatory delivery, including coordination of research on key issues.

Outputs will include:

Knowledge-sharing events, including conferences

Publications (including the forthcoming book 'Regulatory Delivery: Global Best Practice')

Research programmes and practical testing

Structure and membership

It is proposed that INDR brings together regulators, academics and businesses as members of the network. The network will be based for a trial period at the Centre for Socio-Legal Studies, University of Oxford and led by Professor Chris Hodges and Graham Russell, Director of Regulatory Delivery, Business, Energy and Industrial Strategy, UK Government.

The success of INDR is dependent on participation by all sides of the triangle, with each contributing to the experience forum. Invitations to become part of the INDR are being extended to selected governments, academics, expert organisations and commercial business entities.

In terms of practical applications, by early 2018 INDR was already beginning to take shape, with its initial 'home' at the Centre for Socio-Legal Studies, a research centre at the Law Faculty of the University of Oxford. And by May 2018, a face-to-face seminar had taken place in Oxford that brought together the thoughts of World Bank, OECD and others regarding comparative Regulatory Delivery approaches and the Role of Standards, as well as the sorts of research topics INDR might pursue.

Challenges for Regulatory Delivery were also recognised, as indeed Florentin Blanc (OECD) highlighted at the 2018 seminar:

- Intrinsic: the links between regulation/regulatory delivery and outcomes are complex and not straightforward.
- Regulatory delivery is about changing behaviour. This is complex as there are a variety of factors that shape behaviour (even for a single person) depending on issues, context etc.
- It is rarely (if ever) possible to run 'experimental evaluations' and to make them reliable would require considerable size and time because of the number of variables that need to be controlled for, and because of delays in effects.
- Quality and reliability of data differs considerably between different regulatory domains, and even inside them. For example OSH fatal accidents vs. occupational disease or vs. food-borne disease incidence.
- The availability of funds to address data quality.

At the same event, Robert Madelin, former Director General of DG Connect and DG Sante in the European Commission, highlighted the complexity of the situation and recognised the need for an organisation such as INDR:

> There is no single driver for regulation or rules. People change as does the ambient culture. In a world of transparency and multi-pluralism the question has to be asked 'who will implement the rules'? How also do you motivate non-mandatory regulatory compliance – in other words how do you ensure consumer satisfaction is balanced by sufficient indications of risk? Is there a danger of businesses gold-plating their risk profiles and adding unnecessary cost? INDR is positioned at the heart of change and the time is ripe for this initiative.

By this time, Srikanth Mangalam was firmly on board as an Executive Committee Member, with special responsibility for the identification of research projects. The concept of INDR as a membership organisation was also evolving. It was regarded as axiomatic that participation in INDR should be non-partisan, and not an opportunity for lobbying but provide an equal voice for all participants to engage in objective consideration of policy and best practice. It was promulgated that membership of INDR should be open to the following:

- Government Regulators
- Independent or quasi-autonomous regulators
- Academics
- Expert Organisations, for example regulatory trade bodies
- Commercial Business Entities
- Individual Experts/Fellows, for example specialist consultants to WTO etc, by invitation of the Executive Committee.[7]

Invitations to membership of INDR were sent to interested individuals and organisations in late 2018, and the INDR Advisory Board met in February and April 2019, with the progress of INDR being discussed. Planning began for an Oxford Conference for October of 2019, and the three days of the international conference covered INDR's progress as well as the RDM and an exploration of Ethical Business Practice (EBP) and Ethical Business Regulation (EBR). The highly successful conference attracted 80 attendees from across the globe and covered topics such as the challenges faced in digital regulation and those differences experienced in the application of the RDM in different geographic regions.

With the onset of the global Covid-19 pandemic, various INDR activities had to be cancelled or transferred online. Nevertheless, Chris and other team members participated in a number of conferences and seminars, including, amongst others, a conference on the RDM organised by the Malaysian Productivity Corporation, a Joint Digital Technology Symposium with the Internet Commission, an OECD Network of Economic Regulators webinar and the OPSS Biannual Inspection Reform conference, which was fully virtual in 2020.

[7] INDR Draft Structure document (June 2018).

As the pandemic persisted, INDR activities adapted further and a two-day on-line regulatory course for international Directors and Senior Leaders was held in late June 2021, concentrating on the RDM and with an agenda that covered:

Scene Setting and Governance Frameworks

- Why is regulatory delivery necessary? What are its objectives? What are the prerequisites for effective regulatory delivery?
- Governance frameworks: understanding the basis on which a regulatory agency is formed and an exploration of current powers, structures and controls and whether they are appropriate and sufficient.

Culture and Accountability

- Accountability: the accountability mechanisms that are currently operating and an exploration of those which may be missing. Attendees debate whether these relationships are adequate, appropriate and effectively controlled and also the responsibility of the agency to build capacity for those it is accountable to.
- Culture: exploring the internal culture of the regulator's organisation, and why cultures may vary, including an exploration of the values of the organisation, the nature of the leadership and the competency of the officers.

Intervention Choices and Ethical Business Regulation

- Intervention Choices
- EBR

Despite the constrictions of travel bans and working-from-home rules, Chris's thinking never stopped, and various concepts were explored regarding the development of INDR, including a form of Regulatory Institute ('the concept I have applied is one of feedback and improvement – both personal and ultimately, through harvesting of the feedback, to further development of the RDM' – CH, February 2021). Chris was also simultaneously developing the concept of Outcomes Based Cooperative Regulation (OBCR), building on the basic EBR tenets.

Although INDR membership fees were paused during the pandemic, that did not prevent activity on the governance front. In July 2021, INDR was established as a private limited company, with Chris once more taking the lead. It will not be surprising to anyone who has attempted it how long it takes to deal with the bureaucracy of setting up companies, websites and bank accounts, but Chris's patience was rewarded.

Once INDR was firmly established as an independent entity, planning began in earnest for the November 2021 INDR Conference, which was truly hybrid – in person in Oxford and also available on-line. It was at this conference that Chris first spoke publicly about OBCR – at that time headed Outcomes-based, Ethical Cooperative Regulation, with an emphasis on the mechanisms of cooperation:

(a) trust, values, ethics, evidence;
(b) shared purposes and outcomes;
(c) co-creation, responsibility, accountability, consequences, intervention;
(d) behavioural science and its implications for regulation and 'enforcement'/intervention.

Chris expressed his thinking on this as follows in his paper 'Supporting Cooperative Behaviour' in February 2022:

> Humans achieve more when we cooperate. The history of our species has followed an historical trajectory away from defensive and aggressive competition towards increasing cooperation. The cooperative mode of (social) interaction has developed integrally, linked with developments in our psychological reliance on ethical values, forms of engagement (institutions) and the evidence supporting levels of trust that others will act as expected. These mechanisms currently need to be strengthened and reinvented in order to avoid the risks that we currently face, which are now existential to our species.[8]

In his initial paper, *An Introduction to Outcome Based Cooperative Regulation (OBCR)*,[9] Chris summarises some of the core evidence for how we should aim to engage in business, regulatory, community, social and international contexts, emphasising the need for tools like common purposes, agreed ethical values and principles, means of providing reliable evidence, mechanisms for co-creation and coordination of roles, responsibilities, problem identification and problem solving, and mutual accountability.

Given the unstable global political situation prevailing at the time of writing this chapter, the degree of prescience that Chris displayed amongst his conclusions is remarkable:

> We should strengthen cooperation as an essential means of resistance to threats to destabilisation:
>
> (a) International perceptions of threat – driving cybersecurity, terrorism.
> (b) Threats to life and health – disease, migration.
> (c) Socio-economic perceptions of threat – inequality, lack of economic security.
> (d) Build communities – start with the right size of populations to generate social community; governance of some issues in some countries are too large or too small.
> (e) Avoid perceptions of closed elites: moderate between expertise, competence, knowledge, involvement, values, feelings.[10]

And so the journey continues. Currently, INDR has a constituency of over 200 senior regulators, regulatory experts and academics. Chris's thinking continues to evolve, and it is a great pleasure to know that his ideas are gaining traction at the highest levels of government. Let us see what the next chapter of his life contains!

[8] C Hodges, 'Supporting Cooperative Behaviour' Research Paper no 2022/2 (February 2022), available at indr.org.uk.

[9] C Hodges, *An Introduction to Outcome Based Cooperative Regulation (OBCR)* (7 February 2022) available at www.indr.org.uk.

[10] Hodges (n 8).

INDEX